Teaching
the
Learning Disabled
Child

Teaching the Learning Disabled Child

NORRIS G. HARING
University of Washington

BARBARA BATEMAN
University of Oregon

with
GEORGE B. GLEASON
and
DOREEN KRONICK

PRENTICE-HALL, INC., ENGLEWOOD CLIFFS, N.J. 07632

Library of Congress Cataloging in Publication Data

Haring, Norris Grover (date).
   Teaching the learning disabled child.

   Includes bibliographies and index.
   1. Slow learning children. I. Bateman, Barbara D.,
joint author (date). II. Gleason, George E., joint author (date).
III. Title.
LC4661.H353   371.9'26   76-15965
ISBN 0-13-893503-3

© 1977 by Prentice-Hall, Inc., Englewood Cliffs, New Jersey 07632

The Prentice-Hall Series in Special Education
William M. Cruickshank, Series Editor

Printed in the United States of America

10 9 8 7 6 5 4 3 2 1

PRENTICE-HALL INTERNATIONAL, INC., *London*
PRENTICE-HALL OF AUSTRALIA PTY. LIMITED, *Sydney*
PRENTICE-HALL OF CANADA, LTD., *Toronto*
PRENTICE-HALL OF INDIA PRIVATE LIMITED, *New Delhi*
PRENTICE-HALL OF JAPAN, INC., *Tokyo*
PRENTICE-HALL OF SOUTHEAST ASIA PTE. LTD., *Singapore*
WHITEHALL BOOKS LIMITED, *Wellington, New Zealand*

Contents

PREFACE, vii

Part I

1   INTRODUCTION, 3

2   KEY FIGURES IN THE FIELD OF LEARNING DISABILITIES, 20

3   THEORIES OF ACADEMIC LEARNING—RESEARCH IN EDUCATION, 58

Part II

4   EDUCATIONAL IDENTIFICATION, ASSESSMENT, AND EVALUATION PROCEDURES, 95

5   DIAGNOSTIC-REMEDIAL AND TASK-ANALYTIC REMEDIATION, 123

6   DIRECT INSTRUCTION—DISTAR, 165

v

Part III

7   SYSTEMATIC INSTRUCTIONAL PROCEDURES, 205

8   CLASSROOM ADMINISTRATIVE ORGANIZATION, 275

Afterword

A PARENT'S THOUGHTS FOR PARENTS AND TEACHERS, 303

INDEX, 331

Preface

    Education must assume *some* of the responsibility for the learning problems children have, and we must recognize that not all teachers are "superteachers." There are those who need relatively complete teaching packages with a systematizing guide or academic teaching processes. Although these packages do not exist yet—except in a variety of bits and pieces—we know several authors involved in developing them. Perhaps soon some group of educators will synthesize the knowledge, skills, and materials we need. Until then, teaching learning disabled children still will be very much a job requiring creative individual arrangements within the systematic guidelines of each teacher's own choosing. We have written this book to offer such systematic guidelines to the teacher who is new to the learning disabilities area. We would welcome comments and suggestions on those aspects you find particularly valuable—or in need of change.

    We have selected and discussed some of the increasing number of educational assessment and instructional tactics commonly in use by experienced teachers. From our many contacts with teachers of children with learning disabilities, we provide their comments about methods most commonly employed. Teachers' reports—both positive and negative—about each method are based on a number of factors. However, we have found that some teachers strongly prefer one method to all the others without any evaluative data other than the feeling that that method simply seems more natural. We have included methods and/or procedures that are supported at least by *some* data, albeit "soft" data in some cases.

Many teachers prefer such complete teaching packages as DISTAR; others prefer more generic procedures such as applied behavior analysis and precision teaching. These preferences seem to depend on the individual characteristics the teachers and the situations in which they work, representing a great variety. We therefore have presented a variety of methods, strategies, and procedures for beginning students in regular or special education who anticipate teaching children with learning disabilities during their careers.

This, then, is an initial *methods* book that introduces methods and includes a separate chapter discussing contributors to the research and theoretical bases for them. Carefully selected references also are provided.

Despite the fact that regular primary teachers are becoming increasingly effective in teaching the early academic skills and in employing behavioral technology, media, and materials, they will need assistance in dealing with learning disabilities. We believe this volume provides exactly the assistance necessary.

We hope that any revision of this effort will add more data from applied research projects on and practical refinements or elaborations of the methods we present here. Our greatest problem in education has been the lack of systematic research and refinement of the instructional tactics we have been using for years. We must become more precise in developing individual instructional plans for children and more concerned with measuring each child's progress as he or she progresses through that plan.

ACKNOWLEDGMENTS

This volume represents the combined efforts of a dedicated team of writers and editors, secretaries, and other production staff members. Without the diligence and cooperation of these workers this book would not have become a reality.

We wish to thank Tracy Singer and John Bush, whose editorial pencils on various drafts of the manuscript made the final draft so much better. Patricia Nolen gave many excellent suggestions that greatly improved the section on reading instruction. Connie G. Pious helped us to make a few revisions we considered necessary. Similar thanks for editorial assistance must go to our highly skilled Prentice-Hall production editor, Alice C. Harvey.

Finally and very importantly, we thank Patricia Druliner for her contributions to Chapter 6. All of these people have been a pleasure to know and to work with.

Part I

Introduction

1

The phenomena that we refer to as "learning disabilities" are derived partially from our own culture, which places so much emphasis on learning academic skills. In a different society, where "success" depends less on the ability to make one's way through school, such phenomena may be unknown or unimportant. But to say that these phenomena are related to a particular culture must not in any way minimize their significance. To the child who has a learning disability, to the teacher who must enable the child to learn without a painful struggle, learning disabilities present very real and sometimes devastating problems.

The very early auditory and visual perceptions required for reading, spelling, and computation are slower to develop naturally in some children than in others. To effectively teach children in whom these early perceptions have not been developed naturally, intervention or teaching must be individualized, and the child's experience must be associated with positive results. If early experiences with instruction require correct academic responses and the child experiences failure, he or she becomes very susceptible to developing resistance to reading, spelling, and computation. Two or three years of repeated failure can cause learning behaviors in the classroom that for all practical purposes can be seen and defined as learning disabilities.

Most teachers want all their students to learn effectively. In fact, discussions so frequently heard in education reflect this concern: they focus on how differently children behave and learn. They learn at different rates and with different styles, and they have different motivations. There is much talk about arranging the curriculum and the teaching to accommodate these differences. Yet we still teach with fairly stock arrangements. Attempts toward truly individualized instruction are few and many of them are awkward.

Many children who are labeled "learning disabled" are in truth instructionally disabled. That is, they are children who have no neurological disorder at all, but who have had a series of unfortunate, usually inadvertent, experiences in learning preacademic and academic tasks. As often as not, these disabling experiences have stemmed from early pressures on the child to make preacademic responses or from his or her not receiving satisfying results from the normal inquiries the child makes in preacademic activities. On the other hand, although a child may have no clinically observable signs of neurological disorders, he or she certainly may have very subtle learning disabilities that cannot be readily accounted for by poor instruction. These learning problems seem to persist in a very small number of children, even though their curriculum has been individualized and they have received systematic instruction. These children, with or without minimal brain dysfunction, are learning disabled. We believe that these children *can* be taught by precision teaching procedures. These procedures are discussed in detail in Chapter 7.

Two case studies have been included here to illustrate the difference between the "learning disabled" and the "instructionally disabled" child. The studies of Rick and Marvin were provided by Kathleen Liberty, who prepared them when she was with the Regional Resource Center for Handicapped Children in Eugene, Oregon. Ms. Liberty is now a research teacher at the Experimental Education Unit, University of Washington.

CASE STUDIES

Rick and Marvin, both of normal intelligence, were diagnosed as children with extreme learning problems, particularly in reading, in the fall of 1971. The school district in the small Oregon town where they attended school provided minimal assistance to the youngsters, who were reading 2.5 and 2 grade levels below their age group, respectively. The boys were given remedial reading classes for 20 minutes daily. Judy Bowers, the teacher assigned to this class, had no special training in teaching reading; consequently, assistance from the Regional Resource Center for Handicapped Children was requested. Kathleen Liberty worked with Ms. Bowers in program design and evaluation for the three weeks after classes were resumed in the fall and before the two boys were assigned to the remedial reading class.

The similarities between Rick and Marvin seemed to be great. Neither exhibited any behaviors that were considered disruptive or inappropriate. Both children were diagnosed as having difficulty combining sounds to pronounce words correctly (blending). When the probes designed by Ms. Bowers were applied to the remedial program for the two boys, however, the results showed an interesting and important difference in their particular disabilities.

The materials used to teach blending skills to Rick and Marvin were probes sequenced by the arrangement of consonants and vowels. Combinations of consonants and vowels included C-V-C probes (three-letter nonsense words like "nup," with consonant-vowel-consonant order); C-C-V-C probes (four-letter nonsense words like "snup"); and three-, four-, and five-letter real words. The nonsense words forced the pupils, who had extensive sight word vocabularies, to sound out unfamiliar words. The students both began reading in the Miami Linguistic Readers series. They were to progress to the Harper and Row basal level readers after completing the seven-book Miami series.

Each child was timed for one minute on his blending probe every day. After the test, the pupil repeated all incorrectly answered and non-answered words. He then wrote them on flash cards and was asked to study the cards at home or in his regular classroom before the next day's reading session. Rick began blending C-V-C words at a low rate. In five weeks of data-taking, he had met the goal for this skill and was moved to more advanced blending probes. By the end of 10 weeks, Rick had reached his goal for the project. In oral reading he moved quickly from grade level 2.5 in the Miami series to the Harper and Row texts. The total project consisted of 12 weeks, at the end of which Rick returned to his regular classroom reading. Frequent checks proved that he continued to progress normally in his class.

Marvin's results were quite different. Like Rick, he began the first probe with C-V-C words and achieved a rather low rate of correct responses. Although his correct rate accelerated somewhat, his error rate fluctuated greatly. The charts show that Marvin did not make significant progress in the number of correct responses even when he was given easier C-A-C (consonant–letter "a"–consonant) and C-I-C (consonant–letter "i"–consonant) probes. By the end of the school year, Marvin was only reading on the second-grade level in the Miami series.

Although both pupils had been diagnosed as having learning disabilities with severe reading problems, their performances in the remedial reading classroom were qualitatively and quantitatively different. Although both began with similar error rates, Rick quickly covered three grade levels; while Marvin continued to make errors, Rick's errors soon dropped. Even with easier probes, Marvin's rate of correct answers never rose above 60 percent.

With remediation, Rick was able to return to his regular classroom program. He is a child who can be seen more accurately as having an instructional disability. Marvin, however, progressed little at a much higher cost in teaching time than was used for Rick. Obviously, remediation of Marvin's reading problem will take more time and effort. He is a bona fide learning disabled pupil. In small communities like Rick's and Marvin's, the variety of assistance for learning disabled children must be commensurate with the existing variety of pupil problems. It is essential that learning disabled children like Marvin be identified and given even more specific, intensive instructional intervention than those children who simply may have an instructional problem, as did Rick.

> *A distinction made on the basis of type and duration of remediation needed provides a solution to the labeling problem by providing diagnoses that are both descriptive and functional* (Liberty, 1973). Italics added.

These case studies support the view that diagnostic procedures and the definitions that follow from them must distinguish reliably between the child who has an instructional disability and the one who is truly learning disabled. The view itself can be generalized to cover all diagnoses and definitions, particularly for conditions such as learning disabilities, which so often have been vaguely or contradictorily described. Definitions that are not based on direct measures of child performance on academic tasks are not functional; they may name, or even partially describe, a condition, but they do not suggest the means to remediate it. Such definitions, therefore, are of limited value to teachers.

Definitions

The term "learning disabilities" came into existence in the late 1950s and early 1960s when material began appearing in professional journals in the areas of special education and exceptional children. Prior to 1965 almost nothing was done to apply research findings from either medicine or psychology to the problem of teaching a child described as "learning disabled." The "slow learner" was forced into the pattern of failure because no special effort was made to program instruction for whatever deficits the child experienced. We may never know how many children were labeled such diverse things as "dyslexic," "aphasic," "hyperactive," "autistic," "mildly retarded," "brain injured," nor what effects such labels had on those so tagged.

Recently, however, some very important questions have been raised about at least one consequence of using one of these labels. We refer to the encouraging news that the widespread practice of medicating "hyperactive" children is undergoing considerable scrutiny. Physicians, educators, legislators, parents, and others are deeply concerned not only about the safety or advisability of prescribing drugs to control behavior when long-term studies of such practices are generally lacking, but also about the "rightness" of this treatment and the ethical questions rising from it. Estimates vary considerably concerning the number of children with behavior or learning disorders who are being medicated to control their behavior. McIntosh and Dunn (1973) state that ". . . well over half of the children classified as having SLD [specific learning disability] are required to take drugs to make them behave better." According to Sroufe and Stewart (1973), more than 150,000 children are being medicated, and the number is on the rise. Ayllon, Layman, and Kandel (1975) cite a figure of 200,000; Krager and Safer (1974) say at least 300,000. Whatever estimate one accepts, the figures are by no means inconsequential.

Not surprisingly, physicians are under some pressure from distraught parents or teachers to prescribe for some children "something . . . anything!" to decrease the kinds of behaviors that can make a home or classroom a certain bedlam. For some children, bringing behavior under control through drugs may in fact spare the child from physical abuse by parents who cannot cope with the behavior and vent their frustrations on the child. In such cases, one could consider using the stimulant medication as a stopgap measure, in conjunction with ongoing therapy for the family, while alternatives to the drug intervention are developed (Beck, 1975).

However, as educators we believe that the most serious educational consequence of widespread use of medication is that articulated so well by Sroufe and Stewart: ". . . the use of the drugs lowers the motivation of parents and teachers to take other steps to help the child." Fortunately, there are some signs in the professional literature that educators are asking one of the critical educational questions about medication: Are these drugs the best means to improve *academic* performance? The study by Ayllon, Layman, and Kandel is a seminal controlled investigation of the relative effects of medication and behavioral programming on controlling hyperactivity and changing academic performance. The behavioral program not only worked as well as the medication in controlling hyperactivity but also improved academic performance in math and reading. A similar study completed at the University of Washington (Shafto and Sulzbacher, in press) produced the same results with a younger child.

We have digressed from the topic of labels to reiterate our belief that their consequences often can be anything but helpful to the child labeled; we used one label to illustrate that point.

The quest to discover a cause to explain an observed effect (etiology) has lead to the hypothetical categorizing or labeling of children who have failed in some way or another to meet the expectations for the "normal" child in the classroom. Such labeling and expectations too often affect not the remediation of the problem, but the way in which the person who accepts the label (the teacher, for example) responds to the child. Person A labels Person B and acts in a certain way because of characteristics attributed to B. Person B, who may well have been neutral toward Person A, now reacts in terms of how Person A behaved, and in doing so confirms A's beliefs about B (Fine, 1970). The classrom teacher may seek diagnostic solace as a means of rationalizing programming inadequacies (Lovitt, 1967). Since a child's classroom failure is due to some medical or psychological dysfunction, no teaching obligation follows for altering the present program's stimulus or consequence conditions, or considerations of an "instructional disability" in the teacher's classroom techniques. Hence the child channeled into such a pattern rarely can do anything to change the process. In a sense, a built-in failure factor operates on a wide scale in public education.

The process of defining the concept of learning disabilities began with the differentiation of *exogenous* and *endogenous* retardation by Alfred A. Strauss and Laura Lehtinen-Rogan in 1947. The exogenous category included mental retardation due to neurological defects or actual structural brain damage. The endogenous category referred to children who exhibited behaviors much the same as the other category but without any hard signs of retardation or brain damage. This evidence began to break down the idea that mental retardation was a homogenous state. Investigators from the medical field and neurological sciences tended to use the term "minimal cerebral (or brain) dysfunction" (Clements, 1966). Those interested in educational services for exceptional children, especially those in the field of special education, began to develop a functional and behavioral definition focusing on environmental factors rather than neurological disorder. One of the first educational definitions developed by Kirk and Bateman (1962) stated:

> A learning disability refers to a retardation, disorder, or delayed development in one or more of the processes of speech, language, reading, writing, arithmetic, or other school subjects resulting from a psychological handicap caused by a possible cerebral dysfunction and/or emotional or behavioral disturbances. It is not the result of mental retardation, sensory deprivation, or cultural or instructional factors.

This definition was later refined by Kirk (1968) to omit reference to etiology and to focus on behavioral manifestations:

> A learning disability refers to a specific retardation or disorder in one or more of the processes of speech, language perception, behavior, reading, spelling, writing, or arithmetic.

Another educationally oriented definition that has been used by the Council for Exceptional Children, Division for Children with Learning Disabilities, was presented by Ray Barsch (1967):

> A child with learning disabilities is one with adequate mental ability, sensory processes, and emotional stability who has specific deficits in perceptual, integrative, or expressive processes which severely impair learning efficiency. This includes children who have central nervous dysfunction which is expressed primarily in impaired learning efficiency.

Still another definition oriented to perceptual and perceptual-motor handicaps was developed by the Classification of Exceptional Children Project conducted by Nicholas Hobbs (1975). This project grew out of a concern held by Elliot Richardson, then Secretary of Health, Education, and Welfare, regarding the serious problems that can result from inappropriate classification and labeling of children. The title of this particular chapter (11) "Learning Disabilities," contains the following definition (developed by the committee of Joseph Wepman, William Cruickshank, Cynthia Deutsch, Anne Morency, and Charles Strother) of specific learning disabilities:

> "Specific learning disabilities," as defined here, refers to those children of any age who demonstrate a substantial deficiency in a particular aspect of academic achievement because of perceptual or perceptual-motor handicaps, regardless of etiology or other contributing factors. The term *perceptual* as used here relates to those mental (neurological) processes through which the child acquires his basic alphabets of sounds and form. The term *perceptually handicapped* refers to inadequate ability in such areas as the following: recognizing fine differences between auditory and visual discriminating features underlying the sounds used in speech and the orthographic forms used in reading; retaining and recalling those discriminated sounds and forms in both short- and long-term memory; ordering the sounds and forms sequentially, both in sensory and motor acts (Wepman, 1968); distinguishing figure-ground relationships (Frostig, Lefever, and Whittlesey, 1961); recognizing spatial and temporal orientations; obtaining closure (Kirk and Bateman, 1962); integrating intersensory information (Birch and Leford, 1964); relating what is perceived to specific motor functions (Kephart, 1963). Impairment of the processes involved in perception may result from accident, disease, or injury; from lags in development; or from environmental shortcomings. Impairment of perception may distort or disturb the cellular system and/or the normal functions of one or more sensory systems (Wepman et al., 1975).

Problems of terminology arise when two different disciplines attempt a common description of the child to accommodate different purposes for obtaining diagnostic information. The physician will naturally view a child's problem as a medical one, attempting to obtain diagnostic information relative to preventing or reducing causative factors. The educator, on the other hand, needs a more functional and behavioral definition for managing and remediating the child's problem relative to the classroom environment.

Many fields have contributed to both the knowledge and confusion surrounding learning disabilities. Whether or not communication between professional groups is improving is difficult to discern. There are, however, signs that it is. Special education, a field that developed from medicine and psychology to provide educational opportunities for handicapped and exceptional children, is in the center of the "learning disabilities" turmoil and is hampered by the same confusion in terminology and jargon as other fields. But it was research in special education and the development of precise instructional methods for handicapped children that began to break down the accepted categories and labels as individual differences in learning problems were discovered. A statewide study in North Dakota declared:

> Most learning problems in elementary school . . . are neither emotional
> nor physiological in origin: They are simply children's defensive reactions
> to curricula that appear irrelevant and to teachers who are overly punitive
> or judgmental (Silberman, 1968).

The varieties and type of "learning disabilities" and behavioral
correlates of brain dysfunction appear to be infinite. In fact, every "learning disability" may be unique to each individual. There is absolutely no
need for new definitions or categories of learning disabilities. The Task
Force II report (Haring, 1969) on educational, medical, and health-related
services for children with minimal brain damage presented the idea that
"definitions should vary as they are designed to facilitate educational
adaptations within a particular content and must identify behavioral
components that are functional to educational treatment" (Haring and
Bateman, 1969). A definition presented to strengthen the professional
opinion of the person making the definition generates the search for
educational panaceas, rather than the recognition of the problems and
systematic procedures of diagnosis, intervention, and remediation. In
recent years, the "Madison Avenue" approach to remedial programs has
flooded the educational market with many fancy and complex programs
that do more to help the designer's pocketbook than the child's learning
problem. If a child can be molded to fit a given category, then the program
designed to remediate that specific category can be used. Instead of factual
information about how to design a remedial program, the classroom
teacher gets "Madison Avenue hype" about the problem-solving capability
of certain materials, which is more closely related to an aspirin commercial
than to valid, empirical evidence.

Parent Groups

One of the driving forces behind improving educational opportunities and clarifying the diversity of definitions were parent groups acting
to obtain both legislation and working alliances with professional groups.
As in other areas of exceptionality, parents have played an integral role
in initiating programs. Results of a national survey of learning disability
programs (Richards and Clark, 1968) showed that over half the states
reporting listed parental pressure as a basic motivation for implementing
a program for learning disabled children.

Parents' group action in the field of learning disabilities represents
a "grass roots" political movement for getting action in a specific area of
need. For many years, well-to-do parents of learning disabled children who
could not function in the public schools arranged for tutorial help or care
in private residential schools. When federal laws for handicapped children were enacted, many of the children with learning disorders were
assimilated into classes for the educable or moderately retarded, or in slow
learner-emotionally disturbed classes. Parents tended to be dissatisfied
with these classes, which did not meet their children's educational needs.

Some of the parents joined to form a few private schools for their children. During the 1950s and 1960s training schools throughout the nation were opened for the dyslexic, minimally brain damaged, learning disabled, and others. These were expensive undertakings for both the parents and educators who were interested in developing and researching materials and methods for the learning disabled. Many could not afford these schools, but nonetheless demanded quality education for their children. Parental interest in the reason why their children were unable to succeed in school led to the formation of parent groups who worked together in this specific problem area of education.

The California Association for Neurologically Handicapped Children was incorporated in 1960, and in 1969 had 3,600 members (McCarthy and McCarthy, 1969). The Association for Children with Learning Disabilities (ACLD), chartered in Illinois in 1964, has expanded to chapters in 29 states with over 12,000 members. The Council for Exceptional Children (CEC) established a special division of Children with Learning Disabilities in 1967. These groups were inspired and encouraged by the success of parent and professional groups working for the mentally and physically retarded.

During the 1960s the term "minimal brain dysfunction" was broadly accepted in professional circles to describe children with certain perceptual and learning problems. Those diagnosed by medical or psychological personnel as being minimally brain damaged or dysfunctional did not qualify for typical special education programs. These children seemed to exist in a "never-never land" between normalcy and retardation. However, parent groups such as the ACLD and coalitions of parents and prominent special educators began to work for legislation on state and federal levels to provide professional training and research for learning disabled children.

In 1963 planning began for the establishment of a three-phase task force to study the status and needs of children with minimal brain dysfunction and/or learning disabilities. Group action by parents, followed by involvement of federal agencies and a large number of organized professional groups (primarily medical with the inclusion of some educators and a few psychologists), focused more attention on these children. Four agencies sponsored the task force: 1) the National Institute of Neurological Diseases and Blindness, U. S. Department of Health, Education, and Welfare, 2) the Easter Seal Research Foundation, National Society for Crippled Children and Adults, 3) the U. S. Office of Education, Department of Health, Education, and Welfare, and 4) the Neurological and Sensory Disease Control Program, Division of Chronic Diseases, U. S. Public Health Service. Task Force I, a committee of primarily medical and psychological personnel headed by Dr. Samuel Clements, dealt mainly with terminology and identification. This is the task force that adopted the term "minimal brain dysfunction" as a result of its study on the terminology and identification of learning disabilities. It established a detailed list of the symptoms that might characterize a child with minimal brain dysfunction syndrome, set up some guidelines for diagnostic evaluation of children, and compiled an extensive bibliography.

The two subsequent task forces were directed more specifically toward special education and educational programming for the learning disabled. The Task Force II report (Haring, 1969) made specific suggestions about 1) educational identification, assessment, and evaluation procedures, 2) educational administration and classroom procedures, 3) professional preparation for teachers of the learning disabled, and 4) related legislation. Another division of Task Force II, chaired by C. Arden Miller, specified medical, psychological, learning, and language problems encountered in learning disabled populations. Also included was information for parents, community workers, and teachers about the kinds of medical care facilities available to the affected child or adult. Task Force III (Chalfant and Scheffelin, 1969) provided the most comprehensive review of the literature relating to the behavioral consequences of central nervous system processing dysfunction in children.

The interest of government agencies in the problems of children with learning disabilities is indicated by the formation of the three task forces just discussed. Their outstanding reports have contributed to the understanding of educators and researchers in the field of learning disabilities.

LEGISLATION

The amorphous nature of the category "learning disabilities" has led to a rather confused concern on the part of educators toward the children placed in this category. The confusion has carried over into the legislation necessary to provide special facilities and education for these children. Public education for all children has long been a laudable tradition in the United States. Citizens have come to believe that all children are educated by public schools because the law decrees that it should be done, but in more recent years it has become apparent that *some* children are not educated even when attending school and that *some* children are not allowed to attend the public schools to be educated.

PARENTAL AND PROFESSIONAL GROUPS

The interest of parents in their children who were unable to succeed in school led to the formation of concerned parent groups, and professional organizations also began to show more interest in educational problems. Legislators became increasingly aware of the pressure exerted by such parent groups and professional organizations. State and federal government agencies began to form study committees on the learning disabled child, and legislators initiated laws and bills providing public school facilities and programs for children with learning disorders. Despite such action, by 1968 "approximately one-third of the states had made no provisions for the child with learning disabilities" (Haring, 1969), and the remaining two-thirds of the states had services either directly or as part of legislation for handicapped children. Very few of the state laws referred specifically to learning disabilities (or a related term) and even fewer described programs that should be set up or how children should be diagnosed. Some school districts throughout the country have established local programs, receiving funds from state special education "umbrella" laws, but programs on a national scale began only in 1970. Hearings by both houses of Congress on learning disabilities revealed that many of those writing and testifying for passage of the bills were parents of children with learning disabilities who were members of parent organizations.

Federal Legislation—Title VI

Services available to children with learning disabilities are provided under Title VI of the Elementary and Secondary Education Act, amendments of 1970. The act authorized the Bureau of Education for the Handicapped to serve handicapped children, who are defined as "mentally retarded, hard of hearing, deaf, speech impaired, visually handicapped, seriously emotionally disturbed, crippled, or other health impaired children who by reason thereof require special education and related services" (Title VI). Children with learning disabilities were sometimes considered under this law as falling into the category of "other health-impaired children"—if neurological impairment or brain injury could be proven. Therefore, in some areas of the country federal funds were made available for public school special classes to include the learning disabled.

The purpose of the Children with Learning Disabilities Act of 1969 was to amend Title VI of the Elementary and Secondary Education Act, thereby providing a new program for children with learning disabilities. The definition which is the basis of the act is as follows:

> For the purpose of this new program, "children with learning disabilities" are defined as children having a disorder in one or more of the basic psychological processes involved in understanding or using language, spoken or written, which disorder manifests itself in imperfect ability to listen, speak, read, write, spell, or do mathematical calculations. This term does not include children with learning problems which are primarily the result of visual, hearing or motor handicaps, or mental retardation, of emotional disturbance, or of environmental disadvantage (Hearings on Children with Learning Disabilities Act, 1969).

A FUNCTIONAL DEFINITION

In early 1970, President Richard Nixon signed into law Public Law 91-230, which amended Title VI legislation to include learning disabled children. Part G of Title VI of P.L. 91-230 authorized a five-year program with funds for research, training of teachers, and establishment of model centers for testing and educational improvement of children with learning disabilities. The definition adopted by the act, however, is more amenable to administration than to educational planning. It is a legalistic term that pinpoints the problem for administrative use.

For this volume, we define a learning disability as *a behavioral deficit almost always associated with academic performance and that can be remediated by precise, individualized instructional programming.* This definition does not conflict with the basic federal legislation and provides a flexible, pragmatic focus on the educational needs of a child in terms of observable behavior without ruling out possible dysfunctions or disorders in perception or neural process.

Child Service Demonstration Program Grants

As of July 1, 1971, Child Service Demonstration Grants were awarded through Title VI to educational agencies in eight states: California, Colorado, Mississippi, New Jersey, Ohio, Utah, Washington, and Wisconsin. The initial funding for these programs was $125,000 to initiate and maintain quality service programs for as many children as possible. Local districts, private agencies and facilities, and other institutions were encouraged to enter into cooperative efforts with state agencies to develop model demonstration programs that hopefully would multiply throughout the state.

The passage of comprehensive legislation by the federal government concerning nearly every level of disabling condition and related educational services has been followed in suit by state legislation. The well-known Elementary and Secondary Education Act (ESEA), Public Law 89-10 passed in 1965, was the beginning of direct federal aid to education. The Morse-Carey amendment to P.L. 89-10 became Title VI, providing direct aid to programs for handicapped children awarded on a formula basis (McCarthy and McCarthy, 1969). The Learning Disabilities Act of 1969 codified existing programs for the handicapped and provided for funding specifically for program development for learning disabled children.

Perhaps this federal legislation will help to bring order out of the chaos that presently exists in state legislation. In the past, lack of direction from the federal government, confusion about definitions of the learning disabled, and inflationary problems have often tied up bills in committees and study groups. There is no unity in existing programs, and considerable confusion persists about questions of facilities, teacher certification, class size, and the like. Often state laws are couched in very general terms and leave room for considerable disagreement as to interpretation. For instance, the law in the state of Oregon mandates special education "for those children having 'extreme learning problems' " under the special education umbrella. Special education includes "special instruction for handicapped children in or in addition to regular classes, special classes, special schools, special services, home instruction, and hospital instruction." In Florida, the Superintendent of Public Instruction has the authority to establish criteria to guide the development and operation of special programs (Kass, Hall, and Simches, 1969). "Florida law mandates the provision of special classes, instruction, facilities for related services, or a combination thereof for all exceptional children. This includes children with 'specific learning disability.' No further program description is provided."

Litigation—Labeling and Tracking

One of the most important issues concerning educational services for disabled children has surfaced in fairly recent court decisions concerning placement and labeling in special education, techniques of psychological diagnosis, and the role of parents in the public educational process. Some writers in the field of special education (Martin, 1972; Abeson, 1972) feel that educational opportunities for exceptional children will be achieved by establishing a strong legal basis. Federal and state legislation is certainly one vehicle for reaching this goal. But another effective means of obtaining increased educational service and opportunity is through the court system.

Parents and professional groups have brought both specific and class action suits against school districts and the state based primarily on the belief that the due process clause of the fourteenth amendment to the United States Constitution is being violated. The landmark case that most clearly articulates the specific issues was Judge Skelley Wright's decision (1967) in *Hobson* v. *Hanson,* Washington, D. C. Judge Wright ruled against the use of tracking systems as a method of placing children in special and regular classes. The tracking system is widely used in many school districts; it places children according to standardized test results, which are usually inappropriate for use with large portions of students due to class, socioeconomic background, race, and ability level differences. In the *Hobson* decision, it was held that black and other minority students could not be placed "according to environmental and psychological factors which have nothing to do with innate ability" (269 F. Supp. 40, 1967).

Children forced into lower tracks because of poor performance on such tests are labeled "slow learner" or "learning disabled" or "educable retarded." In the *Hobson* decision, group testing devices used to diagnose educational ability levels were rejected as invalid for placement or labeling purposes. Clearly, new techniques designed to test individual ability were needed to solve the problem. The issue of tracking and labeling is essentially not whether to do it, but whether these methods do or do not provide quality educational services. In *Covarrubias* v. *San Diego Unified School District* damages were sought for deprivation of equal protection against special placement until the procedures were changed. Parents are challenging school districts for the first time to provide quality education for *all* children. Citizens do not generally complain to school officials unless they feel that something is basically wrong with the system; that their child is suffering in some fashion; or, indeed, that their child is being damaged permanently (Cruickshank, 1972). The mandate is clear and it is up to the educational community to meet the needs of the larger community.

PURPOSE AND ORGANIZATION OF THIS VOLUME

Federal and state laws, court rulings, and public awareness are changing the role of public education. A case for or against learning disabilities being caused by instructional methods and administrative placement techniques will not be made in this volume. The authors are concerned with one basic issue: quality education for all children no matter what the child's handicapping condition. The philosophy of "education for all" is becoming a reality in many states, such as Washington and Oregon, by legislative mandate. The learning disabled child must be educated in the regular classroom if special education services are to be extended to the severely handicapped populations that have not been served in public education prior to passage of legislation requiring education services for all children.

This book is an attempt to provide a comprehensive view of the field of "learning disabilities" and to offer educational techniques and procedures on how to teach children with specific academic problems in the regular classroom with or without resource personnel.

Both the design and purpose of this volume have undergone a series of changes and evolutions. The final format evolved after nearly a year of researching the literature and attempts at correlating data in an integrative model of human behavior and educational technology. Perhaps the greatest problem in the field of learning disabilities is the wide philosophical and ideological gulf between cognitive and behavioral psychology. The first part of this volume traces the history of the rapid development of the concept of learning disabilities by considering both the contributions directly to the field and contributions applicable to the field. The gap in the literature and thinking about learning disabilities tends to diminish when a cybernetics and organismic model of human behavior and cognition is introduced. Such a model is possible when isomorphisms, that is, one-to-one correlations between elements of two groups, are discovered in both the goals and the data of behavioral science and research in the various aspects of systems theory.

In Chapter 2, the work of some "pioneers" in the field of learning disabilities and the theories they generated are considered. Chapter 3 is a discussion of work in academic learning theory, but focuses on work that led to the development of behavioral technology widely used throughout the United States today. These chapters aim at a means of developing meaningful, interdisciplinary action in serving learning disabled children. This is necessary not in the interest of advancing a new theory, but in providing a synthetic framework in which the relationship of behavioral and systems technology can be gained. General system theory was developed by a biologist, Count Ludwig von Bertalanffy, who sought a means of integrating and unifying the various levels of science. The science of human behavior was developed by several individuals, including B. F. Skinner, with the goal of discovering the principles and laws that govern the behavior of human beings. R. Buckminster Fuller has suggested that generalized principles exist that apply to the behavior of all systems. It is in this spirit that Part I of this volume is presented.

The second part of this volume is a presentation of some methods and tools of assessment, evaluation, and remediation currently in use throughout this country. The material hopefully is of use to classroom teachers and resource personnel alike in developing and understanding various assessment tools and in selecting a curriculum designed for the needs of the individual student. Chapter 4 is a brief historical analysis of assessment methods that have been and are being used in determining a child's specific problem. Chapter 5 is a summary review of some of the materials and curricula currently on the market for use with learning disabled children. Chapter 6 is an overview of a successful instructional system developed by Drs. Siegfried Engelmann and Wesley Becker, which reveals the change in thinking about learning disabilities as an education problem best handled by precise teaching techniques.

The third part of this work covers information generated by research in the experimental and applied analysis of behavior that is the beginning of a comprehensive instructional technology. Chapter 7 is in some ways the chapter that either "makes or breaks" the book. There we describe developments in educational technology from both the behavioral and systems views that make possible systematic instructional procedures allowing for the individualization of instruction necessary for effective prevention and remediation of learning disabilities. Chapter 8 offers information concerning administration and organization of classrooms considering the ecology of the classroom and new ways of administrative decision-making.

The afterword to the volume is a parent's story of living with and providing for a learning disabled child. It not only gives the reader a break from the authors' obsessions with technology development, but furnishes another necessary viewpoint on the learning disabled child and the struggle for educational equality by a parent for her child.

Whether or not this volume contains any "truths" is beyond the authors' ability to determine. The monumental problem of providing educational opportunities to children with specific learning problems, be they of cognitive, emotional, or behavioral origins, is our concern. Much confusion has come about over the nature of learning disabilities, the relevancy of etiology, and methods and procedures of remediation;

although we would like to believe that this is both a comprehensive and categorical volume, such an assertion would be sheer self-deceit. However, to suggest that this book represents a light at the end of the tunnel of confusion is not a flight of fancy. Systematic and behavioral research in education has provided a technology of instruction that has proven effective in programming learning experiences for the child with learning problems. This volume is only part of the process of opening educational opportunities to all children.

REFERENCES

ABESON, A., Movement and momentum–government and the education of handicapped children. *Exceptional Children*, 1972, *39*, 63–66.

AYLLON, T., D. LAYMAN, and H. KANDEL, A behavioral-educational alternative to drug control of hyperactive children. *Journal of Applied Behavior Analysis*, 1975, *8*:2, 137–146.

BARSCH, R., Memorandum from Ray H. Barsch to Advisory Council Members, Officers, and Committee Chairman of the CEC Division for Children with Learning Disabilities, 1967.

BECK, G. R., Personal communication, 1975.

BIRCH, H. G., and A. LEFORD, Two strategies for studying perception and brain damaged children. In H. G. Birch, ed., *Brain Damage in Children*. Baltimore: Williams & Wilkins, 1964.

CHALFANT, J. C., and M. A. SCHEFFELIN, *Central Processing Dysfunctions in Children: A Review of Research* (NINDS Monograph No. 9). Washington, D.C.: USGPO, 1969.

Children with Learning Disabilities Act of 1969. Hearings before the General Committee—Education, and Labor, House of Representatives. Washington, D.C.: USGPO, 1969.

CLEMENTS, S. D., *Minimal Brain Dysfunction in Children: Terminology and Identification*. Phase one of a three-phase project (NINDB Monograph No. 3). Washington, D.C.: U.S. Department of Health, Education, and Welfare, 1966.

CRUICKSHANK, W. M., Some issues facing the field of learning disability. *Journal of Learning Disabilities*, 1972, *5*, 380–388.

FINE, M. J., Considerations in educating children with cerebral dysfunction. *Journal of Learning Disabilities*, 1970, *3*, 132–142.

FROSTIG, M., D. W. LEFEVER, and R. B. WHITTLESEY, A developmental test of visual perception for evaluating normal and neurologically handicapped children. *Perceptual Motor Skills*, 1961, *12*, 383–394.

HARING, N. G., ed., *Minimal Brain Dysfunction in Children, Phase Two, Educational, Medical, and Health-Related Services*. Washington, D.C.: USGPO, 1969.

HARING, N. G., and B. D. BATEMAN, Introduction. In N. G. Haring, ed., *Minimal Brain Dysfunction in Children*. Washington, D.C.: USGPO, 1969.

HARING, N. G., and R. W. RIDGWAY, Early identification of children with learning disabilities. *Exceptional Children*, 1967, *33*, 387–395.

HOBBS, N., (ed.) *The Futures of Children,* Vol. 1. San Francisco: Jossey-Bass, 1975.

KASS, C. E., R. E. HALL, and R. F. SIMCHES, Legislation. In N. G. Haring, ed., *Minimal Brain Dysfunction in Children.* Washington, D.C.: USGPO, 1969.

KEPHART, N. C., *The Brain Injured Child in the Classroom.* Chicago: National Society for Crippled Children and Adults, 1963.

KIRK, S. A., Illinois test of psycholinguistic abilities: its origin and implications. In J. Hellmuth, ed., *Learning Disorders.* Vol. 3. Seattle: Special Child Publications, 1968.

KIRK, S. A., and B. BATEMAN, Diagnosis and remediation of learning disabilities. *Exceptional Children,* 1962, *29,* 1973.

KRAGER, J., and D. SAFER, Type and prevalence of medication used in the treatment of hyperactive children. *The New England Journal of Medicine,* 1974, *291*:21, 1118–1120.

LIBERTY, K., Disparate performances of LLD children. Unpublished manuscript. Experimental Education Unit, Child Development and Mental Retardation Center, University of Washington, Seattle, Washington, 1973.

LOVITT, T. C., Assessment of children with learning disabilities. *Exceptional Children,* 1967, *39,* 233–242.

McCARTHY, J. J., and J. F. McCARTHY, *Learning Disabilities.* Boston: Allyn & Bacon, 1969.

McINTOSH, D., and L. DUNN. Children with major specific learning disabilities. In L. M. Dunn, ed., *Exceptional Children in the Schools* (2nd ed.). New York: Holt, Rinehart & Winston, 1973.

RICHARDS, L. J., and A. D. CLARK, Learning disabilities: a national survey for existing public school programs. *Journal of Special Education,* 1968, *2,* 223–226.

SHAFTO, F., and S. SULZBACHER, Treatment tactics with a hyperactive preschool child: Stimulant medication and programmed teacher intervention. *Journal of Applied Behavior Analysis,* in press.

SILBERMAN, C., *Crisis in the Classroom.* New York: Random House, 1968.

SROUFE, L., and M. STEWART, Treating problem children with stimulant drugs. *The New England Journal of Medicine,* 1973, *289*:8, 407–413.

WEPMAN, J., The modality concept—including a statement of perceptual and conceptual levels of learning. In H. Smith, *Perception and Reading.* Newark: University of Delaware Press, 1968.

WEPMAN, J., W. CRUICKSHANK, C. DEUTSCH, A. MORENCY, and C. STROTHER, "Learning disabilities." In N. Hobbs (ed.), *The Futures of Children,* Vol. 1. San Francisco: Jossey-Bass, 1975.

Key Figures
in the Field
of Learning Disabilities
2

To gain historical perspective and understanding about the problem and development of learning disabilities, we should be aware of the contributions of some of the key figures whose work has been instrumental in the attempt to educate learning disabled children. Until recently, the child trapped in a fog between normal and handicapped has received little attention from educators. The growth of recognition of these special children, whose problems appear to be due to disorientation in perceptual or conceptual processes that are necessary for academic success, has been a steady one for the past 30 years. Today all fields that contribute knowledge to the establishment of programs of effective remediation are near convergence into integrated modes of communication that will enhance the education of learning disabled children. Actually the term "learning disabilities" did not begin appearing in the literature regularly until the 1960s, due mainly to the reaction against the labels of "brain damaged" and "brain injured" from both parent groups and professionals. Perhaps the confusion and degrees of specialization that took place in the field of special education necessitated the development of a concept that could clarify and bring about a measure of unification. The "learning disabled child" has proved to be such a concept. We have already witnessed the wide variety of attempted definitions and classifications that have been made. Now we shall trace some of the major developments dealing specifically with learning disabilities. Hopefully, tracing these theoretical positions, which have influenced classroom procedures for learning disabled children, will give the reader a better understanding of the problems involved in the assessment, diagnosis, and remediation of learning disabilities.

Four major trends can be seen in the field of learning disabilities: psychoeducational (perceptual-motor and visual theorists), the psycholinguistic (language disability theorists), the neuropsychologcial (brain processes theorists), and the behavioral theorists. Although none of the approaches remains completely discrete, differences of opinion and interpretation of scientific data have not always made communication between various practitioners smooth. Points of integration are being arrived at and the process of synthesizing research information is now occurring. But the student of learning disabilities should have a thorough background as to the lines of development and the major contributors to both theory and practice.

PSYCHOEDUCATIONAL APPROACHES

Heinz Werner and Alfred Strauss

Two of the first researchers to begin clarification of the category of learning disabilities were Heinz Werner and Alfred Strauss. Strauss, a refugee from Hitler's Third Reich, came to the United States in 1937 to the Wayne County Training School in Northville, Michigan, where he began to collaborate with an earlier refugee from Nazism, Dr. Heinz Werner. Together Werner and Strauss began to lay the cornerstones for the entire field of learning disabilities.

It was probably through his early training in neuropsychiatry that Strauss developed an interest in various kinds of mental deficiency. His work with Dr. Kurt Goldstein, a pioneer in the field of brain damage, was probably instrumental in formulating his later ideas. Goldstein's research (1929, 1936, 1939) with brain injured soldiers after World War I set the course for Strauss's work with Heinz Werner. Goldstein had found in his patients, whom he called "traumatic dements," the psychological characteristics of concrete behavior, meticulosity, perseveration, figure-background confusion, forced responsiveness to stimuli, and catastrophic reaction (Cruickshank and Hallahan, 1973a). Werner and Strauss were interested in learning whether or not the same psychological symptoms and behaviors found in brain injured adults occurred with children. Using Goldstein's research and early research by Strauss as a basis, they discovered nearly all of the characteristics described by Goldstein in brain injured children, focusing on hyperactivity and distractibility as prominent behavioral manifestations. Throughout the literature, the hyperactive, distractible child has been referred to as exemplifying "Strauss syndrome."

Although their early studies (1933) dealt with severely retarded children, Werner and Strauss began to study brain injured, mentally retarded children with milder forms of intellectual impairment. This led to the establishment of two categories of retardation: *exogenous* and *endogenous*. An exogenous child presented mental retardation due to neurological factors; the endogenous child's retardation was due to familial environmental factors. Strauss and Werner considered a child exogenous when no evidence of mental retardation was present in the immediate family and if the case history indicated a prenatal, natal, or postnatal disease or injury to the brain.

These categorizations and the research that produced them were not well accepted and were quite intensively criticized by several professionals. Sarason (1949) pointed out that diagnosing a child as brain injured (or exogenous) on the basis of behavioral manifestations results in a circular argument if one bases an etiology for brain injury on these same behaviors. Birch (1964) charged that Strauss and Werner based their classification on "necessarily incomplete and often fragmentary evidence." Whether or not this differentiation shows the cause of either of these syndromes has not been the key issue. The differentiation between *organic* and *minimal* brain damage was probably the most influential in creating a discrete category called "learning disabilities." After studying changes in IQ between the two groups, in which it was found that endogenous children gained 4.0 points in IQ during institutionalization while the exogenous children declined 2.5 points (Kephart and Strauss, 1940), Werner and Strauss (1940) recommended the lessening of inessential stimuli and the strengthening of essential stimuli in the environment of the exogenous child. This consideration of specific educational methods for the exogenous child formed the basis of further work by Strauss, Laura Lehtinen-Rogan, and Newell Kephart, in which specific behaviors of exogenous children were researched.

In 1947, Alfred Strauss and Laura Lehtinen-Rogan published their classic work on brain injured children, *Psychopathology and Education of the Brain-Injured Child,* in which they combined the results of Goldstein's (1927) studies with educational techniques based on Gestalt psychology. This is considered by most authorities to be the first comprehensive presentation on minimal brain dysfunction. In this volume they described the brain damage syndrome in terms of distractibility, hyperactivity, perseveration, and disturbed perception, while attempting to formulate an etiological base. Of the brain injured child they said, "He presents a picture of a child who is extremely mobile in attention and activity, unduly attracted by the doings of others or by the presence of normally inconspicuous background stimuli, inconstant and variable in interest, lacking persistence and sustained effort" (Strauss and Lehtinen-Rogan, 1947). Observations such as these led to the establishment of four criteria employed by Strauss and Lehtinen-Rogan to distinguish the brain injured child (1947):

1. Evidence in the medical history that shows insult of some nature to the brain before, during, or after birth.
2. The presence of neurological signs (now referred to as "soft" signs), which may indicate brain lesion.

3. If the psychological disturbance is of such severity that a measurable retardation of intellectual growth is observed, the immediate family history must be essentially normal and indicate that he (or she) is the only one of the siblings thus afflicted.

4. When no mental retardation exists, the presence of discrepancies or deviations of psychological development can be discovered by the use of certain qualitative tests for perceptual and conceptual disturbances.

It is from this last criterion that the phenomenon of learning disabilities as it is known today is diagnosed.

In viewing the educational process for the brain injured child, Strauss believed firmly in the totality of brain function and the essential inseparability of input and output. His educational process included providing the child with the opportunity to experience the normal ability to focus attention undisturbed by environmental distractions, and encouraging the child in seeking to duplicate the experience independently, thus becoming fortified against weaknesses that interfere with the total learning process. Materials specially selected and prepared for the child were used, as well as methods of teaching, which compensated for or avoided processes that would severely impair development of the individual. Emphasis was placed on analyzing the child's failure to succeed on a task in order to simplify, restructure, or recast the task requirement according to the child's pattern of mental abilities and limitations. Strauss drew much of his educational procedures from Gestalt psychology, especially when dealing with problems in conceptual behavior. Other methods were strictly his own. The shaping of the classroom environment to exclude extraneous sights and sounds was one of the first uses of the engineered classroom. The utilization of motor activity mentioned by Strauss opened new areas of research. According to James and Joan McCarthy (1969), "With occasional exceptions or shifts in stress, this pattern largely dominates the thinking in the field of learning disabilities today."

The work of Werner and Strauss, no matter what its reception from the medical and psychological fields, had a powerful effect on the closely related fields of mental retardation, special education, and learning disabilities. These men were among the first clinical researchers to advance evidence and methods for determining individual differences among mentally retarded children in ability and ways of processing input information. According to Hallahan and Cruickshank (1973), this led to one of the most significant contributions in the field of learning disabilities—functional analysis as a basis for prescriptive educational methods.

Many of the pioneers in the field of learning disabilities were associated with Strauss either at Wayne County Training School or later at the Cave Schools in Racine, Wisconsin, and Evanston, Illinois. Among these people were Newell Kephart, William Cruickshank, Ray Barsch, and Samuel Kirk. (All of these individuals' contributions will be considered in this chapter.) Needless to say, the research and educational methods developed initially by Heinz Werner and Alfred A. Strauss, and later by Laura Lehtinen-Rogan and Newell Kephart, provided the impetus for a field that has seen faster development than any other related area.

Newell C. Kephart

Newell C. Kephart, one of the original members of the Werner-Strauss research group, stressed perceptual-motor development in the education of the learning disabled child. While at Wayne County Training School, Kephart coauthored several studies with Strauss (Kephart and Strauss, 1940; Strauss and Kephart, 1939, 1940) and eventually collaborated with Strauss on revising the original Strauss-Lehtinen-Rogan volume in 1955. But perhaps the most significant contribution to litera-ture in the field of learning disabilities was Kephart's volume *The Slow Learner in the Classroom* (1960, 1971), which presented his basic philosophy and suggested remedial and educational techniques for children with perceptual-motor difficulties.

Because he believed motor activities to be the first patterns acquired by the child, Kephart suggested that adequate motor development proceeding sequentially must be established before perceptual organization can begin. As motor development progresses, more complex activities such as perception, symbolic manipulation, concept formation, and others will develop. The child first locates a sense of self in time and space before efforts result in that acquisition of information that constitutes learning. If a child cannot, because of some disruption in the developmental period, establish a stable world of three-dimensional space, a perceptual handicap in dealing with the environment may develop. Kephart holds that these perceptual-motor problems are reinforced by our modern, restricted environment. Children do not develop such basic abilities as eye-hand coordination, temporal-spatial translation, and form perception. The child should experience a learning process that begins "to build up an image of his (or her) own body, a visual and kinesthetic awareness of how he (or she) fills the space within his (or her) own skin. This awareness is basic to motor control" (Radler and Kephart, 1960). Failure in school achievement is thought to be related to deficits in these basic perceptual-motor abilities.

According to Kephart, an adequate body image is essential to a child's development. *Laterality*, or "the inner sense of one's own symmetry," is learned by the child's continual experimentation with movement. The human body is bilaterally symmetrical, anatomically and neurologically designed to develop right-left orientation (Kephart, 1970). The distinction of left and right and the differentiation and control of the two sides of the body are essential for adequate development of body image. As laterality develops, the child begins to perceive the environment. *Directionality* is the projection of laterality into space (Radler and Kephart, 1960). A child begins to perceive the relationships of objects to the body, then relationships between objects. All movements in space are established with reference to the body. This leads to balance and perceptual-motor coordination. Perceptual-motor coordination refers to a monitoring in terms of the meaningful aspects of perceptual data. Here we find the central concept involved with Kephart's remedial programs— feedback mechanism. When the organism responds to an environmental stimulus, the response is fed back into the total perceptual process to adjust the ultimate ouptut. As perceptual and motor learning develop, feedback is utilized to correct the responses to and perception of the environment. According to Kephart, a learning disability can be detected when a child begins to fail repeatedly in activities directly related to the defect. The continuing failure causes the defect to become enlarged. Proper programming and training emphasizing a sequential development of motor generalizations is necessary for remediation. Failure in this way can be seen as the inability to use kinesthetic feedback properly, or to process motor responses in such a way as to obtain feedback for repetition of an act. Kephart's remedial programs, reflecting his early connection with Strauss, implement ideas of engineered classrooms with use of chalkboard training, rail walking, balancing, ball play, music, and the like. Utilizing his theoretical stance, Kephart's curriculum stresses the developmental relationship of movement to perception and perception to higher thought processes. The need to teach generalized skills is stressed, for Kephart believed that splinter skills (skills developed in advance of basic skills) can not be generalized and do not lead to further development.

William Cruickshank

William Cruickshank's work with learning disabled children began as a modification of the procedures of Strauss and Lehtinen-Rogan. Cruickshank's interest in this problem developed directly out of tutorial relationships with both Werner and Strauss, and was given first thrust in the field of cerebral palsy as a way to try to replicate that which the earlier authors had done, but to do it on a neurologically handicapped population with normal or near normal intelligence. A doctoral dissertation (1950) by Jane Dolphin, a graduate student of Cruickshank's, provided a scientific transition substantiating the Werner and Strauss concepts about exogenous children. The Dolphin dissertation, coupled with other research studies by both Dolphin and Cruickshank (1951a, 1951b, 1951c, 1952) with an experimental group of cerebral palsied children who ranged from below normal to above normal IQs, showed that when compared with nonhandicapped children, the cerebral palsied group displayed the same psychological characteristics found by Werner and Strauss in their exogenous, mentally retarded subjects (Cruickshank and Hallahan, 1973b). These and related studies led Cruickshank to study intellectually normal children to make a conceptual transition from children with actual brain damage to children who display similar behavioral patterns but have no measurable neurological impairments. These children had been labeled "minimally brain damaged," "perceptually handicapped," "hyperactive," and, later, "learning disabled."

During the late 1950s in Montgomery County, Maryland, Cruickshank and a team from Syracuse University set up a demonstration pilot study "to investigate the value and effect of a nonstimulating classroom environment, specially prepared teaching materials, and highly structured teaching methods upon the learning problems and school adjustment of hyperactive, emotionally disturbed children with and without clinically diagnosed brain injury" (Cruickshank, Bentzen, Ratzburg, Tannhauser, 1961). The main aims of the study were to evaluate the utility of teaching methods developed in experimental situations for brain injured children for this more specific population, and then to carry out the study within the framework of a public school system.

Each child chosen for the study underwent a thorough diagnosis including psychological evaluation, physical and neurological examinations, psychiatric evaluation, and other related diagnostic tests. Cruickshank maintains that learning disorders and their resulting behaviors are generally dysfunctions in the neurological processes of growth, development, and maturation—even when there is no measurable tissue damage. Beginning with his work with cerebral palsied children (Cruickshank and Dolphin, 1951), Cruickshank's experience covers a wide spectrum of the field of brain injured children. Because of his diversified experience, he was one of the first practitioners to urge the establishment of interdisciplinary research and of finding means of communication to integrate concepts from research into the operational level of the classroom teacher. Another point of emphasis throughout his work has been the importance of studying individual differences in the learning process and developing methods of individualized instruction. Regarding the identifying or labeling of the child with learning problems, Cruickshank offers an important insight:

> The importance of labels should not be underestimated. The academic concern is only one aspect, perhaps even the least important in terms of the child . . . the label affects what is expected of the child, elicits feelings in the adult about the child, often even before the adult and the child have interacted, and can subvert the child's chance to interact as a child with an adult who chooses to interact with the child as being *brain injured*, in which case the child is the victim of whatever myths, fantasies, or associations that adult may have about brain injury (Cruickshank and Paul, 1971).

Cruickshank makes it clear that a child's abilities and disabilities are understood and communicated, not by labeling but by thorough diagnosis. The work done in Montgomery County represents one of the early, indepth attempts at diagnosis, methods of instruction, classroom management techniques, and research applications for gaining insights into the remediation of learning disabilities. The introduction of kinesthetic teaching methods has proved essential to the learning experience of many children. The volume, *A Teaching Method for Brain-Injured and Hyperactive Children,* deals in depth with these methods and applications.

Raymond H. Barsch

Raymond Barsch's approach to the learning process and to perceptual-motor activity closely parallels that of Kephart. Barsch has devised a curriculum called *Movigenics,* a theory of movement developed from the "study of the origin and development of patterns of movement in man and the relationship of those movements to his learning efficiency" (Barsch, 1968). The theory is a synthesis of research, clinical experience, and established laws of behavior in an attempt to gain a view of the totality of human performance and to account for all the various components of the totality. Barsch presents 10 basic constructs of the movigenic theory (1968):

1. The fundamental principle underlying the design of the human organism is *Movement Efficiency.*
2. The primary objective of Movement Efficiency is to economically promote the survival of the organism.
3. Movement Efficiency is derived from the information the organism is able to process from an energy surround.
4. The human mechanism for transducing energy forms into information is the percepto-cognitive system.
5. The terrain of movement is space.
6. Developmental momentum provides a constant forward thrust toward maturity and demands an equilibrium to maintain direction.
7. Movement Efficiency is developed in a climate of stress.
8. The adequacy of the feedback system is critical in the development of Movement Efficiency.
9. Development of Movement Efficiency occurs in segments of sequential expansion.
10. Movement Efficiency is symbolically communicated through the visual-spatial phenomenon called language.

To paraphrase Barsch:

Humankind is designed to move. The totality of one's being is organized into a harmony of interrelated anatomical, neurologic, chemical, physiologic, organic, glandular, and psychological segments and elements in a magnificent unity. The basic biologic organization of the human system is directed toward movement. Movement is internally continuous and externally situation directed to enhance the survival potential of the species. Since each person is a moving organism, the efficiency of one's movement becomes the measure of survival potential in one's environment, or "energy surround." All living organisms live in an energy surround consisting of the energies that are the primary sources of stimuli with which the organism must contend. Movement efficiency is derived from the information the organism is able to process from an energy surround. A person is constantly surrounded by energy forms in ever-changing motion. Under this constant stress and bombardment, the human organism obtains information to support survival. Human beings thrive on information and are constant seekers of data. Data are essential to life. We are dynamic beings capable of converting raw data from energy forces into information. The task of converting energy into information is carried out through the transduction process by the six processing channels, the senses: taste, touch, feeling, smell, sight, and hearing. As sensory information is coded neurally in the brain, a sensitivity system develops. This system, or mode of perception, is the transformation of the senses into the processing systems that lead to perception. The sensitivity (or percepto-cognitive) system is the avenue of access for information. The percepto-cognitive system consists of six modes of perception: the auditory, the visual, the kinesthetic, the tactual, the olfactory, and the gustatory. The information the organism encounters is discriminated, distributed, classified, and organized by the *cognition sequence*. This process of cognition is a four-stage action—sensitizing, perceiving, symbolizing, and conceiving. The cognitive sequence is the means by which we economically expand the knowledge of ourselves and the environment. We must learn to move in cognitive space as well as in physical space. Space is the terrain in which we must evolve survival strategies and develop movement efficiency. As we must learn to find directional alignment by controlling movement against gravitational pull and to center ourselves in relationship to the energy surround, we must begin to explore and measure cognitive space. The developing person is projected into a progressively more complex world of space. This momentum of development is generated by the climate of stress in which we exist. Stress is everywhere, and we try to seek a movement efficiency with which the stress situations can be tolerated. In learning to deal effectively with the constant bombardment from the environment, we rely upon a monitoring system to "feed back" correcting information to maintain some form of steady state. The efficiency of the feedback (or percepto-cognitive) system is essential in the development of movement efficiency. This development occurs in a sequential progression. Each unit of behavior, each organ of the body, each system within the hierarchical structure of experience proceeds from a simple form to more refined and articulated forms. Communication is expression and interchange with others of the experience of our own "space world." Language is the utilization of symbols to define and communicate the existing state of movement efficiency.

This highly refined philosophic view leads Barsch to the conclusion that a learning disability is a "feedback perturbation" encountered in the developmental sequence. Using his theoretical framework, Barsch developed a curriculum to allow a child wtih a learning problem to explore and experience being in space and integrate these experiences into progressively more complex behaviors.

For Barsch, perception, movement, and language constitute an indivisible, dynamic triad for curriculum implementation. Extending the space-movement orientation to academic programming, he has devised a space-oriented approach to reading, spelling, mathematics, and writing based upon the reciprocity between gross and fine motor functions within the learner.

The child with a learning disorder may be viewed as a child who fails to confirm the basic hypothesis upon which the mainstream curriculum is based (Barsch, 1965). To find a set of hypotheses that will allow the child to learn, the environmental factors composing the learning situation must be manipulated to bring the child to an optimal learning level. Barsch presents two volumes (*Achieving Perceptual Motor Efficiency*, 1967, and *Enriching Perception and Cognition*, 1968), that specifically deal with structuring an effective curriculum according to the theory of movigenics. In viewing Barsch's work, it is advisable to keep in mind his view that there must be a team approach to learning disabilities.

With this in mind, Barsch can be viewed in his own terms as a "multidiscipline professional."

G. N. Getman

Getman and his colleagues (1964) have developed a visuomotor training program based on a model of the visual processes conceptualized by Skeffington (1926). The model evolved from clinical evidence of physiological behavior measured by optometrists, and principles of human behavior proposed by psychologists, neurologists, and educators. The model shows four circles representing performance areas emerging into one central function—vision. The four visual processes are:

1. Antigravity Process—the total motor system utilized for location, exploration, and organization of the individual within the environment. It is all those modes of movement of self through space.
2. Centering Process—the constant visual and kinesthetic appraisals of the relationships between self and environment.
3. Identification Process—the labeling that evolves through the manipulation of objects.
4. Speech-Auditory Process—communication skills.

The four circles emerge in a center section that is vision. Getman states:

> Visualization, as it is being considered here, is an emergent, a derivative and a culmination of all action systems represented in the model. It is in this developmental level that overt performance can be translated into covert behavior (1965).

Accordingly, Getman's theory implies that communication between individuals is the process of sharing or trading visualizations. Visualization is not acquired as a separate skill; rather it must be a synthesis of these

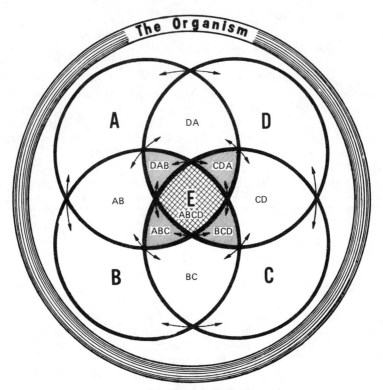

A: THE ANTI-GRAVITY PROCESS
B: THE CENTERING PROCESS
C: THE IDENTIFICATION PROCESS
D: THE SPEECH-AUDITION PROCESS
E: THE EMERGENT: VISION

Figure 2-1. *The Visual Processes.*

From Hellmuth, Jerome (ed.), *Learning Disorders,* Vol. I, Special Child Publications,
Seattle, Washington.

systems within the individual. To develop the process, all skill areas must function separately and together.

From this model (Skeffington's), Getman builds a model that shows how perceptual skills develop. This is Getman's attempt to validate his belief that there must be a "visuomotor system of hierarchical dominance" for skill in learning. This model is a guideline for mind-body training designed to assist children toward their maximum cognitive growth (McCarthy and McCarthy, 1969).

The model is a pyramidal hierarchy of seven levels. The anchor level is the *Innate Response System,* which includes the tonic neck reflex; the startle reflex (an alerting mechanism); the light reflex (an adaptive mechanism of adjusting pupil size to light); the grasp reflex (this "grasp and manipulate system" is related to attention span); the reciprocal reflex (thrust and counterthrust mechanisms essential to the freedom and faculty of movement); the stato-kinetic reflex (the mechanism of productive balance of systems indicating readiness to act); and the myotatic (the mechanism from which proprioception and kinesthesis develop). This Innate Response System is part of the human design and is present at birth. In the newborn infant this system of reflexes is a "mechanism of response" at a true S-R level. All reflexes working together become the interconnecting nets of the feedback system. These nets, which are not completely inherited, "are established through movement, the awareness of movement, and control of movement." Getman

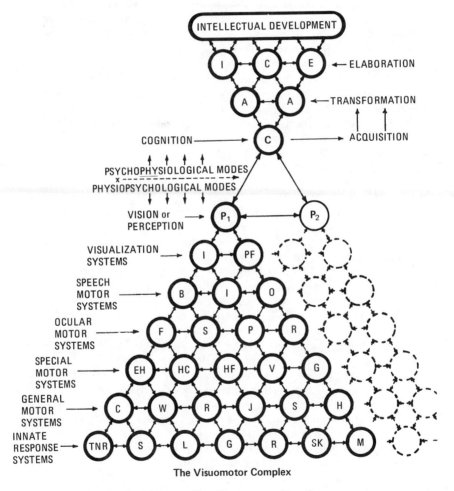

The Visuomotor Complex

Figure 2-2. *The Visuomotor Complex.*

From Hellmuth, Jerome (ed.), *Learning Disorders,* Vol. I, Special Child Publications, Seattle, Washington.

emphasizes that the psychologies of learning "too frequently overlook the physiological action systems," and the total body must be understood.

The second level of the model is the *General Motor System,* including creeping, walking, running, jumping, skipping, and hopping, which can aid the teacher in helping the child to develop the "minding body." Locomotor activities such as these provide the explorations and extensions necessary "for reciprocal balance and unity of mobility" of visual mechanisms that guide the child in movement.

The third level, *Special Motor Systems,* is a synthesis of the first two systems or levels. Included are eye-hand relationships, combination of the two hands, hand-foot relationships, voice, and gesture relationships. Children, Getman explains, are frequently given very specialized tasks before they have developed the two lower levels sufficiently. Skills developed on the third level can occur only when the lower level skills are developed. This echoes Kephart's warning about "splinter skills" (1960, 1971).

The fourth level, the *Ocular Motor System,* is the area of integration and balance of eye movements. Performance of this skill must include control and learning across stationary lines of print. This system is composed of relationships that "determine the learning and rhythms of combinations of the two eyes and the two circuits of performance behind the eyes." The components of this level are fixations (quick perception of a target); saccadics (movements of eyes from one target to another); pursuits (following moving targets); and rotations (moving both eyes in all directions).

The fifth level, or *Speech Motor System,* is composed of both speech motor and auditory integrative systems. This level illustrates that a child's speech pattern starts with babble and imitations of others, and finally develops to original speech. To Getman the significant aspect of this level is that "skill in visualization cannot really be obtained without the interplay of the vision-language processes," and vice versa.

The next level, or *Visualization Systems,* is the immediate intersystem relationships by which we gain the ability to visualize, or "picture in the mind's eye." This consists of an immediate intersystem relationship that enables one to perceive or "see" an object by its feel, or sound, and past-future relationships, which allow the individual to review past experience and preview what will occur. Utilization of visualization skills helps the child to analyze the structure of his or her experience (here-now) in relationship to the past experience (here-yesterday) and future experience (here-tomorrow). The process provides an organization and "a closure of related information" that is called a perceptual event. This is the experience that results from the reduction of all data synthesized from all lower levels of the hierarchy. This act of perception, according to the model, takes two forms: a single perceptual event or a construct "loaded with different but related aspects or components of the informational input." When these two separate perceptual acts are compared, the result is the next level of the model—*cognition.* The cognitive act is the *psychophysiological* acquisition of new knowledge. Further intellectual development includes abilities such as analogs and abstractions, imagination, creativity, and expression.

This developmental hierarchy is programmed into practical lessons for a development curriculum (Getman, Kane, Halgren, McKee, 1964), which emphasizes many of the same techniques developed by Kephart and Barsch.

Marianne Frostig

One of the early researchers who started her own private school for children with learning difficulties (Marianne Frostig Center for Educational Therapy), Frostig emphasizes an educational approach that develops or corrects visual perception in children who have suffered neurological impairment (Frostig and Horne, 1965). The center is private, non-profit, and operated by the Foundation of Educational Therapy for Children. It has three major purposes: research and development; training of school psychologists and educational therapists; and service to children and their parents (psychological evaluation; education focused on ability training and academic skills and content in classroom, small group, and tutorial settings; psychotherapy, both individual and group; and parent counseling and psychotherapy). A careful diagnosis and assessment is made of each child's strengths and weaknesses in six developmental areas: sensory-motor, perception, language, higher thought processes, and social and emotional development. Four specific tests are recommended by Frostig for this assessment: Wepman Test of Auditory Discrimination (Wepman, 1958); Illinois Test of Psycholinguistic Abilities (Kirk, McCarthy, and Kirk, 1968); Frostig Developmental Test of Visual Perception (Frostig, Maslow, Lefever, and Whittlesey, 1964), and the Wechsler Intelligence Scale for Children (Wechsler, 1949). These tests are supplemented by observation and interviews, achievement and mastery tests, and other psychological and medical tests whenever indicated. Test results are correlated with the six developmental areas as partial guides in developing individual remedial programs. In addition to these tests, sensory-motor functions and emotional-social adjustments are evaluated. In children for whom no cause can be found for retarded development in one or more of the six areas, Frostig assumes there is a "developmental lag."

The materials developed for visual perceptual training by Frostig are based on a test constructed at her center. These materials ameliorate specific disabilities assessed by the test and are a focus for readiness training. Frostig's research tends to confirm Piaget's (1952) theory that perception is the major developmental task of the child between the ages of three and seven and one-half years of age. The Frostig test has revealed that learning problems in a great many children result from difficulties in visual perceptual development. The test measures five areas of visual perception:

1. Eye-motor coordination—measures the child's ability to coordinate vision with movements of hand and/or body, such as in forming letters, drawing figures.
2. Figure-ground perception—measures the child's ability to distinguish particular forms or words within a visual pattern.
3. Constancy of shape—tests the child's ability to recognize a shape, letter, or word when it appears in different colors, positions, or print sizes.
4. Position in space—measures the child's ability to distinguish a form from its reverse, or when it appears in an unusual position.
5. Spatial relationships—measures the ability of the child to recognize the position of objects or letters in relation to each other.

From the results of this test, Frostig and her coworkers have devised specific training in each of the five areas of visual perception, and also programs for gross and fine muscle coordination, training eye movements, and enhancing body image and concept. Frostig declares that the program's goal is "the integration of the child's psychological functioning" (1964). In pursuing this goal, Frostig points out four areas of difficulty that the educator must handle in working with learning disabled children. First is the amelioration of lags and inadequacies in development; this involves selection of specific training programs for specific disabilities. Second, the remedial teacher is to teach the child according to strengths and weaknesses. Third, the teacher aids the child in emotional and social development. The fourth task is to ameliorate global and pervasive disturbances, such as impulsivity and distractibility, through techniques of classroom management, which include focusing attention, providing structure, and promoting ego growth through reduction of anxiety.

In summary of the Frostig program, Frostig and Maslow state:

> Overall changes in behavior, I.Q., or academic progress probably reflect the changes brought about by the total environmental influences, and are due to a multiplicity of factors. But it seems likely that the efficacy of developmental ability training programs can be inferred from the differential changes in specific sub-test scores (1969).

Bryant Cratty

Bryant Cratty is another researcher making progress into understanding perceptual-motor behavior and its consequences in gaining the ability to learn efficiently. Like most other researchers interested in the development of human behavior, Dr. Cratty hypothesizes a developmental model to help him explain and "predict the manner in which the infant and child change as a function of age." This model relies on "data from factor analytic studies of human performance as well as information from research in which intellectual, motor, perceptual, and verbal aspects of given samples of behavior have been compared." Cratty emphasizes the relationship between motor and perceptual behavior. In describing the formation of relationships in the matrix of a child's behavior, Cratty speaks of bonds that are "functional connections between attributes that in the child's life have previously been operating independent of one another" (1970). The model, a "latticework" of bonds and channels resembling an arbor or a tree, consists of six axioms and the supporting postulates that are the philosophical foundation for Cratty's work on the integration and differentiation of behavior. Certain phases of Cratty's model seem to be central to the problem of learning disabilities and how they occur. For instance, as the child develops, there is normally a proliferation of attributes (ability traits reflected in scores obtained from tests of motor, perceptual, verbal, or cognitive skills). However, intellectual deficits impede this proliferation process and render the total attribute structure less specific and complex (1970). This appears to be analogous to finding an actual neurophysiological insult, a cerebral dysfunction that inhibits the child from developing in an orderly, sequential manner.

Another way in which the learning process is inhibited occurs "when for a variety of reasons, a blunting of a total classification of attributes or of individual attributes occurs" (1970). There are myriad ways in which "attributes may be either retarded, terminated, or otherwise reduced in efficiency." As these deficits may result in or be the result of some type of deprivation, Cratty notes that there is an "optimum time" to provide learning experience that will allow development of a specific attribute or group of attributes. Likewise, overemphasizing the experience of any group of attributes may hinder or delay the development and emergence of "ability traits within another classification" (1970).

In the development of behavioral attributes, functional connections or bonds are formed between the various behavioral manifestations that may have been previously independent of one another. The formation of a bond may, Cratty states, be the emergence of an entirely new attribute within a classification. The bonds develop cognitively and behaviorally. Cratty postulates that the role of the educator is "at times to aid the child to form useful bonds between previously unassociated attributes and is at other times to aid him in terminating useless bonds" (1970). In normal children, bond formation is a steady growth process, and failure of this function impedes learning. Remediation of this interference depends on the "effectiveness of educators, or curriculum developers, and of parents . . . in the facility with which they can identify those bonds that are dependent on other bonds." In relation to learning disabilities, Dr. Cratty postulates:

> At times educators must aid a child to strengthen bonds between facets of his behavior that may be indistinct either because of some kind of maturational delay or sensory-motor or cognitive deficits or because of lack of practice.

This theoretical stance about the differentiation and integration of behavior is the result of Cratty's background in physical education and research in physical development of the blind, mentally retarded and neurologically impaired. Cratty's interest is based in perceptual and motor development and its relationship to the human personality. In an attempt to review the literature of experimental data on relationships between movement and cognition and between movement and perception, he draws several conclusions that relate to learning disorders. Cratty infers that improved motor efficiency may result in improved academic performance of children with learning disorders due to reinforcement of self-concept. Research has proved "motor tasks aid in development of certain perceptual processes." For example, hand-eye coordination is essential to precise hand movements in writing. Further, Cratty postulates that a properly applied curriculum of movement experience assists hyperactive children in learning better control of their classroom adjustment behavior. Through his review Cratty suggests:

> In the future it is believed that communication between clinicians and experimentalists will be improved if the latter takes into consideration the individual differences within their subject-populations rather than studying groups of undefined children to whom general labels are assigned.

Cratty's stance on the effectiveness of motor education and the perceptual process came from experience in the physical education of children with various types of learning problems. In his book, *Perceptual and Motor Development in Infants and Children* (1970), he begins the complex task of describing the origins of perceptual-motor behavior in the human infant with the movement evident prior to birth and follows with an analysis of infant reflexes. Cratty traces motor development from the first reflexes necessary to maintain the life process through the "gross motor attributes in early childhood" to the adolescent period. Suggestions are made as to specific ways in which the teacher can help the child to develop both motor and perceptual skills throughout the development sequence. In *Motor Activity and the Education of Retardates* (1969), Cratty offers detailed curriculum guides ranging from relaxation techniques to adjust the arousal level to the motor activities that will aid a child to gain the confidence necessary to develop the maximum of individual ability. Cratty states:

> A human is a single integrated organism. For convenience, we frequently fragment his behaviors in order to study them more closely or to attempt to change them in various ways. At the same time, we should remain aware, however, of the manner in which verbal, perceptual, motor, and cognitive behaviors may be interrelated (1967).

PSYCHOLINGUISTIC APPROACHES

Samuel Tory Orton

The case that appears to involve the earliest recognition of *minimal cerebral dysfunction* is credited to H. C. Bastain, a British neurologist. In 1869 he described the phenomenon of word-deafness and word-blindness when referring to a patient who could hear well but was unable to recognize spoken words, and to a patient whose vision was adequate but who failed to recognize printed words (Tarnapol, 1969). Although many instances of this neurological condition and others had been reported in medically related literature, there was little interaction between medical and educational fields.

Perhaps the first direct insight into the remediation of language disabilities was made by Samuel Tory Orton, a neurologist and psychiatrist, in his work with dyslexic children. In 1925 he specified the difference between the syndrome of developmental reading disability and mental retardation or brain damage. Basing his theories and treatment on studies of injuries to the dominant brain hemisphere in adults, Orton made deductions about neurological language development problems in children with no signs of actual brain damage. Through his work with symbolic language, or "a sign or series of sounds which has come to serve as a substitute for an object or a concept and can thus be used as a means of transferring ideas," Orton found that language problems began with reading disabilities and extended to writing disabilities, developmental word deafness, motor speech delay, abnormal clumsiness, stuttering, and combinations of these syndromes. The one common factor he found in these six problems he termed "strephosymbolia," meaning twisted symbols, and is defined as a difficulty of the mind in properly sequencing and organizing the order of letters and sounds into words. "Specific reading disability" was Orton's term for the inability to learn to read rapidly and efficiently at the mental age level expected and at the achievement level reached in other subjects. The remediation programs offered by Orton in his book, *Reading, Writing, and Speech Problems in Children,* utilize a systematic phonics program reinforced with kinesthetic aids.

Samuel Kirk

The stress on actual neurological aspects of learning disabilities began to vary among researchers in the late 1950s. Samuel A. Kirk developed the philosophy that the primary goal of educators must be to assess accurately the behavioral aspects, not the causes, of the child's disability, and/or develop individual learning potential (Kirk, 1962).

Kirk has turned his attention to children with learning disorders and has shaped his philosophy to deal specifically with this population. It is his contention that learning processes are directly linked with the psycholinguistic processes. Nearly all learning disorders are manifested in problems of reading, writing, spelling, arithmetic, and reasoning, and hence are related to human language usage. Kirk assumes that learning disorders occur when there is a breakdown within the child's internal communication system, or psycholinguistic processes. Somewhere between the child's process of obtaining information (through visual or auditory means), synthesizing those data and conceptualizing them, and the expression of ideas, some inner process (neurological) must be malfunctioning if a child fails to learn.

Hypothesizing that if one were able to "pinpoint" various stages of these psycholinguistic processes and devise tasks or tests that would assess the functioning of each area, one might be able to determine from the test profile where the breakdown in this internal communication is occurring, Kirk reasoned that a remediation technique could then be prescribed to strengthen the area of weakness and ameliorate the learning disorder. With this in mind, Kirk selected a theoretical learning model by Osgood (Osgood, 1957; Osgood and Miron, 1963), who had done extensive work in communication theory and psycholinguistics. Osgood's original model illustrated a behavioral act as being divided into two stages (decoding and encoding) and three levels of organization (projection, integration, representation). Although Osgood's model is a clear illustration of how information is received and transmitted by the brain, it does specify a particular stage for memory, which Kirk considered a necessary part of the psycholinguistic process. Using the work of Dorothy Sievers (1955) and James McCarthy (1957), a combination of the theoretical model and new empirical evidence was used to devise a clinical model from which tests could be generated. The clinical model evolved from a model conceived by Wepman, Jones, Black, and Pelt (1960), which utilized levels of functioning in the central nervous system, and the Osgood model to delineate a series of steps in the psycholinguistic process. These steps are incorporated in the Illinois Test of Psycholinguistic Abilities (Kirk, McCarthy, and Kirk, 1968), which has proved an effective test profile for diagnostic purposes.[1] The test profile indicates those areas of the child's psycholinguistic processes that are normal or superior and those that are defective and for which remedial treatment would be prescribed and applied. Through his work on ITPA, Kirk (1968) has developed a particular stand on learning disabilities. He says:

> *Learning disabilities* has been presented as a behavioral and educational concept, referring to development discrepancies in the communication processes of children. These include disorders or delay in development in

[1] Not all writers agree with this view of the ITPA. For a discussion of some of the critical views, see Chapter 4.

one or more of the processes of speech, language, perception, reading, writing, spelling, and arithmetic, sometimes with associated behavioral disorders.

These learning disorders are grouped into three categories: 1) academic disorders, 2) nonsymbolic disorders, and 3) symbolic disorders. A reading problem is an academic disorder but originates from a nonsymbolic disorder (McCarthy and McCarthy, 1969). Research (Bateman, 1965; Kass, 1966; Ragland, 1964; McLeod, 1965) validates this position. Kirk's work has proved that ITPA is a useful tool for distinguishing between symbolic and nonsymbolic disorders associated with the management of learning disabilities, specifically diagnosis for remediation purposes, in contrast to assessment for classification or categorization.

Joseph Wepman

Joseph Wepman, whose early work with speech and hearing defects lead him to major research and theories on aphasia (inability to use words as symbols of ideas), has been a great influence in the area of learning disorders. By 1960 he had evolved a learning model that, like Osgood's, stressed multilevel and multistage functions. Specifically, however, Wepman's model mentions three separate levels of operation for both input and output (sensory/motor) modalities: on the input side are the reflex, the perceptual, and the conceptual levels; on the output (motor) side are the reflex, the imitational, and the thought and language levels. Mediating these input/output modalities, of course, is the central nervous system, which coordinates input with appropriate output. Thus, for example, ideas or concepts are perceived through auditory stimulation; they are processed as such by the brain, and the result is appropriate thought or speech resulting not from the auditory stimulation alone but from what those sounds come to symbolize as ideas or concepts.

For Wepman, the importance of this model lay in the idea that disorders of speech are modality bound and are not the result of any single defect in any one area of the brain. Rather, disorders in speech could be traced basically to three areas: input and sensory dysfunction (agnosia); faulty symbol formulation (aphasia); and dysfunction in response transmission to end organs (apraxia). Therapies, consequently, should follow pinpoint diagnoses of areas of dysfunction. Following this reasoning, in 1961 Wepman, along with Lyle V. Jones, developed the Language Modalities Test for Aphasia, designed to locate disorders in input modalities (auditory and visual), output modalities (oral, graphic, or gestural), and symbol systems.

Helmer Myklebust

A major researcher in the area of language deficits is Helmer Myklebust. Through his early work with deaf and autistic children, Myklebust became interested in how auditory deficits affected the total learning process of the child (1954, 1964, 1965, 1967). After extensive work with learning disabled children, Myklebust became convinced that their problems must be caused by neurological damage, which altered the processes, or *the neurology of learning,* and provoked psychological disturbances manifested in behavioral disorders. In 1960 Myklebust and Boshes proposed that the term "psychoneurological learning disability" be used to designate the problem for this group of nonlearning children. In his arguments for the term's acceptance, Myklebust explicates the basic idea of his approach to learning disabilities. A classification is needed, he and his colleague state:

> which clearly indicates that learning processes have been altered and that this modification is due to neurological dysfunction, that it is the neurology of learning which has been impaired and the result is a *disability,* not an *incapacity,* in learning.

> Another important consideration is that initially the manifestations most often are behavioral, not neurological; the more observable symptoms are psychological in nature (Myklebust and Johnson, 1967).

Along with other researchers (Birch and Lefford, 1964), Myklebust advances a psychoneurological model that presents the brain as a transducer converting one type of information to another. Using this model as a guide to understanding learning processes, learning disabilities are "the psychological concomitants of neurological deficits." Brain systems (auditory, visual, tactile, and so on) operate either semi-independently or in direct relation to one another. To understand any dysfunction that may arise in any system, each system must be investigated separately, the combination of systems must be understood, and the integrative function of all systems must be seen.

Myklebust's orientation to the etiological causes of learning disabilities requires that careful differential diagnoses in intellectual, neurological, and medical areas be made of the child before a remedial program is planned. To pinpoint a deficit in learning, Myklebust has devised a measure that he calls the *Learning Quotient.* It incorporates measures of intellectual potential, physiological maturity, and experience to obtain a more inclusive and valid measure of a child's potential level of intellectual functioning. The rationale used is that traditional measures of deficiencies are viewed only in terms of school subjects and the extent of the deficiency is determined on the basis of the number of years the child falls below expectancy level. This method fails to incorporate both verbal and nonverbal facets of learning. Myklebust's formula for the Learning Quotient is:

$$\frac{\text{Mental Age} + \text{Life Age} + \text{Grade Age}}{3} = \text{Expectancy Age}$$

A battery of achievement tests is given in reading, spoken language, written language, and in nonverbal learning. When each of these achievement scores is divided by the child's expectancy age, the result is a ratio expressed as a Learning Quotient. Myklebust (1967) summarizes the purpose of the Learning Quotient as follows:

> The Learning Quotient serves as a measure of discrepancy between expectancy and achievement in various ways: in perception, conception, motor function, language, and in any aspect of nonverbal learning that can be adequately determined in terms of age scores. It adds precision to the concept of learning disabilities by providing a basis for statistical studies in which behavioral functions can be correlated with other factors, educational, psychological, and medical.

Myklebust's program of remediation was developed with Doris Johnson and is described in *Learning Disabilities: Educational Principles and Practices* (Myklebust and Johnson, 1967). It features individual program planning for the disabled child, teaching to the child's tolerance level (no overstimulation), and applying objective methods to the description, evaluation, and modification of human behavior.

Katrina de Hirsch

Katrina de Hirsch, director of the Pediatric Language Disorder Clinic at the Columbia Presbyterian Medical Clinic in New York City, has been active in clinical treatment of language disturbances in children for more than 20 years. De Hirsch's published work reveals a background rooted in Gestalt psychology and the attempt to find relationships between difficulties in oral speech, trouble with printed language, and ego disorganization due to maturational delays and perceptual problems.

De Hirsch claims in her early work that the "ability to experience and to respond in terms of Gestalten is one of the basic conditions in the successful handling of language . . ." (1954). Children with learning problems involving speech delay, dyslalia, dyslexia, hyperkinesis, or aphasia encounter trouble at nearly every level of integration. De Hirsch hypothesizes that the difficulty is with structuralization and organization of gestalten, or the ability of the individual to respond to a given array or constellation of stimuli as a whole. Following the work of Max Wertheimer and Wolfgang Kohler, de Hirsch points out certain practical difficulties related to basic language problems.

The problem of developmental language disorders is the focal point of all academic learning disorders. All problems in poor reading, writing, and speech, according to de Hirsch, arise from what Weiss calls "central language imbalance." The children on whom de Hirsch seems to focus in her work are those who appear to have normal or above normal intelligence, but who began to speak later than the average child, whose motor speech patterns are poor, and who have difficulty with finer motor acts and laterality because of unstable temporal and spatial organization. Among these children the problems of dyspraxis (difficulty in penmanship), dyslexia (difficulty in comprehending printed language), and speech delay and dyslalia (problems in oral speech) occur frequently. These children rated 20 to 30 points higher on the performance section of the Bellevue-Wechsler intelligence test than on the verbal section and were unable to establish a functional superiority of one side over the other, with the dyslexic child often encountering crossed laterality and difficulty in left-to-right discrimination, which is a prerequisite for reading the English language.

Another factor in de Hirsch's early work that was later explored and developed was the concept of body image, which was seen "to be consistently primitive in children suffering from severe language disorders" (1954). The concept of plasticity developed by Dr. Lauretta Bender in dealing with childhood schizophrenia is applied to children with language disorders. Ego orientation is the ability to develop an image of the self derived from one's experience of the body in relationship to the environment and to its various parts. The child who is plastic suffers from "a developmental lag of the biologic process from which subsequent behavior evolves by maturation at an embryological level" (Bender, 1960). As described by Dr. Bender, a developmental lag leads to pervasive anxiety and neurotic defense mechanisms. De Hirsch makes the assumption that this phenomenon is significant in the development of specific language disabilities.

Following her gestalt orientation, de Hirsch emphasizes the need to view each individual child as a whole. She sees the role of the clinician as evaluating neurophysiological, linguistic, and affective aspects of communication and the complex interactions between them. De Hirsch (1967) writes:

> A great many youngsters are damaged on both the physiological and the psychological levels of integration. Classifying all language deficits as related either to organicity or to psychosis does not do justice to the complexity of the clinical phenomenon.

Since language is the fundamental means of interpersonal communication, language skills are requisite for successful social behavior and personal interaction. Reading, to de Hirsch, is "successful response to visual forms of language," and the goal of reading is understanding the graphically fixed language units (1963). Although a clinician and a practitioner of the clinical approach to language problems, she offers an analysis of integrated reading performance useful for the classroom teacher. The reading process includes a number of partial performances:

1. Perceptual grasping of letters and word configurations.
2. Evocation of inner speech.

3. Comprehension of syntactical relationships.
4. Construction of anticipatory schemata as to what the sentence is going to say.
5. Assimilation of content into already existing frameworks.

Reading involves both integrative and differentiating processes. A successful reader, states de Hirsch, must be able to grasp the whole of the content and to analyze the various parts. The analysis of wholes and the integration of parts move forward simultaneously, and the combination of the two makes for good reading. Her clinical investigation seems to show that dyslexic children have trouble with organization, not only of complex linguistic forms, but also with more basic motor, visual-motor, and perceptual schemata. She suggests that remedial methods should facilitate the organization of small or large gestalten and link the visual to the auditory image of the word.

Katrina de Hirsch's work covers nearly every aspect of language and language disorders from speech pathology to problems of reading and writing. She remains near Samuel Orton's position that there is a close relationship between all aspects of language function in child development. The movement toward pinpointing specific learning difficulties in language developments that are either "organic," involving actual dysfunction of the brain in reception of environmental data, or psychopathological, involving ego disorientation, is central in her work.

THE NEUROPSYCHOLOGICAL APPROACH

Although some educationally and clinically oriented psychologists have developed theories of learning disabilities based on brain functioning, a few individuals have done pioneer research on various forms of brain damage and the psychological correlates of brain dysfunction. Many learning disability theorists refer to psychological or neuropsychological aspects of learning disabilities, but most do so to strengthen their educational conceptualizations rather than to provide a solid basis for understanding brain-behavior relationships. It also is true that much of the work done has been performed with many methodological restraints. Pinpointing, locating, and measuring the effect of a brain lesion is an art still in the early stages of development. Problems in knowing how a child's brain develops and how specific dysfunctions affect various behaviors loom as obstacles yet to overcome; research in the mechanisms of brain behavior correlates has yet to be applied readily to educational problems. Of the contributors in this area, several are outstanding. Drs. Ralph Reitan and Arthur Benton are perhaps the two key figures. Although only Reitan's work is mentioned here, the reader interested in this area is encouraged to look at both men's work.

Ralph Reitan

Extensive research with brain damaged subjects using psychological testing, psychometric evaluation, and strict experimental design has lead Dr. Ralph Reitan of the Neuropsychology Laboratory, Child Development and Mental Retardation Center at the University of Washington, to direct interest to the area of learning disabilities, or minimal cerebral dysfunctions. Dr. Reitan's early work evidences his great interest and time investment in controlled investigation of problems involving actual brain damage varying from studies of aphasia to tests of the validity of various psychological and neurological tests to evaluate brain damaged subjects.

According to Homer Reed, Jr. (1970) of The Tufts-New England Medical Center, Reitan's research on the "effects of brain lesions on intelligence and adaptive abilities in human beings provides the best single body of literature with which to document the influence of brain damage on intelligence." Using the technology available through pioneers in the measurement of intelligence, such as Binet, Thurstone, Guilford, and Wechsler, and applying these measurement techniques to specific physiological problems isolated by researchers such as Broca, Goldstein, Halstead, and others, Reitan began to provide statistical data about the effects of brain lesions on intellectual and behavioral abilities. This research has a greater scope than has been the case for other investigators because of the large number and variety of psychological tests used. Also of vital importance is the careful data and statistical analysis employed to assess performance and evaluate specific neurological and psychological problems. Reed (1970) lists the major findings of these studies:

1. Psychological tests regularly show the deleterious effects of brain damage on intellectual and adaptive abilities.
2. Higher order cognitive abilities such as concept formation and problem-solving skills have proven more vulnerable to lesions than simpler behaviors such as motor speed.
3. Language functions are more greatly impaired by lesions in the left cerebral hemisphere than are spatial or manipulatory skills.
4. The opposite is true for lesions in the right cerebral hemisphere.
5. The effects of the normal aging process have a close relationship to the effects of brain damage on psychological abilities.
6. Test results of brain damaged children and adults who have incurred brain damage early in life indicate psychological abilities that differ from those who sustained brain damage in adulthood.
7. Standard IQ tests do not reveal the effects of brain damage as well as do other types of tests.

The relationships of brain function and behavior are of great importance to the classroom teacher because he or she has the responsibility of shaping and modifying academic and social behaviors. Reitan and Heineman (1968) suggest that methods must be developed "whereby the condition of the brain, particularly as it relates to behavior, may be evaluated." In considering the brain as the principal organ of adaptive behavior, it is only logical to presume that the more tenuous grasp of a specific ability by a brain damaged child as compared to a normal child should be more readily subject to disorganization by any type of adverse influence (Reitan, 1966). Often the classroom teacher is confronted with labels such as hyperactivity, distractibility, impulsivity, and so on, to describe certain behavioral manifestations of children whose learning disorders and behavioral problems are thought to result from minimal cerebral dysfunctions even though there is no gross impairment of intellectual functioning. The concept of "minimal brain damage" came into use because clinical psychologists tried to devise a way of identifying children whose behavior suggested cerebral damage whether or not positive neurological evidence was available from their methods of examination.

Dr. Reitan has initiated research (Reitan and Boll, 1973) to discern the extent to which children with minimal cerebral damage show deficits similar to those of brain damaged children as contrasted with the performance of normal children. In the initial study a child who showed no indications of structural cerebral damage did show some impaired efficiency in the functioning of the left cerebral hemisphere that could be viewed as mild cerebral dysfunction. The absence of indications of structural cerebral damage, Reitan points out, may be a good indication of this child's potential for developing higher level abilities, since the evidence found may be related only to a lag in the development of normal brain-behavior relationships. These results, Reitan asserts, point out the need for this child to receive one-to-one tutorial assistance to overcome the deficits encountered in primary verbal information-processing skills and to avoid falling behind in academic progress. A child with some impairment to the left cerebral function and corresponding difficulty in processing verbal information should be treated in a special manner with regard to verbal communication, according to Reitan. Slow, deliberate, repetitive speech would be effective in helping the child to appreciate the information that is being communicated. This special handicapping situation requires that the information communicated per unit of time be minimized and that redundancy of content be emphasized. The classroom teacher should avoid overloading the child with verbal information in order to increase the child's ability to respond and comprehend. Reitan and his associates have found that even children who progress normally in academic situations sometimes show mild neuropsychological deviations, and the early identification of these impairments eventually may foster the best possible development.

The significance of this type of investigation is that until now no systematically obtained information was available with respect to the type of progress that can be expected, behaviorally and academically, from children who are either brain damaged, mentally retarded, or learning disabled. Dr. Reitan believes that until there is information relating known conditions of cerebral impairment to well-documented behavioral and academic performance, it will be difficult to assess the effectiveness of remedial programs for children with various types of disabilities due to the lack of criterion information to compare these programs.

A consideration of the behavioral correlates of brain functions, and their relationships to practical performance in the classroom situation and in everyday living, necessarily requires at least a brief introduction to the structure of the brain (Reitan, 1970). Even a general understanding of the anatomical and neurological organization of the nervous system improves one's comprehension of the consequences of dysfunctions within the system. Reitan emphasizes the importance of educators' understanding that communication through language and the ability to organize effectively one's visuo-spatial environment constitute two of the most basic types of behavioral functions involved in any type of efficient social performance. These developmental skills require constant integrity of neurological organization that maintains brain-behavior relationships. The way in which one plans a successful educational program for a learning disabled child may in part be determined by an understanding of how minimal brain damage alters behavior. The neuropsychologist must be able to translate neurological findings into information that is directly applicable to the classroom situation and to the design of specific educational programs. Psychological and neurological test results must be correlated to classroom performance levels and academic behaviors. Terms such as perception, motivation, learning, success, and failure are only tools to explain why and how individuals differ in their interactions with the environment. Less interested in the principles that underlie the brain-behavior relationship, the classroom teacher is faced with the social and practical significance of the consequences as well as with planning a course of action that will reduce the difficulties the individual faces in responding effectively to the demands of his or her environment (Reed, 1970). Dr. Reitan's work to date on minimal cerebral dysfunction and his future work in the area of learning disabilities may begin to provide the data necessary for correlating the influence of brain damage on intellectual functions with the practical problems facing the classroom teacher in designing effective programs of intervention and remediation.

THE BEHAVIORAL APPROACH

Much of this volume contains information both on the development of the behavioral approach to educating the learning disabled child and the most contemporary procedures used by behaviorally oriented practitioners. Therefore, we will only mention two behaviorally oriented researchers in this section. In the next chapter the development of the behavioral approach will be considered more fully. Classroom research and the search for procedures and methods of instruction for children with learning disorders has led many researchers to adopt and advance behavioral concepts and principles. Refinement of research techniques in the classroom and the applicability of the experimental analysis of behavior suggested certain educational procedures and caused long-time educational researchers, such as Wesley Becker, Richard Schiefelbusch, Frank Hewett, and the authors of this volume, to become more behavioral in their research. This is especially true of those whose orientation changed from clinical to educational, and whose remedial tactics changed from an emphasis on discovering etiological factors to one considering observable behavior and its precise measurement.

Frank Hewett

Although Frank Hewett's work deals with a specific population—emotionally disturbed children—his contribution to the area of learning disabilities is vital. Hewett does not enter into the debate on definition or etiology of "minimal cerebral dysfunction" or "specific learning disability" or "central processing system dysfunction." Instead, he seeks educational strategies that will allow a wider portion of public school children to learn efficiently and effectively.

Hewett believes that the actual incidence of emotional disturbance in school-age children in the United States is greater than the highest estimate of 10 percent (Bower, 1962). Further, he is "perplexed and appalled" by diagnostic practices, and questions the utility of such practice in the classroom. In an attempt to link diagnosis and description with educational operations, Hewett and his colleagues conceived a developmental hierarchy of educational tasks delineating seven stages of learning and the tasks that must be accomplished at each level if efficient learning is to occur.

This concept of a hierarchy of educational tasks is an attempt to narrow the gap between theory and practice in planning educational strategies for children with learning disorders. The basic assumption underlying the hierarchy holds that an effective educational program for children with learning disorders depends on establishing a point of meaningful contact between teacher and child (Hewett, 1964). The initial point of contact should be the establishment of educational goals and a methodology of achieving these goals that focuses on the child's learning ability. Hewett states:

> All such children (emotionally disturbed) are ready to learn something and despite their deviate behavior, the major educational goal is to get them ready for school while they are actually in school.

Selection of an educational strategy or a methodology, Hewett contends, is based on the manner in which these children are viewed. The sequence devised by Hewett is a statement of the developmental goals strategy, which expresses "in a continuous, interrelated educational context" the goals of the psychodynamic-interpersonal, sensory-neurological, and behavior modification strategies.

The psychodynamic-interpersonal strategy is concerned with causative factors based on psychoanalysis and the psychoeducational approaches of Freud and his followers. Hewett's (1968) position regarding this strategy is:

> As appealing as the specificity of diagnosis, labeling, and training associated with the sensory-neurological strategy may be to the educator, when it results in educational narrowness and rigidity it may have serious drawbacks . . . Being told by a physician or neurologist that a given child is "dyslexic" or has "strephosymbolia" may cause the teacher to decide that an ominous problem really precludes the child's being helped in the classroom.

The final strategy that Hewett incorporates into the development sequence is the behavior modification strategy, which attempts to find *what* behavior actually interferes with the child's learning. The teacher using this strategy is more concerned with changing aversive behavior than participating in the debate "over whether symptom removal constitutes a cure or mere masking of the real problem." Hewett warns that although "behavior modification offers a powerful methodology," it does not offer essential educational goals involving developmental or educational implications.

From these three strategies and what Hewett considers the need for a comprehensive "generalist approach" to education because of the overlapping of specialized fields, a developmental strategy has been formulated by the staff of the Neuropsychiatric Institute School in the Center for Health Sciences of the University of California at Los Angeles. This strategy is concerned specifically with describing a developmental matrix that consists of "the essential behaviors and competencies all must possess if they are successfully to learn in school" (Hewett, 1968). This developmental sequence of educational goals hypothesizes that for learning to be initiated successfully, the child must pay attention, respond, follow directions, explore, discover his or her environment independently, and function effectively with others in that environment. Readiness for school depends upon learning these behaviors in an orderly sequence from infancy to school age. The lowest levels of this hierarchy are not discrete and do not develop independently of one another, but there is a continuous sequence of the developing learning process, which leads to mastery of self-care and intellectual skills and to self-motivation in learning.

Hewett's developmental sequence is a synthesis of the work on developmental stages of Kephart, Doll, Havighurst, Piaget, Sigmund Freud, Anna Freud, Erickson, Maslow, and Sears into operations directly related to classroom learning. The sequence involves an orderly progression and a statement of the goals of the developmental strategy. Each level of the hierarchy contains its own specific goal that relates to the

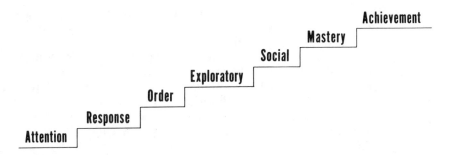

Figure 2-3. *A Developmental Sequence of Educational Goals.*

Child Development & Mental Retardation Center, Media Services.

rest of the hierarchy both upward and downward. The first four levels prepare the child for learning. The *attention level* is the first step in initiating learning behavior. The ability to focus on relevant cues in the environment is fundamental in all learning. When attention results in a child's acting upon this information, the second level, *response,* is reached. Noticing and doing make possible the child's ability to follow directions and develop *order* in his or her patterns of attention and response. The more systematic these patterns become, the easier it is for the child to *explore* the environment and thus make sense of the world. When a command of these four levels—attention, response, order, and exploration—is gained, a child is ready to develop socially and intellectually. On a *social* level the child learns to relate and interact with people in a meaningful way. Success in school is a delicate fabric of success in social relationships. Approval and acceptance of the peer group are essential for mastery of basic vocational and intellectual skills. Learning disabilities are usually encountered on the *mastery* level. Hewett (1968) states:

> The inability of the child to utilize his intellectual capacity to care for himself and develop basic intellectual skills constitutes a mastery level problem and is commonly seen among children with emotional problems. . . . Disturbed children also may fail to learn to read, write, spell, and do arithmetic in keeping with their chronological age and intelligence. These failures more often than not are the result of attention, response, order, exploratory, and social problems, which have kept the child out of the mainstream of socialization in the community and school.

The final level of the sequence is *achievement,* or development of self-motivation in learning. Achievement of educational goals at one grade level provides the basis for further, more complex learning.

Hewett makes clear that the developmental sequence serves as a source for the educational goals necessary for efficient, orderly learning. He then provides his ideas on one methodology to achieve these goals, drawing pragmatically from behavior modification techniques. The developmental sequence provides the framework for understanding what a child needs to be ready for school and to function well in the classroom, and the methods of attaining these goals.

Hewett sees as a central problem in public education the children who have not achieved the four basic goals of attention, response, order, and exploration. These children cannot deal with the stress of failure that they encounter in school, and without intervention their lack of readiness continues to inhibit their school performance, thereby increasing the stress of failure. To succeed in teaching any child, the teacher must be highly oriented toward success and must firmly believe that despite a lack of readiness to be in school, every child is ready to learn "something"; if "nothing" is learned, the fault lies in the teaching program (1968). Effective teaching requires the understanding of appropriate tasks for the child, tasks that are given within an understandable theoretical structure.

Hewett provides what he describes as a "learning triangle," which suggests three essential elements for success in teaching emotionally disturbed children. The *task* is related to attainment of a goal and to the development sequence; this involves selecting educational tasks within the ability of the student. By *reward,* Hewett refers to a positive consequence that tends to maintain or increase the strength or frequency of behavior associated with accomplishing tasks related to the achievement of educational goals in the developmental sequence. The *structure* of the educational situation dictates limitations that determine the reward. Hewett claims that structure is the degree of teacher control in the learning situation.

Hewett's work elucidates diagnostic techniques and the development of educational programs that insure individual learning and improvement along the developmental sequence. Each level of the sequence and the tasks needed to aid the teacher in the classroom situation are explored. Hewett develops a comprehensive model and program for the engineered classroom and supplies data from his work in the Santa Monica (California) Unified School District to support his views.

Steven Forness

Steven Forness is Hewett's coworker at the Neuropsychiatric Institute, University of California at Los Angeles, where he is the special education director in the Department of Psychiatry. His published work reveals an in-depth interest in the utility and limitations of behavior modification as a method of classroom management and motivation. Forness advances the view that the teacher can be a "learning specialist" or "a researcher." The classroom teacher should be aware of the reinforcers available in the school environment and should be able to use them systematically in an effective manner. The behavioristic approach, according to Forness, all too often has been misunderstood and misused because of the emphasis on tangible rewards and the failure to utilize systematic observation and methods of collecting data. The techniques of recording and charting behavioral data are precise methods of pinpointing and changing behaviors, which allow the teacher to perform more systematically. Charting consists of recording the frequency of behavior over a period of time on a graph or chart to determine behavioral trends. These techniques were developed by experimentalists in laboratory situations, but are useful to the classroom teacher in shaping a classroom environment that is more predictable, systematic, and individualized. In this way the learning process is more open and accessible to both the student and to the teacher.

The central point Forness makes about classroom management and charting techniques is that since many things are happening in the classroom simultaneously, it is difficult to process meaningful information on a single problem. Teachers trained in observation and recording of classroom behavioral data are able to discover trends on which further decisions and teaching strategies can be planned. If the teacher notices that a particular problem recurs at certain times each day, an intervention strategy can be focused upon the before or after events that maintain the behavior during those periods more easily than aiming in shotgun fashion at the entire classroom day. Charting this information provides a baseline by which the effectiveness of behavioral intervention can be measured.

This approach to classroom management and initiation and maintenance of the learning process, Forness says, offers the teacher and the school psychologist methods of becoming aware of what is available in the school situation to remediate learning problems. Forness focuses on two points available to all classroom situations—teacher attention and high frequency behaviors. He points out that teacher attention is used most often in an unsystematic manner. In a classroom situation when things are apparently running smoothly, some children receive teacher attention only for misbehavior. Forness (1970b) states:

> If Johnny, who has been sitting quietly, suddenly gets up and runs over to the window, however, the teacher focuses attention (and by implication her concern at that point) on Johnny and asks him to return to his seat. The unwitting message to the child is that out-of-seat behavior is rewarded by a show of attention and concern.

This view is based on the assumption "that both adaptive and maladaptive behavior are learned through interaction with observable stimuli in the environment and, thus, that stimuli can be manipulated to alter behavior." In regard to learning disabilities, specific learning disability, minimal brain dysfunction, or neurotic learning inhibition, the shift in education is away from conceptualization and toward observable behavior and immediate environmental events that can alter behavior. In this manner the teacher can become aware of "high frequency behaviors," or "tasks in which a child engages most often that can be used to get him [or her] to engage in tasks he [or she] does not often willingly perform." This is a restatement of the Premack Principle (1959)—high frequency behaviors may be used to reinforce low frequency behaviors. A student may work on a history assignment for half an hour to gain five minutes of listening to rock and roll records on earphones. The significance is that a teacher can respond consistently and initiate reinforcement that allows learning to take place. The charting of classroom behavior and use of baseline data serve as positive guidelines for reinforcement and behavioral intervention. Children easily can be taught to chart their own classroom behavior, thus gaining an awareness of what they are doing in the classroom environment.

Forness also focuses on the limitations and liabilities of the behavior modification approach. He lists three limitations that are either inherent in the theoretical pattern itself or lie in misapplication of theory by practitioners. First, learning theory does not guide the teacher in determining educational goals. Second, a view of motivation as exclusively extrinsic in nature is limiting in scope. Third, the operational definition of reinforcement ignores certain of its cognitive aspects. Forness suggests, like Hewett, that the behaviorist often overlooks the task of making behavioral goals compatible with developmental levels of learning. Academic goals, he suggests, must look within the total learning situation and focus on the "nature and structure of the task to be learned," which are of greater importance "than the behavioristic principles of learning, for example, reinforcement and practice." Finally, Forness discusses the use of extrinsic and intrinsic motivation. He points out that although the theoretical behavioral approach maintains that "desire or motivation can be manipulated simply by applying consequences when the organism behaves in a desired fashion," evidence shows that much behavior in a child apparently results not from extrinsic motivation but from motivation intrinsic to the task at hand.

A child's attempt to master the environment through exploration and discovery is motivated intrinsically. Programs that utilize intrinsic motivation, such as Hewett's, violate the purely behaviorist approach. However, intrinsic motivation should be at the top of the reinforcement hierarchy; unless the teacher is willing to consider intrinsic motivation or at least work toward that goal, he or she may be creating a situation of "reinforcement overkill" in which more powerful reinforcers than necessary are brought to bear. Forness sees obvious advantages from, and much good work being done with, behavior modification in remediating learning disorders, but he emphasizes the need for refining methodology so that it deals directly with the problems being faced. Whereas a child labeled "retarded" or "learning disabled" is often a victim of "the system," the educator must be careful that the child is not victimized further by misused methodology or unorganized programming. Behavior modification is useful only so long as the learning process is allowed to develop without obstruction.

SUMMARY

It is impossible to mention the work of everyone who has contributed to the field of learning disabilities. In fact, one of the most meaningful developments resulting from the thinking in the field is the concern for cooperation among disciplines, all contributing knowledge to the problem of the learning disabled child. A multidisciplinary and integrative approach clearly is necessary for the development of effective, comprehensive programs for the prevention of learning disabilities and for intervention and management procedures that will help learning disabled children. The correlation of behavioral research with educational and neuropsychological-neurophysiological research will advance the state of knowledge about how a child's brain develops and what relationships may exist between behavior and possible neural or perceptual dysfunctions.

Because of the work of the individuals discussed in this chapter, the learning disabled child is no longer a forgotten person. In following chapters, we shall see how these contributions have helped to develop an educational technology and systematic set of instructional procedures that hopefully one day will allow a specific academic or perceptual disorder to be remediated while the child remains in the regular school classroom.

REFERENCES

BARSCH, R. H., *Achieving Perceptual Motor Efficiency*, Vol. 1; *Enriching Perception and Cognition*, Vol. 2. Seattle: Special Child Publications, 1967 and 1968.

————, Six factors in learning. In J. Hellmuth, ed., *Learning Disorders*. Vol. 1. Seattle: Special Child Publications, 1965.

BATEMAN, B., *The Illinois Test of Psycholinguistic Abilities in Current Research: Summaries of Studies*. Urbana: University Illinois Press, 1965.

BENDER, L., Genetic data in evaluation and management of behavior disorders in children. *Diseases of the Nervous System*, 1960, *21*:2.

BIRCH, H. G., ed., *Brain Damage in Children: The Biological and Social Aspects*. Baltimore: Williams & Wilkins, 1964.

BIRCH, H. G., and A. LEFFORD, Two strategies for studying perception in "brain damaged" children. In H. G. Birch, ed., *Brain Damage in Children: The Biological and Social Aspects*. Baltimore: Williams & Wilkins, 1964.

BOWER, E. M., Comparison of the characteristics of identified emotionally disturbed children with other children in classes. In E. P. Trapp and P. Himmelstein, eds., *Readings on the Exceptional Child*. Englewood Cliffs, N.J.: Prentice-Hall, Inc., 1962.

CRATTY, B. J., *Developmental Sequence of Perceptual-Motor Task*. New York: Educational Activities, Inc., 1967.

CRATTY, B. J., *Motor Activity and the Education of Retardates*. Philadelphia: Lea & Febiger, 1969.

————, *Perceptual and Motor Development in Infants and Children.* New York: The Macmillan Company, 1970.

CRUICKSHANK, W. M., F. A. BENTZEN, F. H. RATZBURG, and M. T. TANNHAUSER, *A Teaching Method for Brain-Injured and Hyperactive Children.* Syracuse, N.Y.: Syracuse University Press, 1961.

CRUICKSHANK, W. M., and D. P. HALLAHAN, Alfred A. Strauss: pioneer in learning disabilities. *Exceptional Children,* 1973, *39,* 321–327.

CRUICKSHANK, W. M., and J. L. PAUL. The psychological characteristics of brain-injured children. In W. M. Cruickshank, ed., *Psychology of Exceptional Children and Youth* (3rd ed.). Englewood Cliffs, N.J.: Prentice-Hall, Inc., 1971.

DE HIRSCH, K., Differential diagnosis between aphasic and schizophrenic language in children. *Journal of Speech and Hearing Disorders,* 1967, *32,* 3–10.

————, Gestalt psychology applied to language disturbances. *The Journal of Nervous and Mental Disease,* 1954, *120,* 257–261.

————, Two categories of learning difficulties in adolescents. *American Journal of Orthopsychiatry,* 1963, *33,* 87–91.

DOLPHIN, J. E., *A study of certain aspects of the psychopathology of children with cerebral palsy.* Unpublished doctoral dissertation. Syracuse, N.Y.: Syracuse University, 1950.

DOLPHIN, J. E., and W. M. CRUICKSHANK, The figure-background relationship in children with cerebral palsy. *Journal of Clinical Psychology,* 1951a, *7,* 228–231.

————, Pathology of concept formation in children with cerebral palsy. *American Journal of Mental Deficiency,* 1951b, *56,* 386–392.

————, Tactual motor perception of children with cerebral palsy. *Journal of Personality,* 1952, *20,* 466–471.

————, Visuo-motor perception of children with cerebral palsy. *Quarterly Journal of Child Behavior,* 1951c, *3,* 198–209.

FORNESS, S. R., Behavioristic approach to classroom movement and motivation. *Psychology in the School,* 1970b, *7,* 356–363.

————, Educational prescription of the school psychologist. *Journal of School Psychology,* 1970a, *8,* 96–98.

FROSTIG, M., *Movement Education: Theory and Practice.* Chicago: Follett Educational Corporation, 1970.

FROSTIG, M., and D. HORNE, An approach to the treatment of children with learning disorders. In J. Hellmuth, ed., *Learning Disorders.* Vol. 1. Seattle: Special Child Publications, 1965.

————, *The Frostig Program for the Development of Visual Perception.* Chicago: Follett Educational Corporation, 1964.

FROSTIG, M., and P. MASLOW, Treatment methods and their evaluation in educational therapy. In J. Hellmuth, ed., *Educational Therapy.* Vol. 2. Seattle: Special Child Publications, 1969.

FROSTIG, M., P. MASLOW, D. W. LEFEVER, and J. R. B. WHITTLESEY, *The Marianne Frostig Developmental Test of Visual Perception, 1963 Standardization.* Palo Alto, Cal.: Consulting Psychology Press, 1964.

GETMAN, G. N., The visuomotor complex in the acquisition of learning skills. In J. Hellmuth, ed., *Learning Disorders*. Vol. 1. Seattle: Special Child Publications, 1965.

GETMAN, G. N., E. R. KANE, M. R. HALGREN, and G. W. McKEE, *The Physiology of Readiness, an Action Program for the Development of Perception for Children*. Minneapolis: Programs to Accelerate School Success, 1964.

GOLDSTEIN, K., *Die lokalisation in der grosshirnrinde. Handb. norm. pathol. physiologie*. Berlin: J. Springer, 1927.

————, The modification of behavior consequent to cerebral lesion. *Psychiatric Quarterly*, 1936, *10*, 586–610.

————, *The Organism*. New York: American Book, 1939.

————, Uber aphasie. *Schweizer archiv fur neurologie und psychiatrie*, 1962, *19*:1.

HALLAHAN, D. P., and W. M. CRUICKSHANK, *Psychoeducational Foundations of Learning Disabilities*. Englewood Cliffs, N.J.: Prentice-Hall, Inc., 1973.

HEWETT, F. M., *The Emotionally Disturbed Child in the Classroom*. Boston: Allyn & Bacon, 1968.

————, A hierarchy of educational tasks for children with learning disorders. *Exceptional Children*, 1964, *31*, 207–214.

KASS, C. E., Psycholinguistic disabilities of children with reading problems. *Exceptional Children*, 1966, *32*, 533–539.

KEPHART, N. C., *The Slow Learner in the Classroom* (2nd ed.). Columbus, Ohio: Charles E. Merrill, 1971.

KEPHART, N. C., and A. A. STRAUSS, A clinical factor influencing variations in I.Q. *American Journal of Orthopsychiatry*, 1940, *10*, 343–350.

KIRK, S. A., *Educating Exceptional Children*. Boston: Houghton Mifflin, 1962.

————, Illinois test of psycholinguistic abilities: Its origins and implications. In J. Hellmuth, ed., *Learning Disorders*. Vol. 3. Seattle: Special Child Publications, 1968.

KIRK, S. A., J. J. McCARTHY, and W. D. KIRK, *Illinois Test of Psycholinguistic Abilities* (rev. ed.). Urbana: University of Illinois Press, 1968.

McCARTHY, J. J., *Qualitative and quantitative differences in the language abilities of young cerebral palsied*. Unpublished doctoral dissertation. Urbana: University of Illinois, 1957.

McCARTHY, J. J., and J. F. McCARTHY, *Learning Disabilities*. Boston: Allyn & Bacon, 1969.

McLEOD, J., *Some psychological and psycholinguistic aspects of severe reading disability in children*. Unpublished doctoral dissertation. University of Queensland, Australia, 1965.

MYKLEBUST, H. R., *Auditory Disorders in Children*. New York: Grune & Stratton, 1954.

————, *Development and Disorders of Written Language*. New York: Grune & Stratton, 1965.

————, Learning disorders—psychoneurological disturbances in childhood. *Rehabilitation Literature*, 1964, *25*, 354.

MYKLEBUST, H. R., and O. JOHNSON, *Learning Disabilities: Educational Principles and Practices*. New York: Grune & Stratton, 1967.

ORTON, S. T., *Reading, Writing, and Speech Problems in Children.* New York: W. W. Norton, 1937.

OSGOOD, C. E., A behavioristic analysis of perception and language as cognitive phenomena. In J. S. Bruner, ed., *Contemporary Approaches to Cognition.* Cambridge, Mass.: Harvard University Press, 1957.

OSGOOD, C. E., and M. S. MIRON, eds., *Approaches to the Study of Aphasia.* Urbana: University of Illinois Press, 1963.

PIAGET, J., *The Origins of Intelligence in Children.* New York: International Universities Press, Inc., 1952.

PREMACK, D., Toward empirical behavior laws: I. positive reinforcement. *Psychological Review,* 1959, *66,* 219–233.

RADLER, D. H., and N. C. KEPHART, *Success through play: How to prepare your child for school achievement and enjoy it.* New York: Harper, 1960.

RAGLAND, G. G., *The performance of educable mentally handicapped students of differing reading ability on the ITPA.* Unpublished doctoral dissertation. Charlottesville: University of Virginia, 1964.

REED, H. B. C., JR., Brain damage, intelligence, and education. *National Business Education Quarterly,* 1970, *38,* 19–27.

REITAN, R. M., Brain structure and brain function. *National Business Education Quarterly,* 1970, *38,* 5–12.

———, The needs of teachers for specialized information in the area of neuropsychology. In W. Cruickshank, ed., *Syracuse University Special Education and Rehabilitation Series.* Syracuse, N.Y.: Syracuse University Press, 1966.

REITAN, R. M., and T. J. BOLL, Neuropsychological correlates of minimal brain dysfunction. *Annals of the New York Academy of Sciences,* 1973, *205,* 65–88.

REITAN, R. M., and C. HEINEMAN, Interactions of neurological deficits and emotional disturbances in children with learning disorders: methods for their differential assessment. In J. Hellmuth, ed., *Learning Disorders.* Vol. 3. Seattle: Special Child Publications, 1968.

SARASON, S. R. *Psychological Problems in Mental Deficiency.* New York: Harper & Row, 1949.

SIEVERS, D. J., *Development and standardization of a test of psycholinguistic growth in preschool children.* Unpublished doctoral dissertation. University of Illinois, 1955.

SKEFFINGTON, A. M., *Papers and Lectures.* Duncan, Okla.: Optometric Extension Program, 1926–1965.

STRAUSS, A. A., Beitrage zur enisteilung, entstehung und klinik der schwersten schwachsinnsforme. *Arch. of Psych. u. Nerv.,* 1933, *9,* 693.

STRAUSS, A. A., and N. C. KEPHART, Behavior differences in mentally retarded children as measured by a new behavior rating scale. *American Journal of Psychiatry,* 1940, *96,* 1117–1123.

———, *Rate of mental growth in a constant environment among higher grade norm and border line children.* Paper presented at American Association on Mental Deficiency, 1939.

STRAUSS, A. A., and L. S. LEHTINEN-ROGAN, *Psychopathology and Education of the Brain-Injured Child.* New York: Grune & Stratton, 1947.

TARNOPOL, L., *Learning Disabilities.* Springfield, Ill., Charles C Thomas, 1969.

WECHSLER, D., *Wechsler Intelligence Scale for Children*. New York: Psychological Corp., 1949.

WEPMAN, J. M., *Auditory Discrimination Test*. Language Research Associates, 1958.

WEPMAN, J. M., L. V. JONES, R. D. BOCK, and D. V. PELT, Studies in aphasia: background and theoretical formulations. *Journal of Speech and Hearing Disorders*, 1960, 25, 323–332.

WERNER, H., and A. A. STRAUSS, Causal factors in low performance. *American Journal of Mental Deficiency*, 1940, 44, 163–168.

Theories of Academic Learning—Research in Education

3

INTRODUCTION

In a sense, the concept of the learning disabled child was generated by research in the field of special education. As a scientific discipline, special education developed from attempts by medicine and psychology to describe and define the causes of learning disorders and provide programs to meet the educational needs of handicapped children. Dr. Frank Hewett (1972) states that the emerging discipline of special education has found itself "in the middle of a complex, multi-disciplinary maze, the choice points of which are labeled in such alien jargon and which involve such sophistication with extra-educational concepts that an efficient, understandable route to the ultimate goal (for example, a useful, practical educational program for the child) is most difficult to arrive at." Attempts to classify or pigeonhole the child with a learning disability met dismal failure because most diagnostic and research designs offered no means of effective or remedial procedures. Through a series of historical accidents, American psychologists and educators have belonged to and have been primarily influenced by the school of thought that believed intelligence (basic cognitive structures) to be innate, hereditary, and unchanged by experience (Bateman, 1964). The learning disabled child offered the psychologist and the educator a direct challenge to the accepted principles of learning. In fact, knowledge of the principles of learning, the laws of behavior, and the necessity of systematic scientific inquiry into their application is a necessity for the special educator and regular classroom teacher alike.

Research in education has been conducted from several perspectives. One, as we have seen, has been in the area of special education of handicapped children; another has been experimental psychology—studying the processes of learning, skill acquisition, transfer of training, and such in laboratory situations. The relationship of these two types of research has become clearer and more tangible in recent years. In considering the phenomenon of the learning disabled child, it is advisable to explore the history of learning research to trace the findings from laboratory research to the emergence of actual classroom practices. Research in learning is of specific importance when intervention procedures for learning problems in the classroom are generated.

The history of experimental psychology and its influence on educational practices are somewhat ambiguous. The impetus to reach scientific agreement on problems in various environmental settings has not been always obvious or intentional. Only when the scientific method is applied in educational settings can educational research interlock with other scientific disciplines. In theory, there have been two approaches to learning disabilities. The first assumes that the child has an organic or neurological disorder of some nature and diagnostic research must uncover exactly what causes that disorder to remediate the problem. The second, which stresses an educational diagnosis based on observable behaviors that leads to direct intervention strategies, is an instructional approach. These two approaches are not mutually exclusive. All experimental data on learning must be evaluated for their applicability in solving problems and in the design of new and more efficient educational procedures.

Since the early 1900s American psychologists have been diligently studying the process of learning and what constitutes learning behavior. The transition from basic research in learning theory to actual classroom techniques has been rough but steady. Throughout the years of the development of various learning theories, the classroom teacher has not always accepted the sophisticated and complex theorizations. Since the mid-1960s scientifically based techniques of educational programming and remedial intervention have emerged. No longer must a classroom teacher use random, unsystematic methods. Teachers have needed not new philosophies or theories of learning but actual proven techniques on which to base instructional programming.

Because the authors are more interested in improving the quality of classroom instruction, a bias toward behavioral techniques in educational settings will become obvious throughout this book. In any field the history of scientific development is one of refining that field's procedures for assessing the relationships between independent and dependent variables. This progress has always involved sharpening procedures of direct observation, avoiding introspective and inferential judgments whenever possible, establishing observable control over variables, and experimental (systematic) manipulation of one independent variable at a time. Substantial advancements in education can be made if educators will use these procedures for evaluating the interrelationships between independent classroom variables of learning and the dependent variables of performance.

ASSOCIATIVE AND COGNITIVE
TRADITIONS IN PSYCHOLOGY

To define learning is a useless task, but to understand learning as the fundamental process of life is useful indeed. Public education is one way of exchanging information by which a child gains the skills needed to live an effective and productive life. There are many levels of learning behavior and many variables that influence learning. From simple signal learning, or the establishment of a conditioned response, to high level problem-solving behavior by which the generalized principles governing the relativity of all systems of behavior are understood, the total process of learning must be considered in the design of an efficient public education system.

Accomplishments in elucidating the types and varieties of learning abilities need to be explored. The study of learning problems began with the desire to know the environment, the forces of nature, and the relationship of the individual to both. Psychology had its sources in the basic desire for knowledge of the matrix of human behavior. As psychology advanced in capabilities, certain basic laws of learning behavior were discovered. Modern experimental psychology utilized advances in the physical sciences, especially physics, to become emancipated from the philosophical double binds of early psychology, in which all inferences were based solely on the personal experience of the individual. The study of the history of learning theory traces its main theoretical developments from the psychology of learning as applicable to academic situations.

The theoretical and historical roots of experimental psychology are necessary parts of the classroom teacher's repertoire if the scientific method and contemporary tools of measurement are to be applied to the classroom. Any amount of expertise in the classroom is dependent upon the amount of sophistication the educator possesses as to the actual theoretical and historical bases for contemporary classroom methodology. This is not to suggest that every teacher should be a trained psychologist or scientist, but since a teacher deals each moment of classroom time with learning behavior, to be deficient and unsophisticated in the field is to preempt successful teaching with lack of skill. Successful classroom teaching is a learned skill. A teacher is an agent of change, a catalyst who aids students in making transitions necessary to establish behaviors that facilitate the steady growth of the learning process. A classroom teacher's awareness of the many levels of learning behavior becomes the single most important skill he or she develops.

Nearly all research in learning in the United States has developed out of two main theoretical positions—associative and cognitive. Learning research further generated learning models out of which definite methods of classroom instruction are derived. It is important that teachers develop an understanding of learning theory "to become aware of the premise upon which their own teaching methods are based" (Garry and Kingsley, 1970). Any method to initiate and maintain learning behavior in the classroom is based on an idea or theory of how individuals acquire skills and knowledge. Contemporary research is revealing the process of how learning occurs, whereas much previous research documented the conditions essential for learning to take place.

What Is a Theory?

In the broadest sense, a theory is a systematic interpretation of an area of knowledge (Hill, 1963). Research in learning that follows basic research design is an attempt to build a formal, logical structure to explain learning behaviors. The history of learning theory reveals that formal systems develop as the result of informal systems (verbal interpretation with research design) that precede them. Behaviorist researchers continually have stressed the need for a system of learning behaviors inferred from precise analysis of stimulus and response relationships. Behavioral learning theory allows greater research precision and is generally more compatible with scientific approaches as used in the natural sciences. Cognitive, or field, theory historically has been interested in exploring the particular human characteristics of intellectual processes and the ways in which complex problems are solved. The cognitive theoretical approach has tended to appeal to applied psychologists in both clinical and educational situations.

Associationism

The two great theoretical traditions in learning theory once were separated by rather sharp distinctions, but as research became more sophisticated some avenues of agreement were found. The associationist tradition has its roots as far back as Aristotle, David Hume, and nineteenth-century British psychologists such as James Mill and his son John Stuart Mill. Following Thomas Hobbes and John Locke, the philosophical basis for associationist psychology, empiricism, made the association of ideas the fundamental concept of learning and knowledge. The empirical is that which pertains to experience, or which pertains to the methods of results based on observation or experiment (Misiak, 1961). From empirical philosophy the British associationists began to build "the structure of the new physiological psychology" that developed in the United States beginning in the early 1900s (Boring, 1950). According to the associationist paradigm, when mental processes occur together, links or associations are formed in the central nervous system. When an event arouses one of the associations, others also tend to be aroused. The associationists were primarily interested in the way in which "complex ideas" form in the mind as a result of sensory input. To acquire a new idea, an individual must have contiguity of sensory impressions and repetition of these contiguous sensory events.

The Lockean point of view has been, and is still, dominant in the Anglo-American psychology (Allport, 1955). All of what is called scientific psychology both in laboratory and clinical research is founded in the basic assumptions of Lockean associationism. The Lockean empiricist is Aristotelian, believing that what is external and visible is more fundamental than what is not. The mind is "tabula rasa"—a blank slate—at birth. Therefore, what happens to the individual, or the effect of the environment on the individual, is what is important in understanding human function and learning. All basic stimulus-response models developed out of this philosophical stance. Ivan Pavlov's research in Russia during the 1920s was developed by American psychologists in the Lockean tradition, such as James Watson and Clark Hull.

The basic associationist assumptions also led to the experimental research in the United States initiated by Edward Thorndike, who began his experiments with trial-and-error learning in animals. Thorndike hypothesized a set of principles that explained changes he observed in the learning process. His law of exercise postulated that stimulus-response bonds were necessary for learning to occur. Otherwise, a response must occur in the presence of the stimuli. The primary law of learning, according to Thorndike, was the *law of effect,* which stated that learning was strengthened not only by the contiguity of stimulus-response bonds, but by the effects that followed the response. Thorndike discovered in his work with animals that correct responses are progressively strengthened by immediate delivery of "motive satisfiers." Gagne explains this as follows:

> When confronted with a novel situation, the motivated learner engages in various "tries" to attain satisfaction. Sooner or later, largely by chance, he makes a set of responses that lead to motive satisfaction (1970).

Thorndike's work paved the way to reinforcement theory and operant conditioning techniques as researched by men such as Edwin Guthrie, Clark Hull, and B. F. Skinner (all of whom shall be discussed later).

Thorndike's experimental work with animal trial-and-error learning led him to research in academic situations using experimental methods. William Estes (1954) states that to his knowledge Thorndike offered "the first interpretation of mental development in terms of learning theory." Thorndike in a real sense can be considered one of the initial researchers in the application of experimental methodology to the study of academic learning behavior.

Another development in the early 1900s that has made perhaps the greatest impact on academic learning theory was the work of James B. Watson. Watson became the spokesman for the movement in American psychology that studied objective human behavior using experimental methodology in lieu of inference about consciousness. He asserted that behavior is "a matter of conditioned reflexes, that is, responses learned by what is now called classical conditioning." Dispensing with subjective feeling states and consciousness as the study of psychology, the behaviorist tradition, with its emphasis on environment rather than heredity as the explanation of intelligence, gradually became the prevailing approach to learning in the United States. Henry Misiak (1961) comments:

> The Behaviorist school presented an Associationist explanation of behavior. The old laws of association, applied originally only to mental operations, were transformed by this school into laws of behavior and were invoked to explain the stimulus-response relationship.

As the behaviorist tradition developed, Edwin Guthrie remained closest to Watson's original, radical view of learning behavior. Guthrie, like Watson, was a contiguity theorist, who emphasized the stimulus-response bond formation rather than reinforcement of the stimulus-response event. The relationship of the Watson-Guthrie and the Thorndike-Skinner theoretical stances will be explained shortly. For now it is important to keep in mind that out of the British associationist philosophy, with emphasis on empirical evidence, developed the behaviorist approaches to learning that dominate classroom research today.

Cognitivists

Opposed to the associationist trends is the gestalt tradition of Max Wertheimer, Wolfgang Kohler, and Kurt Koffka. The central theoretical difference is reflected in the cognitive idea that learning is an active process of discovery and comprehension of relationships, of building an organization, or hierarchy, of sensory experience. Whereas Locke was the source of the associationist tradition, the German philosopher Gottfried Leibniz was the source of the cognitive tradition. For Locke, the organism reacted when stimulated; for Leibniz, and later Kant, it was self-propelled. In other words, the person is the source of acts, not merely a responder to acts. Leibniz, followed by the gestaltists, postulated the human mind as being active rather than passive in nature. The entire developmental history of psychology cannot be dichotomized this way, but it is useful to see that various viewpoints in contemporary psychology have developed out of these two philosophical traditions.

A year before James Watson leveled his first edict to American psychology, Max Wertheimer presented a challenge to the traditional psychology of Germany. Unlike Watson's objections that psychology concern itself with objective behavior and forego discussions of consciousness, Wertheimer objected to the process of analysis and fragmentation of consciousness in order to study or conceptualize the whole. Wertheimer's challenge to psychology was that we perceive the world in gestalten, or dynamic wholes, rather than mosaics or parts that are put together through the perceptual process into a whole. From Wertheimer's concept of gestalten developed the interest in figure-ground relationships, or the way in which gestalten "come to stand out as distinct entities separate from the background against which they appear" (Hill, 1963). The appearance of objects in perception is the product of a *synthetic process* that is regulated by the psychological *laws of perception*. Two factors constitute the objective conditions of this process: 1) the objective structure of the object, or the constancy of its objective properties; and 2) the psychological framework of the subject, that is, the system of "cognitive structures" as well as the "set" of the subject (Gobar, 1968). Thus, cognitive theories of learning presented by the gestaltists were formulated in terms of perception. Learning, in the cognitive paradigm, is not a matter of adding new connections and subtracting old ones in a digital fashion, but rather of changing one gestalt to another in an analogous manner. Such a shift in perceiving gestalten involves insight in which the field of experience is reorganized to allow awareness of the whole situation in a new, synthetic fashion. This type of learning can be either spontaneous or the result of a series of gradual, partial insights. The importance of this kind of cognitive activity is in problem-solving behavior in which the individual must perceive and discover a solution by either perceiving or recognizing a pattern that is organized cognitively into the appropriate gestalt.

Gestalt, or field, psychology in America has had less impact than behaviorism; by the time the German gestaltists imported their theories in the 1930s behaviorism had already won the favor of experimental psychologists in American circles. Thus, as Edwin Boring notes, "many American psychologists did not understand them, for they were protesting against something that was no longer important in America" (1950). Some psychologists came to embrace gestalt concepts in America as a "cognitive theory," but the whole array of gestalt concepts has never been accepted. In place of planning, foresight, or purpose, American cognitive theorists (such as Edward Tolman) prefer the more static conception of cognitive maps or sets. Contemporary individuals who have made invaluable contributions to education out of this tradition include Jean Piaget and Jerome Bruner.[1]

---

[1] For readers who wish to become better acquainted with the different perspective of the cognitive theorists, we recommend the following volumes:

J. S. BRUNER, *The Process of Education* (New York: Vintage Books, 1963).

J. S. BRUNER, *Toward a Theory of Instruction* (New York: W. W. Norton, 1968).

J. S. BRUNER, R. R. OLIVER, and P. M. GREENFIELD, and others. *Studies in Cognitive Growth* (New York: John Wiley, 1966).

J. PIAGET, *Language and Thought of the Child*, 3rd ed. (New York: Humanities, 1962).

J. PIAGET, and B. INHELDER, *The Psychology of the Child* (New York: Basic Books, 1969).

For clarity's sake the differentiation must be made anew between field theory and learning theory. Learning theory, as viewed in this chapter, is the scientific approach to learning behaviors, "which has grown out of the American functionalist-behaviorist tradition and which is associated historically with the names of Pavlov, Thorndike, Loeb, Jennings, Watson, and Carr, and contemporarily with the names of Hull, Guthrie, and Skinner" (Estes, 1970). The behaviorally oriented learning theorists reason that concepts of learning must develop and be confirmable in terms of the predictability of observable behaviors. Learning theorists have constructed their paradigms in a quite straightforward manner utilizing experimental data.

Field theorists, on the other hand, secure their main sources of information from inferences made on observations of people in social situations that treat the individual as a whole. The gestalt workers claim that a person learns as a result of the way in which the environment is perceived, and that there are basic laws determining the organization of perception. In a sense, learning theory and field theory initially dealt with different problems. The learning theorists, following the basic S-R research paradigm, began with a carefully defined experimental situation in which learning behavior could be observed and measured. From research data, gauging the rate or amount of change in the target behavior, the learning theorist then generalized a conceptual model to test further the reliability of the experimental data in other analagous situations. Estes and colleagues (1954) point out that comparison of learning and field theories is a difficult enterprise because both use different data language. Learning theory has developed a more centralized, formal system of describing and predicting learning behaviors in given situations; whereas field theory has maintained a more global view of human behavior in approaching problems of learning. The field approach places emphasis on cognitive operations and development of perception in understanding relationships between stimuli and the environment. The behaviorist tradition started by utilizing only observable, overt behavior for research design and began to ascertain and formulate laws relating behavior changes to multiple independent variables that related directly to the learning situation. It should be reiterated once more, however, that the sharp theoretical distinctions that once existed are disappearing as research on learning becomes more sophisticated. Differences that were initially methodological and philosophical begin to fade as theoretical stances are applied to actual classroom situations, and learning theory begins to elucidate actual learning abilities.

The remainder of this chapter will focus on the development of the analysis of behavior and classroom procedures that have been applied successfully to remediate learning problems. Claims that the behaviorists are more interested in advancing methods and techniques of measurement of psychological science than in applying research data to social problems often have been made. By tracing the theoretical and practical roots of behaviorism to the present state, the application of behavioral procedures by the classroom teacher may be better understood. The authors do not wish to underestimate the importance of recent work by other approaches to the field of education, but it is beyond the scope of this volume to include all the work that has been done. We will focus on the historical factors involved with the transition from laboratory work in learning theory to the development of systematic procedures for intervention and remediation in the classroom, specifically in special education classrooms.

Educational research in learning disabilities began with early work with brain damage, but the most significant problem was not the *fact* of brain injury. It was, instead, the *presence* of certain behaviors in the child's repertoire that made learning difficult or impossible (McCarthy and McCarthy, 1969). Not until fairly recent years has classroom research begun (Haring and Phillips, 1962; Becker, Madsen, Arnold, and Thomas, 1967) to document problem behaviors and systematic methods of remediation that are applicable to regular public school classrooms. To gain a better perspective of behavioral techniques, such as the functional analysis of behavior, behavior modification, and precision teaching, we shall "go back to the roots."

FROM LEARNING THEORY TO CLASSROOM RESEARCH—A BRIEF HISTORY

Only since the 1930s has the field of education begun to utilize scientific research design to explore the learning potential offered by public education. Psychologists interested in learning behavior have worked steadily and diligently researching educational techniques in spite of usually uncooperative environments. Because of the difficulty in accepting experimental design in regular classroom situations, much of the initial work in academic learning theory was accomplished in special education classrooms, or in clinical or laboratory settings. But success with the mentally retarded and emotionally disturbed has proved the far-reaching benefits of the behavioral approach in education. These advances cannot be overlooked in a time when educational innovation is an absolute necessity in finding a means to solve the multitude of problems facing our society.

Behaviorist research historically has emphasized the need for objective, experimental design in learning research. This has allowed the theoretical stance to be flexible enough to change with new data. Research generates new theory by testing the initial hypothesis for reliability and validity. In Gestalt, or field, psychology "little or no attempt is made to control or manipulate the situation" (Garry and Kingsley, 1970). Behaviorist research, on the other hand, has always required rigid control to determine the relationship between independent and dependent variables. Learning theory has been produced by research in human behavior and is constantly changing to accommodate new information. The validity of a theory rests upon the kind and extent of predictions that can be made in utilizing that theory. In this way, one scientific method produces a system of factual data by which existing knowledge can be organized into consistent systems.

The most powerful systematic methods of classroom instruction have been developed through the evolution of behavioral research. Because the behaviorist focuses on what the learner does rather than how it is done, reliable techniques for initiating and maintaining a high frequency of learning behavior have been discovered. The history of the behaviorist approach to academic learning theory clearly illustrates the dynamic capabilities that have developed.

Watson and Guthrie—Early Behaviorism

James B. Watson's attack (1914) on the lack of objective research in psychology was the beginning of the American tradition of behaviorism. Watson wanted psychology to be a scientific system, not a philosophically speculative one. Psychology's task, as Watson viewed it, was to study what people do, not what they think or feel. The dismissal of consciousness (thinking and perception) as subject matter for scientific research seemed welcome to American psychologists. Watson began his work on the most elemental level, studying strict stimulus-response relationships. He used no theory and utilized only the bare minimum of reliable data in the form of Pavlov's stimulus-response research in Russia. Behaviorism after Watson became the psychology of stimulus-response (Boring, 1950).

Watson's view of learning is heavily influenced by the classical conditioning paradigms based on the study of reflexology. The genetic characteristics of man, according to Watson, are exemplified in "certain stimulus-response connections called reflexes" (Hill, 1963). This constitutes the entire inherited behavioral matrix. New connections within this inherited matrix occur through the conditioning process, following Pavlov's original research paradigm. According to the basic classical conditioning theory, if a second stimulus occurs along with or just before the stimulus for the reflex response, after several pairings the new stimulus alone will produce the response. Watson's treatment of skill acquisition and acquisition of knowledge emphasizes simple stimulus-response bond formation through the principles of frequency and recency. *Frequency* implies that the more one makes a given response to a given stimulus, the more likely that the same response will be made to the stimulus again. *Recency* implies that the more recent a response to a given stimulus, the more likely the response will be made again. The process of learning thus involved eliciting the proper sequence of words in response to a question or other conditioned stimulus.

Watson's views were simplistic and his analysis was not thorough. The importance of his work was his stance on making psychology an objective science utilizing logical thoroughness (although his work lacked the depth he seemed to imply was possible). We shall see, however, that Watson's rejection of traditional psychology caused most American learning theory to become truly behavioristic.

Edwin Guthrie is the researcher who remained closest to Watson's original behaviorist (S-R) position in developing learning theory. The basic principle of Guthrie's system is the principle of association: "a combination of stimuli which has accompanied a movement will, on its reoccurrence, tend to be followed by that movement" (Guthrie, 1952). This is the core of Guthrie's contiguity theory of learning—we repeat what we learn and we learn what we do. Utilizing puzzle box experiments with animals, Guthrie developed his learning theory along the lines of classical conditioning techniques, contending that the responses in any situation will be reproduced on the occasion of the presentation of an analagous situation.

The learning situation—any stimulus-response situation—is composed of a great many stimuli and responses out of which conditioning, or learning, can be generated by the principles of substitution and contiguity. By contiguity Guthrie implied that for a stimulus-response bond to form, the relationship must develop sequentially in time. Stimuli can be external or internal to the organism. For example, a boy learning the multiplication tables encounters various attracting and distracting stimuli in the room. Sounds occurring at the instant (the teacher's voice or his own repeating of the problem), the movements of his fingers and hands as he writes the problems and answers on the paper, and all the other various stimuli that are impinging upon his sense organs are being associated with the movements and responses he is making. Each response the boy makes modifies the learning situation. Some responses are cues for further activity (getting pencil and paper ready); some sustain action or attention; others cause the termination of the stimulus situation (correctly answering the problem).

Guthrie claimed that learning is complete on each trial, and the strength of the association will not gain through repetition, as full strength occurs on the first connection. This is an "all-or-none" or digital conception of learning. Following this line of thought, Guthrie reasoned that correct performance is a result of associating correct responses with appropriate cues. Learning then proceeds by stimulus substitution in S-R units. Guthrie breaks down the overall skilled, or learned, performance to add plausibility to his argument. A skilled act is made up of many specific small movements. The learner either makes a connection with one of the components of the overall skilled activity, or it is not made at all. If the association is made, there is no variation in strength to the connection. Thus, the learning situation involves an enormous number of specific stimulus-movement connections. Improvement in any skill requires a gradual accumulation of specific movements or parts that occur suddenly.

The weak point of Guthrie's theoretical stance is his rejection of reinforcement, or reward. Guthrie implies that we learn not by success or reward, but simply by doing. Drive and motivation arouse the learner and cause activity, but are seen as relatively unimportant to learning. Guthrie contended that the probability of a response occurring again is increased in a charge that preserves the last S-R bond in any given situation. Changes in the stimulus situation may be made by the experimentor (or the apparatus) following the occurrence of the response to be conditioned, or may be a result of the stimulus consequences of the organism's response itself (Boring, 1950). There is no way of predicting, Guthrie claims, whether any particular stimulus following an S-R will serve as "a bond-protecting reinforcement."

In contiguity theory as formulated by Guthrie, the role of "reinforcement" is to terminate a present stimulus condition through the behavior elicited by the reinforcing stimuli. This follows the logic of contiguity theory, which reasons that conditioning is strictly simultaneous. The basis for contiguity learning theory is the associationistic philosophical tradition. Guthrie attempted to give the associationist paradigm of learning firm physiological roots. His ideas of stimulus-response reflexology are taken from Pavlov's classical conditioning experimentation. Pavlov's experiments showing actual pairing of unconditioned and conditioned stimuli were taken by Guthrie to be physiological proof of association. He states, "We assume that all behavior is brought about through neural activity. But neurological explanations are of very little use in explaining most behavior." Although Guthrie never utilized neurological explanations of behavior, his underlying physiological paradigm is governed by the all-or-none theory of neural connection. From the level of neural connections to the level of stimulus-response to actual intellectual or conceptual learning experience, Guthrie does not deviate from the all-or-none theory. Hill (1963) states, "Whereas for Watson, a stimulus-response connection is something that varies in strength and grows stronger with practice, for Guthrie it is an all-or-nothing bond. The connection is either present or absent, with no intermediate variation in strength."

Thus, we can see that Guthrie, like Watson, attempted to present a structural basis of behavior utilizing neural contiguity or the temporal connection between neurons as a basis. As Gobar (1968) makes clear, this is to commit a *genetic fallacy*, or "the fallacy that functional simplicity at a lower level constitutes the sufficient explanation of morphological complexity at higher levels." Guthrie's attempt to make all human behavior absolutely empirical from a functional physiological level leaves little room for the explanation of complex learning behaviors outside the rather rigid mechanistic all-or-nothing paradigm.

The result of Guthrie's work was not the presentation of research data, but rather, like Watson, to generate interest in the growing behaviorist approach to the study of human learning. While Guthrie's system does not stand up as a formal deductive theory, his contributions to understanding practical learning situations are valuable. Guthrie's methods for breaking habits appear often in the literature and are repeated time and again by educational psychologists dealing with deviant behavior. His classic example of the 10-year-old girl who could not learn to hang up her coat upon entering the house until her mother instructed her each time she threw her wrap on the chair to go back outside, return to the house, and hang up the coat properly, is often repeated throughout the literature on conditioning. Guthrie's central contribution was that, more than any other major learning theorist, he emphasized the precise analysis of stimulus-response events. He particularly emphasized the role of movement-produced stimuli—the sensations produced by our own movements. These are instrumental in thought, the coordination of sequences of behavior, and responses to stimuli that are no longer present.

Both Watson and Guthrie emphasize the *theory of contiguity* in their work, while remaining behaviorists in the general sense of the term. Both of these men disdained the notion that reward had any effect on what was learned. In this respect they differed from other behaviorists (such as Thorndike and Skinner), who primarily were interested in the nature of the reinforcing event or stimuli. *Contiguity theory* stressed that learning depends on the temporal continuity of stimulus-response bonds.

Neither Guthrie nor Watson ever actually did experimental research in classroom or academic learning, so the application of their theories to the classroom situation has no empirical evidence of success or failure. There is simply no way to know. No long and active tradition or research has developed within the framework of Guthrie's theory. The contemporary behavioral researchers in education draw much from the philosophical orientations of both these men, however, especially in the use of analysis of behavioral events and the use of continuous measurement.

Thorndike and Skinner—The Evolution of Experimental Analysis of Behavior

Edward L. Thorndike must be considered the first American learning theorist and was a protegé of William James, a leading theorist in modern psychology. Thorndike's work with both animal and human learning makes him the initial developer of American educational psychology. William Estes (1970) says of Thorndike:

> To my knowledge, the first interpretation of mental development in terms of learning theory was undertaken by Thorndike (1931). Thorndike proposed to account for the progressive increase in intellectual capacity from lower organisms to man in terms of quantitative increase in the number of available associative connections.

Thorndike was an innovator in the field of experimental animal psychology. His early work, published in *Animal Intelligence* (1898), is recognized as one of the first objective studies of animal behavior. The experimentation with cats in problem boxes is perhaps his most well-known study. A hungry cat was confined to a cage designed so the cat could open the door by pulling a string inside the cage. A morsel of fish was placed outside the cage. Observing the cat learning to open the cage led Thorndike to several conclusions. First, he concluded that it was not an "intelligent" understanding of the relationship of string-pulling and door-opening, but a sequential "stamping-in" of the stimulus-response connection between recognizing the string and pulling it. Second, he concluded that particular responses are followed immediately by a "motive satisfier" and are thus strengthened. This happened, of course, when the cat was rewarded with the food after escaping from the box. Thus, Thorndike postulated the "law of effect," that animal learning is a gradual discrimination of correct responses.

The contribution to education from this work manifests itself through techniques rather than actual data. Thorndike concerned himself with basic, practical methodology in research. All experimentation relied on careful observation of behavior under controlled conditions. The main concern of the research was to discern what events caused the gradual strengthening of stimulus-response bonds. Above all, Thorndike attempted to pattern the laws of learning after the formalized system of physics. Through his research work and published writings, three important aspects of Thorndike's work formed a basis for work in American learning theory:

1. Association between stimulus and response.
2. Objective observation of overt behavior.
3. Establishment of the basic laws of learning.

As a behaviorist, Thorndike differs from Watson and Guthrie basically on the problem of "reinforcement" or "reward." Watson's *law of frequency* and Guthrie's basic formulation of stimulus-response learning do not differ greatly from Thorndike's *law of exercise*. It is generally accepted that stimulus-response bonds are strengthened by the response occurring in the presence of the stimuli. Thorndike, however, stated that the primary law of learning was the *law of effect*. This said that the "stamping-in" of stimulus-response connections depends on the effects that follow the response, not merely the contiguity of the stimulus-response bond. Any S-R connection, Thorndike reasoned, could be strengthened if it is followed by a "satisfier." Likewise, a connection can be weakened by an event following a connection called an "annoyer." Thus, the presence of satisfying or annoying events determined whether the S-R connection would be "stamped-in" or "stamped-out."

Thorndike was criticized by more strict behaviorists for the use of seemingly subjective language for describing the connection process. But Thorndike, although using terms such as "satisfier" and "annoyer," remains objective in his definition of these phenomena. He states:

By a satisfying state of affairs is meant one which the animal does nothing to avoid, often doing things which maintain or renew it. By an annoying state of affairs is meant one which the animal does nothing to preserve, often doing things that put an end to it (1931).

In this way the animal remains in the "is-does" paradigm and does not concern itself with feeling states.

Thorndike's experimental work in trial-and-error learning and great quantities of his writing have had more effect on educational practice than practically any other learning theory. All modern connectionist (associationist) theories of learning draw heavily on Thorndike's work. The explicit nature of his theory contributed to its application in classroom situations. The effect on educational practice was threefold. First, Thorndike, unlike previous theorists, not only devoted time to theoretical aspects of learning, but he began to pay attention to applied aspects and classroom situations. Second, he recognized that the learner was an individual ready to make certain responses, capable of varying his or her responses, and trying to respond to the aspects of a stimulus situation that appeared familiar with a response previously successful in similar situations. Finally, Thorndike established two component parts of the learning situation—the teacher must identify the basic elements of the task and present them with least confusion, and upon occurrence the correct response should be rewarded. This presents the beginning of task analysis in educational practice. The elements of any task are presented in a way that provides the most favorable opportunity for eliciting correct responses, which then can be rewarded.

Another, and perhaps the greatest, effect on education was Thorndike's (1924) experimental study that tested the claims of formal discipline advocates. Thorndike compared the school records of over 13,000 high school students to determine whether the study of Latin, or other formal learning disciplines, had any direct effect on reasoning ability. The results showed that several studies had more impact on reasoning ability than Latin, but no subject greatly improved overall performance. The result signaled the beginning of the end for the doctrine of formal discipline, and a movement toward curriculum innovation. The resulting great increase in curriculum planning led to an overreaction in the attempt to design an ultra-practical curriculum that would simulate situations in "real" life. Whatever the shortcomings, the overall effect of Thorndike's challenge to traditional programming has resulted in a vast reorganization of teaching and classroom design, which has greatly benefited American education.

Thorndike's contribution, regardless of his limitations in presenting a formal theory of learning, is the establishment of utilitarian methods in the classroom that are derived from actual practice. This represents the first attempt at a well-organized learning situation that considers the individual learner and individual ability.

As inferred, Thorndike's was not a systematic theory. The work of B. F. Skinner involves an extension of the connectionist theory that is more systematic both in theory and application. The relationship of Skinner and Thorndike is that of a contemporary thinker whose views are closely analogous to a great pioneer's. Both men disdain high level theorization in the formulation of their systems. In fact, Skinner is quite explicit about the nature of his antitheoretical stance. He denies that his systematic treatment of behavior is a theory at all, but rather an elucidation of the controls exercised for centuries without ever being formally presented. Skinner (1969) writes:

> The word "theory" was to mean "any explanation of an observed fact which appeals to events taking place somewhere else, at some other level of observation, described in different terms, and measured, if at all, in different dimensions"—events, for example, in the real nervous system, the conceptual system, or the mind.

The basic assumption made by Skinner is that behavior (and therefore learning) is lawful. He argues that theories utilizing levels of description other than what is occurring have not stimulated good research in learning. The function of a scientific analysis of behavior is not to provide a theory per se, but to reveal a systematic interpretation of human behavior based upon the generalized principles, or laws, of behavior by which predictions validly can be made. Thus, theory and practice become synonymous. The application of scientific data to a practical situation should prove either the validity or invalidity of the laboratory data obtained to modify or change certain behavior. A synthesis of the laws of behavior based on the dependent variables and the independent variables can be expressed in quantitative terms that yield a comprehensive patterning of the organism as a behaving system. Going further, Skinner states that he is not anti-theorist, but he does reject the hypothetico-deductive method. Claiming that "behavior is one of those subject matters which do not call for hypothetico-deductive methods," Skinner reasons that if hypotheses appear (a tentative explanation of events that cannot be observed directly) the investigator has turned his or her attention to inaccessible events (1969).

From this paradigm Skinner formulates his laws of operant conditioning. He agrees with Thorndike's "law of effect," and the attempt to chart the process of behavioral change on a "learning curve." Thorndike's discovery of a quantitative process in behavior, similar to the processes of physics and biology, reveals behavior change over a period of time that cannot be made by simple observation. Learning curves do not, however, elucidate the *basic process* of how behavior is "stamped-in." The curve is the result of certain fundamental processes involving the interaction of dependent variables in evoking responses, but it is not the most direct means of recording these processes. Both the frequency of response and the consequences must be recorded. To understand what Thorndike called "stamping-in," Skinner began to study the *consequences of behavior*. He states that the "barest possible statement to be made about the stamping-in process is that a consequence made contingent upon certain, measurable properties of behavior can cause the frequency of that behavior to increase." This way, single responses are not the unit of study; rather predictive science studies a class of responses that are referred to as *operants*. The term emphasizes the fact that the behavior operates upon the environment to generate consequences (1953).

The difference between respondent behavior, which is the study of the reflexology of physical behavior elicited by a specific stimulus, and operant behavior, which needs no particular stimulus, is crucial to understanding. Skinner speaks of operant behavior as being emitted by the organism rather than elicited by stimuli. Most common behavior can be classed as operant; walking, talking, working, and playing are all composed of operant responses. The emphasis in Skinner's work is thus the switching from the direct analysis of particular stimuli to the analysis of environmental conditions that influence behavior and learning. No longer are vague notions of stimulus-response connections used. Instead, Skinner deals with the rate at which any operant is emitted under a given set of conditions.

Learning, Skinner informs us, depends on the contingency of reinforcement. In the learning situation a response is made deliberately contingent upon the occurrence of some other response that precedes it and that has a high probability of being made. Thus, the ability of a pigeon in a Skinner box to obtain food is made contingent upon the pressing of a lever. There are many types of arrangements of contingencies, but all involve the common factor that the learning activity is made to be preceded systematically by the occurrence of a selected event. When this event exerts control over the activity, Skinner says that learning has occurred. For an operant to be "stamped-in," Skinner implies that the learned activity must take place in such a way that aftereffects are made contingent upon its occurrence (Gagne, 1965 and 1970).

The main area of Skinner's concentration is the independent variable and the schedule of reinforcement. Behavior, to Skinner, obeys the laws of probability, rather than being an all-or-none situation as postulated by Watson, Guthrie, and Thorndike. Contingencies of reinforcement are sometimes studied by constructing a model of a reinforcing environment (Skinner, 1969). Skinner's greatest contributions have been exemplifying ways of systematically pinpointing the behavior to be modified, developing techniques by which behavior can be modified, and pointing out the importance of the independent variables constituted by the immediate environment. Learning, or problem-solving behavior, is defined as "finding, storing, and using again correct rules." Behavior shaped by a given contingency occurs in a given way with a given probability because the *behavior has been followed by a given kind of consequence in the past.* This is to say that behavior is *not* always under the control of prior stimuli.

Thus, Skinner studies behavior, including the central behavioral process of learning, by an experimental analysis consisting of viewing changes in probability (or rate of response) as a function of manipulated variables. The emphasis is not on trial to trial, but on behavior occurring in time and recorded cumulatively. Skinner sees the behavioral processes revealing, through experimental analysis, a technology of behavior through which modern science can discover the means to solve the multifaceted problems of contemporary society. Skinner (1971) writes:

> Psychology as a basic science has failed to supply a conception which recommends itself to specialists in other fields of human behavior. . . . The experimental analysis of behavior may be on the point of doing so . . . It is not concerned with testing theories but with directly modifying behavior . . . It is less interested in the topography or structure of behavior than in the variables of which it is a function. It usually confines itself to the more convenient variable, but the interaction between organism and environment represented by the concept of contingencies of reinforcement has great generality.

Two of Skinner's graduate students at Harvard, Nathan Azrin and Ogden R. Lindsley, began applying operant techniques in social situations in the mid-1950s. In design and technique the experiments closely resemble laboratory work being done by Skinner with rats and pigeons. A change to human subjects, psychotic patients and the mentally retarded, represented the move from the laboratory and animal subjects to human and social problems. Operant work transferred from the laboratory to human subjects at the lowest level of the mental scale, such as institutionalized retardates, attempted to avoid the fallacy of morphological simplicity in the transfer from rat to man. The primary purpose of this initial work was mainly to gather data on operant conditioning of human subjects. Azrin began developing *behavior modification* techniques in the early 1960s at Anna State Hospital in Illinois. During the next four years, assisted by Teodoro Ayllon, he devised and experimented with *token economy systems* of reinforcement, utilizing original experimental data from laboratory and animal research.

The application of the experimental analysis of behavior has been accelerating rapidly since the early 1960s. Whereas Skinner has been criticized for overspeculating and taking his interpretations far beyond his data, the application of the principles of behavior modification to classroom settings is providing new data to fill the gap. Education has benefited greatly from four areas of Skinner's work: environmental effects on free operant behavior; schedules of reinforcement; programmed instruction; and the emphasis of precise control and measurement of behavior in the individual case.

Through Skinner's zeal to implement the experimental analysis of behavior, the psychology of learning is beginning to reveal patterns of human behavior, both developmentally and existentially, that can guide teachers in classroom instruction. The basic Skinnerian paradigm of stimulus-response-reinforcement is proving of great utility in the classroom and is so simple a method that it requires no great expenditure of time for special training. The structure of the stimulus-response-reinforcement relationship is evident in the classroom when a teacher hands a child a book and asks the child to read. If the child reads correctly, praise or reinforcement is given. According to the paradigm, the praise reinforces reading behavior, and the probability of correct reading at a future time is increased.

Before returning to the experimental analysis of behavior in this chapter, we must explore the difference between behavior therapy and experimental analysis in the evolution of learning theory.

Hullian Theory—Behavior Therapy

All learning theorists cannot be covered systematically in this volume. However, it is necessary to point out several recognized theoreticians and researchers who have made outstanding contributions to learning theory. Clark L. Hull is recognized as a leading innovator of *deductive behavior theory,* a major force in psychology in the late 1940s and the early 1950s. Hull, whose theoretical work is considered the most elegant formulation to date, attempted systematically to define the nature of the learning process in terms of drive-reduction and reinforcement. His basic postulate states that the strengthening or the establishment of a connection between responses of an organism and particular stimulating conditions is dependent on two events—the close proximity in time of the stimulus and the response, and reinforcement, a rewarding state that produces reduction of drive or need (Garry and Kingsley, 1970). If a drive or need is reduced, all previous behavior is reinforced. A specific response that produces drive reduction not only strengthens the relationship between the specific stimulus-response unit (law of effect), but also strengthens cross-connections with all other stimuli occurring at that time (substitution). Such an oversimplification of basic Hullian theory is unavoidable here, given the complex nature of his theorization. Skinner's argument against Hull's formulation was that he (Hull) placed the variables that were found to operate between stimulus and response inside the organism as a central process, rather than in environmental contingencies that control behaviors.

Hull's original work followed a basic stimulus-response paradigm function, but as his research developed, his conceptual stance shifted closer to that of Guthrie. Skinner (1961) claims that this was a transition from stimulus-response priority to consideration of the contingencies of reinforcement, although Hull did not use those terms. The prime weakness of Hull's theorization was the deductive approach to the study of contingencies. Also, certain studies showing learning taking place in the absence of observable reward tended to challenge Hull's ideas as well as Guthrie's. Whatever the drawbacks, Hull's work and his basic postulates generated much experimentation by colleagues and followers, such as Neal Miller, O. H. Mowrer, K. W. Spence, and R. R. Sears.

Hull's theoretical formulations are quite similar to those of both Guthrie and Thorndike. In a sense Hull's work began to bridge the gap between Thorndike's law of effect and Guthrie's antireinforcement view. The unifying factor in the work of all three men is the idea of contiguity of stimulus-response. Hull's system represented a major attempt at a synthesis of the traditions that guided a great part of American research on learning prior to 1940—associationism, conditioning, and law of effect theory (Estes, 1970)—but because of the limitations it has been superseded by the Skinnerian paradigms for the experimental analysis of behavior.

A major reformulation of Hull's theory, including the concept of inhibition, by Kenneth W. Spence has had a marked influence on work in the area of mental retardation. Interest in discerning the differences between mentally retarded and normal populations seems to have grown out of the Hull-Spence system.

Most of the applications of the Hull-Spence theory in the area of retardation have not attempted to determine the parameters of theoretical functions, but to make comparisons between groups of normal and retarded subjects on single response measures, which might reflect differences in theoretically significant variables provided all of the relevant factors have been held constant in a comparison (Estes, 1970). The significance of the application of the Hull-Spence system, despite its logical failures, is the movement of learning theory into the area of mental development with regard to retardation. Whatever their shortcomings, Hull's theories provide a basis for conceptual tools through which the roles of learning processes and the motivational variables that determine performance can be analyzed.

The most direct application of the Hull-Spence system to the study of learning process was done in the field of mental retardation by David Zeaman and Betty House. From their study of visual learning discrimination patterns in retarded children, they formulated a two-stage discrimination process based on the following assumptions:

1. Any given stimulus display represents a variety of dimensions beyond most controlled by the experimenter, but the uncontrolled dimensions usually are irrelevant to a discrimination problem.
2. A subject attends to only one dimension at a time.
3. Cues for instrumental learning are those aspects of the stimulus that are being attended to.

The modification of the Hull-Spence system, which is essentially a single-stage model, resulted in a two-stage model applicable to discrimination learning. From research results, Zeaman and House discovered that if the mastery of a discrimination were simply a matter of the steady divergence of strengths of correct and incorrect habits as a function of learning trials, they would have no basis for predicting the observed forms of what they called "backward learning curves." The backward learning curve is a method of data analysis used to replace group learning curves as a more representative measure of individual performance change. Instead of taking the reference point for each subject from the initial trial, the backward learning curve takes the point of reference from when the subject meets the criterion of correct performance. To elucidate the full properties of the Zeaman-House theory would necessitate presenting the mathematical form of their theory. A full presentation can be found in the William K. Estes book, *Learning Theory and Mental Development* (1970). The importance of Zeaman's and House's discoveries are that rules of learning in mentally deficient children are relatively independent of intelligence level. They suggest that individuals of differing intelligence levels vary in the probability of attending to revelant stimulus dimensions at the beginning of a new problem. In working with the mentally retarded, they concluded, it is important to shape the learner to attend to relevant stimulus conditions. This approach, although still emphasizing reinforcement and conditioning, differs from the operant system developed by Skinner in that it places much emphasis upon the inference of underlying processes from the individual performance, rather than emphasizing empirical relationships between observed behavior and controlled variables. The Hullian tradition has offered complex, formal, mathematical models concerning learning performance, but much of the utility of the theorization is lost in the ambiguous nature of the data language and logical construction of the models.

RESEARCH DESIGNS

Most educational research has been conducted under what might be called an *experimental psychology* design, that is, identifying and testing experimental and control groups, treating the experimental groups, testing both groups again, and analyzing the differences between them. This type of research tends to be information oriented rather than problem oriented, and no suggestion for implementation of actual instructional methods is generated. Another type of research is *correlation,* which involves measuring relationships of certain behaviors in a given population. Historically most of the research in education falls under one of these two categories. However, another research design, the experimental analysis of behavior, which stresses the functional analysis and modification of behavior, is being used increasingly, especially in the area of learning disorders and remedial intervention. This design provides control of antecedent conditions often overlooked in the first design and also gives direct information about the performance of the individual child. Problems in the application of research data to various educational and training situations appear to be solved by the experimental analysis of behavior where other research designs and learning theories have not been successful. The difference in research design can be viewed as applied versus basic. Basic research is characterized as information oriented and not directly relevant to immediate practice in the classroom situation (Mueller, 1972). Analytic behavior application is the process of applying sometimes tentative principles of behavior to the improvement of specific behaviors, and simultaneously evaluating whether or not any changes noted are indeed attributable to the process of application (Baer, Wolf, and Risley, 1968). Applied research studies variables that can be effective in improving behavior in a social situation. Research into the nature of paired-associate learning and transfer of learning (to be discussed shortly) is interested more in determining *why* behavior is changed or learning takes place than in the ways of facilitating learning and behavioral change through continuous measurement and evaluation.

Transfer of Training

Transfer of training research began in the United States with the classic work of William James, *Principles of Psychology* (1890), which challenged the theory of formal discipline. This theory advocated that memory and reasoning are trained skills enhanced by learning foreign languages, mathematics, and using rote techniques to "discipline the mind." James, followed by Thorndike, led the initial attack on the doctrine of formal discipline that led to a great volume of research and studies on the problem of transfer of training.

Transfer of learning means that experience or performance on one task influences performance on some subsequent task (Ellis, 1965). Transfer of learning is said to take three forms: 1) performance on one task may aid performance on a second task, which is *positive transfer;* 2) performance on one task may inhibit performance of a subsequent task, which is *negative transfer;* and 3) there may be no effect of one task on another, which is *zero transfer.* Concern with the effects of antecedent events, or previous learning, on the present learning situation is implicit in this paradigm. Most educational programs are based on the assumption that what is taught in the classroom will transfer to new situations.

Most of the research on the transfer of training has been basic research "aimed at determining *why* transfer occurs" (Ellis, 1965), that is, discovering the variables that influence transfer. The method of research is the hypothetico-deductive system using "experimental design" as defined by R. A. Fischer. This type of research is designed to test a specific hypothesis or theory and to provide statistical data to prove or disprove it. Research design is usually the experimental group-control group, or pretest-posttest variety. Laboratory research aimed at developing laws of behavior became increasingly popular beginning around

1930. It was felt that a science of human behavior could be developed best through careful laboratory studies of the learning process. The problem arose when the gulf between learning theory and educational practice began to emerge. Learning theory research followed the Hull-Spence system to formalize the factors that influence learning. Only recently have problems of ways best to facilitate transfer of learning in the classroom been considered. One of the best discussions of this topic is found in Kathryn A. Blake's book, *Teaching the Retarded* (1974).

Paired-Associate Research

Paired-associate learning research developed out of application of the stimulus-response paradigm to verbal behavior. One of the earliest systematic studies of learning was done in the 1890s by Herman Ebbinghaus. In studying the conditions of memorization, Ebbinghaus discovered that certain types of material are memorized more easily than others because of meaningfulness or familiarity of the material. He used nonsense syllables consisting of two consonants joined by a vowel, such as teg, tak, ref, to provide a material free from previous association. Utilizing nonsense syllables, Ebbinghaus began his experimental studies of memory, retention, and recall by measuring the effects of variables such as length of series and order of presentation. This research method led others to study verbal association and develop empirical research techniques. The basic work by Ebbinghaus revealed that memorization of a single syllable was directly influenced by the presence of other syllables. The learning of any single association was shown to be affected by the *interference* of other associations within and outside the list.

The method by Ebbinghaus is one of two procedures most frequently used for studying the effects of memory in the learning of verbal material. His *anticipation method* requires a list of nonsense syllables to be presented for a standard period of time at a uniform rate. The second procedure is the *paired-associate* method. In the basic paired-associate learning trial, the subject is presented with a stimulus-response pair repeatedly. After each presentation, the subject is tested. If single paired-associate items are considered in isolation, say the relationship between an English word and the corresponding word in a foreign language, the process of acquisition would be the same as in classical conditioning. Theoretically, during one training trial associations of the paired stimulus-response would be established in the short-term memory, and after several trials, in the absence of interference, transfer to long-term memory would occur. However, research has shown that paired-associates are rarely, if ever, learned in this way. Often the process can be shortened if the learner discovers a feature of the stimulus member of the pair that evokes an already existing chain of associations and brings to mind features of the response member.

Gagne claims that this type of verbal behavior constitutes a three-link chain, which "involves a previously learned connection (FIX) that includes the spoken or written response 'fix.' . . . it contains a mediating (or coding) connection that may be supplied either by the learner or the instructor, that puts together the other two links" (Gagne, 1970). The chaining link may be of any sort as long as it supplies a direct connection between the stimulus word and the correct response.

The similarity of tasks involved in paired-associate learning to the tasks students perform in school is widely recognized. Research using the paired-associate design has been interested mainly in discovering the relationships between learning, practice, and recall (Betts, 1966). Studies of stimulus generalization (Guttman, 1963), stimulus predifferentiation (Miller and Dollard, 1941), and learning set (Harlow, 1959) have attempted to prove behavior theory as developed by Hull and Tolman, but applicability either to classroom practice or research has been limited. Perhaps the most direct contribution of the paired-associate and transfer of learning research has been in the area of programmed instruction. The development of a workable educational technology can be witnessed in the development of programs that require students to respond to sequences of problems organized on the basis of learner responses. However, no systematic procedures for instruction were generated from this type of research even though concern for application of knowledge or about transfer was present.

The Experimental Analysis of Behavior

One of the central problems with studies in transfer of learning was the failure to specify the precise variables producing transfer. Even more recent experimentation using the paired-associate design or the experimental psychology design has actually contributed little to the needs of education. Perhaps this can be best viewed in the field of special education. Max Mueller (1972), director of the Division of Innovation and Development of the Bureau of Education for the Handicapped, noted:

> The majority of educational research conducted in the field of special education has been tied to what one might call an experimental psychology design. . . . Although this design is appropriate to many problems, it tends to discount, or, at least, inadequately control the antecedent condition, the comparability of those groups, and the individual differences within the groups . . . . we are giving support to projects in the area of the functional analysis and modification of educational behavior. This is a strategy of research which is being used increasingly by those researchers in the education of the handicapped.

As we have seen, the experimental analysis of behavior developed out of Skinner's work in operant conditioning. An emphasis on rate of occurrence of repeated instances of operant behavior distinguished the experimental analysis from kinds of psychology that observe one or more of the following practices (Skinner, 1969): 1) behavior is taken to be the sign or symptom of inner activities, or central processes; 2) behavior is held to be significant only in meeting certain standards or criteria, such as "problem solving," or "environmental adaptation"; 3) changes in probability of response are treated as if they were, in fact, responses or acts; that is, to discriminate is not to respond but to respond differently to two or more stimuli; 4) the dimensions studied, although quantifiable, are not related in any simple way to probability of response; 5) inner events of which behavior is said to be a sign are measured by various techniques from which the data obtained are loosely controlled experimental spaces and the "scores" taken as measures are to be arbitrary features of what the experimenter hypothesized; and 6) instead of studying behavior, the subject's statements of what might be done, or impressions of a situation and such, are recorded and studied.

One task of the experimental analysis of behavior is to discover all the variables of which probability of response is a function. A stimulus is described in the language of physics. The operant practitioner does not follow the reasoning of classical conditioning or traditional stimulus-response psychologies in believing that a stimulus forces the individual to respond. Even though the stimuli may be difficult to specify, the researcher does not resort to inner states or personal inference. The stimulus is usually the independent variable manipulated or changed by the experimenter to determine its effect on the dependent variable, which is usually a measurable aspect of behavior. *Contingencies of reinforcement* are important features of independent variables studied in an experimental analysis. Reinforcement may be contingent on rate of response or change. The term "contingent" implies that there is a resultant rather than a merely temporal relationship between what one does and what happens afterward. The contingencies of our environment control our behavior and predictably can influence our responses. In fact, most of our behavior is controlled by contingencies of one sort or another. A teacher's credentials are contingent upon completion of a course of study. We occupy our homes contingent upon rent or mortgage payments. The management of contingencies whether in a laboratory or classroom stiuation becomes a powerful tool to facilitate behavior change. Management of contingencies is a systematic approach in using reinforcement. Ogden Lindsley (1964) adapted Skinner's basic reinforcement paradigm (stimulus → response → reinforcement) to a more explicit classroom version. He identified four components of a contingency management system: E^a is the antecedent event; M is the movement (the response to be measured); A is the arrangement of reinforcement (its presentation schedule); and E^s is the subsequent event designated as a consequence (reinforcement) of the response.

$$E^a \rightarrow M \rightarrow A \rightarrow E^s$$

The more clearly environmental contingencies are defined, the more likely an individual will emit appropriate responses. When contingencies between appropriate responses and reinforcing stimuli become more established, appropriate responses to discriminative stimuli rapidly increase and inappropriate responses disappear. Thus, by discovering the variables of which a response is a function, irrelevant and inappropriate responses can be eliminated, and appropriate responses can be strengthened.

An important difference between the experimental analysis of behavior and other research designs should become clear. Such a field as the systematic analysis of contingencies of reinforcement does not need a theory. Skinner (1969) states:

> Unlike hypotheses, theories, and models, together with the statistical manipulations of data which support them, a smooth curve showing a change in probability of a response as a function of a controlled variable is a fact in the bag . . .

The Applied Analysis of Behavior

The application of operant techniques and the experimental analysis of behavior in situations outside the laboratory to social problems has marked a new era in behavioral research. The distinction between *applied* and *basic* research has become clear over the years as research produced useable data. While both applied and basic research ask what controls the behavior under study, nonapplied research is likely to look at any behavior and at any variable that may conceivably relate to it (Baer, Wolf, Risley, 1968). On the other hand, applied research looks directly at what variables can be effective in improving or modifying a specific target behavior. The behavior studies using applied research are seen to be significant socially rather than merely convenient for study. The change, or the differentiation between applied and basic research, is seen by the emergence of a post-Skinnerian scholarly publication, *The Journal of Applied Behavior Analysis* (JABA), from the original operant publication, *The Journal of the Experimental Analysis of Behavior* (JEAB). The birth of the new publication was necessitated by research begun in child development and preschool retardate behavior by Sidney Bijou and Florence Harris at the University of Washington, as well as Lindsley's and Azrin's work with psychotic patients. Donald Baer, Montrose Wolf, and Todd Risley, who worked with Bijou and Harris at Washington, established the model for applied behavioral research in JABA's first issue and thus set the trend for nearly all ensuing research.

The application of the experimental analysis of behavior to classroom situations was a natural result. Classroom research historically had been neither systematic nor precise. With an effective research design, studies have been made not only concerning children with physical or mental handicaps, learning deficits, or socioeconomic disadvantages, but in regular classrooms as well. Researchers utilizing the applied analysis of behavior are more interested in developing procedures that are effective in modifying deviant behavior than in advancing a theoretical stance. They echo Skinner's antitheoretical position, maintaining that applied research will produce effective procedures for the improvement of specific behaviors (Baer, Wolf, and Risley, 1968).

Programs utilizing the applied analysis of behavior in various classroom settings are flourishing at several universities, such as at the University of Kansas, whose program began in 1965 when Vance Hall, Wolf, Baer, and Risley all moved from the University of Washington. The move was assisted by Richard Schiefelbusch and Norris Haring, who also obtained the services of one of Skinner's top students, Ogden R. Lindsley from Harvard, to coordinate research at the university's Child Rehabilitation Unit. The same year that these energetic young researchers went to Kansas, Haring accepted a position as Director of the Experimental Education Unit at the University of Washington. With this change of personnel the Kansas program grew rapidly in applying operant techniques in various situations. Programs were initiated in public education, home settings, community centers, preschool, and day care. Lindsley developed the first "precision teaching" courses in the Kansas School of Education, and Hall and Wolf developed models for conducting classroom research. The impetus of the Kansas group has been to develop a workable technology of behavior by quantifying procedures that can be used to produce reliable results in specific situations.

The Juniper Gardens program is one of the best known attempts to design operant programs at the community level. Juniper Gardens, a black housing project in the poorest section of Kansas City, provided a social laboratory for the Kansas group's research needs—the development of new technologies. It also set the pace for programs in the control of human behavior. Plans included nearly all levels of social interaction from preschool to neighborhood traffic problems. Lead by Risley and Hall, the Juniper Gardens experiment may prove to be the beginning of operant techniques applied to community design.

Since the early 1960s, research in operant techniques to modify behavior problems in children has been conducted at the University of Washington. Behavior modification procedures were first designed by Florence Harris and her associates, Wolf and Baer, at the Developmental Psychology Laboratory. This group concentrated on the development of normal pre-school behaviors, primarily social in nature, through the appropriate use of social reinforcement by adults and peers. In 1966 Sidney Bijou began experimenting with token economy systems in working with mentally retarded children. Operant techniques proved successful in increasing the rates of academic performance among developmentally retarded children (Birnbrauer, Wolf, Kidder, and Tague, 1965; Bijou, 1966). In conjunction with this research, Norris G. Haring and his associates (Haring, 1972; Haring and Hauck, 1969a, 1969b; Haring and Hayden, 1968; Haring and Lovitt, 1967) have been developing techniques on direct application of operant principles to classroom situations now being used at the Experimental Education Unit of the

Child Development and Mental Retardation Center. The systematic form of instruction being developed deals with two basic procedures: analysis—pinpointing the relationship between the child's observable behavior and environmental factors that evoke it; and systematic procedures for altering events influencing that behavior so it may change in a beneficial direction. Haring's interest in operant procedures shows a unique change in a person trained in Hullian psychology, whose research with the mentally retarded in engineered classrooms and in curriculum design in special education has led him directly to the applied analysis of behavior.

Wesley Becker is another researcher whose work showed a steady movement to the applied analysis of behavior from his original research stance using clinical and factor analytic methods. Dr. Becker is a member of the University of Oregon faculty, where he was joined by other applied analysts such as Gerald Patterson, Owen White,[2] and Steven M. Johnson. Becker's book, *Parents are Teachers,* is a classic work in the attempt to educate parents in using operant techniques. Dr. Patterson's research (Patterson and Reid, 1970) demonstrates how to change behavior in aversive interactions between two members of a family in a manner that facilitates overall cooperative behavior in the family. Parents were first provided with a manual and then taught to observe and record behavior occurrences of themselves and their children. After this step all family members were taught intervention procedures, and formal procedures for interaction with specific behaviors were instituted and maintained until the response data from direct observation and family agreement exhibited changes in behavior patterns.

Becker also has contributed significantly to classroom management procedures, his research spanning nearly 20 years. Believing that "as many as 80 to 90 percent of the children typically referred by the teacher to psychologists, social workers, or special education classes can be handled most effectively by the regular classroom teacher," Becker has worked steadily in developing behavior modification programs that are directly applicable to the regular classroom. With Seigfried Engelmann, he has devised a behavioral program that has had significant success in improving the academic performances of economically disadvantaged preschool and first grade children (Becker, Engelmann, and Thomas, 1971).

These programs are by no means the only ones currently operating, but they do represent the move from the security and irrelevance of traditional university psychology laboratories into the mainstream of society. However, developments in programmed instruction, engineered classrooms, precision teaching, and educational technology are direct extensions of early work by learning theory researchers and the continual refinement of research findings. Application of the experimental analysis of behavior to educational settings may be the most fruitful result of behavioral

---

[2] Dr. White is now the coordinator of Planning, Development, and Evaluation at the Experimental Education Unit, University of Washington.

science. The search for learning abilities and instructional disabilities has provided information on what actually constitutes a learning disability.

Let us now turn to a specific application of operant procedures in the area of learning disabilities.

Assessment of Children with Learning Disabilities

One of the first systematic applications of experimental analysis of behavior to the area of learning disabilities was made by Thomas C. Lovitt at the University of Washington's Experimental Education Unit. Lovitt's work cannot be considered theoretical, but his formulation of precise methods of collection and utilization of classroom data has direct practical application to the child with a learning disability. There is a need for effective assessment procedures that could eliminate the unfortunate consequences of some traditional referral methods by suggesting how teachers *can* remediate a child's learning disability. Often, traditional referrals label a child and supply medical or psychological "explanations" of the child's behavior. If the child arrives at school with a noneducational explanation for his or her academic failure, the teacher may feel there is nothing educational to be done about the failure; the teacher therefore sees no need to alter the programming or classroom methods. Lovitt suggests a four-point diagnostic procedure (Lovitt, 1967). The program consists of 1) baseline assessment, 2) assessment of behavioral components, 3) assessment based on referral, and 4) generalization of assessment. With this method, diagnosis and treatment are based on direct observation, not on the inference that one deviant behavior is caused by a syndrome of interrelated events. Treatment, therefore, concentrates on modifying explicit behaviors, not on searching for correlated unrevealed behaviors. Responsibility for successful change rests with the programmer, who in most cases is the classroom teacher.

Since changing behavior is the primary interest of every teacher, the initial procedure is to analyze the behavior of the child upon entering the classroom situation. This proposed diagnostic procedure is called baseline, and it provides a continuous assessment of behavior over a given period until a stable measure of performance is obtained.

The second phase of the evaluation process is "the assessment of those behavioral components that maintain and modify behavior." For instance, Lovitt suggests that the first component, antecedents of behavior (the stimulus materials presented to children), must be considered in order to find a program that will accelerate individual performance. The programmer, supplied with individually relevant data such as preferred rate or duration or preferred type of reader, can design programs based on these or other stimulus dimensions, such as preference in rate and size of visual presentation, or timbre and intensity of auditory delivery (Lovitt, 1967). The second behavioral component to be measured is the response behaviors of the child both topographically (quantification of responses) and functionally (the effect of these responses on the environment). Lovitt stresses the need for the functional analysis, which reveals the relationships of behavior to its controlling environment. Whereas topographical analysis is a static measure, functional analysis is dynamic. Utilizing these together, the programmer can obtain a more objective measure by having data on both rate and duration of behavior. A third component is the temporal arrangement of the consequences of behavior. The rate of teacher interaction with individual children and the simultaneous plotting of student performance rate provide data for arrangement of teacher interaction to maintain high performance rate. Some students may require little interaction, others with contingency deficits may need a high rate of teacher interaction. The final behavioral component to be assessed is the environmental consequences that maintain behavior. The importance of structure as it relates to the classroom is observable in the systematic scheduling of activities, and the general and systematic orientation established between the child's behavior and its consequences. The teacher should establish a flexible structure and plan instruction to emphasize the consequences of performance. This will allow the individual with learning disabilities diverse experiences in the hierarchy of consequences by which behavior can be brought under control.

The third aspect of the assessment process is the referring agent, either the teacher or parent as well as the child. According to Lovitt, there always exists a possibility that the managerial and programming skills of the adult may be as incompetent as the learning skills of the child. It often is expedient for the diagnostician to deal directly with the adult's programming disability rather than with the child's performing disability. By involving the referring agent in the evaluation process, the diagnostician can collaborate in the determination of target behaviors specified for remediation.

The fourth aspect is the emphasis on generalization of diagnostic information. The final outcome of the evaluation process should be to provide the referring agent with information that can be implemented immediately into programming procedures. Frequently, diagnostic information cannot be translated into functional academic programs because classroom teachers have not been able to design them with the data they receive from standardized tests, couched in clinical jargon. Lovitt points out that an assessment should include both the child's performance rate and details about environmental contingencies that were in effect during assessment. Data must include both topographical and functional analysis of behavior. The instructions given during the evaluation, the exact material that was given the performer, the events that followed the child's responses, and the child's responses to the various programs all must be considered, according to Lovitt. Diagnostic generalization becomes effective only when data are relevant to process and product rather than to product alone.

Lovitt's work reveals a direct application of the experimental analysis of behavior to the problem of learning disabilities. Specific remedial techniques will be discussed in a later chapter. The trend toward application of methods derived from research on learning theory is obvious. With the direct assessment of such behaviors as rates of reading, computation, or listening and speaking, and the functional application of modification procedures, progress is evidenced immediately and empirically. Instead of labeling a child, learning deficits are used as criteria for remediation. Lovitt's contribution to the diagnosis of academic learning disorders has been to provide a clear, precise method of evaluation that facilitates direct educational programming and remediation.

CONCLUSION

Often, attempts to scientifically validate a theoretical bias lead only to mystification of the person who attempts to apply the data or technique outside the strict controls of the laboratory. The person who does the research learns the most from it and is best able to change and implement the research findings. If education is to change effectively in relationship to advances in technology and applied science, classroom research must "clarify[ing] . . . controlling relationships" (Skinner, 1971). Education has been slow to change because it has maintained behavior originating from feelings, mental states, character, and other internal processes. Only in recent years has the intervening role of the environment been recognized as important in shaping and maintaining behavior. Learning in part involves decision-making behaviors by which an individual learns to respond to the environment to gain maximum reinforcement. Decisions in the classroom, by teacher and student, all too often do not consider the full extent of the contingencies involved. A learning disability can begin as a pattern of negative reinforcement due to lack of environmental awareness by the controlling agent, the parent or teacher. Thus, a child often cannot solve problems because the imposed environmental limitations make a solution improbable or highly unlikely.

The work of the researchers who have been discussed attempts to delineate the progress made in applying the generalized principles of behavior to academic situations. Although not all research has been covered in this chapter, the material should convey a definite pattern, or trend, toward effective and efficient practices in modifying classroom behavior to benefit the individuality and human integrity of each student.

It is no accident that we mention the student's individuality and integrity. So often in the past, behavioral technology has been criticized—mistakenly, we believe—for denying or ignoring these considerations. The technology is criticized on the grounds that the behavior manager always is doing something *to* the learner and that the learner is merely a passive receiver of these ministrations. But of all the approaches to changing behavior—in this case, changing behavior through teaching—the behavioral approach is the least vulnerable to such criticism because the approach *requires* a response from the learner and interaction between the manager and the pupil. Moreover, the technology demands that instructional and other cues be arranged to increase the probability that responses will occur. Cues that are arranged for the benefit of the individual learner are likely to respect his or her individuality and integrity. One can say that in the strictly conditioned response studies, the "subject" is a passive receiver, but in the higher cognitive activities one finds in a school setting—and in this book we are talking about such activities—the child is an active participant in the behavioral approach.

REFERENCES

ALLPORT, G. W., *Becoming: Basic Considerations for a Psychology of Personality.* New Haven: Yale University Press, 1955.

BAER, D. M., M. M. WOLF, and T. R. RISLEY, Some current dimensions of applied behavior analysis. *Journal of Applied Behavior Analysis,* 1968, *1,* 91–97.

BATEMAN, B. D., Learning disabilities—yesterday, today, and tomorrow. *Exceptional Children,* 1964, *31,* 167.

BECKER, W. C., *Parents Are Teachers.* Champaign, Ill.: Research Press, 1971.

BECKER, W. C., S. ENGELMANN, and D. R. THOMAS, *Teaching: A Course in Applied Psychology.* Chicago: Science Research Associates, Inc., 1971.

BECKER, W. C., C. H. MADSEN, C. R. ARNOLD, and B. A. THOMAS, The contingent use of teacher attention and praise in reducing classroom behavior problems. *Journal of Special Education,* 1967, *1*(3), 287–307.

BETTS, M. L. B., *Relationships Among Learning, Practice, and Recall.* Final Report, Cooperative Research Report, Project No. S–169. Cambridge, Mass.: Harvard University, 1966.

BIJOU, S. W., A functional analysis of retarded development. In N. R. Ellis, ed., *International Review of Research in Mental Retardation.* New York: Academic Press, 1966.

BIRNBRAUER, J. J., M. M. WOLF, J. D. KIDDER, and C. E. TAGUE, Classroom behavior of retarded pupils with token reinforcement. *Journal of Experimental Psychology,* 1965, *2,* 219–235.

BLAKE, K., *Teaching the Retarded.* Englewood Cliffs, N.J.: Prentice-Hall, Inc., 1974.

BORING, E. C., *A History of Experimental Psychology,* 2nd ed. Englewood Cliffs, N.J.: Prentice-Hall, Inc., 1950.

ELLIS, H., *The Transfer of Learning.* New York: The Macmillan Company, 1965.

ESTES, W. K., *Learning Theory and Mental Development.* New York: Academic Press, 1970.

ESTES, W. K., S. KOCH, K. MACCORQUODALE, P. E. MEEHL, C. G. MUELLER, W. N. SCHOENFELD, and S. W. VERPLANCK, *Modern Learning Theory.* New York: Appleton-Century-Crofts, 1954.

GAGNE, R. M., *The Conditions of Learning.* New York: Holt, Rinehart & Winston, 1965, revised 1970.

GARRY, R., and H. L. KINGSLEY, *The Nature and Conditions of Learning.* Englewood Cliffs, N.J.: Prentice-Hall, Inc., 1970.

GOBAR, A., *Philosophic Foundations of Genetic Psychology and Gestalt Psychology: A Comparative Study of the Empirical Basis, Theoretical Structure, and Epistemological Groundwork of European Biological Psychology.* The Hague: Martinus Nijhoff, 1968.

GUTHRIE, E. R., *The Psychology of Learning.* New York: Harper & Row, 1952.

GUTHRIE, E. R., and A. L. EDWARDS, *Psychology, a First Course in Human Behavior.* New York: Harper & Row, 1949.

GUTTMAN, N., Laws of behavior and facts of perception. In S. Koch, ed., *Psychology: A Study of Science, V.* New York: McGraw-Hill, 1963, 114–178.

HARING, N. G., A Program Project for the Investigation of Procedures of Analysis and Modification of Behavior of Handicapped Children. Progress Report for Grant No. OEG-0-70-3916 (607). Submitted to the U.S. Department of Health, Education, and Welfare, Office of Education, 1972.

HARING, N. G., and M. HAUCK, Improved learning conditions in the establishment of reading skills with disabled readers. *Exceptional Children,* 1969a, *35,* 341–352.

———, *Contingency Management Applied to Classroom Remedial Reading and Math for Disadvantaged Youth.* Proceedings of the Ninth Annual Research Meeting (Cosponsored by the Department of Institutions, Division of Research, State of Washington, and University of Washington, School of Medicine, Department of Psychiatry), 1969b, *2,* No. 2, 41–46.

HARING, N. G., and A. H. HAYDEN, Programs and facilities of the Experimental Education Unit of the University of Washington Mental Retardation and Child Development Center. In M. V. Jones, ed., *Special Education Programs Within the United States.* Springfield, Ill.: Charles C Thomas, 1968.

HARING, N. G., and T. C. LOVITT, Operant methodology and educational technology in special education. In N. G. Haring and R. L. Schiefelbusch, eds., *Methods in Special Education.* New York: McGraw-Hill, 1967.

HARING, N. G., and E. L. PHILLIPS, *Analysis and Modification of Classroom Behavior.* Englewood Cliffs, N.J.: Prentice-Hall, Inc., 1972.

———, *Educating Emotionally Disturbed Children.* New York: McGraw-Hill, 1962.

HARLOW, H. F., Learning set and error factor theory. In S. Koch, ed., *Psychology: A Study of Science, 2.* New York: McGraw-Hill, 1959, 492–537.

HEWETT, F. M., Introduction to the behavior modification approach to special education. In N. G. Haring and A. H. Hayden, eds., *The Improvement of Instruction.* Seattle: Special Child Publications, 1972.

HILL, W. H., *Learning: A Survey of Psychological Interpretations.* San Francisco: Chandler Publishing Company, 1963.

HULL, L. L., *Essentials of Behavior.* New Haven: Yale University Press, 1951.

———, *Principles of Behavior.* New York: Appleton, 1943.

JAMES, W., *Principles of Psychology.* Vol. 1. New York: Henry Holt and Company, 1890.

LINDSLEY, O. R., Direct measurement and prosthesis of retarded behavior. *Journal of Education,* 1964, *147,* 62–81.

LOVITT, T. C., Assessment of children with learning disabilities. *Exceptional Children,* 1967, *34,* 233.

McCARTHY, J. J., and J. F. McCARTHY, *Learning Disabilities.* Boston: Allyn & Bacon, 1969.

MILLER, N. E., and J. DOLLARD, *Social Learning and Imitation.* New Haven: Yale University Press, 1941.

MISIAK, H., *The Philosophical Roots of Scientific Psychology.* New York: Fordham University Press, 1961.

MUELLER, M. W., Trends in research in the education of the handicapped. In N. G. Haring and A. H. Hayden, eds., *The Improvement of Instruction.* Seattle: Special Child Publications, 1972.

PATTERSON, G. R., and J. B. REID, Reciprocity and coercion: two facets of social systems. In C. Neuringer and J. L. Michael, eds., *Behavior Modification in Clinical Psychology.* Englewood Cliffs, N.J.: Prentice-Hall, Inc., 1970.

SKINNER, B. F., *Beyond Freedom and Dignity.* New York: Alfred A. Knopf, 1971.

———, *Contingencies of Reinforcement: A Theoretical Analysis.* New York: Appleton-Century-Crofts, 1969.

———, The flight from the laboratory. *Current Trends in Psychological Theory.* Pittsburgh: University of Pittsburgh Press, 1961.

———, *Science and Human Behavior.* New York: The Free Press, 1953.

THORNDIKE, E. L., *Animal Intelligence: An Experimental Study of the Associative Processes in Animals.* New York: Macmillan, 1898.

———, *Human Learning.* New York: Century, 1931.

———, Mental discipline in high school studies. *Journal of Educational Psychology,* 1924, *15,* 1–22.

WATSON, JOHN B., *Behavior: An Introduction to Comparative Psychology.* New York: Holt, 1914.

ZEAMAN, D., and B. J. HOUSE, The relation of IQ and learning. In R. M. Gagne, ed., *Learning and Individual Differences.* Columbus, Ohio: Merrill Books, 1967, pp. 192–212.

Part II

Educational Identification, Assessment, and Evaluation Procedures [1]

4

A thorough description and evaluation of all the procedures and instruments currently used in the educational identification and assessment of children with learning disabilities is beyond the scope and intent of this book. Rather, the attempt here is to describe some prevalent practices and to make recommendations about possible future directions.

The choice of procedures used in the identification and evaluation of children with learning disabilities depends on many factors, such as the examiner's philosophy regarding the nature and purpose of educational diagnosis, the professional training and skills of the examiner, the time and funds available for diagnosis, laws or regulations regarding tests used in determining a child's eligibility for special services, possible limitations imposed by the child's age and disabilities, the use of diagnostic data for research purposes, and many other variables.

To treat even briefly the varied procedures and tests, it has been necessary to use headings that are only crudely descriptive. The headings in no way are meant to reflect anything other than one method of classifying some of the many educational/assessment techniques currently in use. These headings, which provide the basis for the organization of this

[1] This chapter appeared in Bateman, B. D., and R. L. Schiefelbusch, Educational identification, assessment, and evaluation procedures. In N. G. Haring, committee chairman and ed., *Minimal Brain Dysfunction: National Project on Learning Disabilities in Children.* Public Health Service Publication No. 2015. Washington, D.C.: USGPO, 1969. Our thanks to Richard Schiefelbusch for allowing us to use this material.

chapter, are: 1) procedures to determine whether a child has a learning disability—that is, whether there is a need of, or eligibility for, an educational program designed for children with learning disabilities; 2) procedures to determine the specific kind of educational or teaching program to be provided once eligibility and/or placement has been determined, and 3) functional analysis of behavior.

PROCEDURES FOR DETERMINING ELIGIBILITY OR CLASSIFICATION AS A LEARNING DISABILITY

Early identification of potential learning disabilities, *before* they are manifested as failure in school, and the diagnosis of manifest disabilities *after* school failure require somewhat different orientations and are discussed separately in the following sections. A primary distinction is that measures of academic functioning in the strictest sense cannot be obtained on preschool children, so the concept of discrepancy between academic performance and potential cannot be employed.

Identifying Potential Learning Disabilities in the Preschool Years

As is true in many areas of health, education, and welfare today, there is increasing emphasis on early identification of potential learning disorders, with the intent of providing preventive programs. The role of medical evaluation looms necessarily large at the early ages because 1) there has been no opportunity for school learning problems to occur, 2) psychological tests at the early ages are generally less reliable than at older ages, and 3) although few educational-psychological institutions have established screening programs that reach large numbers of preschoolers, these children *are* seen by medical personnel.

A few communities are initiating preschool and nursery screening projects that involve cooperative efforts by medical, psychological, and educational personnel. Data from such projects hopefully will alleviate our current paucity of knowledge about subtle prognostic signs in young children (Beery, 1967). Many of these youngsters are seen by medical personnel first—often when parents begin to note such symptoms as delayed language, hyperactivity, poor motor coordination, lack of responsiveness, or uncontrolled temper outbursts.

Nursery school personnel also encounter some of these children, but at the present time there is little consensus about appropriate educational programming for two-, three-, and four-year-olds showing these atypical behaviors. Recommendations include variations of "Don't do anything, he is normal and will outgrow it," "She can't tolerate limits so remove them," "Socialize her," and "He needs very firm discipline and careful structuring of an early educational program." Our knowledge of accurate prediction and prevention of learning disabilities in three- and four-year-olds is inadequate; we need:

1. Further dissemination of information describing children with learning disabilities to all agencies and personnel in early contact with these children.

2. Data on recommendations made and their relationship to the children's subsequent development. Parent groups could assist in determining what kinds of recommendations are actually being made by professionals and what outcomes accrue.

3. Funding of community screening projects involving multidisciplinary approaches that offer unique opportunities for service, training, and research.

4. Development of reliable and valid psychological tests for this age level, even though such efforts are filled with problems. Behavioral observations and normative developmental data will probably continue to comprise the bulk of our objective assessment techniques.

Among standardized tests used in psychological assessment of suspected learning disorders in three- and four-year-olds are the Illinois Test of Psycholinguistic Abilities, the Beery-Buktenica Test of Visual-Motor Integration, the Draw-a-Man, the Stanford-Binet Intelligence Scale, the Basic Concept Inventory, the Wechsler Intelligence Scale for Children, the Wechsler Preschool Primary Scale of Intelligence, and the Frostig Developmental Tests of Visual Perception. (See appendix on Academic Achievement and Diagnostic Tests at end of this chapter.)

Many more systematic evaluation techniques are available for the kindergarten age group. At this level the interdependence of identification and definition becomes both complex and important. Educators readily recognize that definition plays a large role in the identification techniques employed, but it is just as true that we often define that group we are *able* to identify. Traditional school readiness tests most readily identify the child of below average ability. A major difficulty in identifying a child with potential specific learning difficulties at the five-year level is differentiation from the generally slow learning child. The concept of discrepancies within the child's levels of cognitive and perceptual growth is important here, in contrast to the concept of discrepancy between estimated potential and actual functioning. Kindergarten teachers asked to describe the children of average or high intelligence whom they feel are likely to have trouble meeting the academic demands of first grade frequently mention short attention span and "immaturity." Techniques are being developed to assist kindergarten teachers in refining their differentiation of generalized retardation or immaturity and specific learning problems. At present there are few data to suggest unequivocally that formal testing is more successful in finding potential problems than is sophisticated teacher observation (Haring and Ridgway, 1967).

A notable preliminary study of predicting future academic failure of kindergarten children is that of de Hirsch, Jansky, and Langford (1966). From an original battery of 37 tests, a Predictive Index of 10 tests was able to identify 91 percent of the kindergarten children who later failed at the end of second grade. These 10 tests are:

1. Pencil Mastery (ratings of grasp and control based on age expectancy).
2. Bender Visual Motor Gestalt Test (six of nine figures used and scored on response to essentials of gestalt, degree of differentiation, and ability to organize figures in space).
3. Wepman Auditory Discrimination Test (20 alternate pairs).
4. Number of Words (total number of words used in story telling, after Dorothea McCarthy, *The Language Development of the Preschool Child,* University of Minnesota Child Welfare Monograph 4, 1930).
5. Categories (ability to produce generic names of three clusters of words).
6. Horst Reversals Test (only matching of letter sequences was employed).
7. Gates Word-Matching Test (abbreviated version).
8. Word Recognition I (ability to pick from a pack of successively presented cards the words "boy" and "train," which had been taught at the beginning of the session).
9. Word Recognition II (identifying same words exposed on the table with eight others).
10. Word Reproduction (writing from memory as much of the two words as can be recalled).

The authors point to certain limitations in the study, for example, the small number of children who failed. Nevertheless, it is an effort to refine objective methods of identifying potential learning disabilities at the kindergarten level.

There is little doubt that before long it will be possible to identify accurately a substantial proportion of those five-year-olds who, in the absence of intervention, will later fully qualify as children having learning disabilities. A marked increase in the number and extent of such screening efforts will probably appear. If so, two questions will loom: 1) whether it is possible to provide adequate and appropriate preventive programs for the children so identified, and 2) whether the increased referral rate will be a significant problem. If parents and teachers expect a child to have learning problems because of identification in a screening project, will that expectation produce an otherwise nonexistent disability? The incidence of learning disabilities is sure to rise with the increased use of screening measures. A point of diminishing returns may be reached, therefore, in identification of subtle learning problems.

Group tests used in kindergartens to identify youngsters with potential learning problems include Screening Tests for Identifying Children with Specific Language Disability (Slingerland), Detroit Tests of Learning Aptitude, and many other instruments. Most of the tests at the three- and four-year levels are also appropriate at the five-year level (e.g., Frostig Developmental Tests of Visual Perception, Beery-Buktenica Visual-Motor Test of Integration, and others).

Useful individual tests at the kindergarten level include the Predictive Index (de Hirsch), Dyslexia Schedule (McLeod), the Illinois Test of Psycholinguistic Abilities (Kirk and McCarthy), Basic Concept Inventory (Engelmann), and others such as those included in the test appendix.

Determining Learning Disabilities in School-Age Children

Within the framework of many educational definitions of learning disabilities, the diagnostician frequently explores 1) a possible discrepancy between measures of intellectual, cognitive, or academic potential and current level of performance; 2) dysfunction in the learning processes; and 3) absence of other primary factors such as mental retardation, cultural, sensory, and/or educational inadequacy, or serious emotional disturbance.

To determine that a significant discrepancy exists between academic potential and academic functioning, it is necessary to assess both and to examine the difference. Neither assessing potential nor evaluating what constitutes a significant discrepancy is an entirely straightforward, objective procedure, however. The usual way to assess academic potential is through an individual test of intelligence such as the Binet or WISC. In spite of all the difficulties inherent in the fact that performance on such tests is influenced by the very factors one is looking for (learning disability, educational deprivation, and so on), there is to date no widely accepted superior method of estimating academic potential. A predictive problem arises when correlation between academic potential and academic achievement is relatively low. Such a predictive index may reveal little as to the nature of a disability. Yet this is sometimes necessary to show a large enough discrepancy that will make the child eligible to receive special educational services.

Measuring academic achievement is considered (correctly and incorrectly) somewhat more objective than measuring intellectual potential. Scores on standardized achievement tests, school grades, retention in a grade, teacher referral, and the like all may be accepted under some circumstances as adequately valid and reliable indicators of achievement. Proper cautions are required in cases where a severe reading disability is reflected in achievement scores in other areas such as arithmetic reasoning, where group administration procedures fail to prevent copying, where the achievement test content is not highly correlated to a particular curriculum or its objectives, and in related circumstances.

Tests used in assessing academic achievement include standard achievement batteries such as the California, Stanford, and Metropolitan commonly used in schools. The Wide Range Achievement Test is most frequently used as a quick individual exam, although two sections of it may be used with a group. Specific reading achievement tests include the Gates series of tests, the Gray Oral Reading Tests, and many other similar instruments. Special tests on arithmetic and spelling achievement are also available, but are used comparatively infrequently.

How large must be the discrepancy between potential and functioning levels to constitute a learning disability? That question sometimes is answered arbitrarily for the diagnostician by existing state or school regulations. For example, at least one state requires a two-year discrepancy between mental age and reading age before the child is eligible to receive special help. This has the obvious advantages of being objective and of covering the large majority of severe reading disabilities in the lower and middle grades. The disadvantages of rigidity in unusual cases and the imposition of a minimum of two years of nearly total reading failure before services can be initiated are equally obvious. According to some educational definitions, a first grader whose achievement is perhaps only a few months below the expected level (mental age or some function thereof) may qualify if other evidence suggests that the problem is becoming more severe and if intervention is possible. Questions are often raised about the very bright child who is achieving at grade level but who shows a large discrepancy between potential and functioning. In fact, achievement-oriented parents are sometimes more concerned about such a child than are school personnel.

The diagnostician may wish to examine whether the child shows disorders in the learning processes. Here the diagnostic procedures are often more subjective or clinical and include the use of instruments less well standardized, in a normative sense, than the common measures of potential and achievement. This portion of the diagnostic process may be described as the assessment of psychological correlates of the disability. For instance, gross deficiencies in auditory memory, spatial concepts, sound discrimination, time orientation, and such would be considered disorders of learning processes that could be related to school achievement problems.

Some of the tests used in exploring possible disorders of the learning processes are closer to criterion-referenced than to norm-referenced instruments, in underlying philosophy if not in actual format. For instance, comparatively few normative data are available on such factors as sound blending or letter reversals. These might be thought of as "either-or" rather than strictly "developmental" aspects of learning. A child's sound blending ability either is adequate to perform the task of recognizing a word from its separated sound components, or it is not. A large number of the tests employed in this phase of diagnosis may be described as primarily visuomotor or auditory-vocal. This distinction is similar to that between performance and verbal items. Also, a growing number of tests are appearing that are related to tactile-kinesthetic functions, intersensory integration, and spatial-temporal awareness.

Tests related to auditory-vocal functioning include the Illinois Test of Psycholinguistic Abilities (1961) subtests of auditory decoding, auditory-vocal association, vocal encoding, auditory-vocal automatic, and auditory-vocal sequential; Parsons Language Sample; Basic Concept Inventory; Mecham Verbal Language Development Scale; the Roswell-Chall Auditory Blending Test; and the Learning Methods Test.

A diagnostician may be concerned with ruling out mental retardation, serious emotional disturbance, and educational, sensory, or cultural inadequacy as primary factors in the disability. In-depth consideration of serious emotional disturbance and sensory deprivation, which require other than educational techniques and personnel, will not be discussed here. This is but one reason the team or clinic approach is essential within this concept of diagnosis. Case history information may be helpful in assessing possible educational and cultural deprivation. Finally, the distinction between mental retardation and learning disabilities is usually made on the basis of intelligence test scores, large discrepancies within the various learning processes, and the availability of educational services for the two distinct classifications. Whether a distinction always can and should be drawn between mental retardation and learning disabilities has now become academic, at least within the medical and clinical definitions that require that children with substantially below average intelligence be excluded from the category of learning disabilities. Other educational definitions specifically allow latitude in "estimating potential intelligence" regardless of test scores. Even so, it remains a troublesome question for local educators struggling with placement problems.

The role of referent groups, for instance the classroom, must be evaluated carefully in some suspected learning disability cases. Placed in a class where the mean ability level is extremely high, a child of average intellectual functioning may appear to be performing quite poorly. This is not an infrequent problem for average children of highly achievement-oriented parents. It often becomes important for the diagnostician to ascertain the general achievement level of a school or particular classroom to understand why the child's performance level has been perceived by the teacher or parent as less than adequate. It is also possible, although seldom observed or noted, that severe learning disabilities may go undetected in a child of very high ability placed in a low or low average classroom or school.

PROCEDURES FOR PLANNING
EDUCATIONAL TECHNIQUES AND PROGRAMS

Once it has been established through various assessment procedures that a child does have a learning disability, the primary educational question—What do we do about it?—is next. This is not to say that entirely different tests or procedures must now be employed, but rather to suggest that new questions must be considered. The issue is no longer whether the child has a disability; the issue is what should be done about it. Specific educational recommendations must be forthcoming.

The question of the efficacy of inferring remedial procedures from the diagnostic processes to be described still awaits definitive, data-oriented resolution. In this discussion it is assumed that making specific educational recommendations for the use of materials or techniques other than those routinely employed in the regular classroom is a necessary and legitimate part of this phase of educational assessment. But it must be noted that the research on aptitude-treatment interaction (that is, the lack of it) fails to support this assumption.

The process of psychoeducational diagnosis conducted to make recommendations for prescriptive or individualized teaching is based, implicitly or explicitly, on a model of cognitive-perceptual functioning (Strother, 1966). The diagnostician uses some sort of model to guide him or her in choosing areas to be assessed. Popular and representative models (such as the central processing model) utilize computerlike categories of the child's functioning or potential dysfunctioning: input (sensory modalities and attention), integration (intersensory and associative), output (motor and vocal response systems), storage and retrieval (memory), and feedback, plus others (for example, Gallagher, 1962). Just as diagnostic tests can be described in terms of the portion of the cognitive-perceptual map they explore, so remedial techniques and materials can be described and related to each other and to tests in terms of the cognitive-perceptual areas they are designed to exercise or develop (Frostig, 1967). Thus, one of the main jobs of the diagnostician operating within this framework has been to know tests and relatable remedial techniques and materials that cover all the major areas of dysfunction found in children with learning problems.

For example, a child might have a problem described in global behavioral terms by the teacher or parent as an inability to follow verbal instructions. The diagnostician then must be prepared to observe and assess such possible specific areas as dysfunctions in temporal sequencing, auditory closure, auditory discrimination (probably with help from audiologic disciplines), comprehension of the structure and function of various linguistic patterns, speed of auditory perception, immediate auditory memory, attention to auditory stimuli, integration of auditory symbols and visual referents, and so on (Myklebust, 1954; Reichstein and Rosenstein, 1964).

The problem might be of a different sort in which totally different tests or types of observation would be appropriate. If, for instance, the difficulty was poor handwriting, the diagnostician might be required to assess such diverse functions as fine muscle control, eye-hand coordination, visual perception, or body image. If the disability showed up as difficulty in acquiring sight vocabulary, tests of visual memory or aptitude for learning through tactile-kinesthetic reading might be necessary.

In short, the diagnostic-remedial, or psychoeducational (as it is sometimes called), approach to children's learning problems requires that the diagnostician know what receptive (or perceptual), integrative (or cognitive), expressive (or response) processes allegedly underlie complex behavioral products such as reading, speaking, or writing, and be prepared to assess these areas in as much depth as necessary to find specific deficits and to plan strategies for reducing or circumventing these disabilities.

There are variable degrees of precision in diagnosing different areas of dysfunction. The following illustrative example shows various points at which a tester might stop assessing and begin making recommendations.

Barry was referred to the school's psychoeducational diagnostician by his third grade teacher, who reported that he seemed capable of doing better work than he was currently doing. The diagnostician might have proceeded as described below.

1. Administration of the WISC revealed Barry's verbal I.Q. to be 120 and his performance I.Q. as 103. Barry's reading grades were consistently D, and his last achievement test showed that he was reading at 2.3 grade level, even though he is nine years old.

At this point the diagnostician might stop and simply conclude that Barry is eligible to receive remedial reading under state or district regulations, and so recommend.

2. Further examination of the WISC scaled scores revealed that Barry scored significantly poorly (Newland and Smith, 1967) in coding, digit span, and information. Further reading tests showed that he read very rapidly and inaccurately, freely supplying incorrect words, which seemed to him to be in context. His knowledge of phonics and word attack skills was limited to moderate mastery of simple consonant sounds. He showed total confusion on vowels. His sight vocabulary was generally adequate for second grade and definitely stronger for distinctive words such as "elephant" or "balloon" than for the troublesome "when," "with," "they," and the like.

The diagnostician might stop at this point and recommend that Barry be given a phonically oriented remedial approach with special emphasis on careful attention to each word part, also concluding that Barry needs work in attending (digit span), perceptual speed training (coding), and so on.

3. Since Barry's cluster of low WISC subscales is not at all uncommon in that type or types of reading problems called "dyslexia," and since his reading difficulties in sound-symbol association, differentiation of similar words, and so on also are not inconsistent with dyslexia, the diagnostician might continue testing with other instruments. Dominance testing also might be done since this is said by many to be related to dyslexia. Other test options might include the ITPA, the Bender, the Frostig. If Barry showed deficiencies in auditory-vocal sequencing and visual-motor sequencing, some diagnosticians would then say with greater certainty that the boy was "dyslexic." The Bender and Frostig might well reveal some visual-motor perceptual problems. The Purdue might then be

administered to gain further information about the perceptual-motor aspects of Barry's problem.

This process of further, related testing might continue indefinitely, limited only by time and the diagnostician's knowledge of available tests. If the test results continued to be consistent with the dyslexia hypothesis and in particular showed up visual-perceptual and body image problems, additional recommendations for Getman, Kephart, Frostig, or other remedial programs might be made. Such remedial recommendations are again limited only by the diagnostician's knowledge of what is available and the availability of a capable tutor familiar with the materials.

This procedure of further testing and interrelating findings on one test to those on another and exploring related disabilities can be continued with ever increasing sophistication and remoteness from the presenting symptom of inadequate word attack skills in reading. A point of diminishing returns might be reached in this pursuit for several reasons, however. Among them are:

1. Inadequate factor analytic studies of definitions and relationships among functions tested by the commonly used instruments.[2]
2. Inadequate knowledge of relationships between functions or processes tested (for example, spatial relations) and other behavioral disabilities such as spelling or writing.
3. Lack of refined, differentiated, systematic remedial procedures for these "process" disabilities.
4. Inadequate verification of the efficacy of "process" training in overcoming other behavioral disabilities, a problem that might be rephrased in terms of the sufficiency for and necessity of "process" (underlying disability) training prior to or concomitant with direct remediation (for example, teaching short vowel sounds).

In general, the rationale for this kind of extensive diagnostic exploration is that the child possibly has some kind of correlated or underlying "process" disability that so far has prevented adequate response to ordinary teaching skills. This correlated disability should be remediated first (for example, auditory closure taught or auditory memory improved); then the child can more easily learn the skills (such as phonic

---

[2] To give one example: The ITPA has been critically reviewed by writers who argue that its diagnostic, predictive, and programming values are questionable; and that because validity and reliability are not conclusively established, one must exercise caution in using this instrument. Among the criticisms offered are that the ITPA does not always measure discrete, mutually exclusive abilities; it is not as effective with children under six as with children over six; and the functions it seeks to identify do not correlate with "relevant school criteria." Most of the critics of the ITPA suggest that more studies of this instrument must be undertaken. The reader who wishes to explore this issue further is directed to the following citations in this chapter's reference list: Hammill and Larsen (1974), Kaluger and Kolson (1969), McIntosh and Dunn (1973), Newcomer and Hammill (1975), Ryckman and Wiegerink (1969), and Weener, Barritt, and Semmel (1967).

word attack skills). This rationale is used by the "teach to weakness and improve it" proponents (for example, Kirk, 1966). The "teach to strength" proponents (such as Cohn, 1964) advocate the above kind of diagnostic testing to find intact areas so that instruction can be redirected to those channels or processes through which the child learns more readily. Some advocate direct remedial teaching, usually on an individual basis, in specific areas of weakness *and* simultaneous restructuring of instruction, usually on a group basis, so that the child is exercising and learning through the intact perceptual-cognitive processes.

Two separate questions, which are not always treated as separate, are *what* to teach and *how* to teach it to the child with learning disabilities. Some psychoeducational diagnoses appear to have dealt more extensively with the *how* than with the *what* of teaching these children. Consequently, the *what* of teaching has sometimes been trivia. For instance, some practitioners have come to question the educational relevance of large amounts of remedial bead stringing, puzzle assembling, and so on (Engelmann, 1967).

These kinds of tasks are attempts to fulfill prescriptions for the development of visual memory or visual closure, and the like. But the diagnostician may have neglected to ask what tasks the child needs to learn for which visual memory or closure is required. If that question had been asked, it is possible that different recommendations might have been forthcoming and that the tasks generated would more nearly resemble the important educational outcomes desired. The child might, for example, be exercising or developing visual memory by using letters or number symbols rather than beads.

To inventory the tasks a child needs to be taught requires survey instruments and procedures such as parent or teacher interview techniques that are highly specific and behaviorally oriented. For instance, it is of no help to anyone for the diagnostician to state that the child needs remedial reading. This general *what* is obvious. The problem is determining the specific *what* within the large realm of behaviors or tasks called reading that the child needs to learn. Similarly, a parent's report that the child needs to become more independent at home is of little help. The diagnostician must be prepared to establish that the child cannot dress independently or groom or does not ever play alone, and so on. Comparatively few survey instruments of this specific behavior-to-be-learned type are available. Among the few are phonics inventories, direct interviews, and social competency measures, such as the social maturity scale of the Valett Developmental Survey of Basic Learning Abilities, the Vineland, the PAC, and the Cain-Levine Social Competency Scale. In the language area, items from the auditory-vocal automatic and vocal encoding subtests of the ITPA perhaps represent specific tasks that should be taught directly to the child who is deficient in them. These are the kinds of tests about which the diagnostician can say to the teacher, tutor, or parent, "Teach the failed test items as directly as you can." They are viewed as important tasks that the child cannot yet perform, and they seem next in line to be learned, either developmentally or in terms of priority due to the nature of the task (Valett, 1967).

FUNCTIONAL ANALYSIS OF BEHAVIOR

Functional analysis of behavior as an approach to children's learning disabilities overlaps both identification and planning through incorporation of procedures for describing specific deviant behaviors and through provision of a system—both scientific and methodological—for planning and executing remedial strategies.

Functional analysis is a method of evaluation based on thorough behavioral assessment of individual performance. It has been adapted to the task of analyzing complex behaviors observable in behavior disorders, socialization, or academic performance during skill acquisition (for example, in reading). Although its use is recent, functional analysis has been applied systematically in at least three settings or arrangements pertinent to learning disabilities: 1) arrangements within highly controlled environments such as specialized treatment facilities (laboratories), 2) arrangements within natural environments accomplished through direct or indirect programming by the behavioral scientist, and 3) arrangements in natural environments accomplished by practitioners or parents who have been trained by the behavioral scientist.

In each instance, the evaluation analysis is similar in structure and strategy, that is, the data employed are a record of actual, explicit events—the antecedent events, the responses of the subject, and consequent events temporally related to the responses.

The general strategy of evaluation is essentially a two-step procedure first of obtaining baseline data (a pretreatment measurement of the performance or behavior pattern) on the specific behavior to be changed and then assessing the conditions that maintain the behavior. These conditions include the stimulus events, the responses, the contingency system, and the consequences within the learning environment in which the child is to perform. To illustrate briefly, if a child is referred for hyperactivity the first step in the evaluation procedure is to determine what behaviors are observable in his hyperactivity, e.g., foot tapping and ear pulling, and then to observe and count instances of those behaviors per minute (or other time unit) under a range of conditions. When the baseline data (rate of specific behaviors over several observations) are obtained, the second step is an assessment of the environmental conditions that cue and consequent foot tapping and ear pulling.

Baseline

The diagnostic procedures for establishing a baseline of relevant performance presuppose that the evaluator knows precisely what class of specific behavioral units to assess. For instance, forms of vocalization, body movements, object manipulations, acquisition of sight vocabulary, completion of assigned work, or disruptive behaviors in the classroom might be the target behaviors to be studied. "Pinpoint" recording can be attained when specific behaviors are observed. Either simple or complex units can be recorded per unit of time, enabling behavioral rates to be established for a specified number of response classes. The topography (form or exact description) of relevant behaviors also can be described selectively or generally. Specification of the *topography* of the responses is important to subsequent plans for modifying the behavior, and the *rate* is important as an indicator of the effectiveness of the contingencies used during training.

The aim in establishing baselines for relevant behaviors is to establish the total range of variability for the child under different conditions or stimulus arrangements. Thus the baseline should not be a product of one observation, but rather should be based upon a continuous assessment of behavior over a period of time until a functional range has been obtained. The evaluator also should be concerned not only with the reliability of baseline performances but with the validity of his evaluations. This is largely assured by the objective nature and the quantification of the observations. In addition, the recorded behaviors can be exactly matched to those the evaluator will subsequently seek to modify. Therefore, the validity and the predictive value of the recorded data should be appreciably higher than those derived from standardized tests that sample a range of performance and are used as indirect or inferred indicators for performances in the behavior areas in question.

Analysis of Behavioral Components

The second aspect of the proposed evaluative process is the assessment of those behavioral components that maintain and modify behavior, i.e., *antecedent* or *stimulus* events, behavioral *movements* or *responses,* the *contingency system* used to program consequences, and the *consequences* which are contingent upon a specified behavior (Lindsley, 1964; Lovitt, 1967).

Antecedent or stimulus events. The baseline recording procedure described above alerts the teacher to the child's pattern of behavior. The baseline data also provide useful information for the teacher in planning specific instructional arrangements. If this is to be the intent, the baseline data should be obtained from responses made to events similar to those to be used later in changing the behavior. Since the evaluator cannot recreate the learning history of the child step-by-step, he may instead observe the child's response rates or patterns (preferences) to a variety of classroom materials, to the behavior of peers, and to the teacher's modes of instruction and interaction. For example, the evaluator can obtain valuable information by letting the child select his own preferred rate of visual or aural presentation, the intensity or brightness of the aural or visual stimuli, and/or the configuration or size of the visual stimulus (Lovitt,

1967). Teachers in aural rehabilitation classes do this routinely when they let the child set the loudness level on auditory training equipment. Another method is to vary arbitrarily the stimuli (such as the loudness) and to observe the changes in the child's responses. Changes in the materials and in modes of instruction will produce changes in response patterns; consequently these must be held constant while observations and measurements are made to determine the baseline levels of responding.

Movement or response behaviors.   As various stimuli are presented, changes in the child's responses must be continuously recorded. Stimulus events themselves thus give additional diagnostic meaning to the response levels and variability. Response changes may be noted in rate of speaking or moving, the length of response units, or the extent of sustained responding.

Reinforcement or contingency system.   Many of the educational and social deviations displayed by children with learning disabilities could result from infrequent or sporadic contingencies or reinforcements. Although most normal children seem to prosper on a fairly lean schedule of reinforcement, many children with behavioral deficits often fail to respond, or respond at very low rates on intermittent schedules. The contingency rates required to accelerate or to maintain the desired behavior are important indicators are for subsequent instructional programming and should be assessed. For example, a normal child may achieve well with only the 6-week's grade as reinforcement while the child with learning disabilities might require charting progress in performance every day and even every hour.

Subsequent or consequent events.   It is necessary to identify an individual's hierarchy of consequences—those particular commodities or events that either increase or decrease his rates of performance. Those consequences should be selected which ultimately will be available in the child's home or school and whenever possible they should take the form of the complex social consequences that will eventually control his behavior (Lovitt, 1967). But it is often necessary initially to use simple, tangible consequences. For most children a variety of reinforcers is likely to have consequence value. The first objective then is to select commodities that will have consequence value and thus will accelerate the child's rate of response.

Tokens, points, or checkmarks are sometimes used as currency which enables a child to select and "purchase" his own tangible or social reinforcers. In this way consequent events may have greater strength for evoking and sustaining effort. Contingencies and social reinforcers in such a learning situation are under the direct control of the adult.

The Dyadic Unit

In many diagnostic evaluations it may be necessary to assess the referring agent—the teacher or parent—as well as the referred child

(Lovitt, 1967). Often it is the pattern of interaction between the child and adult rather than just the child's behavior which must be modified. More specifically, it may be desirable to consider the stimulus-response chains or pattern within the dyadic (two-person) unit. The two members of the unit provide sequential contingencies for each other. Each provides preceding responses which become stimuli for the next response of the other, and each establishes the contingency and the subsequent event (feedback) to the other as well. In the classroom, for example, some teachers respond to a child only when he is emitting undesirable behavior, an action which simply increases the probability of more of the same behavior. Rather, they should be reinforcing him for the desired behaviors to increase the probability of these desirable behaviors.

This discussion of functional analysis is limited to behavioral assessment and does not treat the behavior modification procedures derived directly from the assessment data gathered. Application of behavior modification techniques necessitates consideration under remediation or program implementation. A bibliography of behavior modification literature pertinent to learning disabilities is included, however.

Generalization of Evaluation

The intent in studying behavioral functions should be to effect an optimum environment for learning. In terms of the diagnostic remedial approach discussed earlier this necessitates rephrasing to state that the purpose of the diagnosis is to plan remediation. Given the information specified above, the teacher or clinician presumably should be able to plan for a stable, effective learning environment. The teacher should seek to generalize the arrangement of effective learning conditions to an extended time frame and to a range of formal and informal settings. This can be done by maintaining a cumulative record of performance data in order to make ongoing educational decisions.

FUTURE CONSIDERATIONS

This brief overview of the educational appraisal of learning disabilities has been divided broadly into two types of procedures—those for determining that a learning disability exists or is likely to develop and those for planning intervention strategies or remedial steps to minimize the effects of the disability. Both approaches address themselves on occasion to specific academic bits of behavior, such as learning or teaching short vowel sounds, but there is still ample room in the field of educational appraisal of learning disabilities for greater attention to the systematic determination of precise educational deficits. Most traditional achievement testing is far too global. Among the promising future trends in the evaluation of learning disabilities will be greater attention to the development of specific educational-oriented, deficit-oriented, and criterion-referenced instruments that will answer with greater precision the question of what the child needs to learn next. This emphasis, of course, brings the field of learning disabilities into very close or overlapping contact with general education, and mutual contribution to improvement of all instructional practices and prevention of learning disabilities is expected. Functional analysis is a powerful process for decision-making, because with these procedures the educator is able to determine the functional variables of learning.

REFERENCES

BEERY, K. F., *Preschool Prediction and Prevention of Learning Disabilities*. Final Report, 1967, Project Nos. 6-8742 and 6-8743, Grant Nos. OEG 4-7-008742-2031 and OEG 4-7-008743-1507. Washington, D.C.: U.S. Department of Health, Education, and Welfare, Office of Education, 1967.

COHN, R., The neurological study of children with learning disabilities. *Exceptional Children*, 1964, *31*, 179–185.

DE HIRSCH, K., J. J. JANSKY, and W. S. LANGFORD, *Predicting Reading Failure: A Preliminary Study of Reading, Writing and Spelling Disabilities in Preschool Children*. New York: Harper & Row, 1966.

ENGELMANN, S., Relationship between psychological theories and the act of teaching. *Journal of School Psychology*, 1967, *2*, 93–100.

FROSTIG, M., The relationship of diagnosis to remediation in learning problems. *International Approach to Learning Disabilities of Children and Youth*. Tulsa, Okla.: The Association for Children with Learning Disabilities, Inc., 1967.

GALLAGHER, J. J., Educational methods with brain-damaged children. In J. H. Masserman, ed., *Current Psychiatric Therapies*. New York: Grune & Stratton, 1962.

HAMMILL, D. D., and S. C. LARSEN, The effectiveness of psycholinguistic training. *Exceptional Children*, September 1974, 5–14.

HARING, N. G., and R. W. RIDGWAY, Early identification of children with learning disabilities. *Exceptional Children*, 1967, *33*, 387–95.

KALUGER, G., and C. J. KOLSON, *Reading and Learning Disabilities*. Columbus, Ohio: Charles E. Merrill, 1969.

KIRK, S. A., *The Diagnosis and Remediation of Psycholinguistic Disabilities*. Urbana: Institute for Research on Exceptional Children, University of Illinois, 1966.

LINDSLEY, O. R., Direct measurement and prosthesis of retarded behavior. *Journal of Education*, 1964, *147*, 62–81.

LOVITT, T. C., 1967a. Assessment of children with learning disabilities. *Exceptional Children*, 1967, *34*, 233–240.

McCARTHY, D., *The Language Development of the Preschool Child*. University of Minnesota Child Welfare Monograph 4, 1930.

McINTOSH, D. K., and L. M. DUNN, Children with major specific learning disabilities. In L. M. Dunn, ed., *Exceptional Children in the Schools* (2nd ed.). New York: Holt, Rinehart & Winston, 1973.

MYKLEBUST, H. R., *Auditory Disorders in Children: A Manual for Differential Diagnosis.* New York: Grune & Stratton, 1954.

NEWCOMER, P. L., and D. D. HAMMILL, ITPA and academic achievement: a survey. *The Reading Teacher,* May 1975, pp. 731–741.

NEWLAND, T. W., and P. A. SMITH, Statistically significant differences between subtest scaled scores on the WISC and WAIS. *Journal of School Psychology* 1967, *5,* 122–127.

REICHSTEIN, J., and J. ROSENSTEIN, Differential diagnosis of auditory deficits—a review of the literature. *Exceptional Children,* 1964, *14,* 42–44.

RYCKMAN, D. B., and R. WIEGERINK, The factors of the Illinois Test of Psycholinguistic Abilities: a comparison of 18 factor analyses. *Exceptional Children,* October 1969, 107–113.

STROTHER, C. R., The needs of teachers for specialized information in the area of psychodiagnosis. In W. M. Cruickshank, ed., *The Teacher of Brain-injured Children.* Syracuse University Special Education and Rehabilitation Monograph Series No. 7. Syracuse, N.Y.: Syracuse University Press, 1966.

VALETT, R. E., A developmental task approach to early childhood education. *Journal of School Psychology,* 1967, *5,* 136–147.

WEENER, P., L. S. BARRITT, and M. I. SEMMEL, A critical evaluation of the Illinois Test of Psycholinguistic Abilities. *Exceptional Children,* February 1967, 373–380.

Additional Sources

ALLEN, R. M., The appraisal of social and perceptual competence of school children. In J. F. Magary, ed., *School Psychological Services in Theory and Practice.* Englewood Cliffs, N.J.: Prentice-Hall, Inc., 1967.

ANDERSON, G. L., and J. F. MAGARY, Projective techniques and the ITPA. In J. F. Magary, ed., *School Psychological Services in Theory and Practice.* Englewood Cliffs, N. J.: Prentice-Hall, Inc., 1967.

BATEMAN, B. D., Learning disorders. *Review of Educational Research,* 1966, *36,* 93–119.

———, Three approaches to diagnosis and educational planning for children with learning disabilities. *Academic Therapy Quarterly,* 1967, *2, 2.*

BENDER, L., Problems in conceptualization and communication in children with developmental alexia. In P. H. Hoch and J. Zubin, eds., *Psychopathology of Communication.* New York: Grune & Stratton, 1958.

BIRCH, H. G., and L. BELMONT, Auditory-visual integration in normal and retarded readers. *American Journal of Orthopsychiatry,* 1964, *34,* 852–861.

BOSHES, B., and H. R. MYKLEBUST, A neurological and behavioral study of children with learning disorders. *Neurology,* 1964, *14,* 7–12.

BRUECKNER, L. J., and G. L. BOND, *The Diagnosis and Treatment of Learning Difficulties.* New York: Appleton-Century-Crofts, 1955.

CLEMENTS, S. D. Come to the wedding. *Academic Therapy Quarterly,* 1967, *2,* 134–138.

————, *Minimal Brain Dysfunction in Children: Terminology and Identification.* Phase one of a three-phase project (NINDB Monograph No. 3). Washington, D.C.: U. S. Department of Health, Education, and Welfare, 1966.

CLEMMENS, R. L., Minimal brain damage in children. *Children,* September–October, 1961, 179–183.

CONNORS, C. K., Information processing in children with learning disabilities and brain damage: some experimental approaches. *International Approach to Learning Disabilities of Children and Youth.* Tulsa, Okla.: The Association for Children with Learning Disabilities, Inc., 1967.

CRUICKSHANK, W. M., ed., *The Teacher of Brain-injured Children.* Syracuse, N.Y.: Syracuse University Press, 1966.

DALEY, W. T., ed., *Speech and Language Therapy with the Brain-damaged Child.* Washington, D.C.: Catholic University of America Press, 1962.

DE HIRSCH, K., Tests designed to discover potential reading difficulties at the six-year-old level. *American Journal of Orthopsychiatry,* 1957, *27,* 566–576.

DILLER, L., and H. G. BIRCH, Psychological evaluation of children with cerebral damage. In H. G. Birch, ed., *Brain Damage in Children.* Baltimore: Williams & Wilkins, 1964.

ENGELMANN, S., *Basic Concept Inventory.* Chicago: Follett Publishing Company, 1967.

FRIERSON, E., and W. BARBE, eds., *Educating Children with Learning Disabilities.* Englewood Cliffs, N.J.: Prentice-Hall, 1967.

HAEUSSERMANN, ELSE. *Developmental Potential of Preschool Children: An Evaluation of Intellectual, Sensory and Emotional Functioning.* New York: Grune & Stratton, 1958.

HARING, N. G., and T. C. LOVITT, Operant methodology and educational technology in special education. In N. G. Haring and R. L. Schiefelbusch (eds.) *Methods in Special Education.* New York: McGraw-Hill, 1967, pp. 12–48.

HELLMUTH, J., ed., *Educational Therapy.* Vol. 1. Seattle: Special Child Publications, 1964.

————, *Learning Disorders.* Vol. 1. Seattle: Special Child Publications, 1965.

————, *Learning Disorders.* Vol. 2. Seattle: Special Child Publications, 1966.

————, *The Special Child in Century 21.* Seattle: Special Child Publications, 1964.

HEWETT, F. M., A hierarchy of educational tasks of children with learning disorders. *Exceptional Children,* 1964, *31,* 207–214.

ILG, F. L., and L. B. AMES, *School Readiness: Behavior Tests Used at the Gesell Institute.* New York: Harper & Row, 1965.

KASS, C. E., Psycholinguistic disabilities of children with reading problems. *Exceptional Children,* 1966, *32,* 533–539.

KIRK, S. A., and W. BECKER, eds., *Conference on Children with Minimal Brain Impairment.* Urbana: University of Illinois Press, 1963.

KIRK, S. A., and J. J. McCARTHY, The Illinois Test of Psycholinguistic Abilities—an approach to differential diagnosis. *American Journal of Mental Deficiency,* 1961, *66,* 399–412.

KLEFFNER, F. R., Aphasia and other language deficiencies in children: research and teaching at Central Institute for the Deaf. In W. T. Daley, ed., *Speech and Language Therapy with the Brain-damaged Child.* Washington, D.C.: Catholic University of America Press, 1962.

LOVITT, T. C., 1967*b*. Free-operant preference for one of two stories: A methodological note. *Journal of Educational Psychology,* 1967, *58,* 84–87.

———, 1967*c*. The use of conjugate reinforcement to evaluate the relative reinforcing effects of various narrative forms. *Journal of Experimental Child Psychology,* 1967, *5,* 164–71.

LOVITT, T. C., H. P. KUNZELMANN, P. A. NOLEN, and W. J. HULTEN. The dimensions of classroom data. Paper presented at a symposium at the Association for Children with Learning Disabilities Annual Convention, Boston, Mass., February, 1968. Copies available from the Experimental Education Unit, Child Development and Mental Retardation Center, University of Washington, Seattle, Washington.

MAHLER, D., *Introduction to Programs for Educationally Handicapped Pupils* (rev. ed.). Sacramento: California Association for Neurologically Handicapped Children, 1966.

MONROE, M., *Children Who Cannot Read.* Chicago: University of Chicago Press, 1932.

MYKLEBUST, H. R., and D. JOHNSON, Dyslexia in children. *Exceptional Children,* 1962, *29,* 14–24.

POWELL, H. F., and N. M. CHANSKY, The evaluating of academic disabilities. In J. F. Magary, ed., *School Psychological Services in Theory and Practice.* Englewood Cliffs, N.J.: Prentice-Hall, Inc., 1967.

RABINOVITCH, R. D., and W. INGRAM, Neuropsychiatric considerations in reading retardation. *Reading Teacher,* 1962, *15,* 433–438.

RAWSON, M. B., *A Bibliography on the Nature, Recognition, and Treatment of Language Difficulties.* Pomfret, Conn.: The Orton Society, 1966.

ROACH, E. G., and N. C. KEPHART, *Purdue Perceptual-Motor Survey.* Columbus, Ohio: Charles E. Merrill, 1966.

SCHIFFMAN, G., Early identification of reading disabilities: the responsibility of the public school. *Bulletin of the Orton Society,* 1964, *14,* 42–44.

SULZBACHER, S. I., T. C. LOVITT, and J. D. KIDDER, Applications of behavior modification procedures by the school psychologist. Division of School Psychology, *Newsletter* of the Washington State Psychological Association, 1967, *4,* 5–7.

SUTPHIN, F. E., *A Perceptual Testing and Training Handbook for First Grade Teachers.* Winter Haven, Fla.: Lions' Research Foundation, 1964.

TAYLOR, E. M., *Psychological Appraisal of Children with Cerebral Defects.* Cambridge, Mass.: Harvard University Press, 1959.

WOOD, N., Evaluation of language disorders in children of school age. In W. T. Daley, ed., *Speech and Language Therapy with the Brain-damaged Child.* Washington, D.C.: Catholic University of America Press, 1962.

ZEDLER, E. Y., A screening scale for children with high risk of neurological impairment. *International Approach to Learning Disabilities of Children and Youth.* Tulsa, Okla.: The Association for Children with Learning Disabilities, Inc., 1967.

ZIMMERMAN, I. L., and H. L. ZIMMERMAN, Individual intellectual evaluation of school children. In J. F. Magary, ed., *School Psychological Services in Theory and Practice.* Englewood Cliffs, N.J.: Prentice-Hall, Inc., 1967.

References on Behavior Analysis and Modification

ALLEN, K. E., D. M. HART, J. S. BUELL, F. R. HARRIS, and M. M. WOLF, Effects of social reinforcement on isolate behavior of a nursery school child. *Child Development,* 1964, *35,* 511–518.

AZRIN, N. H., and O. R. LINDSLEY, The reinforcement of cooperation between children. *Journal of Abnormal and Social Psychology,* 1956, *52,* 100–102.

BAER, D. M., Effect of withdrawal of positive reinforcement on an extinguishing response in young children. *Child Development,* 1961, *32,* 67–74.

——, Technique of social reinforcement for the study of child behavior: behavior avoiding reinforcement withdrawal. *Child Development,* 1962, *33,* 847–858.

BEUTSCH, M., and K. SALZINGER, Operant conditioning of continuous speech in young children. *Child Development,* 1962, *33,* 683–695.

BIJOU, S. Q., Patterns of reinforcement and resistance to extinction in young children. *Child Development,* 1967, *28,* 47–54.

BIRNBRAUER, J. S., and J. LAWLER, Token reinforcement for learning. *Mental Retardation,* 1964, *2,* 275–279.

EYSENCK, H. J., *Experiments in Behavior Therapy.* New York: Pergamon Press, 1964.

FERSTER, C., Arithmetic behavior in chimpanzees. *Scientific American,* 1964, *210,* 98–106.

FERSTER, C., and M. DeMEYER, The development of performances in autistic children in automatically controlled environments. *Journal of Chronic Diseases,* 1961, *25,* 8–12.

GROSSBERG, J., Behavior therapy: a review. *Psychological Bulletin,* 1964, *62,* 73–88.

HARING, N. G., and E. L. PHILLIPS, *Educating Emotionally Disturbed Children.* New York: McGraw-Hill, 1962.

HAWKER, J. R., U. W. GEERTZ, and M. SHRAGO, Prompting and confirmation in sight vocabulary learning by retardates. *American Journal of Mental Deficiency,* 1964, *68,* 751–756.

HEWETT, F., Teaching reading to an autistic boy through operant conditioning. *Reading Teacher,* 1964, *17,* 613–618.

HEWETT, F., D. MAYHEW, and E. RABB, An experimental reading program for neurologically impaired, mentally retarded, and severely emotionally disturbed children. *American Journal of Orthopsychiatry,* 1967, *37,* 35–49.

HIVELY, W., Implications for the classroom of B. F. Skinner's analysis of behavior. *Harvard Educational Review,* 1959, *29,* 37–42.

HOMME, L. H., P. C. DEBACA, J. V. DEVINE, R. STEINHORST, and E. J. RICKERT, Use of the Premack principle in controlling the behavior of nursery school children. *Journal of the Experimental Analysis of Behavior,* 1963, *6,* 544.

KRASNER, L., and L. ULLMANN, *Research in Behavior Modification*. New York: Holt, Rinehart & Winston, 1965.

LEVIN, G., and J. SIMMONS, Response to food and praise by emotionally disturbed boys. *Psychological Reports*, 1962, *11*, 539–546.

——, Response to praise by emotionally disturbed boys. *Psychological Reports*, 1962, *11*, 10.

LINDE, T., Techniques for establishing motivation through operant conditioning. *American Journal of Mental Deficiency*, 1962, *67*, 437–440.

LOVAAS, O. I., and others, Building social behavior in autistic children by use of electric shock. *Journal of Experimental Research in Personality*, 1965, *1*, 99–100.

McCREARY, A. P., Study of association, reinforcement, and transfer in beginning reading. *Journal of Experimental Education*, 1963, *31*, 285–290.

PATTERSON, G. R., An application of conditioning techniques to the control of a hyperactive child. *Behaviour Research and Therapy*, 1965, *2*, 217–226.

PORTER, D., What does learning theory contribute to the classroom? *Audio-visual Instruction*, 1962, *7*, 13–16.

PREMACK, D., Toward empirical behavior laws: I. positive reinforcement. *Psychological Review*, 1959, *66*, 219–233.

QUAY, H. P., J. S. WERRY, M. McQUEEN, and R. L. SPRAGUE, Remediation of the conduct problem child in the special class setting. *Exceptional Children*, 1966, *32*, 509–515.

SALZINGER, K., Experimental manipulation of verbal behavior: a review. *Journal of General Psychology*, 1959, *61*, 65.

SKINNER, B. F., Operant behavior. *American Psychologist*, 1963, *18*, 503–515.

SPIELBERGER, C. D., and others, Effects of awareness and attitude toward the reinforcement on the operant conditioning of verbal behavior. *Journal of Personality*, 1962, *30*, 106–121.

STAATS, A., K. MINKE, J. FINLEY, M. WOLFE, and L. BROOKS, A reinforcer system and experimental procedure for the laboratory study of reading acquisition. *Child Development*, 1964, *35*, 209–231.

STONE, F. B., and V. N. ROWLEY, Changes in children's verbal behavior as a function of social approval, experimenter differences, and child personality. *Child Development*, 1964, *35*, 669–676.

TRAVERS, R. M. W., Research on reinforcement and its implications for education. *Journal of Teacher Education*, 1964, *15*, 223–229.

ULLMANN, L., and L. KRASNER, *Case Studies in Behavior Modification*. New York: Holt, Rinehart & Winston, 1965.

WHELAN, R. J., and N. G. HARING, Modification and maintenance of behavior through systematic application of consequences. *Exceptional Children*, 1966, *32*, 281–289.

ZIMMERMAN, E. H., and J. ZIMMERMAN, The alteration of behavior in a special classroom situation. *Journal of the Experimental Analysis of Behavior*, 1962, *5*, 59–60.

Appendix to Chapter 4:
Tests Used In Identification and Evaluation
of Learning Disorders

The following list of tests includes most of the widely used assessment instruments in the field of learning disorders. This is not, however, a comprehensive or exhaustive list. Those tests marked with an asterisk (*) were the most frequently mentioned instruments in an informal survey in which 43 professional persons responded regarding the tests they used or recommended in diagnosing learning disorders (Joan C. Fertman, personal communication, May 1967).

The tests are organized according to the following general headings:

  I. Intelligence Tests.
     A. Global.
     B. Verbal and/or Vocabulary.
     C. Visuo-Motor (Performance).
 II. Perceptual Tests—Visuo-Motor.
III. Academic Achievement and Diagnostic Tests.
     A. Reading.
     B. Spelling and Arithmetic.
 IV. Diagnostic Language Tests.
  V. Screening and Readiness Tests.
 VI. Social Competence Tests.

I. INTELLIGENCE TESTS

A. Global

Stanford-Binet Intelligence Scale: Combined L and M form, third revision. Houghton Mifflin, 1960. Individually administered test of intelligence with IQs for ages 2–0 through 18–0.

* *Wechsler Intelligence Scale for Children* (WISC). Psychological Corporation, 1949. Individually administered test of intelligence providing separate verbal and performance scores with norms for ages 5–0 and 15–0.

A Quick Screening Scale of Mental Development. Psychometric Affiliates, 1963. Provides a rough estimate of a child's level of mental development with norms from 6 months to 10 years.

Merrill-Palmer Scale of Mental Tests. Harcourt, Brace & World, 1926–31. Individually administered test of general intelligence for young children.

Wechsler Preschool & Primary Scale of Intelligence (WPPSI). Psychological Corporation, 1967. Individually administered test of intelligence providing separate verbal and performance scores with norms for ages 4–0 to 6–6 (overlapping the WISC in the age range 5–0 to 6–6).

Minnesota Preschool Scale. Teacher's College, Columbia University, Educational Test Bureau, 1940. Individually administered test of intelligence (similar in content to the Binet-type test) yielding verbal, nonverbal and total IQ from 18 months to 6 years.

Time Appreciation Test. Western Psychological Services (Buck, J.N.). Ten-minute intelligence test for children, assessing only concepts of time.

Kent Series of Emergency Scales. Psychological Corporation. Quick estimate of mental ability used to verify other testing in the age range of 5 years through adult.

B. Verbal and/or Vocabulary

Full Range Picture Vocabulary Test. Psychological Test Specialists (Ammons, R.B.), 1948. Individually administered, nonverbal test of intelligence for ages 2–6 through adult.

* *Peabody Picture Vocabulary Test* (PPVT). American Guidance Service, 1959. Individually administered test of verbal intelligence estimated by measuring receptive vocabulary for ages 1–9 to 18–0.

Pictorial Test of Intelligence. Houghton Mifflin (French, J.L.), 1964. Individually administered test of intelligence including 6 subtests with norms from 2–6 to 8–6.

Lorge-Thorndike Intelligence Tests. Houghton Mifflin, 1954–62. Verbal test of intelligence.

C. Visuo-Motor (Performance)

Columbia Mental Maturity Scale, revised edition. Harcourt, Brace & World, 1959. Individually administered test of intelligence requiring no verbal responses and minimizing motor responses; heavily weighted with visual discrimination and concept development for mental ages 3–0 to 10–0.

* *Draw-A-Man Test.* World Book Company (Goodenough, F.), 1926. Quick estimate of intelligence that can be used clinically to make assessments of personality and body image factors for ages 3–3 to 13–0.

Raven Progressive Matrices. Psychological Corporation, 1938, 1947. Nonverbal test series designed to aid in assessing mental ability in solving problems presented in abstract figures and designs for ages 5–0 to 11–0 (1938) and mentally retarded adults (1947).

Leiter International Performance Scale. Western Psychological Services, 1948. Individually administered, nonverbal test of intelligence for ages 2–0 through adult.

Arthur Point Scale of Performance Tests, revised form II. Psychological Corporation, 1943. Individually administered nonlanguage performance scale for measuring intelligence for ages 4–0 to adult.

II. PERCEPTUAL TESTS—VISUO-MOTOR

Left–Right Discrimination and Finger Localization. Hoeber-Harper (Benton, A.L.), 1959. Includes research, reviews, methods of administration and norms from 6–0 to 9–0 for the tests of left-right discrimination and finger localization.

Harris Tests of Lateral Dominance. Psychological Corporation, 1955. The manual of examining procedures brings together a number of easy-to-administer tests of lateral dominance including measures of eye, hand, and foot dominance for ages 7–0 to adult.

Memory-for-Designs Test. Psychological Test Specialists (Graham, F.K. and Kendall, B.S.), 1960. Test of visual memory.

* *Benton Revised Visual Retention Test.* Psychological Corporation, 1955. Individually administered test designed to assess memory, perception, and visual-motor functions for ages 8–0 to adult.

Beery-Buktenica Visual-Motor Integration Test. Follett Publishing Company, 1967. Tests of visual-motor integration through geometric form copying for ages 1–9 to 15–11, with separate norms for males and females.

* *Frostig Developmental Tests of Visual Perception.* Consulting Psychologists Press, 1961. Test of visual perception including 4 subtests for ages 3–0 to 10+.

* *Bender Visual Motor Gestalt Test for Children.* Western Psychological Services, 1962. Individually administered test of form copying with the score yielding both quantitative and qualitative assessment for ages 5–0 to 10–0.

Lincoln-Oseretsky Motor Development Scale. Western Psychological Services, 1955. Individually administered test measuring a wide range of motor skills, eye-hand coordination, and so on for ages 6–0 to 14–0, with separate norms for males and females.

* *Purdue Perceptual-Motor Survey.* Charles E. Merrill (Roach, E.G. and Kephart, N.C.), 1966. Individually administered survey providing an indication of the child's level of perceptual-motor development recommended for grades 1 through 4.

Minnesota Percepto-Diagnostic Test. Western Psychological Services, 1963. Individually administered test using gestalt designs scored for degrees of rotation for children and adults; designed to detect type of reading disability and/or emotional disorder.

Ayres Space Test. Western Psychological Services, 1962. Performance test for children and adults with visual perception impairment, with normative data provided for ages 3–0 to 10–0.

Road Map Test of Direction Sense. Western Psychological Services (Money, J.). Measures ability to orient to right or left, toward and away, and apply to two-dimensional plane for ages 7–0 to 18–0.

III. ACADEMIC ACHIEVEMENT AND DIAGNOSTIC TESTS

A. Reading

Gates Primary Reading. Western Psychological Services, 1958. Group tests of word recognition, sentence reading, and paragraph reading for grades 1 and 2.

Gates Advanced Primary. Western Psychological Services, 1958. Group tests of word recognition and paragraph reading for grades 2 and 3.

* *Gates Reading Survey.* Western Psychological Services, 1958. Group test including work knowledge, comprehension, and speed for grades 3 to 10.

Gray Oral Reading Test. Bobbs-Merrill, 1963. Individually administered reading test that is a useful supplement to silent reading tests for grades 1.0 to 12.0.

Gilmore Oral Reading Test. Harcourt, Brace & World. Ten graded paragraphs yielding 3 scores—accuracy, comprehension, and rate—for grades 1 to 8.

Durrell Analysis of Reading Difficulty. Harcourt, Brace & World, 1955. Reading tests yielding an analysis of *how* the child reads and where he or she has difficulty, for grades 1.5 to 6.5.

Spache Diagnostic Reading Scales. California Test Bureau, 1963. Battery of interdependent tests measuring specific components of reading ability from grades 1.0 to 8.0.

Roswell-Chall Diagnostic Reading Test of Word Analysis Skills. Essay Press, 1959. Tests child's knowledge of letter sounds, their combinations into words, and the ability to apply phonic rules for grades 2.0 to 4.0 (informal).

Roswell-Chall Auditory Blending Test. Essay Press, 1963. Test of sound blending for grades 1.0 to 5+ (informal).

Botel Reading Inventory. Follett Publishing Company. Three tests evaluating word recognition, word opposites, and phonics.

Monroe Diagnostic Reading Tests and Supplementary Tests. C.H. Stoelting Company. Reading test battery consisting of any silent reading comprehension test, Gray Oral, Iota Word Recognition, Word Discrimination Test, and supplementary diagnostic tests.

McKee Inventory of Phonetic Skill. Houghton Mifflin. Reading test measuring phonic skill.

A Quick Phonics Readiness Check for Retarded Readers. (Schach, V. G., *Elementary English,* 39, 1962, 584–586.) Includes tests of auditory discrimination, sound blending, and auditory memory (very informal).

Learning Methods Test. The Mills Center, 1512 E. Broward, Ft. Lauderdale, Fla., 1955. Designed to aid the remedial reading teacher in determining the student's ability to learn new words by four different teaching methods.

Dolch Basic Sight Vocabulary Test. Garrard Press.

Phonics Knowledge Survey. Harcourt, Brace & World (Durkin, D., and L. Meshover), 1964. Phonics test to be administered by teachers.

Durrell-Sullivan Reading Capacity and Achievement Tests. Harcourt, Brace & World. Two parallel tests at each level reveal discrepancies between understanding of spoken language and understanding of the printed word for grades 2.5 to 6.0.

Doren Diagnostic Reading Test. American Guidance Service (Doren, M.), 1956. Group test of word recognition skills.

B. Spelling and Arithmetic

Buswell-John Diagnostic Test for Fundamental Processes in Arithmetic. Bobbs-Merrill. Individual test in which child works aloud to determine *how* answers are obtained.

Wide Range Achievement Test, revised edition. Psychological Corporation (Jastek, J. and Bijou, S.), 1965. Short test of oral word reading, spelling, and arithmetic achievement, with norms from kindergarten through college.

Diagnostic and Remedial Spelling Manual. Teacher's College, Columbia University, Bureau of Publications, 1940. Individual Diagnostic Program including 9 tests for grades 1.0 to 6.0.

Lincoln Primary Spelling Test. Educational Records Bureau 1960–62. Three distinct but overlapping levels of spelling words so that the same test with different words can be used with children of independent schools (grades 2 to 4) and those of public schools (grades 2 to 5).

IV. DIAGNOSTIC LANGUAGE TESTS

Parsons Language Sample. (Spradlin, J.E. *J. Speech* & *Hearing Dis.,* Monograph Supplement No. 10, January, 1963, 8–31, 81–91.) Individually administered test of language, including 7 subtests that sample language behavior according to a Skinnerian model.

Basic Concept Inventory. Follett Publishing Company (Engelmann, S.), 1967. Based on an "educational deficit" rather than "diagnostic-remedial" approach to language deficiencies in children. Suitable for preschool and primary children or others with severe receptive language difficulty. May be used with culturally disadvantaged and auditorily impaired children.

* *Illinois Test of Psycholinguistic Abilities.* University of Illinois Press (Kirk, S.A. and McCarthy, J.J.), 1961. Individually administered test of language, including 9 subtests with language ages from 2–0 to 9–6 (now being revised).

Verbal Language Development Scale. Western Psychological Services (Mecham, M.J.), 1959. Measures language age, expansion of Vineland Social Maturity Scale for ages infant to 15 years.

Orzeck Aphasia Evaluation. Western Psychological Services, 1964. Comprehensive evaluation of apraxia, agnosia, and sensory suppression.

* *Auditory Discrimination Test.* Language Research Associates (Wepman, J.M.), 1958. Individually administered test of auditory discrimination ability for speech sounds in single words for ages 5–0 to 8–0. Requires concepts of same and different.

Examining for Aphasia, second edition. Psychological Corporation (Eisenson, J.). Basic standardized procedure for systematic exploration of the language functions of aphasics for use with adolescents and adults.

Templin-Darley Screening and Diagnostic Tests of Articulation. Bureau of Educational Research and Service, 1960. Diagnostic and Screening tests of articulation for ages 3–0 to 8–0.

Halstead-Wepman Aphasia Screening Test. (*J. Speech & Hearing Dis.,* 14:9, 1949.) Useful in testing for verbal communication disorders.

The Sequenced Inventory of Communication Development. University of Washington Press. (D. Hedrick, E. Prather, A. Tobin), 1975. An assessment instrument based on recent research on normal acquisition of language, the SICD covers receptive and expressive language including grammatical structure.

V. READINESS AND SCREENING TESTS

Screening Tests for Identifying Children with Specific Language Disability. Educators Publishing Service (Slingerland, B.H.), 1962. Three sets of screening tests to detect symptoms of possible specific language disability in average children in the primary grades.

The Predictive Index. Harper & Row (de Hirsch, K., Jansky, J.J., Langford, W.S.), 1966. A diagnostic test of potential reading disabilities comprised of 10 subtests to be given to kindergarteners.

Detroit Tests of Learning Aptitude. Bobbs-Merrill. Battery of 19 tests with separate mental age norms and subtests for ages 4–0 to adult.

The Anton Brenner Gestalt Test of School Readiness. Western Psychological Services, 1964. Group test that assesses readiness for school.

Diagnostic Test to be Administered by Teachers to Discover Potential Learning Difficulties of Children (Peterson, W.). In J. Hellmuth, ed., *Special Child in Century 21.* Seattle: Special Child Publications, 1964, 271–273.

Dyslexia Schedule (McLeod, J.). Bulletin of the Orton Society, 1966. Operational means of defining children with dyslexia.

The Vallett Developmental Survey of Basic Learning Abilities. Consulting Psychologists Press, 1966. Contains 229 developmental test items with educational relevance arranged sequentially under such headings as visual-motor coordination and concept development.

Kindergarten Evaluation of Learning Potential (KELP). McGraw-Hill (Wilson, J.A.R. and Robeck, M.C.), 1967. Helps teacher measure learning potential on the basis of classroom learning.

First Grade Screening Test. American Guidance Service (Pate, J.E. and Webb, W.W.), 1966. To identify first graders in need of special assistance to make sufficient progress to be ready for second grade.

Evanston Early Identification Scale. Follett Publishing Co. (Dillard, H. and Landsman, M.), 1967. A quick, objective screening system for human figure drawing, yields classification as high, middle, or low risk. For use in kindergarten or early first grade.

VI. SOCIAL COMPETENCE TESTS

Progress Assessment Chart (Social-Emotional First Aid Teaching Sets) SEFA. N.A.M.H., 30 Queen Anne St., London, W. I., England (Gunzburg, H.C.), 1963. For use with mentally retarded children providing a behavioral checklist of need for training in four main areas—self-help, communication, socialization, and occupation.

Caine-Levine Social Competency Scale. Consulting Psychologists Press, 1963. Behavioral rating scale of 44 items to estimate the social competence of trainable mentally retarded children.

Vineland Social Maturity Scale, revised. Psychological Corporation (Doll, E.A.), 1953. Binet-type age scale designed to measure the successive stages of social competence from infancy to adult life.

Preschool Attainment Record. American Guidance Service (Doll, E.A.), 1966. Global appraisal of attainment of children ages 6 months to 7 years in ambulation, manipulation, rapport, communication, responsibility, information, ideation, creativity.

Diagnostic-Remedial and Task-Analytic Remediation [1,2]

5

Diagnosis of learning disabilities must, in an educational setting, lead to remediation. In the last chapter we examined two major diagnostic approaches to educational remedial planning—the diagnostic-remedial and the functional analysis of behavior (task-analytic) approaches. Since the current, organized learning disability movement began in the early 1960s three distinguishable approaches to teaching learning disabled (LD) children have emerged—the etiological, the diagnostic-remedial, and the task-analytic (Bateman, 1967b).

The contributions and limitations of each of these three approaches to teaching reading to learning disabled children will be reviewed briefly, and a fourth approach proposed—one that suggests that many learning disabled children have certain characteristics which require a very precise and careful teaching of decoding if they are to master initial reading skills. This fourth approach combines task-analytic programming of reading instruction with research on the learning processes of learning disabled children and proposes aptitude-treatment interaction as a viable premise on which to rest the combination.

This chapter focuses primarily on the remediation of reading dis-

[1] The authors express deep gratitude to Janet Derby for her generous and substantial assistance in the preparation of this chapter.

[2] Most of the material in this chapter is adapted from Bateman, B., Teaching reading to learning disabled children. In L. Resnick ed. *Theory and Practice of Early Reading*. Lawrence Erlbaum Associates, Hillsdale, N.J. (in press).

abilities because the vast majority of children with learning problems have difficulty in reading and most of the special training programs, such as perceptual programs, which have been promoted for use with learning disabled children are said to facilitate reading improvement. In actual practice, many programs for learning disabled children are indistinguishable from remedial reading programs. This problem is compounded by the fact that in some states, such as Oregon and Minnesota, the state reimburses school districts for services labeled learning disabilities programs, but not for those labeled remedial reading. Thus, this chapter also explores various parts of the relationship between remedial reading and learning disabilities.

THE CHILDREN

In current discussions of learning disabilities, two litanies are necessarily recited—that the field has grown phenomenally and the fact that this growth has occurred without an accepted definition of learning disabilities. One definitional dispute is over whether learning disability necessarily implies a deficiency in academic performance. Few definitions specifically state that it does; yet it is hard to imagine that many children are or should be regarded as learning disabled when their school performance is satisfactory.

Professionals remain unable to agree on a definition, but in practice the overwhelming majority of children labelled learning disabled are having difficulty in reading beyond what would be predicted by experienced teachers taking into account such factors as apparent intelligence, home background, and so on. Many also have writing and spelling problems; some are perceived as hyperactive; some as poorly coordinated; some as having receptive and/or expressive difficulty with spoken language; a few show finger agnosia, and so forth. The list of possible accompanying difficulties is nearly endless. Arguably a few children who have learned to read with no more than the usual difficulty may have been labeled learning disabled. If so, they are not within the scope of the present discussion, as it is clear that teaching them to read is not different from teaching any other children.

IS THERE A NEED FOR REMEDIAL INSTRUCTION IN OUR SCHOOLS?

What are the remedial needs of our nation's children? Are they as pressing as some would lead us to believe?

Reading

The HEW report of the National Advisory Committee on Dyslexia and Related Disorders (1969), entitled *Reading Disorders in the United*

States, declares that eight million children—one child out of every seven —in America's elementary and secondary schools will not learn to read adequately. In a typical class of 28 students, four children will have difficulty learning to read. Up to 15 percent of the total school population—apparently with adequate intelligence and emotional stability— still exhibit difficulties in learning to read within a reading program that proves effective for most children.

Every year from 2 to 10 percent of the nation's school children are not promoted due to academic failure. Based on the cost of one year of schooling for one child, the cost to the taxpayers of a 5 percent retention rate is $1.7 billion per year.

Former United States Commissioner of Education James Allen (1969), in his famous "Right to Read" speech, said that one of every four students nationwide has significant reading deficiencies. *The Federal Register* of April 29, 1975, states that "According to a 1970 Harris survey, approximately 18 million Americans are functionally illiterate, lacking even minimal reading skills" (p. 18551). About half of our unemployed youth in the age range of 16 to 21 years are functionally illiterate. In New York City, three-fourths of the juvenile offenders are two or more years retarded in reading. The United States Armed Forces instigated a program to teach reading called Project 100,000 when it found that 68.2 percent of its inductees fell below the seventh grade level in reading and academic ability.

Even though many retarded readers of average intelligence function adequately in other areas during their primary school years, the problem soon expands. As years of reading failure compound and build up a feeling of inadequacy and dissatisfaction with school, a child's overall academic work is severely threatened. The further a child progresses in school, the more success depends upon the ability to read. The HEW report also points out that reading disabilities impose incalculable social and economic consequences upon the individual and society. Reading failure is a significant factor in the high rate of emotional maladjustment, school dropouts, and juvenile delinquency, and it contributes appreciably to social welfare costs.

LEARNING DISABILITIES VERSUS
REMEDIAL READING

The question of how, if at all, children with learning disabilities differ from those with reading disabilities is currently being debated (Artley, 1975; Lerner, 1975). A disinterested observer might be moved to consider the concept of territorial imperative. Differences are cited and disputed as to teacher training, terminology, views on etiology, and focus of remediation. As yet, the classroom teacher has few, if any, guidelines as to whether Janie, struggling inordinately with learning to read, should be sent to the learning disability or remedial reading teacher. (In fact, evidence is far from clear that either can be counted upon to teach Janie to read, but that is not the issue.) Whether differences may or may not exist between the philosophy and practices of the two disciplines it seems clear that both are concerned with the same children—those children who are failing to learn reading as readily as it seems they should. The label "learning disabled" would not, in all circles, be as readily applied to the children with very mild reading problems as would "remedial" or "corrective reader." With minor exceptions the terms learning disabled and reading disabled apply to the same children and are so used here.

One further preliminary observation is vital. As indicated earlier, many would exclude from the category of learning disabled those children who have not had adequate reading instruction. The assumption of adequate instruction is probably false when it is made regarding conventional whole word, meaning-emphasis instruction (Otto, 1972; Samuels, 1970). The inadequacy of much current reading instruction is becoming so clear that fewer and fewer are heard to claim this lack is but an illusion caused by compulsory attendance or television or the breakdown of the family. A growing number of educators and special educators now hold that a child's failure to learn to read is per se clear and convincing evidence that the instruction was inadequate (e.g., Cohen, 1973; Engelmann, 1969, 1967b). A related position is that even if, at some level of reality, there might be different or additional etiological factors, the educator is nonetheless professionally bound to conceptualize the problem as an instructional one since only instructional variables are under educators' control (e.g., Bateman, 1973; Otto, 1972).

HOW DOES REMEDIATION DIFFER FROM DEVELOPMENTAL TEACHING?

Conventional remediation does differ from developmental teaching, although the distinctions are not always readily apparent. Remediation refers to those things we decide to do to, for, or with a child after we have diagnosed the problem and feel that we know what the child does not know and needs to know. Developmental teaching is the regular program of instruction that all children are exposed to in the general classroom. Developmental teaching presupposes a relative evenness of development and achievement. When this evenness is not present, we often move into remedial teaching. The goal of both remedial and developmental teaching is to assist students in achieving to the limits of their abilities. In some ways remedial teaching is not very different from the everyday instruction of creative, effective teachers, but in some important ways remedial teaching is quite different (see Otto & McMenemy, 1966; and Kottmeyer, 1959). In remedial teaching we often have the advantage of a restricted student-teacher ratio, availability of rich and varied materials, instruction based on individual diagnosis, and freedom to select materials without the restraints of a prescribed curriculum. The chief function of remedial teaching is to remove the effects of inadequate or inappropriate learning. It involves special attention to the reduction of discrepancies among abilities or performance levels and it places more emphasis on some areas than on others. Remedial teaching frequently involves the attempted amelioration of underlying deficiencies in learning. It may isolate and telescope the basic skills of the typical classroom program for the younger pupils, eliminate many supplementary activities, and stress quick mastery of skills.

Because of similarity in goals, many of the same materials are used in both developmental and remedial teaching. Developmental programs regularly used at a lower level may be adapted to meet the needs of the child, or may include remedial materials to be used with children having problems, for example, the *Sound-Order-Sense* auditory perception training program (Semel, 1970). In addition to modified regular materials, many materials have been developed particularly for remedial work. Some were developed specifically for children with one problem and have been found useful in working with other problems or problems of varying severity. For example, Fernald's (1943) kinesthetic tracing technique was first developed for use with extreme or total reading disabilities, but since has been used with children with mild reading and spelling problems.

PHILOSOPHY OF REMEDIATION

The reasons underlying remediation and the diagnostic "model" used both depend upon the philosophy held by the diagnostician, whether that diagnostician is the classroom teacher, a school psychologist, or a concerned parent. The learning-deficiency and teaching-deficiency premises lead to different diagnostic philosophies and procedures as presented in the preceding chapter. Perhaps even more striking are the differences in the remedial positions derived from each.

When the cause for inadequate performance is viewed as a deficiency within the child, the diagnostician sees the reasons as brain damage, mental retardation, sensory deficits, minimal brain dysfunction, lack of motivation, learning disabilities, emotional disturbance, and so on. The important point is that all of these reasons are viewed as something wrong within the child that prevents learning. This view releases the teacher from assuming any responsibility for the poor performance of the child.

If inadequate performance is diagnosed as a deficiency or "difference" within the child, appropriate remediation is tailored as precisely as possible to those individual deficiencies or differences. One purpose of the diagnostic exploration in this framework is to map the relevant variables within or about the child so that the best suited teaching techniques and materials can be found or designed.

When inadequate performance is viewed as the result of inadequate teaching, startlingly different conclusions follow. This point of view obviously places the need for remediation on poor teaching or poor programs, not on something within the child. This diagnostic approach would of necessity be a task-analysis approach. We are immediately thrown into what might be described as a total prevention approach—one implemented not by screening out potentially "deficient" children for different or more intensive teaching, but rather by providing a form of instruction for all children in which all succeed (at different rates) from the beginning. The trend toward placing full responsibility for teaching on the program and the teacher is accelerating rapidly. One of the greatest hindrances to its total acceptance is the unquestioning belief of many educators that no one program or method can successfully teach all children. This faith derives from years of observing inadequate teaching of a thousand types, which indeed did fail with 10 to 35 percent, or even more, of the children. Educators prematurely have accepted the inevitability of failure for millions of American schoolchildren.

The field of learning disabilities has been roundly welcomed into education as a new and eminently respectable reason for our schools' failures—the deficient children are to blame. "They don't learn like they should." But it is just possible that excellent teaching could reduce our present failure rate to one percent or less. In Chapter 6, *Direct Instruction,* we will describe a program that appears capable of doing just that. Other new and very promising approaches might have been selected—their number is rapidly growing. The direct instruction program developed by Carl Bereiter, Sigfried Engelmann, and Wesley Becker was chosen because of its success with thousands of so-called hard-to-teach and high-risk children ("disadvantaged," "retarded," "learning disabled," and so on); its comprehensiveness (a teacher and aide training program plus published instructional materials for teachers and pupils); its scope (reading, language, arithmetic, and more); and its utilization of concept and skill analysis, programming principles, and built-in behavior management techniques. In the final section of this book, systematic instructional procedures based on the applied analysis of behavior and precision teaching will be discussed. Systematic instruction advanced the basic techniques of direct instruction by incorporating precision measurement and behavioral management.

APPROACHES TO REMEDIATION

Once it has been determined that a child is having difficulty learning to read the next step is to diagnose the problem and plan intervention. Two conventional approaches to this process are discussed briefly in the following sections.

Etiological Approach

The only sure way to prevent a child from learning to read is to preclude all opportunity to make the appropriate associations between written letters and the sounds they represent. Therefore the only certain cause of reading failure is the absence of incidental or systematic instruction. For every other alleged cause of reading disability children can be found who put the lie to the theory. Some brain injured children read, as do children with malnutrition, disinterested parents, abnormal EEGs, inadequate lateralization, poor vision, chromosomal abberations, older sisters who achieve well in school, speech defects, finger agnosia, undescended testicles, hyperactivity, lefthandedness, thyroid deficiencies, double hair sworls, low IQs, unresolved oedipal conflicts, jagged ITPA profiles, and every other alleged etiological factor. In light of this, those who use the term "correlates" of reading failure are on safer ground than those who search for "causes." But perhaps neither is on the most direct route to solving the *educational* problem (which is not to say there aren't other problems also well-worth addressing). In one of the most powerful explications of educators' treatment of causes of school failure, Engelmann (1969) describes how we have sought general rather than specific causes and have failed to concentrate on asking *what* precisely is it about reading the child has not been taught. Some formulations of alleged causes of reading failure have educational implications; others do not. Perhaps some that do not, at the present time, will in years to come. We do not here dispute the "truth" of any alleged causes; we do urge that educators and program developers examine the utility, *for their purposes,* of etiological formulations.

A few etiological theories purportedly do lead to teaching strategies. Delacato (1966), for example, includes activities designed to establish hemispheric dominance in his program for teaching reading. Other etiological theories do not purport to have such implications. For instance, few argue that correlational data on family income and reading achievement should prompt reading teachers to give dollars to parents of children in the lowest reading group. A large number of alleged etiologies arguably suggest treatment designed to make children more amenable to instruction—such as correcting visual refractive errors, prescribing ritalin, or using broad spectrum lighting to replace narrow spectrum artificial light—but none of these replaces reading instruction. Numerous reviews of the etiology of reading disorders are available (e.g., Bannatyne, 1966; Blom & Jones, 1971; Westman, Arthur, & Scheidler, 1965).

The relevance-to-teaching position on etiology, espoused here, is treated at greater length by Bateman (1973), Cohen (1973), Engelmann (1969, 1967a) and Otto (1972). They, and others, assert that the etiological classifications most useful to educators are those which specify precisely what the child needs to be taught about reading—short vowel sounds, left to right decoding or sound blending among others. Opponents object that merely knowing a child responds to *b* by saying /d/ (and vice versa) about half the time is not sufficient diagnostic information when some children may respond this way "because" of brain injury, others "because" of inadequate binocular fusion, and still others "because" of poor motivation or other "reasons." This objection is premised on the belief that letter discrimination (or phoneme-grapheme correspondence) can or should be taught differently to children who, for different reasons, have not yet learned it. It is this contention that forms the basis of the position that teaching reading to learning disabled children is different from teaching reading to other children, and it is this position which is critically examined in the remainder of this chapter. The source of severe reading disability, excluding original etiological possibilities, may be viewed as inhering in the child, in the instruction, or in a mismatch between child and instruction. Each of these conceptualizations and the instructional techniques deriving from them will be examined and evaluated.

Diagnostic-Remedial Approach

The view that the child has correlated deficiencies that must be remediated has been the majority position within the field of learning disabilities as it has existed and developed over the past twenty or thirty years. This conceptualization has been known as the diagnostic-remedial approach (Bateman, 1967b), prescriptive-teaching (Peter, 1965), ability and process training (Yesseldyke & Salvia, 1974), psychometric phrenology (Mann, 1971), and even task analysis (Johnson, 1967). Typically the child's cognitive, perceptual, sensory-motor, and other processes are assessed by a variety of psychoeducational instruments, and patterns of strong and weak functioning are ascertained as described in the preceding chapter. Often an effort is made to determine which among the deficits observed is "primary." The observed deficits on psychoeducational instruments are said to be merely correlated with the academic deficiency and causality is specifically disavowed (Kirk, 1972). It is, however, interesting to note that, nevertheless, remediation is planned to overcome or circumvent the correlated deficit with the implicit, if not explicit, hope that so doing will either alleviate the academic problem or lay a foundation for so doing. This procedure suggests the belief may still be closer to causality than to mere correlation.

VISUAL, PERCEPTUAL VISUAL, AND VISUAL-MOTOR PERCEPTUAL TRAINING

Few topics within learning disabilities have been as extensively researched as has the Frostig visual perception training program. Comprehensive reviews of the research (e.g., Robinson, 1972; Wiederholt & Hammill, 1971) reveal that the Frostig training program does tend to increase scores on the Frostig Developmental Tests of Visual Perception and sometimes increases reading readiness scores, but does not improve reading. Illustrative studies finding no relationship between visual-perceptual training and reading are those by Anderson (1972) and Jacobs (1968). Larsen and Hammill's (1975) most recent review concludes that research does not support a necessary relationship between reading and visual-motor integration, spatial relations, visual memory, or visual discrimination, as measured by current instruments. One perceptual test commonly used which appears to differentiate reading of learning disabled children from normal readers is the Bender Gestalt (see e.g., Keogh, 1965; Larsen, Rogers, & Sowell, 1976), but that statistical differentiation holds only for groups of children and is of dubious predictive or educational value. Koppitz (1975) found the Bender Gestalt distinguished control children from learning disabled children, but did not differentiate between those learning disabled children who did have reading problems and those that did not.

Some children do have difficulty learning to name (or give the sound for) letters of the alphabet. Undoubtedly this fact contributes to the popularity of the view that visual discrimination or perceptual training must be needed. But these same children can visually identify hundreds of other objects or events and as Rozin, Poritsky, and Stotsky (1971) and Harrigan (1976) have demonstrated, even young children with severe reading problems can learn as many as 30 Chinese characters in a few hours. This task clearly requires as much or more visual discrimination or perception than learning English letters. Very young children can usually perceive and discriminate letters (Calfee, Chapman, & Venezky, 1972), so the source of difficulty in naming (or sounding) must be sought elsewhere.

Krippner (1973) and Keogh (1974), in two eminently readable reviews, have examined the controversy surrounding optometric, visual, and visual-perceptual training. Both conclude that the controversy is unresolved and will continue at least until better research is available. As to the relationship between visual-perceptual ability and reading, Keogh astutely observes that good visual-perceptual ability may be an outcome of good reading—"that is, as a child learns to read, he develops adequate visual perceptual organization, he masters scanning in a horizontal left-right direction . . ." (p. 227).

Kephart's (1960) motor-perceptual remediation was evaluated in a review of more than 30 studies by Klesius (1972), who found that of 11 studies meeting his criteria for acceptability more than half did not favor Kephart's procedures.

Hammill, Goodman, and Wiederholt (1974) reviewed 76 studies of the Frostig and Kephart programs and concluded that visual- and motor-perceptual training programs have not demonstrated an effect on academic achievement and that the assumption that perceptual-motor inadequacy causes reading problems must be questioned. It should be noted that the Frostig and Kephart programs do not utilize verbal symbols. Delacato's (1966) training method utilizes motor activities such as creeping and patterning to develop hemispheric dominance and thus improve reading ability. Independent studies by Anderson (1965), Robbins (1966), and O'Donnell (1969) failed to find clear support for the still controversial techniques. Balow (1971) reports that after numerous searches of the literature, he found no scientifically acceptable data which demonstrated special effectiveness for any of the physical, motor, or perceptual programs used in the prevention or correction of reading or other learning disabilities.

AUDITORY PERCEPTUAL TRAINING

Sabatino (1973) has extensively reviewed the development and assessment of auditory perception and intervention efforts and noted that in comparison to visual perception, relatively little information is available. He concluded that research has established a correlational relationship between reading failure and auditory functioning and observes that there is general disagreement as to whether auditory perceptual teaching is called for by strengths in auditory perceptual functioning (Johnson & Myklebust, 1967) or by weaknesses (Silver & Hagin, 1967b) or is ever indicated at all (Mann, 1970). No studies were reported which clearly demonstrated auditory perceptual training has a direct effect on reading achievement. Hammill and Larsen's (1974) review found little support in the research literature for the assertions that auditory discrimination, auditory memory, sound blending, or auditory-visual integration as measured are essential to reading. Since three- or four-year-olds can accurately repeat words and patterns of sounds, and even infants can differentiate similar syllables (Eimas, Siqueland, Jusczyk, & Vigorito, 1971), we must agree with Rozin and Gleitman's (in press) conclusion that most pre-literate children have adequate auditory perceptual development for acquiring reading skills and that except in rare cases auditory perceptual training is not important to teaching reading except as teaching reading per se is a form of such training.

It may be too soon to state with certainty that auditory perceptual training is not helpful to the teaching of reading and certainly it may be argued to be of general value. The field may see a decrease in the use of visual and visual-motor perceptual programs and an increase in attention to auditory perceptual training. Therefore, we present in some detail one currently available program, *Sound-Order-Sense* by Elinor Semel (1970). Semel believes auditory perceptual training is important because:

1. Auditory perception plays a key role in efficient reading, cognitive acquisition, and processing of incoming information.
2. Auditory perception skills are basic to the verbal communications that make up a large part of all interpersonal relationships.
3. Auditory perception is becoming more and more important in our world.

All auditory perceptual training efforts are premised, of course, on the belief that listening skills can be enhanced by specific training. Semel's program is based on a three-stage schema of the listening process. The first stage is "responding to stimuli." This is recognizing that there was sound, knowing where it was, what sound it was, how many sounds there were, and whether they were the same. Four skills make up the first stage: *awareness, focus, figure-ground,* and *discrimination. Awareness* relates to attending to a sound—when it started, stopped, or changed. *Focus* is being able to localize a sound or tell from what direction it has come.

Figure-ground is the ability to select a sound from a background of sounds —as in selecting a single voice from many conversations at a party. *Discrimination* is being able to tell differences between sounds—to know whether sounds or words are alike or different, and to tell, for example, where in a word (beginning, middle, or end) a given sound is heard.

The second stage in the listening process is organizing the stimuli. Skills at this stage include knowing the sequence of sounds, the length of time between sounds, and recognizing if and where a particular sound was heard before. The specific skills are sequencing and synthesizing, and scanning.

Sequencing and synthesizing involve being able to repeat a series in the correct order, to repeat a rhythmic pattern, to synthesize or combine separate sounds into words, and to analyze or break a word into its separate sounds. A child who has trouble with sequencing and synthesizing might respond only to the end of a series of directions or be unable to learn a series such as the months of the year.

Scanning refers to the ability to "sift through" the store of auditory information and select materials that are related. For example, rhyming with "hill" requires finding other words that already are stored and end with "ill," such as bill, fill, till, and still. Or, when asked what body part, to sort through the store called "body parts" and select the right one.

The third stage is "understanding the meaning," which is knowing what the sounds and words mean. The particular skills involved at this stage are classification, integration, and monitoring. To understand language in the fullest sense the listener must consider words in context and be able to select the appropriate meaning for that word. The various words must be integrated into meaningful forms, and the significant words must be monitored from all that are heard.

Underlying these three stages of the listening process is memory. A child must be able to remember in order to process the auditory stimuli that are received.

The SOS (Sound-Order-Sense) Auditory Perception Program (Semel, 1970). Believing that improved auditory-perceptual functioning results from systematic, small-step teaching, the SOS program teaches the skills involved in the listening process. Children are taught 1) to discriminate the sounds that make up speech, 2) the order, or sequence, of sounds in words and words in groups, 3) the attributes that give meaning to words, and 4) the interrelation of these elements.

The aim of the SOS program is to develop the child's listening skills to promote the full comprehension of spoken language. Important features of the program include these:

1. It is applicable to children in kindergarten through the second grade, including those in special education classes. It is also useful for older children who have auditory-perceptual problems. It may be used with an entire classroom or with individual children.

2. It does not require extensive specialized training of the teacher in auditory perception. The instructions are complete and only need to be followed carefully but flexibly.

3. The materials are organized in carefully sequenced small steps to insure pupil's success.

4. The remedial procedures are programmed in a sequence from simple to complex.

5. It provides an excellent reading readiness foundation and does not itself require reading ability.

This is a two-year developmental program in auditory perception. Its two levels are each planned for one school year; the levels contain 160 lessons of about 20 minutes each. All lessons include five-minute sections of listening for sound; listening for order (sequence); listening for sense (meaning); and activities that include listening for sound, order, and sense.

The *sound* tasks stress auditory discrimination and figure-ground perception through activities that require the children to make judgments about the similarities and differences in words or word groups. The *order* activities emphasize auditory memory and sequence. For example, the children may be asked to listen for a word that does not fit or to listen to determine if a word has one or two syllables. The *sense* activities teach simple geometric shapes—circle, square, triangle, rectangle—and basic concepts such as plurals, not, big and small, next to, in, and on. The children respond to directions such as, "Mark the ones that are not triangles." Shapes were chosen because they can be responded to by nearly all children.

The children's responses are recorded in a pupil's response book, which is printed with a special process to allow the child to know immediately the correctness of each response. When using a special crayon, if the child responds correctly, the answer box turns gray. If an incorrect response is given, there is no color change. Other materials in the program are records of various sounds in the environment, used as background against which the children listen to sentences given by the teacher, and other recordings used at various places in the order activities. Activity cards are included at each level and are an important part of each lesson. They emphasize the interrelatedness of the auditory-perceptual skills and give the children an opportunity to respond vocally as well as visually and by motion. Color coding allows the teacher to select activities that are felt to fit best on any particular day. The cards are a useful means of integrating the auditory-perceptual activities into classroom activities throughout the day. The teacher is supplied with a comprehensive teacher's guide, which gives clear, day-by-day instructions for implementing the program.

Some children appear to have problems in auditory perception and need additional practice. Such a child might show signs such as the following to alert the teacher:

1. Frequently requests a speaker to repeat what was said.
2. Appears better able to understand what is said by some people than by others.
3. Has difficulty following directions.
4. Has excessive difficulty spelling dictated words, especially in sequencing and phonetic spelling.
5. Has difficulty remembering names, dates, places, tunes, rhythmic patterns.
6. Is easily distracted by extraneous noise and is upset in a noisy environment.

Children who show these signs and make errors in the SOS developmental program probably need additional help. The SOS program has remediation materials to be used concomitantly with the developmental program. There are three response books at each level, one devoted to each of the sound, order, and sense areas. The remediation teacher's guide gives additional suggestions for activities. The teacher's guide of the developmental program also includes guidelines for the teacher to follow to help minimize the problems children will have. These include suggestions such as using consistent attention-getting devices; not presenting too many tasks or directions at one time; and aiming listening activities at the child's level of perception. By following these guidelines and using the appropriate remedial materials along with the regular SOS program, a teacher can help to achieve the aim of developing any child's listening skills to the fullest.

Auditory-Visual Integration

Deficient integration in the sensory systems was proposed by Birch (1962) as causing or relating to reading disability and has been supported by research (e.g., Birch & Belmont, 1964; Lovell & Gorton, 1968; Zurif & Carson, 1970). However, another interpretation is that the revealed auditory-visual matching deficiencies are due to *verbal labeling* problems rather than to cross-modal transfer problems (Blank & Bridger, 1966; Blank, Weider, & Bridger, 1968; McGrady & Olson, 1970; Steger, Vellutino, & Meshoulam, 1972; Vellutino, Steger & Kandel, 1972; *contra* Drader, 1975). Direct teaching of grapheme-phoneme correspondence is one visual-auditory integrative activity clearly supportable at the present time since it is per se part of the reading act.

Multisensory approaches to phoneme-grapheme correspondences. Based on the belief that reading is a process involving several of the sensory systems and that children with severe reading disabilities can be taught best by utilizing all of these systems, several multisensory reading methods have been devised. Fernald's (1943) V-A-K-T (Visual, Auditory, Kinesthetic, Tactile) approach is one, and Gillingham's and Stillman's (1969) method, which is V-A-K (Visual, Auditory, Kinesthetic) is another.

By supplementing the usual auditory and visual stimuli used in teaching reading with kinesthetic or kinesthetic and tactile stimuli, the reading task is intensified and the child receives input from more of his or her sensory systems.

Blau's (1968) variant of the multisensory approach is another method for children with severe disabilities, bypassing the visual modality in the initial stages. Blau's nonvisual AKT method is based on the observation that many disabled readers are more hindered than helped by the visual stimuli of the printed word. The AKT method thus substitutes other types of input for visual input.

The child is blindfolded, then the word is traced on the child's back by the teacher, who also spells it aloud letter by letter. The student learns to identify the letter being traced and often will begin to spell with the teacher. Three-dimensional letters also may be given to trace while the teacher is tracing on the child's back. After the word has been traced on the child's back several times, the child is given three-dimensional letters and, still blindfolded, arranges them in sequence to spell the word. When the blindfold is removed, the child can see what has been done. The word is then written on paper or the chalkboard and on a file card for the child's own use. For some children, once a word is learned with this method, it poses no further difficulty.

Many teachers who have worked with remedial reading problems are familiar with the Hegge, Kirk, and Kirk *Remedial Reading Drills* (1936). Besides providing the teacher with well-organized lists of phonically regular words, the Hegge, Kirk, and Kirk materials give a structured method of teaching reading through a multisensory approach. Basically, the approach is phonic, using visual-auditory-kinesthetic-tactile modalities in the beginning. It is recommended by the authors for use with children who are reading below a fourth grade level, who have severe reading disabilities, who can be taught sound blending, who have no uncorrected visual or auditory problems, and who are motivated and cooperative.

Within the program, the child is first taught the sounds of most of the consonants and short /a/ using the graphovocal method, which requires the child to write the letter from memory and say the sound at the same time. The child moves into the first drills after mastering these single sounds and reads the drills, responding to individual sounds rather than to groups of letters or sounds. All drills are read orally so that the articulation can serve as an aid to learning and so that the teacher can note and correct errors immediately. Accuracy rather than speed is stressed and the drills are done in order without skipping, progress through them being at the child's individual pace.

It is pointed out that the drills themselves do not teach connected reading, so sentence reading is added to supplement the drill material. This can be done as early in the program as the child knows enough words to make sentences; that is, after Drill #1 the child can read, "A sad man had a fat cat." Story reading is not introduced until much later because it is felt that the student in the remedial situation would not be interested in or motivated by stories at a beginning level of difficulty. Therefore, story reading is omitted until the child has finished all of the drills in part one. At this point the child can read fairly regular phonic material at second or third grade level. Picture stories and primers are avoided as reading material, because remedial readers often have become very good picture readers and do not learn to read the words if pictures are there to give them clues.

The drills are divided into four parts:

Part I   Introductory sounds—32 drills
Part II   Combinations of sounds—12 drills
Part III   Advanced sounds—10 drills
Part IV   Supplementary exercises—37 drills.

Each part includes general reviews of previously taught sounds and is concluded with a test covering the particular part. The tests contain examples of each phonogram to check the child's proficiency.

Throughout the program, the teacher is encouraged to use as many of the child's modalities as necessary. Errors in reading words on a drill can be corrected and the proper responses taught by having the child write the word on the chalkboard and say it aloud as it is written. Having the child write it with eyes closed is a more difficult step. The program stresses the importance of having the child say and write the word as separate sounds and then blending the sounds together.

Psycholinguistic Training

The Illinois Test of Psycholinguistic Abilities (ITPA) has been extensively used to diagnose and plan remediation for children with reading and other learning problems. In addition to possible weaknesses in the theoretical underpinnings of its process approach, severe criticism has been directed at the test's reliability, validity, and factorial structure (e.g., Ysseldyke & Salvia, 1974; Ysseldyke, 1973; but see Newcomer, Hare, Hammill, & McGettigan, 1975) and it has also been suggested that remedial activities may not be justified (Hammill & Larsen, 1974; Harris, 1976).

A review of early evidence on the 1961 experimental ITPA (Bateman, 1965) showed that poor readers scored consistently low in auditory and/or visual sequential memory. Both of these tests are at the non-meaningful, automatic-sequential level of language usage. Poor readers were significantly superior to good readers in visual decoding at the semantic or representational level of language usage (Kass, 1966). These findings suggest, consistent with Rozin and Gleitman's (in press) analysis, that poor readers have difficulty with accessing surface and not with accessing meaning. Carroll (1972) suggests, however, that there may not be a pattern of scores on the ITPA characteristic of poor readers.

At the present time there is little, if any, compelling evidence that remediation of psycholinguistic abilities as measured by the ITPA has a direct beneficial effect on reading or other academic performance.

Summary of Diagnostic-Remedial Approach

Ability or process training has come under severe and growing criticism. Bannatyne (1975) has, however, expressed important cautions in uncritically accepting the negative reviews and conclusions as to possible relationships between these abilities and academic achievement.

Ysseldyke and Salvia (1974) have contrasted ability training to task-analytically-derived skills training, discussed in the next section, and fault the diagnostic-remedial approach for: (a) using hypothetical constructs that go beyond observed behaviors, and inferring that they are causes of the observed differences; (b) hypothesizing that processes or abilities are essential prerequisites to skills achievement when some data (e.g., Abt Associates, 1976; Bijou, 1970; Cohen, 1969) show that the skills can be taught directly, and when only correlational (not causal) data suggest a relationship between process and skill; (c) using diagnostic test instruments of questionable reliability and validity; and (d) assuming aptitude treatment interactions that have not been shown to exist. Vellutino (1974) has levelled essentially similar criticism specifically at the reading disability field and concludes that: (a) there is little support for the theory (or its derivative practices) that views reading disability as caused by visual-spatial confusion stemming from neurological disorders; (b) findings supporting the deficient sensory integration hypothesis are equivocal at best; and (c) much more support is available for the hypothesis that reading disability is associated with verbal learning deficiencies. He contends that even so, remedial activity in verbal skills should be directed toward specific aspects of the reading act itself.

At least two essential premises in the diagnostic-remedial approach remain unsupported: (a) the assumed deficiencies in psychological processes can be reliably and validly assessed; and (b) remediation of these processes will result in improved academic performance. Yet, programs based squarely on these premises continue to flourish and to dominate the field among practitioners, if not among academicians and researchers. Harris (1976) suggests this is the situation because research has not had sufficient impact to overcome the three forces he sees as controlling—the "bandwagon," the "pendulum," and the Zeitgeist effects. Ultimately, the tide will be turned by the ready availability of more successful approaches. Some are already here.

TASK-ANALYTIC APPROACH

Careful analysis of the *act of reading* itself, beyond description of possible errors children make, has not previously been of major concern to the traditionalist view of reading and learning disabilities. It is as if the basic assumption that children who read poorly must themselves be deficient has precluded serious consideration of the possibility that in reality the reading instruction was inadequate. The fact that the majority (a decreasing one in recent years) of children have learned to read has apparently been accepted as satisfactory evidence that the teaching was appropriate to the nature of the task. Engelmann (1967b) has aptly observed that if a child learns to read the program is credited, but if she or he fails the child is faulted.

Many factors have had a part in the emergence of reading and learning disability specialists' interest in an analysis of the reading task. In the field of reading itself there has been the growing awareness that children have been reading less and less well in recent decades (Matthews, 1966; Lerner, 1976) and that the method of teaching does indeed make a difference. No longer does the fact of wide intra-program performance differences obscure the fact of important inter-program differences. The recent reversal of the pendulum in the "methods battle" between phonics and the whole-word approaches was initially triggered, some believe, by the public outcry in 1955 over Flesch's *Why Johnny Can't Read.* Chall's *Learning to Read: The Great Debate* (1967) forced even educators to admit the controversy was real. More recently, discrepancies have been noted between the actual data from the U.S. Office of Education Primary Reading Studies (Bond and Dykstra, 1967), such as the stellar performance of the Lippincott phonic-linguistic program (Dykstra, 1968), versus the widely publicized impression that method was not found to be an important variable. Most recently, and yet to have its major impact, is the national evaluation of Project Follow-Through in which one task-analytically derived reading program (DISTAR) was so successful that poverty, high-risk, bilingual (or as some prefer, "semi-lingual") and otherwise usually very low-achieving populations taught by DISTAR read at middle class grade-level norms by the end of third grade (Abt Associates, 1976). The Right-to-Read program may evidence recognition that method does make a difference and that the more successful methods should be implemented. As yet only lawsuits at the small claims court level (Diehl, 1975) have been successfully waged against schools for failing to teach children to read, but the day may come very soon when higher courts will entertain such cases (Stewart, 1971). The success of such cases will depend upon many factors, but proof that methods other than those used might have succeeded will be important (Abel, 1974; Bateman, 1975; Saretsky, 1973).

Other factors moving the learning disabilities field toward an analysis of reading and teaching methods so derived include the rapid development and acceptance of behavioral technology in improving instruction and, not unrelated, the current demand that schools become more accountable for communicating their objectives and their actual accomplishments in teaching basic skills.

Analyses of Beginning Reading

We shall briefly examine several analyses of the beginning reading process that are consistent with outcome data on reading programs and that highlight points of particular relevance for teaching reading to children who, without superb teaching, are likely to encounter undue difficulty in learning to read.

Venezky. Venezky (1975) has defined prereading skills. These skills are of particular importance to the learning disabled because these children are often initially identified as lacking readiness, that is, they have not yet been effectively taught these very skills. He describes the procedure: ". . . [w]e arrive at prereading skills by identifying a complete set of initial reading tasks [objectives] and then defining all of the prerequisite skills for this set of tasks. Then, for a given population of pre-readers, those skills which all or almost all members of the population have mastered are eliminated" (p. 5). The definition of subskills is accomplished by logical analysis of the reading task and by their demonstrated effect on later reading achievement.

Venezky's analysis of sight-word recognition skills revealed three subskills: (a) visual discrimination of letter strings, which in turn requires letter recognition (in which the only problem is orientation), attention to order of letters, and attention to the entire word; (b) association and retention of labels for the letter strings; and (c) retrieval and articulation of labels when shown the strings. His analysis of decoding revealed five subskills: (a) letter differentiation; (b) association of sound and letter; (c) blending sounds; (d) identification of a sound within a word; and (e) sound matching within words.

These subskills were studied in terms of instructional design, and five emerged as the hub of the instructional program: (a) attending to letter order; (b) attending to letter orientation; (c) attending to word detail; (d) sound matching; and (e) sound blending.

In designing the experimental teaching program, emphasis was placed on focusing the learner's attention on relevant features of the task, a strategy of the utmost importance and consistent with Ross's (1976) hypothesis that selective attention deficits are central in learning disabilities.

Venezky notes that many popularly emphasized skills are omitted: letter-name knowledge, fine-motor performance, visual discrimination of objects and shapes, ocular-motor control, and others. Logical analysis reveals that these and other similar skills so commonly taught or insisted upon as a vital part of reading readiness or remediation are not part of reading (although they may be correlated with reading, as is family income). Improvement in them is not accompanied by improvement in reading and they may be demonstrated to be present and sufficiently developed for reading long before reading instruction is ordinarily attempted.

Rozin and Gleitman. Rozin and Gleitman (in press) underscore the fact that even the most comprehensive analysis of fluent adult reading cannot lead directly to a program for teaching beginners. What must be taught to beginners is the residue after eliminating the skills the pre-literate child brings to the instructional situation and those things that will be acquired developmentally through general contact with language. Rozin and Gleitman convincingly demonstrate from research and logic, as does Venezky, that preschool children already possess the visual perception, auditory perception, visual-auditory translation, syntactic, and semantic skills necessary for reading. What they lack and must be taught is the phonological basis of alphabetic orthography. Clinical experience with disabled readers and outcome data on both initial and remedial teaching are totally consistent with Rozin and Gleitman's analysis. They demonstrate a general psycholinguistic relationship: the lower the level of the language feature, the later it becomes accessible. Semantics is easier to access than syntax and syntax is easier than phonology. Within phonology, syllables are easier than phonemes. This principle, combined with historical perspective on the development of written language, leads Rozin and Gleitman to the proposition that the appropriate unit for beginning reading instruction is the syllable. The result is a reading program (Rozin and Gleitman, 1974) in which four teaching steps precede the direct teaching of single phonemes. Those first steps teach: (a) the principle that meaning can be represented visually, (b) logographic (rebus) representations, (c) words are segmentable and written symbols can represent those segments, and (d) each segment (syllable) has a unique writing and syllables recombine and blend to form new words. After these steps the children are taught that syllables can be dissected into parts and work is begun on grapheme-phoneme relationships.

They report that children have no difficulty with the first two steps. Low achievers begin to have problems at the third step (segmenting words) and then with the memory component at the fourth step. Some urban children had not reached the final step of phoneme-grapheme correspondence by the end of the first grade. Although some upper-middle-class children made the syllable to phoneme transition in as little as one month, the experimental group did not surpass controls on phonemic skills at the end of the first year. These disappointing results may reflect program design weaknesses rather than an inappropriate analysis of reading.

Task-analytically Derived Reading Programs

Although all authors of reading programs undoubtedly believe they have given appropriate consideration to the nature of reading, some are more explicit than others about how the program relates to their view of the reading process. One fundamental observation about reading English is that the symbols we read stand for *sounds,* not for objects. We have included only reading programs which clearly and explicitly recognize this alphabetic principle and which have either data, or a reasonable promise thereof, to demonstrate they work. Many additional programs might have been included. DISTAR is of course one of these and is treated in Chapter Six. Auckerman (1971) has described more than 100 approaches to beginning reading and presents much of the available research on them in a highly readable form.

Starter/101.   Starter/101 is designed from task analysis for children who may have or have had difficulty learning to read (O'Keefe, 1970). "The program is essentially the product of our task analysis of the process and potential problem of learning to read. . . . We have delineated, sequenced, and integrated hundreds of specific objectives" (O'Keefe, 1971, p. 55). The program consists of four-step cycles each comprised of: (1) speaking and understanding words to be read in the fourth step; (2) recognizing printing, producing the sound for one letter, both upper and lower cases; (3) combining (blending) sounds; and (4) using learned letter-sounds in new words. Given a range of 22 to 55 hours of instruction, a group of 98 children who had poor school achievement and poor prognosis as to reading averaged a seven month reading gain on the WRAT.

Glass's perceptual conditioning approach.   Glass (1971) provides a rationale, in the form of eight hypotheses, for his perceptual conditioning approach. (1) Decoding should be taught separately from "reading." (2) Meaning should be made irrelevant to decoding instruction and this can be done by teaching decoding using only words whose meaning is already known (and obviously can also be done by using nonsense). (3) Decoding must be taught without context or picture clues so that only decoding skills can be utilized. (4) Since syllabication can be accomplished only *after* a word has been decoded, it should not be part of decoding instruction. (5) Successful decoders do not consciously use rules, so rules should not be taught. (6) Word parts (letter-clusters) are the unit to which successful decoders respond. (7) Correct visual and auditory *clustering* (discrimination of appropriate units of letters and sounds) is vital to decoding. (8) The correct mental set can be conditioned and can cause the decoder to see and respond to the appropriate letter-sound structures.

From this rationale Glass developed an instructional methodology in which whole words are individually presented and the correct mental set is induced by asking, "What letters make _____ sound?" and, "What sounds do the letters _____ make?" The configuration of the whole word is never changed in any way. The decoder is thus perceptually conditioned to see letter clusters which frequently appear in English. Glass argues, as do Rozin and Gleitman (in press), that it is just as easy to learn that three or four letters make a sound cluster as it is to learn one letter makes a sound. Glass recognizes that one cannot necessarily establish from the performance of fluent adult decoders that children should be taught to decode without rules, but nevertheless relies on a study by Burton and Glass (1968) in which it was shown that excellent readers in grades two through five also do not use rules. It should be noted that extrapolation from proficient decoders, even if elementary children, to novices may not be justified.

Formula Phonics. An interesting program to compare with Glass's is Vail's Formula Phonics (1969) which was designed for non-readers and poor readers of all ages and backgrounds. Vail (1971) says, "Certainly middle- and upper-income Caucasian first-graders who have good attendance patterns, who are not immature, and who do not present atypical learning patterns, will probably . . . [read] as well, taught by conventional reading methods, as [by] Formula Phonics" (p. 111). However, Vail's concern, like ours, is for the rest of the children. Regular consonant sounds and rules and long and short vowel sounds are "programmed" into pupils as pre-reading skills, being certain that any incorrectly learned sounds are extinguished. Then regular letter clusters ("pals") are taught. Sounding words is carefully distinguished from reading. Once "programmed," students read orally from material at their highest level of comprehension. When an unknown word is encountered, the teacher then teaches the use of word-attack skills and phonic units programmed earlier by asking the class five questions (the "formula"): "Does the word have: (1) a suffix, (2) silent letters, (3) "pals," (4) any letters which must change their sounds, and (5) how do you work the remaining vowels?" Principles of reinforcement are systematically used. Vail's "pals" and Glass's "clusters" are markedly similar, "programming" and "conditioning" seem related, and total dissimilarity is seen in the treatment of rules in the two programs. Other reading teaching approaches which are consistent with task analysis and/or applied behavioral analysis include the Monterey Reading Program (Baker & Gray, 1972), which utilizes a complex behavioral analysis in monitoring child progress, and the work of Lovitt and Hurlburt (1974) and Haring and Hauck (1969). The application of known principles of learning can also be seen in the construction of certain reading materials such as the *Remedial Reading Drills* (Hegge, Kirk, & Kirk, 1936).

Summary

The programs briefly described in this section have been systematically derived from analyses of reading and/or from behavioral learning principles. None has started from the premise that learning disabled children must be taught unique skills or taught in a unqiue way, with the possible exception of Rozin and Gleitman who use some children's observed difficulty in learning single phoneme-grapheme correspondence as a major part of the rationale for their initial focus on syllables. Like Rozin and Gleitman, Glass and Vail also use clusters of letters, both relying on observed frequency of the clusters, with Glass additionally citing the performance of young, successful decoders as grounds for the larger unit.

Programs such as those cited, most especially DISTAR (described fully in the next chapter), illustrate that a reading failure rate of near zero may be achieved by task-analytically derived programs that do not rely on individual diagnosis of children's psychological strengths and weaknesses. The responsibility for teaching all the essential skills in reading is assumed by task-analytically based programs and no necessary reliance is placed on extra-program training.

Not all task-analytically derived programs nor all demonstrably successful programs were included in this brief review. These were chosen to illustrate task-analytic program derivation and to suggest that some programs *are,* popular mythology aside, far superior to others, in derivation and in outcome data. The same point could have been made, as it has by many others, by reporting the growing body of research (e.g., Bleismer & Yarborough, 1965; Chall, 1967; Gurren & Hughes, 1965) comparing results across programs. Fraught as this kind of research is with practical problems, it is nevertheless clear that intensive, systematic decoding programs result in better reading achievement than do other kinds of beginning reading programs. It is just possible that intensive decoding instruction is even more vital for potential low achievers than for their easy-to-teach counterparts, as teachers have long insisted (see Tobias, 1976).

APTITUDE-TREATMENT INTERACTION

Teachers have long been taught, "There is no one way to teach all children—some need one method, others need another." The often unspoken assumption is that somehow we can consistently and accurately identify those children who need technique A and those who need B. Presumably the secret of this successful matching is in some identifiable characteristics of the children.

In this section we examine the success to date of efforts to match learner aptitudes, traits, or characteristics with reading method.

Modality Instruction

An impressive list of authorities in learning disabilities have recommended that methods of reading instruction should be somehow matched with the child's relative modality patterns. Johnson and Myklebust (1967), Wepman (1964, 1971), and Lerner (1971) have all recommended teaching reading be consistent with the child's strong modality (e.g., auditory learners should be taught by phonics). Kirk (1972) has recommended direct remediation of the weakness. Rupert (undated) suggests initial teaching to the strengths with a switch at some unspecified time to the weakness. Others have suggested teaching to both, concentrating on strengths in group situations and weaknesses in private tutoring; others advocate utilizing the strengths to improve the weaknesses (Johnson, 1967), and so on. (See deHirsch, Jansky, & Langford, 1966 and Silver & Hagin, 1967a for slight variations). This modality-matching advocacy has been so successful that 97 percent of the learning disability teachers in

Illinois who participated in Arter and Jenkins (1975) recent study were familiar with this modality model and 95 percent believed research supported it. Ninety-nine percent of the teachers familiar with it agreed modality should be a major consideration in devising educational prescriptions. The model was reported used frequently or always by 78 percent of the teachers.

Arter and Jenkins (1975) reviewed 15 reading studies to date (Bateman, 1967a; Bruninks, 1968; Bursuk, 1971; Freer, 1971; Harris, 1965; Janssen, 1972; Newcomer & Goodman, 1975; Ringler & Smith, 1973; Robinson, 1972; Sabatino & Dorfman, 1974; Sabatino, Ysseldyke, & Woolston, 1973; Smith, 1971; Tyler, 1974; Vandever & Neville, 1974; Waugh, 1973) which (a) assessed modality strengths and weaknesses, (b) designed or used materials that stress various modalities, and (c) attempted to discover modality-instructional interactions. After a careful critique of the studies, Arter and Jenkins conclude that the findings are remarkably consistent in that fourteen found no interactions and only one (Bursuk, 1971) reported an interaction consistent with modality model predictions. Bursuk studied tenth graders and measured comprehension skills whereas the other 14 studies used elementary age subjects and focused on decoding outcome measures. The interaction Bursuk obtained was due to greater improvement in reading comprehension of auditory learners when they were also taught listening comprehension. Visual learners did not show a transfer from listening comprehension to reading comprehension.

Arter and Jenkins conclude, as have other reviewers (e.g., Ysseldyke, 1973; Vellutino, Steger, Moyer, Harding, & Niles, 1974) that either the modality model is invalid or, given current limitations in educational assessment and programming techniques, it is merely not applicable at this time.

Other Interaction Investigations

Traits other than relative modality patterns have been studied in relation to different kinds of reading instruction. Among these are level of reading readiness (Stallings & Keepes, 1970, which also found a significant modality interaction and was not reviewed by Arter & Jenkins, 1975), reading achievement (Sabaroff, 1963) and introversion-extraversion (Whitehill & Jipson, 1970). (See Berliner & Cahen, 1973 and Bracht, 1970 for reviews of ATI studies, including those just cited.) At this time few specific, definitive answers are available as to interactions between traits, other than modality strength, and beginning reading instruction. Teaching lore, if not hard data, supports the generalization that low ability children benefit proportionately more than do high ability children from tightly structured, systematic, reading programs.

Reed, Rabe, and Mankinen (1970) reviewed studies of teaching reading to brain-injured children, and found 42 articles written during the 1960s which dealt with educational and remedial methods for brain-damaged children. Only nine (covering seven investigations) experimentally evaluated methods; the other 33 described or recommended teaching procedures with no evidence of their merit. After analyzing the seven empirical studies the reveiwers conclude, "Above all, there is no empirical basis for recommending certain pedagogical procedures . . . for brain-injured children as opposed to non-brain-injured children who also may have a learning disability" (p. 396). Although these studies were not designed as aptitude-treatment interaction studies they indicate the absence of a data base for the claim that certain reading methods are better for brain-injured children.

Models for Further Aptitude-Treatment Interaction (ATI) Research

Salomon (1972) is doubtful ATI research can contribute very much to improving instruction because learners can be divided by innumerable, uncorrelated variables. But he believes ATI research can assist in developing better explanations and conceptualizations as to the nature of instruction. He proposes three models which relate directly to the problem of whether learning disabled children should be taught to read differently from other children.

The remedial model. The remedial model is based on a task-analytic view of teaching and can predict ATIs only when (a) task-specific capabilities account for a large part of the variance in learning outcome, (b) the material to be taught is sequentially ordered, and (c) all subordinate objectives on the hierarchy are to be learned as a result of instruction. It assumes the learners will be changed, that is, they will be taught to do what they cannot yet do. This model would predict, for example, that given high and low scorers on visualization and a task which requires attending to certain details to make spatial transformations, the high visualizers would perform better under an activation treatment which merely enables them to do what they already know how to do and low visualizers would perform better under a modeling treatment which taught them the skills they lack.

The compensatory model. The compensatory model does not envision the learner will be changed; rather the treatment will compensate for the deficiency in the learner. If one assumes memory is unlikely to be changed by a treatment, then this model would predict that persons low in memory would perform better in a lecture treatment with quizzes interspersed every five minutes (to reduce the memory requirement) whereas those high in memory would do better in a standard lecture with note taking. According to Salomon, if the personalogical variable can be changed, the remedial model would be preferred.

The preferential model. The preferential model is useful for personalogical variables which represent general "mediating processes" across a variety of tasks and capitalizes on style of information processing, type of motivation, and so forth. The personalogical variables are not unlike those in the compensatory model but the logic of the matching is different. The preferential model would predict that students high on achievement motivation would perform better with achievement-oriented feedback, whereas those high on affiliation-motivation would do better with affiliation-oriented feedback. The unsuccessful modality-reading instruction matching studies reviewed earlier may have been conceptualized as efforts to employ this model, although arguably some investigators may have viewed their work as fitting the compensatory model.

Salomon's review of studies leads him to conclude that (a) when treatments provide the mediators which low performers cannot (do not) provide for themselves, that treatment will depress the performance of those who do provide the mediators themselves, and (b) when treatments capitalize on stronger aptitudes, the high scorers benefit more.

Summary and Implications

The failure of modality-matched reading instruction to show the expected aptitude-treatment interactions need not yet preclude further investigation of other traits in relation to instruction. If learning disabled children do suffer, as Ross (1976) suggests, from selective attention deficits, perhaps they would benefit more than other children from reading instruction which either compensates for that deficit or teaches selective attention directly (Salomon, 1972). In the following section we propose reading instruction for learning disabled children which does just that and does so within the confines of intensive, direct decoding instruction derived from a task-analysis of reading.

A FOURTH APPROACH

Much remains unknown about reading processes, learning disabled children, and reading programs. And yet enough is known, if only it can be implemented, to greatly reduce if not totally eradicate the severe reading problems now so rampant in American schools.

Learning disabled children are those who must be taught by the best reading methods available if they are to succeed. So taught, they can and do learn to read. Therefore, "teaching disabilities" is a more precise term than learning disabilities to describe the cause of their failure when it does occur. Near failure-proof methods for teaching all children to read are already available. Continued failure of schools to employ these programs is at best negligent and at worse malicious. Implementation of the best that is currently available would help mightily; further refinements in these programs would help slightly more.

Beginning Reading Processes

The first step in beginning reading is converting written symbols to their spoken equivalents. Theoretically, this may be done using any unit from paragraphs to single graphemes. Conventional beginning reading programs of the last forty years have used the word as the initial unit to be converted. Both data and logic suggest better reading achievement accrues from using smaller units. The word approach has been defended by inappropriate extrapolation from analyses of proficient adult reading and by claims it maintains children's interest by providing easy access to meaning. But how interesting are Dick and Jane's "ohs" and "looks" and how exciting is memorizing whole words versus "figuring out" new words (Blumenfeld, 1974; Johnson, 1970)? Regardless of the merits of the whole word or meaning-emphasis approach for the majority of children who do seem to learn to read by "osmosis" and without intensive, systematic or structured instruction, the clear fact is this method has been disastrous for learning disabled children. Systematic decoding must be the first step in reading and must be the direct focus of initial instruction for all learning disabled children. Further, it must be recognized that decoding, more than comprehension, is the potential pitfall for learning disabled children.

Task analysis of decoding reveals it contains certain subskills: (a) responding to graphemes or grapheme clusters with appropriate phonemes or phoneme clusters; (b) responding in the appropriate temporal sequence, derived from the spatial order of the written symbols; and (c) blending the phonemes or phoneme clusters into words. Adequate sound-symbol association learning allows the inference that its subskill of letter discrimination was performed and that discrimination in turn allows the inference the child's attention was selectively and appropriately focused on relevant stimulus dimensions.

Two skills are conspicuously absent from a task analysis of decoding: (a) letter naming and (b) picture and/or "context" reading.

Letter naming. Correlations between knowledge of letter names (number known) at the beginning of first grade and reading level at the end of first grade have been reported by Bond and Dykstra (1967) to range between 0.51 and 0.60. However, in a well designed study, Speer and Lamb (1976) have shown that *fluency* (rate) of letter naming correlated 0.79 to 0.85 with reading achievement. Since it is logically evident and empirically established (Samuels, 1971) that letter names do not per se facilitate reading, the fluency factor emerges as even more pertinent. Speer and Lamb predictably found no relationship between gain scores in letter naming and reading achievement. Rate of accurate decoding is probably a more important factor in early reading proficiency than has been recognized in the past (Starlin, 1971). Unfortunately the very children for whom the initial associative learning of sound-symbol relationship is difficult are the same children who obtain less practice and whose fluency is thus doubly hindered.

Picture and "context" reading. Pictures may be used to teach the concept that symbols on paper can signal to us to say something. Programs which utilize rebus writing do just that (e.g., Rozin & Gleitman, 1974; Woodcock & Clark, 1969). Many children do need systematic instruction to understand the concept that speech can be depicted in written form. However, there is no clear evidence that the concept is too difficult to teach using words and letters.

Only if a learning disabled child does not acquire the concept in spite of clean teaching using graphemes or words (a most unlikely event) would it seem appropriate to use pictures. Since learning disabled children, by definition, have more than their share of difficulty in reading, it is foolish to teach unnecessary, extra steps.

The other use of pictures in beginning reading programs is as an aid to comprehension and therefore an "interest-maintainer." The merit of this must be weighed against the fact that humans seem to walk the paths of least effort. Pictures often enable the child to falsely appear to be decoding. Fluent, automatic decoding is a prerequisite to later wholistic comprehension (Laberge & Samuels, 1974), and pictures can, for some learning disabled children, significantly distract the child's attention and energy from the essential task of decoding. The argument that decoding and comprehension initially utilize different cognitive processes and perhaps even different areas of the brain can be made, but for present purposes, the need for attention to be focused on decoding is a sufficiently strong argument to urge that pictures not be employed as a comprehension aid.

A related contention is that pictures are motivating or reinforcing. This is probably true and therefore they should be used *after* successful decoding to provide informational closure and feedback (Gibson, 1970) or whatever other type of reinforcement they can. At least one program (DISTAR) uses pictures this way.

Other context clues are often urged upon children and inevitably lead the child to adopt guessing as a decoding tactic. Proficient adult readers do form hypotheses and expectations about what the next ideas will be—that is not disputed. Our contention is that accurate decoding skills must be acquired before that stage and that guessing strategies interfere, for learning disabled children, with accurate decoding.

Learning Disabled Children

If learning disabled children differ, as a group, from other children in ways relevant to teaching reading, these differences might be described as the need for: (a) systematic aid in attending to the relevant features (shape and position) of the graphemes to be discriminated (Ross, 1976); (b) a greater than usual number of repetitions of correct grapheme-phoneme association; and (c) more systematic reinforcement of new learning.

As indicated earlier, special education efforts to find aptitude-treatment interactions have focused on modality aptitudes and been notably unsuccessful. Literature from other disciplines (e.g., Berliner & Cahen, 1973; Cronbach & Snow, 1969) is not as pessimistic. It is too early to dismiss the possibility that some techniques of reading instruction are particularly beneficial for some children. Learning disabled children, as currently labeled, are not a homogenous group, but to the extent characteristics are shared, these may constitute appropriate personalogical variables for interactional investigation.

The hypothesized lower performance on selective attention to graphemic features and more trials to mastery are characteristics which would be changed through successful intervention and therefore Salomon's (1972) *remedial* ATI model would be appropriate. The model would predict, we believe accurately, that treatments including direct teaching of selective attention and providing numerous repetitions would deter the performance of those non-learning disabled children who already discriminate symbols and need few repetitions. ATI literature seems to suggest the principle that the further away a learner is from mastery of an objective the more the learner benefits from structured, deductive, "ruleg" approaches and conversely, the less yet to be learned, the greater the benefit from "egrule" or inductive approaches (Tobias, 1976). This principle is related to the oft heard generalization that academically able youngsters can learn to read with any approach while difficult-to-teach children need a "structured, phonics" program.

It has not been definitively established that all or even most learning disabled children have these particular deficits. A reasonable interpretation of available data suggest many might. To the extent they do, ATI models should be employed more carefully than in the past in an effort to successfully match these learning characteristics with suitable structured teaching techniques.

Attending to relevant phoneme features. Learning disabled children should be taught the rule that "letters and numbers point *one* way." Everything a child has learned about spatial orientation prior to encountering letters and numbers has been that what something is called is *not* affected by rotation and that one need not therefore attend to how it is "pointed" when naming it. It is hard to know whether to laugh or cry when "severe strephosymbolia" in a ten-year old boy is instantly cured by teaching the "Pointy Rule." It is even harder to answer his somber "Why didn't any of my teachers tell me that?" Admittedly, and remarkably, most children figure out the Pointy Rule even though they do not articulate it. They are masters of incidental learning; learning disabled children are not.

Learning disabled children need practice, to mastery, in discriminating all letters from each other, for example, *b* from *d*. As yet unresolved, but readily determinable, is whether children who require more practice reach mastery more readily by overlearning *b* before *d* is introduced or by initial confrontation with the pair. In either case, learning is made initially easier if other discriminable features (type style, for instance) are added to spatial orientation. Hyman and Cohen (1975) have shown that decreasing the stimulus intensity of the vertical line aids in this discrimination. In short, reversal problems and other letter discrimination failures can be prevented by good pedagogy—even if they do have their origin in "minimal brain dysfunction," in the genes, or in a weak ego.

Greater repetitions to associative mastery. Precise data are difficult to locate, but clinical lore suggests, probably quite accurately, that some learning disabled children require as many as 1500 to 5000 correct associations of initial sound-symbol correspondences before reliable retention will occur. After the first few symbols are learned (that is, the correct sound response invariably given to the letter stimulus) the number of required repetitions drops markedly and will probably approximate that non-learning disabled children. It is difficult to determine, in ordinary teaching situations, whether the repetitions are required because of difficulties in selectively attending, discriminating, or associating. The teacher should therefore cover all bets by special care as to each possibility. Commonly, teachers find it difficult to provide sufficient monitored oral response opportunities to the first symbols before more are introduced. The child's confusion mounts and uncorrected errors proliferate, further compounding the failure cycle. Teachers must be especially alert to the pitfalls of providing off-target practice. Circling a thousand worksheet pictures of things that start with /m/ provides exactly zero practice in looking at *m* and responding with /m/. It is only the latter skill that is part of decoding. The clear implication is that teachers must somehow provide sufficient and appropriate repetitions and must monitor progress very precisely. This is a tall order, but less is not teaching and is not defensible. Letter names double the child's learning burden and do not contribute to reading skill. Therefore, they should be taught only after decoding skills are fairly solid (as done in DISTAR).

The need for reinforcement. Children can be taught to read even though we have not resolved the complex and fascinating disputes between behaviorists and those of other persuasions as to the nature of the acquisition of language skills. But some learning disabled children will not be taught to read without careful use of well established behavioral principles of reinforcement. We must recognize that mastering decoding skills is not sufficiently "intrinsically" rewarding to all children to maintain the necessary effort. We might ardently wish it were or even believe it "should" be. Neither changes the fact that it is not. Reading programs should have built-in procedures for appropriate reinforcement and for visibility and precise monitoring of children's progress. If these are not built in, the teacher must provide them.

Summary

Like other children, learning disabled children bring to school adequate auditory, visual, auditory-visual integrative, syntactic, and semantic skills to learn to read. Like other children, they *do not* need to learn letter names or picture reading to decode. Like other children, they *do* need to be taught the separate, or at least separable skills of decoding sound-symbol correspondence, left-to-right sequence, and sound blending.

Perhaps unlike other children they need programs and teachers that especially emphasize selective attention to relevant grapheme features, provide and require adequate repetitions of grapheme-phoneme correspondences to insure mastery, and systematically utilize principles of reinforcement.

Finally, all our children need accountable schools committed to teaching them to read even if that committment requires, as it does, the relinquishment of handy-dandy cop-outs and the acceptance of demonstrably effective reading programs and teaching techniques.

REMEDIATION OF OTHER SKILLS

Learning disability literature is replete with articles, pamphlets, and books on how to teach arithmetic, handwriting, spelling, language, and other skills to learning disabled children. Many of the suggestions are undoubtedly sound and are sometimes successful with some children. We do not, however, repeat them here because they are readily available elsewhere and because there is no clear and convincing evidence that learning disabled children as a group need or benefit from any different techniques than those that are also most appropriate for all children. To put this view in perspective let us briefly recapitulate what we have said about teaching reading to learning disabled children.

First, the nature of the task of reading English requires that the reader respond to written symbols with the appropriate sounds, that he or she blend those sounds into recognized words, and that both steps be done in the proper sequence. Research, clinical experience, and logic suggest that many children who are labeled learning disabled may need: (a) more specific instruction than other children in attending to the relevant features of letters; (b) more practice repetitions to master the sound-symbol relationships; and (c) more careful and systematic utilization of reinforcement. To the extent these adaptations are necessary to insure success for a particular child one could maintain that that child needed to be taught reading differently from other children. But an even more accurate and productive generalization is that every child is entitled to the amount of direct instruction necessary for him or her to learn the distinctive features of whatever is to be discriminated, to the number of practice trials necessary for mastery, and to that amount and kind of reinforcement necessary to develop and maintain appropriate behaviors.

Thus we reach the same position with respect to teaching reading as we do to teaching arithmetic, spelling, or any other skill to learning disabled children. They need the same careful teaching to which all children are entitled. If they do not receive it, learning disabled children are, by definition, those most likely to fail to learn the skill on their own.

Specific teaching suggestions traditionally offered, such as spelling by tracing each word in clay or writing it in the air or using templates for handwriting or avoiding manuscript in favor of cursive writing, and so on, may, as indicated earlier, be helpful to some children. But we cannot yet demonstrate any means other than trial and error to determine which children might benefit, nor can we conclusively show that learning disabled children are more likely to benefit than non-learning disabled ones. Absent these kinds of data, we believe the soundest current advice to teachers is to utilize the best programs available for all children and do so with particular attention to relevant feature discrimination, adequate practice, and reinforcement.

At the end of this chapter the reader will find a highly selective, very brief list of references to programs and materials helpful to teachers concerned with specific instruction in arithmetic, spelling, handwriting, and communication and language.

DELIVERY OF SERVICES

Once we are familiar with the material and methods that can be used to remediate the problems of students and have also diagnosed what these problems are, the next task is to bring child and remediation together. Delivery of remedial services takes many forms dependent upon the severity of a child's problem, the number of students needing remedial services, the philosophy of administrators of remedial services, and the financial status of the educational body.

Traditionally, remediation has been carried on through either a special class situation where children needing remedial help are grouped together in a separate class, or through the use of an itinerant teacher who spends only part of the day in any particular building, with children needing help coming for specified periods on a regular schedule. In both instances the children are removed from their regular classroom for instruction by a specialist. They are given individual or small-group instruction, which is directed toward solving the learning problems that apparently were too big to cope with in the regular classroom. Although they do provide more individualization, both approaches allow the child to be removed from the regular classroom and labeled as different.

Resource Rooms

The resource room model is an attempt to eliminate the need for the total removal of any child from the classroom on anything but a very temporary basis. A working example is the program developed by the Franklin-Pierce School District, Tacoma, Washington. Here, special education classrooms have been disbanded and the children placed in the regular classrooms. Within each school, classroom counselors trained in classroom intervention techniques, educational assessment, educational programming, and behavior modification techniques are available to work with teachers and individual students. They are supported by highly trained specialists in educational materials and methods, who work from diagnostic centers serving several schools.

Using the resource room concept, when a child whose needs cannot be met is identified by the regular classroom teacher, the resource teacher is called. The resource teacher works with the child, the classroom teacher, and the parents to define the problem, collect the data, and formulate a plan of remediation. The defining and planning are flexible to include co-ordinating health services, psychological assessment, instituting a behavior modification program, or programming special materials to meet the child's individual needs. If the child's needs cannot be identified or met within the school, referral to the diagnostic center may be advisable. This always is done with a specific educational objective; for example, the child is not learning to read using the basal reading system, and an alternative approach is required. The child only leaves the classroom during the time of the problem—during reading period. For the rest of the day the child remains in class for all other activities. At the diagnostic center, efforts are first directed toward finding out why learning is not occurring, and then toward setting up a program to develop whatever skills or behaviors are lacking. The program developed by the center can be carried on within the regular classroom. If it involves special techniques, materials, or methods with which the classroom teacher is un-familiar, the classroom counselor takes the regular class, allowing the classroom teacher to go to the diagnostic center to learn to implement the program. Once the program is developed, the child and the program are placed back into the regular classroom.

The primary advantage of the resource room is that the child is never totally removed from the mainstream of the educational program. The second advantage is that there are no labels attached, no categories into which the child is put. No one is labeled as different, apart from the regular classroom program. The third advantage is that it allows special educators to be specialists in education: to meet the special needs of any or all of the children who need them without imposing on pupils the stigma or the handicap of labels. The fourth advantage is that it gives the classroom teacher an opportunity for continuing in-service train-ing in areas immediately relevant to instructing students in the class-room.

Remediation Within the Classroom

The concept of the resource room moves the remediation of any child's problems into the classroom. In effect, it makes remediation an integral part of everyday good teaching. Very informally, the teacher conducts on-the-spot remediation every day with any child who is having difficulty with a particular task. As the task the child needs help with is pinpointed, the teacher gives the necessary assistance and moves on. This is just a part of regular teaching and does not involve any major adjustment in classroom instruction. Some children may need a more formal, directed effort to solve problems. Some adjustments may have to be made in the classroom in grouping, different materials, or a new technique directed toward solving the problems of a child. But whatever adjustments are necessary are done in the classroom and by the child's classroom teacher. The child is not removed from class, even for a short time. As teachers become more aware of the tasks they are teaching and better can enable their students to master each task before they go on to the next, there will be less need for any drastic adjustment in a classroom, for each child's individual needs already will be receiving attention.

The Pre-First Grade Program

Working on the assumptions that it is easier on the child if he or she does not fail the first time around, and that it is easier on the taxpayer if a child learns when he or she is first taught and does not need later remedial help, the concept of the "pre-first grade" programs was developed. Aimed at prevention, it tries to identify those children who are poor risks for first grade—those likely to encounter difficulties in beginning learning tasks—and places them in a pre-first grade program. With a smaller number of pupils (class size is usually under 20), perhaps with a teacher's aide, and with an awareness that these children need something that they would not get in an ordinary first grade, their teacher teaches them. With good teaching techniques that make sure every child has mastered a task before being moved on, a program solid in basic skills which all children need to succeed in school, and an atmosphere that lets the child know that he or she can learn and that school is a good place to be—the pre-first grade program can be a very successful method of preventing later learning problems. In fact, many children who have gone through such a program were ahead of their first grade counterparts when both groups entered second grade the following fall. If, however, the program is seen as a place to wait until the child is ready to learn, if the curriculum is presented more slowly in a watered-down fashion because these children are not able to go as fast, then the pre-first grade program is only a delay and perhaps a further cause of a child's feeling of failure and frustration.

FINALLY . . .

The diagnostic-remedial approach to learning disabilities views allegedly deficient abilities as the proper focus of teaching. Programs and activities have been developed to train visualization, eye-hand coordination, balance, sequencing, and so on. While the *what* of teaching has been these correlates of academic skills, the *how* of teaching has been dictated by largely trial-and-error efforts to match the child's patterns of strength and/or weaknesses to the materials.

The task-analytic approach teaches basic skills directly without prior remediation of possibly correlated problem areas. The *what* of teaching thus has been the specific skills and subskills directly necessary to achieve the academic objective, and the *how* of teaching is to focus attention on relevant features to be learned and to provide adequate practice and appropriate reinforcement.

The next chapter presents in detail the task-analytically derived DISTAR Language, Reading, and Arithmetic programs which have been carefully designed to teach these basic skills to all children, including learning disabled. To the extent that such successful programs do prevent failure, we may well raise the "Beethoven played in the forest" question— that is, if a child who appears to be "learning disabled" prior to school or while placed in inadequate instructional programs is then placed in a successful program and achieves well, is she or he still "learning disabled"?

SELECTED REFERENCES ON ARITHMETIC, HANDWRITING AND SPELLING, AND COMMUNICATION AND LANGUAGE

Arithmetic

ASHLOCK, R. B., *Error Patterns in Computation: A Semiprogrammed Approach.* Columbus, Ohio: Charles E. Merrill, 1972.

BEREITER, C. *Arithmetic and Mathematics.* Sioux Falls, S.D.: Adapt Press, 1968.

BLAKE, K., *Teaching the Retarded.* Englewood Cliffs, N.J.: Prentice-Hall, Inc., 1974.

D'AUGUSTINE, C. H., *Multiple Methods of Teaching Mathematics in the Elementary School* (2nd ed.). New York: Harper and Row, 1973.

JERMAN, M., Review of research on CAI drill-and-practice programs in elementary mathematics and reading. In N. G. Haring and Alice H. Hayden (Eds.), *The Improvement of Instruction.* Seattle: Special Child Publications, 1972.

MAY, L., *Teaching Mathematics in the Elementary School* (2nd ed.). New York: The Free Press, 1974.

PETERSON, D., *Functional Mathematics for the Mentally Retarded.* Columbus, Ohio: Charles E. Merrill, 1973.

VALLETT, R., *The Remediation of Learning Disorders.* Belmont, Cal.: Fearon, 1967.

VEILLEUX, C., Skill Level Approach to Math (SLAM). Seattle: Experimental Education Unit, College of Education, and Child Development and Mental Retardation Center, University of Washington, 1975.

Handwriting and Spelling

Academic Therapy Quarterly 3 (1), Fall, 1967. (Special issue on diagnosis and remediation of spelling.)

Academic Therapy Quarterly 4 (1), Fall, 1968. (Special issue on handwriting.)

FERNALD, G., *Remedial Techniques in Basic School Subjects.* New York: McGraw-Hill, 1943.

LERNER, J., *Children with Learning Disabilities.* Boston: Houghton Mifflin Co., 1976.

WESTERMAN, G., *Spelling and Writing.* Sioux Falls, S.D.: Adapt Press, 1971.

Communication and Language Skills

DUNN, L. M. and J. O. SMITH, *Peabody Language Development Kit.* Circle Pines, Minn.: American Guidance Services, 1965.

HATTEN, J., T. GOMAN, and C. LENT, *Emerging Language.* Westlake Village, Cal.: The Learning Business, 1973.

LAVATELLI, C. (Ed.), *Language Training in Early Childhood Education.* Urbana: University of Illinois Press (for the ERIC Clearinghouse on Early Childhood Education), 1971.

LEE, L., *Developmental Sentence Analysis.* Evanston, Ill.: Northwestern University Press, 1974.

LEE, L., R. KOENIGSKNECHT, and S. MULHERN, *Interactive Language Development Teaching.* Evanston, Ill.: Northwestern University Press, 1975.

MACDONALD, J., Environmental language intervention: programs for establishing initial communication in handicapped children. In F. Withrow and C. Nygren (Eds.), *Language and the Handicapped Learner: Curricula, Programs, and Media.* Columbus, Ohio: Charles E. Merrill, 1975.

McLEAN, J., Language development and communication disorders. In N. G. Haring (Ed.), *Behavior of Exceptional Children: An Introduction to Special Education.* Columbus, Ohio: Charles E. Merrill, 1974.

RIEKE, J., Communication in early education. In N. G. Haring, ed., *Behavior of Exceptional Children: An Introduction to Special Education.* Columbus, Ohio: Charles E. Merrill, 1974.

SCHIEFELBUSCH, R. (Ed.), *Language of the Mentally Retarded.* Baltimore: University Park Press, 1972.

REFERENCES

ABEL, D., Can a student sue the schools for educational malpractice? *Harvard Educational Review,* 1974, *44,* 416–36.

ABT ASSOCIATES, Education as experimentation: A planned variation model (Vol. III). Boston: Abt Associates, 1976.

ALLEN, J., The right to read. *Reading Newsreport,* 1969, *4,* 29–37.

ANDERSON, W. F., The relative effects of the Frostig program, corrective reading instruction, and attention upon the reading skills of corrective readers with visual perceptual difficulties. *Journal of School Psychology,* 1972, *10,* 387–95.

ARTER, J. A., and J. R. JENKINS, *Examining the benefits and prevalence of modality considerations in special education.* Unpublished manuscript, University of Illinois of Urbana–Champaign, 1975.

ARTLEY, A. S., *The controversy: Reading problem or learning disability: What are the issues?* Paper presented at the Annual Meeting of the International Reading Association, New York, May, 1975. (ERIC Document Reproduction Service No. ED 110 960).

AUKERMAN, R. C., *Approaches to Beginning Reading.* New York: John Wiley, 1971.

BAKER, R. D., and B. B. GRAY, *Monterey Reading Program.* Monterey, Cal.: Behavioral Sciences Institute, 1972.

BALOW, B., Perceptual activities in the treatment of severe reading disability. *Reading Teacher,* 1971, *24,* 513–25.

BANNATYNE, A., A suggested classification of the causes of dyslexia. *Word Blind Bulletin,* 1966, *1*(5), 5–14.

————, Research design and progress in remediating learning disabilities. *Journal of Learning Disabilities,* 1975, *8,* 345–48.

BATEMAN, B. D., Educational implications of minimal brain dysfunction. In F. de la Cruz, B. Fox, & R. Roberts (Eds.), *Minimal Brain Dysfunction.* New York: Annals of the New York Academy of Sciences, 1973.

————, The efficacy of an auditory and a visual method of first grade reading instruction with auditory and visual learners. *College of Education Curriculum Bulletin,* 1967, *23,* 278, Eugene, Oregon: University of Oregon. 6–14. (a).

————, *The Illinois Test of Psycholinguistic Abilities in Current Research.* Institute for Research on Exceptional Children. University of Illinois, 1965.

————, Poor reading instruction and the law. *Reading Informer,* 1975, *3*(1), 17–19.

————, Three approaches to diagnosis and educational planning for children with learning disabilities. *Academic Therapy,* 1967, *2,* 215–222 (b).

BERLINER, D. C., and L. S. CAHEN, Trait-treatment interaction and learning. In F. N. Kerlinger (Ed.), *Review of research in education, vol. 1.* Itesco, Illinois: Peacock Publishing, 1973.

BIJOU, S. W., What psychology has to offer education—now. *Journal of Applied Behavior Analysis,* 1970, *3,* 65–71.

BIRCH, H., Dyslexia and maturation of visual function. In J. Money (Ed.), *Reading Disability. Progress and Research Needs in Dyslexia.* Baltimore: Johns Hopkins Press, 1962.

BIRCH, H., and L. BELMONT, Auditory-visual integration in normal and retarded readers. *American Journal of Orthopsychiatry,* 1964, *34,* 852–61.

BLANK, M., and W. BRIDGER, Deficiencies in verbal labeling in retarded readers. *American Journal of Orthopsychiatry,* 1966, *36,* 840–47.

BLANK, M., S. WEIDER, and W. BRIDGER, Verbal deficiencies in abstract thinking in early reading retardation. *American Journal of Orthopsychiatry,* 1968, *38,* 823–34.

BLAU, H., and H. BLAU, A theory of learning how to read. *The Reading Teacher,* 1968, *22,* 126–29.

BLIESMER, E. P., and B. H. YARBOROUGH, A comparison of ten different beginning reading programs in first grade. *Phi Delta Kappan,* 1965, June, 500–504.

BLOM, G. E., and A. W. JONES, Bases of classification of reading disorders. In E. O. Calkins (Ed.), *Reading Forum.* (NINDS Monograph No. 11, U.S. Public Health Service Publication No. 0–418–318). Washington, D.C.: U. S. Government Printing Office, 1971.

BLUMENFELD, S. L., *The New Illiterates—and How to Keep Your Child from Becoming One.* New Rochelle, N.Y.: Arlington House, 1974.

BOND, G. L., and R. DYKSTRA, The cooperative research program in first grade reading instruction. *Reading Research Quarterly,* 1967, *2,* 5–142.

BRACHT, G. H., Experimental factors related to aptitude-treatment interactions. *Review of Educational Research,* 1970, *40* (5), 627–45.

BRUININKS, R. H., Relationship of auditory and visual perceptual strengths to methods of teaching word recognition among disadvantaged Negro boys. (ERIC ED 043 721, 1968).

BURSUK, L. A., Sensory mode of lesson presentation as a factor in the reading comprehension improvement of adolescent retarded readers. (ERIC ED 047 435, 1971).

BURTON, E., and G. G. GLASS, *Students' conception of their decoding skill.* Paper presented at the Educational Research Conference, 1968.

CALFEE, R., R. CHAPMAN, and L. VENEZKY, How a child needs to think to learn to read. In L. Gregg (Ed.), *Cognition in Learning and Memory.* New York: John Wiley & Sons, 1972.

CARROLL, J. B., Review of the ITPA. In O. K. Buros (Ed.), *Seventh Mental Measurements Yearbook,* Vol. 1, Highland Park, N.J.: Gryphon Press, 1972.

CHALL, J., *Learning to Read: The Great Debate.* New York: McGraw-Hill, 1967.

COHEN, S. A., Minimal brain dysfunction and practical matters such as teaching kids to read. In F. de la Cruz, B. Fox, & R. Roberts (Eds.), *Minimal Brain Dysfunction.* New York: Annals of the New York Academy of Sciences, 1973.

————, Studies in visual perception and reading in disadvantaged children. *Journal of Learning Disabilities,* 1969, *2,* 498–507.

CRONBACH, L. J., and R. E. SNOW, Individual differences in learning ability as a function of instructional variables. Final Report, 1969, School of Education, Stanford University, Contract No. OEC–4–6–061269–1217, USOE.

DEHIRSCH, K., J. J. JANSKY, and W. S. LANGFORD, *Predicting Reading Failure.* New York: Harper & Row, 1966.

DELACATO, C. H., *Neurological Organization and Reading.* Springfield, Ill.: Charles C. Thomas, 1966.

DIEHL, K., The workshops were wonderful. *Reading Informer,* 1975, *3*(1), 14–15; 24.

DRADER, D. L., The role of verbal labeling in equivalence tasks as related to reading ability. *Journal of Learning Disabilities,* 1975, *8,* 154–57.

DYKSTRA, R., The effectiveness of code—and meaning—emphasis beginning reading programs. *Reading Teacher,* 1968, *22*(1), 17–23.

EIMAS, P. D., E. R. SIQUELAND, P. JUSCZYK, and J. VIGORITO, Speech perception in infants, *Science,* 1971, *171,* 303–6.

ENGELMANN, S. E., *Preventing Failure in the Primary Grades.* Chicago: Science Research Associates, 1969.

————, Relationship between psychological theories and the act of teaching. *Journal of School Psychology,* 1967, *5* (2), 93–100 (a).

————, Teaching reading to children with low mental ages. *Education and Training of the Mentally Retarded,* 1967, *2,* 193–201 (b).

Federal Register, April 29, 1975, 18551.

FERNALD, G., *Remedial Techniques in Basic School Subjects.* New York: McGraw-Hill, 1943.

FLESCH, R., *Why Johnny Can't Read and What You Can Do About It.* New York: Harper & Brothers, 1955.

FREER, F., *Visual and auditory perceptual modality difference as related to success in first grade reading word recognition.* Unpublished doctoral dissertation, Rutgers University, 1971.

GIBSON, E. J., The ontogeny of reading. *American Psychologist,* 1970, *25,* 136–43.

GILLINGHAM, A., and B. STILLMAN, *Remedial Training for Children with Specific Disability in Reading, Spelling, and Penmanship* (2nd ed.). Cambridge, Mass.: Educators' Publishing Service, 1969.

GLASS, G. G., Perceptual conditioning for decoding: Rationale and method. In B. Batement, ed., *Learning Disorders,* Vol. 4. Seattle: Special Child Publications, 1971.

GURREN, L., and A. HUGHES, Intensive phonics vs. gradual phonics in beginning reading: A review. *The Journal of Educational Research,* 1965, *58,* 339–46.

HAMMILL, D. D., L. GOODMAN, and J. L. WIEDERHOLT, Visual-motor processes: Can we train them? *The Reading Teacher,* 1974, *27*(5), 469–78.

HAMMILL, D. D., and S. C. LARSEN, The relationship of selected auditory perceptual skills and reading ability. *Journal of Learning Disabilities,* 1974, *7*(7), 429–35.

HARING, N. G., and M. A. HAUCK, Improving learning conditions in the establishment of reading skills with disabled readers. *Exceptional Children,* 1969, *35,* 341–52.

HARRIGAN, J. E., Initial reading instruction: Phonemes, syllables, or ideographs? *Journal of Learning Disabilities,* 1976, *9*(2), 74–80.

HARRIS, A. J., *Individualizing first grade reading according to specific learning aptitudes.* New York: Office of Research and Evaluation, Division of Teacher Education of the City University of New York, 1965.

———, Practical applications of reading research. *The Reading Teacher,* 1976, *29*(6), 559–65.

HEGGE, T., S. A. KIRK, and W. KIRK, *Remedial Reading Drills.* Ann Arbor, Michigan: George Wahr Pub. Co., 1936.

HYMAN, J., and S. A. COHEN, The effect of verticality as a stimulus property on the letter discrimination of young children. *Journal of Learning Disabilities,* 1975, *8*(2), 98–107.

JACOBS, J. N., Visual perceptual training programs. *Educational Leadership Research Supplement,* January, 1968.

JANSSEN, D., Effects of visual and auditory perceptual aptitudes and letter discrimination pretraining on word recognition. Doctoral dissertation, Pennsylvania State University, 1972. University Microfilms 73–21, 267.

JOHNSON, D., Educational principles for children with learning disabilities. *Rehabilitation Literature,* 1967, *28,* 317–22.

JOHNSON, D. J., and H. R. MYKLEBUST, *Learning Disabilities, Educational Principles and Practices.* New York: Grune & Stratton, 1967.

JOHNSON, M., *Programmed Illiteracy in Our Schools.* Winnipeg: Clarity Books, 1970.

KASS, C. E., Psycholinguistic disabilities of children with reading problems. *Exceptional Children,* 1966, *32,* 533–39.

KEOGH, B., Bender-Gestalt as a predictive and diagnostic test of reading performance. *Journal of Consulting Psychology,* 1965, *29,* 83–84.

KEOGH, B. K., Optometric vision training programs for children with learning disabilities: Review of issues and research. *Journal of Learning Disabilities,* 1974, *7,* 219–31.

KEPHART, N. C., *The Slow Learner in the Classroom.* Columbus, Ohio: Charles E. Merrill, 1960.

KIRK, S. A., *Educating Exceptional Children.* Boston: Houghton-Mifflin, 1972.

KLESIUS, S. E., Perceptual-motor development and reading—A closer look. In R. Aukerman (Ed.), *Some Persistent Questions on Beginning Reading.* Newark, Del.: International Reading Association, 1972.

KOPPITZ, E. M., Bender Gestalt test, visual aural deficit span test and reading achievement. *Journal of Learning Disabilities,* 1975, *8,* 154–57.

KOTTMEYER, W., ed., *Handbook for Remedial Reading.* St. Louis: Webster, 1959.

KRIPPNER, S., Research in visual training and reading disability. In B. Bateman (Ed.), *Reading Performance and How to Achieve It.* Seattle, Washington: Special Child Publications, 1973.

LABERGE, D., and S. J. SAMUELS, Toward a theory of automatic information processing in reading. *Cognitive Psychology,* 1974, *6,* 293–323.

LARSEN, S. C., and D. D. HAMMILL, Relationship of selected visual perceptual abilities to school learning. *Journal of Special Education,* 1975, *9*(3), 281–91.

LARSEN, S. C., D. ROGERS, and V. SOWELL, The use of selected perceptual tests in differentiating between normal and learning disabled children. *Journal of Learning Disabilities,* 1976, *9,* 85–90.

LERNER, J. W., *Children with Learning Disabilities.* Boston: Houghton-Mifflin, 1971.

———, *Children with Learning Disabilities* (2nd ed.) Boston: Houghton-Mifflin, 1976.

———, Remedial reading and learning disabilities: Are they the same or different? *Journal of Special Education,* 1975, *9*(2), 119–31.

LOVELL, K., and A. GORTON, A study of some differences between backward and normal readers of average intelligence. *British Journal of Educational Psychology,* 1968, *36*(3), 240–48.

LOVITT, T. C., and M. HURLBURT, Using behavior-analysis techniques to assess the relationship between phonics instruction and oral reading. *Journal of Special Education,* 1974, *8,* 57–72.

McGRADY, H. H., and D. A. OLSON, Visual and auditory learning processes in normal children and children with specific learning disabilities. *Exceptional Children,* 1970, *36,* 581–89.

MANN, L., Are we fractionating too much? *Academic Therapy,* 1970, *5,* 85–91.

———, Psychometric phrenology and the new faculty psychology: The case against ability assessment and training. *Journal of Special Education,* 1971, *5* (1), 3–14.

MATTHEWS, M., *Teaching to Read.* Chicago: University of Chicago Press, 1966.

National Advisory Committee on Dyslexia and Related Disorders, *Report to the Secretary of the Department of Health, Education, and Welfare,* August, 1969.

NEWCOMER, P., B. HARE, D. HAMMILL, and J. McGETTIGAN, Construct validity of the ITPA. *Journal of Learning Disabilities*, 1975, *8*, 220–31.

NEWCOMER, P., and L. GOODMAN, Effective modality of instruction on the learning of meaningful and non-meaningful material by auditory and visual learners. *Journal of Special Education*, 1975, *9*, 261–68.

O'DONNELL, P. A., The effects of Delacato training on reading achievement and visual-motor integration. Dissertation Abstracts International, 1969, *30(A)*, 1079–80.

O'KEEFE, R. A., STARTER/101: *A Structured Beginning Reading Program for Young Children*. Morristown, N.J.: Silver Burdett, 1970.

———, STARTER/101 A system for structuring the teaching of reading. In B. Bateman (Ed.), *Learning Disorders: Reading*, Vol. 4. Seattle: Special Child Publications, 1971.

OTTO, W., Adequate reading instruction: Fact or fantasy? *Slow Learning Child*, 1972, *19*(1), 3–11.

OTTO, W., and R. McMENEMY, *Corrective and Remedial Teaching*. Boston: Houghton-Mifflin, 1966.

PETER, L. J., *Prescriptive Teaching*. New York: McGraw-Hill, 1965.

REED, J. C., E. F. RABE, and M. MANKINEN, Teaching reading to brain-damaged children: A review. *Reading Research Quarterly*, 1970, *5*(3), 379–401.

RINGLER, L. H., and I. L. SMITH, Learning modality and word recognition of first grade children. *Journal of Learning Disabilities*, 1973, *6*, 307–12.

ROBBINS, M., The Delacato interpretation of neurological organization. *Reading Research Quarterly*, 1966, *1*, 57–78.

ROBINSON, H. M., Perceptual training—does it result in reading improvement? In R. C. Auckerman, (Ed.). *Some Persistent Questions on Beginning Reading*. Newark, Del.: International Reading Association, 1972.

ROSS, A. O., *Psychological Aspects of Learning Disabilities and Reading Disorders*. New York: McGraw-Hill, 1976.

ROZIN, P., and L. GLEITMAN, The reading process and the acquisition of the alphabetic principle. In A. S. Reber & D. Scarborough (Eds.), *Reading: The CUNY Conference*. New York: Lawrence Erlbaum, in press.

———, *Syllabary: An Introductory Reading Curriculum*. Washington, D.C.: Curriculum Development Associates, 1974.

ROZIN, P., S. PORITSKY, and R. STOTSKY, American children with reading problems can easily learn to read English represented by Chinese characters. *Science*, 1971, *171*, 1264–67.

RUPERT, H., *A sequentially compiled list of instructional materials for remediational use with the ITPA*. Unpublished manuscript, Greeley, Colo.: Rocky Mountain Special Education Instructional Materials Center, no date.

SABAROFF, R., A comparative investigation of two methods of teaching phonics in a modern reading program: A pilot study. *Journal of Experimental Education*, 1963, *31*(3), 249–56.

SABATINO, D. A., Auditory perception: Development, assessment, and intervention. In L. Mann & D. A. Sabatino (Eds.), *The First Review of Special Education*. Philadelphia: Buttonwood Farms, 1973.

SABATINO, D. A., and N. DORFMAN, Matching learner aptitude to two commercial reading programs. *Exceptional Children*, 1974, *41*, 85–90.

SABATINO, D. A., J. E. YSSELDYKE, and J. WOOLSTON, Diagnostic-prescriptive perceptual training with mentally retarded children. *American Journal of Mental Deficiency,* 1973, *78,* 7–14.

SALOMON, G., Heuristic models for the generation of aptitude-treatment interaction hypotheses. *Review of Educational Research,* 1972, *42*(3), 327–43.

SAMUELS, S. J., Letter-name versus letter-sound knowledge in learning to read. *Reading Teacher,* 1971, *24*(7), 604–8.

———, Reading disability? *Reading Teacher,* 1970, *24,* 267, 271, 283.

SARETSKY, G., The strangely significant case of Peter Doe. *Phi Delta Kappan,* 1973, *54,* 589–92.

SEMEL, E., *Sound-Order-Sense,* Levels 1-2. Chicago: Follett Educational Corporation, 1970.

SILVER, A. A., and R. A. HAGIN, Specific reading disability: An approach to diagnosis and treatment. *Journal of Special Education,* 1967, *1,* 109–18 (a).

———, Strategies of intervention in the spectrums of defects in specific reading disability. *Bulletin of the Orton Society,* 1967, *17,* 39–46 (b).

SMITH, C. M., The relationship of reading method and reading achievement to ITPA sensory modality. *Journal of Special Education,* 1971, *5,* 143–49.

SPEER, O. B., and G. S. LAMB, First grade reading ability and fluency in naming verbal symbols. *Reading Teacher,* 1976, *29*(6), 572–76.

STALLINGS, J. A., and B. D. KEEPS, *Student aptitudes and methods of teaching beginning reading: A predictive instrument for determining interaction patterns.* Final Report, Contract No. OEG–9–70–0005, Project No. 9–1–099, USOE, 1970.

STARLIN, C., Evaluating progress toward reading proficiency. In B. Bateman (Ed.), *Learning Disorders: Reading* (Vol. 4). Seattle: Special Child Publications, 1971.

STEGER, J. A., F. R. VELLUTINO, and U. MESHOULAM, Visual-tactile and tactile-tactile paired associate learning in normal and poor readers. *Perceptual and Motor Skills,* 1972, *35,* 263–66.

STEWART, D., *Educational Malpractices: The Big Gamble in Our Schools.* Westminster, Cal.: Slate Services, 1971.

TOBIAS, S., Achievement treatment interactions. *Review of Educational Research,* 1976, *46,* 61–74.

TYLER, J. L., Modality preference and reading task performance among the mildly retarded. *Training School Bulletin,* 1974, *70,* 208–14.

VAIL, E., *Formula Phonics.* Los Angeles: Lawrence Publishing Company, 1969.

———, Formula phonics. A broad spectrum reading method. In B. Bateman (Ed.), *Learning Disorders* (Vol. 4). Seattle: Special Child Publications, 1971.

VANDEVER, T. R., and D. D. NEVILLE, Modality aptitude and word recognition. *Journal of Reading Behavior,* 1974, *6,* 195–201.

VELLUTINO, F. R., *Psychological factors in reading disability.* Paper presented at American Educational Research Association, Chicago, April, 1974.

VELLUTINO, F. R., J. A. STEGER, and G. KANDEL, Reading disability: An investigation of the perceptual deficit hypothesis. *Cortex,* 1972, *8,* 106–18.

VELLUTINO, F. R., B. M. STEGER, S. C. MOYER, C. J. HARDING, and J. A. NILES, Has the perceptual deficit hypothesis led us astray? An examination of current conceptualizations in the assessment and treatment of exceptional children. Paper presented at Annual International Convention of the Council for Exceptional Children, New York, N.Y., April, 1974.

VENEZKY, R. L., *Prereading skills: Theoretical foundations and practical applications.* Theoretical paper No. 54, Madison, Wisconsin: Wisconsin Research and Development Center for Cognitive Learning, 1975.

WAUGH, R. P., Relationship between modality preference and performance. *Exceptional Children,* 1973, *39,* 465–69.

WEPMAN, J. M., Modalities and learning. In H. M. Robinson (Ed.), *Coordinating reading instruction.* Glenview, Illinois: Scott, Foresman, 1971.

———, The perceptual basis for learning. In H. A. Robinson (Ed.), *Meeting Individual Differences in Reading.* Supplementary Educational Monographs, 94. Chicago: University of Chicago Press, 1964.

WESTMAN, J. C., B. ARTHUR, and E. P. SCHEIDLER, Reading retardation: An overview. *American Journal of Diseases of Children,* 1965, *109,* 359–69.

WHITEHILL, R. P., and J. A. JIPSON, Differential reading program performance of extroverts and introverts. *Journal of Experimental Education.* 1970, *38*(3), 93–96.

WIEDERHOLT, J. L., and D. D. HAMMILL, Use of the Frostig-Horne Visual Perception Program in the urban school. *Psychology in the Schools,* 1971, *8,* 268–74.

WOODCOCK, R. W., and C. R. CLARK, *Peabody Rebus Reading Program.* Circle Pines, Minn.: American Guidance Service, 1969.

YSSELDYKE, J. E., Diagnostic-prescriptive teaching: The search for aptitude-treatment interactions. In L. Mann, & D. Sabatino (Eds.), *The first review of special education,* Vol. 1. Philadelphia: Buttonwood Farms, 1973.

YSSELDYKE, J. E., and J. SALVIA, A critical analysis of the assumptions underlying diagnostic-prescriptive teaching. *Exceptional Children,* 1974, *41,* 181–95.

ZURIF, E. B., and G. CARSON, Dyslexia in relation to cerebral dominance and temporal analysis. *Neuropsychologia,* 1970, *8,* 351–61.

Direct Instruction— DISTAR[1,2]

6

with DOUGLAS CARNINE

Direct instruction is an alternative and preventive to conventional remediation. It also may be used, however, as remediation for children who have not been adequately taught by other methods, although most educators agree that it is easier and better to teach well the first time than to remediate after failures. But, one might object, surely all programs are designed to teach well the first time. Perhaps that is the intention, but careful analysis of most programs reveals an appalling confusion between teaching and merely providing an opportunity for children to demonstrate prior learning.

These ordinary "teaching" techniques may be entirely adequate for the child who already knows the meaning of "left" or "next." But there is nothing in these lessons to teach such concepts to a child who does not already have them. Common sense tells us that "teaching" of this kind is

[1] Requests for copies of studies conducted by the Direct Instruction Follow Through Program and questions concerning the direct instruction training program conducted at the University of Oregon can be addressed to Douglas Carnine, Follow Through Program, University of Oregon, Eugene, Oregon, 97403. Questions concerning consulting and workshops in the DISTAR programs or about other direct instruction curriculum (tutorial programs, morphogramic spelling, etc.) should be directed to the Engelmann-Becker Corporation, P. O. Box 10459, Eugene, Oregon, 97401. Information about the Distar programs is available from the publisher, Science Research Associates, 259 E. Erie, Chicago, Illinois.

[2] The authors wish to acknowledge the assistance of Patricia Druliner in preparing this chapter.

ineffective with large numbers of children who most need to be taught. Truly adequate teaching techniques would, by definition, teach all essential skills and concepts to all children, especially to those most in need of teaching, and would not rely on chance or incidental learning. This section presents a new program that seems capable of doing just that. In the DISTAR program, components of effective teaching are built into the instructions to teachers, and everything is clearly spelled out. Nothing is left to chance. However, it should be noted that DISTAR is one of several programs that accomplish the aims of direct instruction and that also might be discussed here.

INTRODUCTION

In 1964 Siegfried Engelmann and Carl Bereiter set up an experimental preschool under a grant entitled, "Acceleration of intellectual development in early childhood." The preschool program tried the developed direct instruction strategies and provided continual information about the need for refinement and modification of the experimental teaching programs. After many groups of children had been taught successfully by the direct instruction programs in reading, language, and arithmetic, the revised materials were published under the name, *Direct Instructional System for Teaching Arithmetic and Reading* (DISTAR).

Direct Instruction and Learning Disabilities

DISTAR's approach is representative of a growing trend in special education that shifts some attention from the child's strengths, weaknesses, or special etiology to an individualized remediation program for the *tasks* the child must learn. For the program's developers, this shift of emphasis away from studying the child to studying the task is the result of an analysis of what teaching really is.

Teachers, like any other practitioners, have a limited set of variables that are their province. Each practitioner must design and evaluate his or her own work on the basis of the variables controlled by that profession. For example, a person's anger could be explained in three different ways, and all of them could be true. A physiologist might explain the anger in terms of the chemical changes taking place in the body. A sociologist might explain it in terms of the pressures inflicted by social institutions. A psychologist might propose traumatic personal experiences. Each of these practitioners is dealing with some aspect of the same phenomenon. None is more right than the others. The pertinent truth in each case is relative to the variables that the practitioner controls. For the physiologist, the relevant variables are chemical; for the sociologist, societal; for the psychologist, personal. Teachers, like other professionals, must define problems, structure solutions, and conduct evaluations in terms of the variables their profession controls. If a problem is defined in terms of other variables, it is no longer a teaching problem. If teachers teach, then the most true and useful assumption they can make is that a child who fails is a child who has not been taught. No other explanation is relevant to the teaching practitioner. If a child's failure is explained in terms of birth history, genetic inheritance, or social and cultural environment, the problem is being defined for other practitioners, not for teachers. These other explanations may be equally true, but they are irrelevant: they do not involve what the teacher has control over—teaching.

> Specific statements of what the child has not been taught represent a sufficient diagnosis in the educational setting. If such statements are not presented, the teacher is not told specifically what to do. Statements about the child's brain injury do not alter one fact about what the child must be taught if he is to achieve specific criteria of educational performance. A diagnosis expressed in terms of the child's perceptual deficiency, his immaturity, or his lack of integrated self-image does not guide instruction. The only facts that are really helpful are facts about performance. Why does the child fail a complex task? Because he hasn't been taught certain skills required by that task (Engelmann, 1969, p. 38).

The assumption that a child learns what has been taught is significant for all of special education, but especially so for learning disabilities. DISTAR's position helps to correct an imbalance in what is essentially a healthy endeavor. Until recently the major focus has been on individual children and their uniqueness: "What is it about this child that has caused learning failure? What are the child's weaknesses? What sort of basic cause do these weaknesses indicate? What kind of special remediation will most benefit this peculiar combination of deficits?" Although etiology and individual differences are important areas of study that contribute to our understanding of the nature of learning, emphasis on this approach has led to a neglect of its complement—those teacher behaviors that can account for success and failure. There has been a tendency for teachers to lay the blame for failure on the child's "malady." If learning does not occur, the child has a learning disability, and because of the disability the child cannot learn. With this circular reasoning the teacher is excused from self-evaluation. Mental retardation, emotional disturbance, brain damage, learning disability—these purportedly account for what the child has or has not learned. What the teacher has or has not done is secondary or forgotten. This stance leads to removing certain children from the domain of education. Again, if the problem cannot be framed in terms of the variables that educators control (what teachers and students do in classrooms), then it is not an educational problem. It falls, instead, in the domain of some other practitioner.

The only explanation left for teachers is the one applicable to their profession: the child has not learned certain skills and the remedy follows —certain skills that have not been mastered must be taught. How does the teacher know what skills the child needs to know? That information comes from an analysis of what the teacher expects the child to be able to do when instruction is completed; in other words, the teacher examines the task that the child must be able to perform. The task is broken down into its component parts and those components are taught in an orderly, straightforward presentation. The task is the same for everyone. Any person who is expected to read must be able to translate visual symbols into words, and must be able to produce those words fluently and comprehend their meaning. Except for the few seriously crippled or sensory impaired, who will need to learn to read through a different modality such as touch, all children eventually will be expected to produce "normal" reading. That task is the same for all children. Where instruction begins on a task ladder depends on the number of skills a child already has been taught.

DISTAR's conceptualization encompasses all essential aspects of the teaching process—analyzing concepts, programming, teaching per se, classroom management, educational materials, and evaluation. It has developed a way of analyzing tasks that isolates the general concept or skill to be taught, and a way to program in which this general case is presented so impeccably that every child can learn it. It has techniques for teaching the general case and strategies for classroom management. This section includes an overview of each of these areas as well as a closeup of the DISTAR programs that have been written.

A visitor to a typical direct instruction classroom during academic work time probably would observe a small group (4 to 10) of the children engaged in quick, enthusiastic verbal exchange with a teacher or aide. The teacher or aide holds a teacher-presentation book and is presenting tasks (arithmetic, language, or reading) to which the children often respond in unison. The pace is fast and both children and teacher stay on the task. The teacher may be using hand signals somewhat reminiscent of a choir director. Visitors often comment on the enthusiasm, the business-like schedule, *and* the noise level. (Up to three groups of children responding out loud as often as 10 times a minute may be startling initially, but observation soon reveals that the children are not distracted by this.) Often the schedule is posted, revealing as many as four or five groups (usually designated by color names and referring to where in a given program the children are working—for example, the reds may be on Day 50 in Reading, Day 62 in Arithmetic, or 59 in Language, while the blues are on Days 80, 84, and 92). These groups are scheduled for 30-minute lessons in each of the three major subject areas. Every child in the class has a lesson in each area every day. However, some schools may use only DISTAR reading; others only DISTAR arithmetic; and so on. The remainder of the school day may be very conventional.

At the present time, DISTAR is used most widely with so-called disadvantaged children, urban and rural, ages four to eight. It is used increasingly with the middle-class primary grades occasionally using high school students with academic difficulties to serve as aides to help administer the program. Some of the most successful remedial reading programs at the secondary level are those teaching DISTAR lessons to high school students who then teach the same lessons to kindergarten or first grade children. Data on the effectiveness of DISTAR are presented in the following section.

Outcome Data

DISTAR appears to be producing school successes in populations that have had large numbers of school failures in the past. Approximately 25 early DISTAR evaluations are summarized in reports by Science Research Associates (1971) and by American Institutes for Research (Kim, Berger, and Kratochirl, 1972). The latter report also discusses the origin, development, and diffusion of the DISTAR direct instruction system.

The academic success of its pupils brought national attention to the DISTAR program and has made it of particular interest to those concerned with hard-to-teach children. One result of this interest was the inclusion of direct instruction in the Follow Through program. Follow Through is a comprehensive kindergarten-through-third grade program for economically disadvantaged children that was intended to compare diverse educational approaches. The approaches were called *model sponsors,* because the sponsors took an active role in implementing their programs in various communities. Gary McDaniels, who designed the final evaluational plan for Follow Through, said:

> The sponsors represented a range of opinion, theory, and rhetoric: Bank Street College in New York City came with a long history of child development philosophy, theory and practice. Siegfried Engelmann came with his learning theory and experience in highly engineered materials and teacher behaviors. Ira Gordon came with his commitments to parent training as the major vehicle for assisting children. Leonard Sealey brought "open education"; David Weikart brought a cognitively-oriented curriculum (McDaniels, 1975b, p. 5).

McDaniels characterized Follow Through, which contained more than 20 sponsors and 180 cooperating communities, as the largest and most expensive social experiment ever launched.

Stanford Research Institute and Abt Associates have conducted a number of studies as part of the national evaluation of Follow Through. Evaluations at the end of the first year of instruction (McDaniels, 1975a) and after four years of instruction with a small sample (Stallings and Kaskowitz, 1974) reported positive academic effects for the University of Oregon Direct Instruction Model, directed by Siegfried Engelmann and Wesley Becker. A more recent, national evaluation report of four-year effects for five communities (Abt Associates, 1976) stated that the Engelmann-Becker Direct Instruction Model had largely achieved the goal of raising the average achievement of economically disadvantaged Follow Through children to a level comparable to that of their middle-class peers. Children in the Direct Instruction model outperformed comparison children on at least some Metropolitan Achievement subtests (MAT) in every community. In the community where children did the most poorly, the sponsor-community relationship was terminated before Christmas of 1972. Consequently, the data from that community did not represent a fair measure of direct instruction effects.

Data collected by the Direct Instruction model are consistent with those reported in the national evaluation and encompass a much larger sample. The data reported by Becker and Engelmann (1976) are based on more than 8,000 economically disadvantaged children who entered the program at the beginning level (kindergarten or first grade, depending on the community) and who had data recorded for more than a year. The communities represent a diverse ethnic background; three are predominantly Native American, two Mexican American, one Spanish, eight black, three white, and three mixed black and white.

Figure 6.1 (Becker and Engelmann, 1976) shows that economically disadvantaged children in the Engelmann-Becker Model who began in kindergarten and completed third grade perform above or close to national norms by the end of third grade for all measures. Using the entry level performance on the Wide Range Achievement Test (WRAT) in Reading, Arithmetic, and Spelling as the baselines, substantial gains against the norms are present for all measures. These gains are displayed in Figure 6.1 as percentiles on a one-fourth standard-score scale. Because percentiles tend to exaggerate differences near the median and underestimate them near the extremes of a distribution, this method of plotting permits the automatic interpretation provided by percentiles, as well as showing the magnitude of the effect in standard score units. Following the practice of the National Follow Through Evaluation, an effect of one-fourth of a standard deviation (using the norm population S. D. as the basis) is considered an educationally significant effect.

The findings presented in Figure 6.1 for the WRAT show the mean percentile of the entry students in Reading, Arithmetic, and Spelling, as well as the gain from this entry level relative to the norm group (the arrows go up). In presenting the data for the MAT, the WRAT entry scores have been used to estimate starting levels. Figure 6.1 shows a gain against the norm group on WRAT Reading decoding skills of one and three-fourths standard deviation units. Low-income students in the projects are nearly *a standard deviation above the norm* in this essential reading skill at the end of third grade. On MAT Total Reading—a measure of vocabulary and reading comprehension—the students fall slightly below the national norm. On both the WRAT and MAT arithmetic tests, the low-income Follow Through students caught up with the national norm. On both spelling tests, they gained appreciably, but still fall a little short of the median of the norm group. On the MAT Language test,

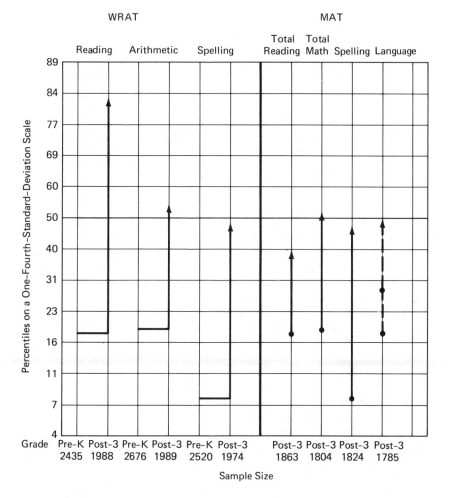

Figure 6.1. Gains against the WRAT and MAT norm groups for Engelmann-Becker Model Low Income students who were tested upon entering kindergarten and at the end of third grade. Since there were no entering kindergarten scores for the MAT, WRAT entering scores were used as estimates for reading, arithmetic, and spelling. The MAT language gain is indicated by a broken line because there is no estimated entry side (Becker and Engelmann, 1976).

they once again are above the median. An analysis of the effects separately by year of entry groups (cohorts) shows a progressive improvement for later starting cohorts (Becker and Engelmann, 1976).

Data on Low Income children in first-starting sites show a closing of the gap with national norms. With one year less in direct instruction, however, the effects across the board are one-quarter standard deviation below those shown for K-sites in Figure 6.1. Thus, first-starting students are above the norm in WRAT Reading, at the norm in MAT Language, one-quarter standard deviation below the norm on both WRAT and MAT Math and Spelling tests, and one-half standard deviation below the norm on MAT Total Reading. There is an obvious and significant advantage in a compensatory catch-up program that has the extra kindergarten year to do the job (as long as the time is used efficiently).

An appropriate question is how these findings stack up against the National Follow Through findings. Abt Associates (1976) have provided the mean scores for 13 [3] Follow Through Sponsors combined in the study of students starting kindergarten in 1970. They also have provided the means for all non-Follow Through (NFT) control groups. The NFT groups are more advantaged than are the FT groups on most demographic measures. As shown in Figure 6.2, NFT groups do better on MAT Total Reading, Total Math, and Spelling than does the average FT student. The Engelmann-Becker (E-B) Model students exceed the average of all Follow Through Sponsors on MAT Reading by one-half standard deviation. They also are ahead of the more advantaged NFT control group. On MAT Total Math, the Engelmann-Becker group exceeds the National Follow Through average by *one full standard deviation*. They also exceed the non-Follow Through control group by nearly as much. On MAT Spelling, which was not emphasized early in the program, Engelmann-Becker students are one-half standard deviation above the national average of Follow Through Sponsors, and one-quarter standard deviation above the non-Follow Through average. On MAT Language, the Engelmann-Becker group clearly has been taught grammatical usage better than the Follow Through average. The non-Follow Through mean for Language is not available at this time.

Becker and Engelmann (1976) also discuss direct instruction effects two and three years after the students leave the program. Engelmann-Becker Follow Through fifth and sixth graders were compared with comparison children in communities that were willing and able to locate Follow Through and appropriate comparison children. In only two of the seven communities involved in the study did the students receive direct instruction in kindergarten. Because of this, the results possibly underestimate what could be achieved if the children had received four, rather than three, years of direct instruction. In the seven communities there were approximately 700 in the Follow Through and 700 in the comparison

---

[3] Responsive Environment Model (Far West Lab), Tuscon Early Education Model (University of Arizona), Bank Street College of Education, Engelmann-Becker Direct Instruction (University of Oregon), Behavior Analysis Approach (University of Kansas), Cognitively Oriented Curriculum (High/Scope), Florida Parent Education Model (University of Florida), EDC Open Education Model, Interdependent Learning Model (NYU), Language Development-Bilingual-Education (South West Lab), Home School Partnership (Southern University and A and M College), California Process Model (California State Department of Education), and a group of five self-sponsored programs.

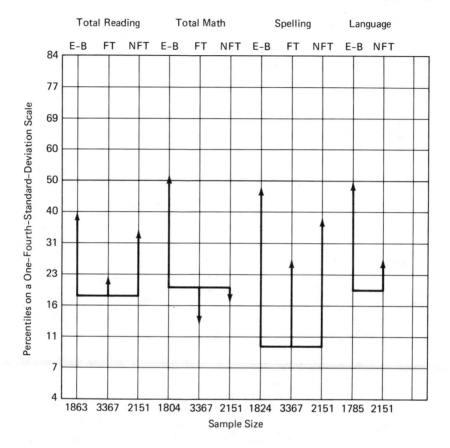

Figure 6.2. *MAT scores at the end of third grade for Low Income students in the Engelmann-Becker program in programs sponsored by 13 Follow Through Sponsors (FT) and in the control groups for the 13 Follow Through Sponsors (NFT).*

The data for Follow Through Sponsors and for their comparison groups are taken from the National Evaluation Study of students entering kindergarten in 1970 (Becker and Engelmann, 1976).

groups. Covariance analyses were used to adjust mean differences in outcome for differences in student sex, mother's education, number of siblings, low-income status, and ethnic background. From 149 total comparisons, 53 differed at the .05 level using a one-tailed test. Only three favored non-Follow Through; 50 favored the Direct Instruction students.

On the WRAT Reading measures, highly significant differences favoring Follow Through were found in 14 of the 20 comparisons. Two other comparisons reached the .07 level favoring Follow Through; and none favored non-Follow Through. On WRAT Arithmetic significant comparisons favoring Follow Through were found for 4 of the 20 measures, and two more were close ($p < .07$); one favored non-Follow Through. On MAT Reading measures 11 of 39 comparisons were significant, favoring Follow Through; and 3 more were close ($p < .10$). No significant differences favored non-Follow Through. MAT Math favored Follow Through significantly for 12 of 40 comparisons; Science for 3 of 10; Language for 2 of 10; and Spelling 4 of 10. In these 70 comparisons, one favored non-Follow Through. The one negative finding, mentioned above, was for WRAT Level 1 Arithmetic. However, the WRAT Level 2 Arithmetic was almost significant in the opposite direction. The only other two negative findings were on the MAT Spelling test, which favored non-Follow Through.

Overall, the results are strongly supportive of an effect of E-B Follow Through that is persisting (in the absence of special programs) two and three years later. The results in reading (both MAT and WRAT) are especially encouraging. In math, there is a strong trend for MAT Math Problem Solving to show significant or nearly significant effects even when other measures of math number facts are going against the Follow Through. This suggests that the problem-solving approach taught in DISTAR Arithmetic has long-term implications. One would expect even stronger results when the students get to algebra, since the DISTAR approach focuses on row functions, which prepares the students well for algebra. The findings in Science are a nice surprise and have a strong effect. They can be attributed to the DISTAR III Reading program, which uses science content to teach students to learn new rules and to apply them in their reading tasks. It should be kept in mind that these effects were largely produced from three years of program impact (first-starting programs). In the one case with a K-starting group, 24 Follow Through fifth graders were compared with 57 non-Follow Through fifth graders. Even with this small sample, 7 of 14 tests were significant or nearly significant ($p < .10$) in favor of Follow Through. In the other K-starting site only MAT Reading scores were available, and these scores showed no significant differences.

Becker and Engelmann (1976) have also examined the academic gains for those Direct Instruction Follow Through children with IQ's below 80 (the pretest average IQ was 73). Figure 6.3 shows that these children gained more than one grade level on WRAT Reading for each year in the program. WRAT Arithmetic data are comparable. IQ gains were 20.8 points from pre-K to post-K; 7.5 from post-K to post-third; 13.0 from pre-first to post-first; and 4.7 from post-first to post-third. (Because of exaggeration caused by statistical regression effects, true gains would be approximately 70 percent of the reported gains.)

In another study (Becker and Engelmann, 1976) a progressive improvement in student achievement resulted from longer participation in the program. Students from the predominantly Native American community who entered the program in kindergarten scored significantly higher on WRAT Arithmetic, MAT Reading, Math, Language, and

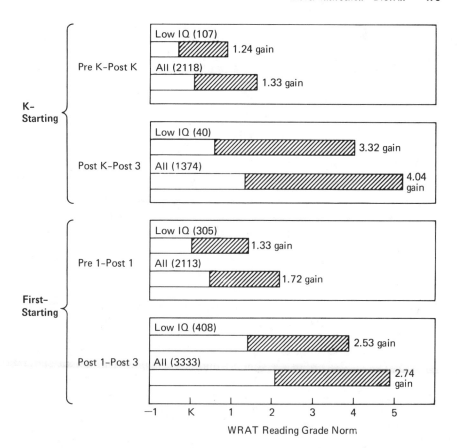

Low IQ = IQ of 80 or less in the Engelmann-Becker Follow Through Program.
All = All children in Engelmann-Becker Follow Through Program.

Figure 6.3. *Reading gains of low IQ, disadvantaged children. Shaded area indicates gain for the time period shown to the left of each chart.*

Spelling than students who entered the program in first or second grade. Students who were in the program four years scored at the 82nd percentile for WRAT Reading, the 58th for WRAT Arithmetic, the 50th for MAT Total Reading, the 66th for MAT Total Math, the 66th for MAT Language, and the 45th for MAT Spelling.

Data on DISTAR effects on average and above average children are very limited. Engelmann and Carnine (1975b) measured performance of average and above average second graders who received two years of DISTAR instruction. The average total reading score was 4.7 on the Stanford Achievement Test at the end of second grade. Questionnaire responses indicated that the students liked the DISTAR Reading Program, felt confident about their performance, and read independently about some of the topics presented in DISTAR Reading III. Data made available by Becker and Engelmann (1973) indicate that non-poor Direct Instruction Follow Through second graders scored at the 4.5 grade level on the WRAT; the low-income second graders' average performance was 3.7. Direct Instruction might not only accelerate middle-class childrens' learning, but also prevent many learning problems currently characterized as learning disabilities.

TEACHING

When a child does things at one point in time that he could not do earlier we are apt to say something new has been *learned*. When someone else's behavior is responsible for a child's new learning, we call the process *teaching*. Teaching is changing what children do or say under particular environmental circumstances.

Teaching Techniques

Teaching is getting a response to occur reliably in the presence of the appropriate stimuli. For example, whenever the child sees the number 7 (stimulus) and the teacher asks "What is this?" (stimulus), the child says "Seven." Any teaching/learning involves three procedures. The first is securing the child's attention. The second is making a clear-cut presentation of the stimulus. The third is reacting to the child's response. When the child makes the correct response, the teacher praises or otherwise rewards that response. This third procedure is based on the principle that systematically rewarded behaviors will recur. When the child makes an error, the teacher corrects. Through reinforced practice, the child knows what is the expected response to that stimulus. (Teaching is essentially the arrangement of stimuli that make learning happen. The teacher presents stimuli; the child responds; the teacher presents other stimuli—either praise or correction.)

Although the arrangement of stimuli is provided in each DISTAR lesson, teacher skill in presenting the stimuli and in reacting to the children's responses is necessary if each child is to be taught. Teaching techniques that have been shown to relate to child behavior are *pacing, feedback* and *corrections, reinforcement* and *signals*. As effective techniques are identified, the feasibility and necessity of training teachers to use these techniques become increasingly important. If teachers demonstrate these skills without training, the training is unnecessary. If they do not demonstrate these skills, however, the question becomes whether they can be trained within a reasonable length of time and at reasonable cost. The teaching techniques, their relation to child performance, and the role of training are discussed below.

Pacing is the rate at which the teacher asks questions and gives instructions. On new or difficult tasks teachers should pause before signaling the children to respond. The pause gives every child enough time to come up with an answer. If the teacher doesn't pause on more difficult tasks, a child may guess or mimic another child's response. The duration of the interval after the children respond and before the teacher asks the next question—which always should be short—defined the fast and slow rates of presentation conditions in a study by Carnine (1976a). Using DISTAR Reading I as the curriculum (Engelmann and Bruner, 1974), he found that during fast-rate presentations when teachers asked about 12 questions per minute, children answered correctly about 80 percent of the time and were off task only about 10 percent of the time. When the teacher asked only four questions per minute the children answered correctly about 30 percent of the time and were off task about 70 percent of the time. The results do not necessarily imply that the faster a teacher presents, the better. As mentioned earlier, a teacher should slow down before requiring the children to respond to a new or difficult task. Grobe, Pettibone, and Martin (1973) reported that a very fast presentation resulted in as much disruption as did a very slow one.

In DISTAR a *correction* is considered as simply more teaching. During *new* learning a correction is never punitive, never an occasion for shame. Neither is it the common guessing game of "Come on, Johnny, think." If the child errs, adequate learning has not yet occurred. This should be conveyed in a matter-of-fact way, so that through more presentation and practice the child can learn the correct response. However, a punitive correction may be used when a child consistently makes errors on tasks that he previously has mastered. Punitive corrections should be used sparingly, but the child should be shown that he is expected to remember and apply what he has learned previously.

To effectively correct errors, the teacher must not only discriminate a mistake from simultaneously occurring correct responses, but also immediately respond to the children appropriately. Carnine (1975b) reported that during arithmetic instruction, correcting errors—in contrast to ignoring them—was associated with more appropriate training and posttest answers. When the teacher corrected errors, the children said the right answer about 70 percent of the time during training and 65 percent of the time during posttest. When the teacher ignored errors, the children said the right answer about 15 percent of the time during training and 15 percent during posttest. Since the arithmetic instruction involved only simple fact teaching, the teacher corrected by giving the answer (providing a model) and repeating the fact question (testing). Other correction procedures are probably more appropriate for more complex tasks.

When children are learning to make multiword responses, chaining and stressing key words in which the teacher responds with the children (leading) probably would be more effective than just a model (Twardosz and Bear, 1973; Risley and Reynolds, 1970). When children must follow several steps to determine an answer, corrections in which the teacher asks questions about the steps tend to be more effective than merely modeling the correct answer (Siegel, 1976; Siegler and Liebert, 1973). In

DISTAR each step is taught separately before the children are expected to follow several steps to solve a problem. Because DISTAR clearly states and frequently reviews the steps, the questions a teacher should ask during correction usually are obvious. Whether modeling, chaining responses, or asking questions about the solution steps, continuing a correction until all children respond correctly and without assistance from the teacher is important (Siegel and Rosenshine, 1973). In summary, proficiency in correcting errors requires that the teacher identify the error, then either model, use chaining and stress key words, or ask questions about the solution steps; and then continue the correction procedure until the children respond appropriately and on their own.

Teachers must not only react appropriately to errors in a small group setting but also anticipate errors to prevent them. When a teacher anticipates an error he or she can precorrect by prompting the children on the aspect of the task that usually causes them difficulty. Fink (1976) prompted two first graders who made frequent decoding errors by asking them to identify the vowel sound before they read the word. He reported that the percent of words accurately read averaged 15 percent without precorrections and 55 percent with precorrections. Teachers also must deal with errors that occur during independent work periods. A teacher can deal with these errors by requiring children to graph their performance and, when necessary, by establishing performance contingencies. Fink and Carnine (1975) reported that arithmetic errors made during an independent work period decreased when the children graphed their performance every day. Walker and Buckley (1974) have reviewed the research literature and discussed procedures for performance contingencies that can be used for independent work.

Although research and discussions concerning *reinforcement* are extensive (e.g., Becker, Engelmann, and Thomas, 1975a), little research has been conducted on praise effects during small group instruction. Kryzanowski (1976) found that when the teacher increased the praise rate during DISTAR Reading I instruction, on-task behavior increased from about 50 to 80 percent. Siegel and Rosenshine (1973), however, reported that praising during DISTAR Language I instruction was not a significant predictor of child achievement. They reported that such other techniques as following the DISTAR Language I lesson plan, correcting mistakes appropriately, requiring the children to respond when the teacher signaled, and pausing before signaling children to respond to a difficult task all were better predictors of student achievement. Teachers proficient in these skills may be applying contingencies that are not reflected in simple approval ratings. Consequently, contingent praise and other easily rated forms of approval are viewed as one technique, but not necessarily the most important one, to be used by DISTAR teachers.

A *signal* can be a hand drop, a clap, a point, a nod, a snap, or other cue that indicates when children are to respond. Signals are intended to produce unison responses in which all the children practice on a skill; yet, since they respond in unison, they do not mimic each other's responses.

A signal also allows a teacher to delay a group's response to a new or difficult task until all children have had time to decide on an answer. Although Siegel and Rosenshine (1973) reported correlational support for the signal's importance during DISTAR Language I instruction, experimental research by Cowart, Carnine, and Becker (1973) indicated a very limited signal effect. When a teacher used signals during DISTAR Arithmetic II instruction (Engelmann and Carnine, 1970), attending occurred 81 percent rather than 57 percent of the time; delayed responding, which would allow late responders to mimic other children's responses, occurred 15 percent rather than 27 percent of the time; and posttest performance averaged 69 percent correct rather than 56 percent. Signal effects during large group instruction also were reported in the same study. When the teacher used signals, the children attended 55 percent rather than 35 percent of the time and responded 80 percent rather than 60 percent of the time. Although the children in the Cowart et al. study were not identified as low performers, subsequent research with low performing children has failed to establish clear signal effects. The lack of consistent data on signaling's importance has not lessened the emphasis on everyone responding during DISTAR instruction but has resulted in less concern about whether all the children begin responding at the same moment. Current research is comparing group responding and individual responding in a small group teaching setting to determine if group responses, rather than all individual responses, result in learning to read more words. This research is important because group responding is central to DISTAR's teaching methodology.

In reviewing the research on relationships between student achievement and classroom teaching variables, Rosenshine (1976) suggested that a direct instruction model best described the variables that correlated with student achievement. In summarizing the effects on primary level, low socioeconomic status classroom performance in reading and math, Rosenshine stated that time spent in group instruction was positively related to achievement; whereas time spent on other activities and working alone was usually negatively related to achievement.

> A drill pattern consisting of questions which the students could answer followed by feedback and subsequent questions was most functional. But clear results were not obtained for various types of questions or types of teacher responses.

> A pattern of direct instruction, consisting of small steps at the student's level and a great deal of work mediated by either the teacher or workbooks, all of which is directed by the teacher, appears most functional (Rosenshine, 1976).

The authors of DISTAR believe that anyone can be a good teacher with specific training; they also think that anyone can be a "fun" teacher. DISTAR developers have included in their programs subject matter that children enjoy: pictures of people eating, unusual animals, and silly mistakes. Certain teacher behaviors—races, fooler games, challenges, creating anticipation, and unpredictably calling on individuals or the group—lend suspense, variety, excitement, and fun to teaching. These behaviors can be learned like any others. The teacher is like an actor; by practicing the role of the fun teacher he or she becomes that teacher.

When children are firm on a group of sounds or numerals, the teacher can race the children to see who can identify the symbol before the teacher does. The teacher seriously emphasizes the desire to win, and when the children win the teacher acts surprised and tells them, "I'm going to study hard so I can win next time." After the children are firm on a skill the teacher can also play a "fooler game," making mistakes deliberately for the children to detect. Students love catching the teacher in a mistake. The teacher can hint about something exciting that is coming later in the lesson. "Wait until you see the take-home for today. It's really something." Fun teaching has great variety. The teacher varies in length of pauses, voice inflections, voice volume, and rate of speech. Variety is added to student response by interspersing group responses with individual turns. The children never know who will be called on next. (Variety is not the only purpose of individual turns. They also are critical in determining if a slower child in a group can perform a skill independently. If the child cannot, additional group practice is needed.) The teacher acts excited and enthusiastic about what is presented, uses the procedures outlined above, and finds that the children are enjoying learning. Some teachers are good at making school fun for children; fewer are so expert at concepts and operations that all children learn. DISTAR has developed procedures and training that enable all teachers to do both simultaneously.

TEACHER TRAINING

The outcome data indicate that a direct instruction system such as DISTAR can enhance child performance and that several teaching techniques may contribute to the system's effectiveneess. The next question is whether training is necessary and if it is, whether prospective and naïve teachers can be trained to implement the techniques adequately. A two-part study (Carnine and Fink, 1976) was conducted. Experiment I determined implementation levels without training and then assessed training effects. Experiment II sought to determine the possible implementation levels for a larger teacher population that was scattered among three different schools and that received training from three different supervisors. Using three naïve teachers as subjects with a multiple baseline design, Experiment I found that the percent of clear and followable signals increased from 29 to 92 percent, 26 to 98 percent; and 29 to 96 percent. The number of questions asked per minute increased from 3.8 to 6.8, 3.8 to 11.8, and 3.6 to 9.4. Although the implementation levels increased after training, they did not equal those of experienced teachers.

Training effects for the 13 teachers in Experiment II were comparable to those in Experiment I, which meant that the implementation level after training was still below the experienced teachers' implementation level. In the corrections study (Carnine, 1975b) the experienced teacher corrected approximately 90 percent of the children's errors, but the prospective teachers corrected only about 60 percent. The data were similar for rate of presentation; the experienced teachers asked 12 questions per minute (Carnine, 1976a), and the teachers in training asked seven per minute. About 75 percent of the prospective teachers' signals were rated as clear and followable. Although the implementation levels for the teachers-in-training were below those of the experienced teachers, training was found to improve implementation. Training that resulted in moderate levels of implementation was found possible for 13 prospective teachers from various schools who received training from different people.

Siegel (1973) reported that when moderate and low DISTAR Language I implementers were trained to correct errors, they used appropriate corrections more often than did control teachers, and their children's adjusted acquisition scores were higher than those of the control children. Experimental studies that measure training effects both in terms of teacher behavior changes and changes in child learning could provide important information about the feasibility and importance of teacher training, not only in a direct instruction system but in other systems as well. The data on training also indicate that measures of program implementation are necessary to evaluate the curriculum in the program. For example, an evaluation of DISTAR in which the teachers were not trained and therefore exhibited low implementation levels for the various techniques would be difficult to interpret. Which effects resulted from the DISTAR curriculum and which resulted from the implementation?

Concept Analysis and Programming

The DISTAR programs just described are based on certain principles of concept analysis and programming. In no way is it essential for everyone who uses DISTAR to be able to analyze and program concepts as the authors have done. However, some knowledge of these areas can be helpful to teachers if they wish to teach a concept or skill not presented in the DISTAR programs and when they need to evaluate other educational teaching sequences or materials. The ideas in this section are unfamiliar to many of us and are, therefore, somewhat difficult.

CONCEPT ANALYSIS

Suppose a five-year-old child suddenly appeared with absolutely no notion of "chair," "red," "vehicle," and "or." Of course, this almost never happens. Most children already know a good deal about what they are supposedly being taught in school, and they have many sources to learn from besides the teacher. This, obviously, is one of the reasons we have so long accepted the nonteaching and poor teaching that pervade our schools. Most children emerge from school knowing some of the things we hoped they would, so we have assumed schools were doing at least a semi-adequate job of teaching. When a child failed to learn we assumed the problem was brain damage, a low IQ, a lack of motivation, a perceptual dysfunction, and so on. A variety of forces and reasons now compel us to question the assumption that our schools have been teaching all children capable of learning.

A child who is capable of learning but has no concept of "chair," "red," "vehicle," or "or" helps us see the teacher's job in better perspective. If a child truly doesn't know something already then how do we teach? Suppose the teacher pointed to a desk chair (wooden, straight backed, oak) and said "chair." Would the child then deduce that the low, fat, soft, round, green, leather object in the dentist's waiting room was the same thing? Hardly. What if the teacher said, "Chairs are what people sit on," and the next picture the child saw was a woman riding a horse?

If to teach "red" the teacher pointed to a red rubber ball and then to an apple, the child might logically conclude that "red" means spherical and that the green balloon is red. How could a teacher present the concepts of "chair," "red," or anything else so that a child could apply them accurately, calling all chairs "chairs" and never calling anything a chair that wasn't? That is what teaching is about—but few can do it.

A teacher does not want to impart rote facts that have no applicability beyond the immediate example presented. A teacher always assumes that what the child learns will allow appropriate function in the presence of a variety of similar situations. A child may never see a problem that requires multiplying 17 by $5\frac{1}{4}$; but if the principles and procedures of multiplication have been taught thoroughly, they can be applied to all problems, including new ones. A well-taught child can respond to the letter "M," whether it is in lower or upper case, in whatever word it appears, and in whatever color or type of print; and that child does not want to say "mmm" when he or she sees "N." Similarly, the child recognizes a car, bus, or truck as a vehicle but does not say "vehicle" when presented with a horse, camel, or donkey.

The teacher intends that the student will learn how to make two kinds of discriminations:

(1) The student will be able to discriminate the set of essential characteristics that defines the concept from the nonessential characteristics. In the vehicle example, the student will learn that a vehicle is man made and takes people places. The other characteristics, e.g., size, shape, and color are irrelevant.

(2) The student must be able to discriminate objects that possess the essential characteristics from those that do not. For example, horses take people places but are not man-made; thus they do not possess both elements of the set of essential characteristics that define vehicles.

The core of DISTAR's contribution to educational programming is analysis of the discriminations that teaching, to succeed, must clarify.

This procedure may be called concept analysis. It is a logical analysis in which three sets of characteristics are identified: 1) the set of characteristics that define the concept, 2) the set that excludes nonexamples from the concept, and 3) the set that is irrelevant.

The set of characteristics is always defined in terms of what the concept is being compared to—the "universe" in which it is presented. The set of essential characteristics change as the instances to which the concept is compared change. For example, we could postulate that the essential characteristics of a square are that it be a closed figure with four sides that are straight and of equal length, connected at four 90-degree angles. However, if a square is compared only to rectangles, some of those characteristics cannot be called essential to squares since rectangles also are closed figures, with four, straight sides, connected at 90-degree angles. What is essential to squares, in this comparison or "universe" is sides of equal length.

Two main considerations determine what goes into any teaching universe. First, the universe must include things with which the concept is likely to be confused. In the square example, rectangle and rhombus would be in the universe, since they are likely to be confused with square. Second, the universe will be determined by how the teaching is to proceed; i.e., how the concept being taught relates to other concepts that will be taught later. In teaching addition, if the aim is to teach only rote facts, then the universe would be all number combinations or facts. If the aim were to teach the mathematical operations involved in addition, however, the universe would contain the following mathematical operations: counting, adding, and subtracting. In the first case rote facts would be discriminated from other rote facts; in the second case a mathematical operation would be distinguished from other mathematical operations.

The reason for requiring that essential characteristics be isolated is that concepts cannot be demonstrated in the abstract. Concepts always are imbedded in some specific example (instance). We cannot touch or see the concept of vehicle but only specific instances of vehicles—cars, buses, trains, and so on. These examples always have many properties— size, location, color, and so on. Those properties essential to the concept of vehicle must be determined (concept analysis), so they can be pointed out clearly and distinguished from those that are not necessary to the idea of vehicle. If this kind of analysis is not done, the programmer inadvertently may use only vehicles that, for example, have four doors, thus teaching the misconception that one of the essential characteristics of vehicle is four-dooredness. The need to determine a concept's characteristics is equalled by the need to determine what are *not* its characteristics. If the examples used to teach vehicle included only those that have the characteristic of taking people places, a child who knows that people can go places on a horse might think that a horse is an instance of vehicle. A child may have the general idea of a concept, but there is no way to know exactly what the boundaries of that concept are unless they are demonstrated—unless instances are presented that are similar to, but not quite the same as, instances of the concept.

DISTAR also applies the rules of concept analysis to the other major type of tasks children are asked to learn—operations. The set of shared characteristics that define an operation has to do with child behaviors rather than with external stimuli. *Skipping* is an operation. For skipping, the set of shared characteristics must exist in the child's movements; whereas the essential characteristics of the concept "red" exist in stimuli that need not involve the child's movements. All the rules for concept analysis apply to operations. The child must learn that skipping has certain characteristics imbedded in many irrelevant characteristics; e.g., skipping is still skipping whether it is done on the sidewalk or in the gym. The child must learn that the essential characteristics of skipping are different from those that define hopping.

Concept learning requires that the student be able to discriminate the set of characteristics that define that concept. After recognizing that set in the clutter of characteristics that make up any instance, the child can recognize when a part of that set is missing.

PROGRAMMING

The authors of DISTAR recognize that both teaching and programming are full-time jobs, but they include programming in the teacher training course so that the teacher has a better understanding of the materials being used and the ability to program, in case some specific has not been programmed. The following is a brief outline of the programming techniques.

First, the programmer must determine the objective, that is, what the child is to know, or in the case of operations, be able to do as a result of the teaching. The programmer then determines the universe based on the two considerations already mentioned: where will the teaching go after this particular concept, and what are the other concepts most likely to be confused with the one being taught? Next, a decision is made about the instances (examples) to be used. The programmer must be sure to include examples of the concepts most closely related to the one being taught; e.g., if teaching square, examples of rectangle and rhombus are included. Carnine (1947a) reported that by selecting a non-instance very close to the instance itself (when the instances range along a continuum) the programmer defines the range of instance values. Students will respond to new stimuli within that range as positive instances and new stimuli beyond that range as non-instances. For example, when geometric forms with one and seven points served as positive instances and forms with eight points served as non-instances, subjects tended to treat stimuli in the range not presented during training—stimuli with three and six points—as positive instances, and to stimuli beyond the range—stimuli with nine points—as non-instances.

When teaching a concept such as square, the programmer also can include non-instances that are less similar to square than rhombus and rectangle. For example, a triangle and various open figures might be conceived as stimuli that lie further from square along a similarity continuum than does a rectangle. Also, such irrelevant characteristics as size, location, color, pattern, and so on, should be varied in both positive instances and non-instances. As mentioned before, varying irrelevant characteristics is intended to avoid teaching a misrule—for example, that squares are closed-figure, *black* lines. The color of the lines is irrelevant, and the instances used should show this. Characteristics that appear in all positive instances but are absent from all non-instances may be treated as essential, whether a teacher intends it that way or not.

> What represents an important dimension of the physical event for the experimenter may not even exist as part of the effective stimulus for the subject. Similarly, the subject may perceive aspects of an experimenter event which have been ignored by, or are unknown to, the experimenter (Prokasy and Hall, 1963, p. 312).

This widely observed phenomenon can be prevented by ensuring that only essential characteristics are present in all positive instances (Miles, Mackintosh, and Westbrook, 1970).

When Carnine (1975c) presented irregular geometric forms with one, two, or three points and containing a dot pattern as positive concepts, the dot pattern controlled responding on a transfer test. When the positive instances lacked dots but the non-instances contained dots, the absence of the dot pattern controlled responding on the transfer test. Only in the third group, when *some* positive instances and *some* non-instances had dots, did the *number of points* control responding on the transfer test.

When two concepts in a universe are very similar, it is more difficult to learn the discrimination between them. Programming techniques can be used to handle these kinds of similar pairs, e.g., exaggerating the difference when the pair is taught. For example, *b* and *d* could be made less confusing by printing *b* in a different type style than *d*—increasing the ways they differ from a mere one (position) to several (slant, thickness, and so on). Carnine (1973) found that children reached criterion significantly faster when matching modified letters than did children who matched standard orthography letters. The benefits of increasing the differences between similar letters has been reported by Hyman and Cohen (1975) and has been incorporated into a fading procedure where the modifications are removed (Oliver, May, and Downing, 1973). Although Trabasso (1963) reported that modifying instances by emphasizing the essential characteristic speeded up acquisition, Carnine (1974c) found that emphasizers did not facilitate learning complex concepts having several essential characteristics.

In any case of similar pairs, one member should be introduced early in the program, so the children have a "fix" on it before seeing the second, similar stimulus or response. Also, a new stimulus should *not* be introduced until the children reach criterion on all previously introduced stimuli. This procedure, called cumulative introduction by Becker, Engelmann, and Thomas (1975b), has resulted in more effective learning than noncumulative procedures (Cheyne, 1966; O'Malley, 1973). Carnine (1976b) reported that both the separation of similar elements (phoneme responses) in order of introduction and the cumulative introduction of each new letter resulted in more accurate letter identifications (Experiment I), more rapid reaching of criterion, and higher posttest scores (Experiment II). The positive effects of separating similar stimuli and responses receive mixed backing in the experimental literature (see Dey, 1970, for a study and brief review).

When a stimulus is presented that is similar to another stimulus in the universe, the two stimuli are presented as a pair to demonstrate the difference between them. The programmer never assumes that the children will notice the single essential characteristic that distinguishes the two stimuli. Granzin and Carnine (1976) reported that presenting stimuli together that differ in only one essential characteristic resulted in more rapid learning than did groupings that differed in several characteristics. They also found that presenting stimuli in pairs was more effective than presenting stimuli one after another. The relative effectiveness of both procedures—presenting minimally different stimuli and presenting stimuli in pairs—was demonstrated for both conjunctive and disjunctive tasks.

Good programming, in addition to anticipating difficult discriminations and preparing for them, allows for a systematic correction procedure. Since a good program teaches all the subskills required in any complex task, a mistake at any point can be corrected by returning to an earlier task. For example, DISTAR reading teaches rhyming patterns such as man, can, fan, ran. If a child later has trouble blending a word beginning with a stop sound, such as *can,* the teacher could say, "Rhymes with "an," starts with *k,* must be. . . ." The importance of teaching the subskills for a more complex task can be demonstrated in two studies—one on decoding and one on fractions. Carnine (1975a) replicated and extended the research of Jeffery and Samuels (1967), Silberman (1964), and Bishop (1964) by showing that teaching the decoding subskills from DISTAR (e.g., sound identification, blending, and saying the blended word at a normal rate) resulted in higher transfer scores—for both regular and irregular words—and required no more instructional time than a whole-word teaching method. In the fractions study, Carnine (1974b) reported that children who learned the subskills for three fraction skills outperformed children who did not learn them. Performance was measured on two transfer tests: one contained new examples of the fraction skills used in training and the other contained related, but untaught, fraction skills.

Finally, the program should include tests that determine whether the students have mastered the preceding steps in the program. If they have not, they repeat the material. The tests are to provide very specific information—what does the student know as a result of the program? To do this, the tests must meet one important criterion: they must test what has been taught and *only* what has been taught. This means that the way the test asks the student to indicate what has been learned must also have been taught. Tests always examine two things: what the student knows (content) and the way it is indicated (response form). If the second part has not been taught, then the student could fail the test for that reason alone. If the content were letter sounds, the form could be, "What is the first sound you hear in this word?" The student would fail if the letter sounds were known but the meaning of "first" was not.

Programming produces a sequence of tasks that—when taught one at time—result in concept learning. The concept is taught through the series of programmed tasks. Teaching focuses on only one of those tasks at a time. Given properly programmed materials, the success of teaching depends upon what happens in that short period during which those tasks are presented.

DISTAR TEACHING PROGRAMS—
LANGUAGE, READING, ARITHMETIC

DISTAR programs in language, arithmetic, and reading are based on concept analysis and programming principles. The format common to all the programs is designed for small group instruction and provides tests to establish the groups and to assist in placement of transfer students. Review lessons and tests are provided throughout. These tests serve a teaching function: they are not for end-of-a-unit grading but are frequent checks that ascertain that the concepts and skills presented have been acquired by all the children. If a child fails a test item, the program specifies the exact lesson to be repeated. As with the correction procedure, the teacher knows precisely what to do to ensure that students know the material and are ready to proceed.

In addition to the in-program tests, criterion-referenced tests also are available (Engelmann, Carnine, and Becker, in press). The tests can be administered by a paraprofessional or other person so that an independent evaluation of child progress is possible. The tests allow for identifying specific skill deficits, placing children in the DISTAR programs, and skipping children ahead in the programs. The tests also suggest remediation assignments for individual children or groups who have not mastered the skills presented.

Although DISTAR is designed for group teaching, it includes some of the advantages of individualized instruction. The programs provide for a great deal of pupil feedback by specifying a minimum amount of teacher presentation time and a maximum amount of student response time. Most lessons include quick checks of individual performance, in addition to group responses. When the group responds in unison, errors or hesitation by one child can be spotted by the teacher. Unison responses are achieved through cues signaling when to respond and what type of response is required. For example, the direction, "Say it fast," tells the students to telescope a previously drawn-out word; and a hand signal tells them when to say the word. The second characteristic of individualized instruction—attention to individual learning problems—is provided in two ways. First, the programs themselves, because they break down complex skills and present the subskills clearly, eliminate many errors that would require individual work. Secondly, for the errors that do occur, there are specific, fast-moving correction formulas that take little time away from the group.

The programs specify what to say, where to point, how to signal the children to respond, when to praise, how to handle incorrect answers, and so on. The format is to be followed exactly, since in many cases a particular skill will depend upon mastery of preceding skills. Thus, the programs resemble a task ladder—each step requires the attainment of the preceding steps. This high degree of specificity is necessary for completely clear teaching of complex skills. Since the teacher does not have to program these skills, however, the time and freedom are available to concentrate on perfecting presentation and to think out remedies for individual academic and behavioral problems.

Language

DISTAR language is designed to teach the language of the classroom to children who, for whatever reasons, have not yet mastered it. Some children do not understand the language the teacher uses. Teachers present new material, but for some children it is not only the material that is new but the *form* of the presentation itself—the language through which it is expressed.

> A teacher cannot teach a complex concept without presenting some examples of the concept and pointing out the characteristics of the example that make it unique. When the teacher presents "water-worn stones," for example, she first identifies the objects by saying "These are stones," then tells what is unique about these stones. The teacher assumes that the children understand the concept smooth, also that they understand the meaning of water-worn, shaped like a disk, and brown. Regardless of what is taught, the teacher will use words that describe the examples, referring to size, shape, color, appearance and so forth. If the children are to learn anything from demonstrations, they must understand the teacher's language. They must have mastered the language of instruction, which encompasses all the basic descriptions used by the teacher to discuss examples of a concept (Engelmann and Osborn, 1969, p. 6).

The following is a brief outline of the types of tasks used in Language I to teach the skills necessary to understand the language of instruction (Engelmann and Osborn, 1976, pp. 2–3).

The first group of tasks, Description of Objects, teaches the following skills:

1. Naming common objects. *(A ball. An ant.)*
2. Making statements that identify common objects. *(This is a ball. This is an ant.)*
3. Making *not* statements. *(This is not a pencil.)*
4. Describing the properties of objects. *(This ball is big. This cup is full.)*
5. Describing positional relations of objects. *(This ball is under the table. This cup is on the table.)*
6. Making plural statements. *(These are girls. These dogs are running.)*
7. Making comparative statements. *(The rock is bigger than the ball. The tree is taller than the bush.)*

The second group, Actions, teaches:

1. Following simple commands. *(Touch your shoe. Stand up.)*
2. Responding with actions to tasks that involve understanding pronouns, prepositions, plurals, tense, and so forth. *(Hold your hand over your head. What is she doing?)*
3. Describing actions illustrated in pictures. *(The boy is running. The dog is eating.)*

Instructional Words is a group of tracks that teach:

1. Words that describe groups of objects *(some, all, none)* and statements that incorporate these words. *(I am holding up some of my fingers. I am holding up all of my fingers. I am holding up none of my fingers.)*
2. Words that are used to ask specific questions *(who, what, where, when).* *(Who jumped over the box? What did the boy do? Where is the box? When did the boy jump over the box?)*
3. Words that describe similarities *(same, different)* and statements that incorporate these words. *(A bird and an airplane are the same because they both fly. A bird and an airplane are different because one is an animal and one is not.)*
4. Conditional words *(or, if)* and statements that incorporate these words. *(I'm going to sing or cry or frown. If the teacher says "go," touch your head.)*
5. The combining word *and* and statements that incorporate this word. *(I am sitting down and touching my nose.)*
6. Words that describe temporal sequence *(before, after)* and statements that incorporate these words. *(You touched your head before you touched your elbow. The woman drove the car after she fixed the tire.)*

The group of Classification formats teach:

1. The class names for animals, vehicles, tools, clothing, food, furniture, containers, plants, and buildings.
2. The names of members of different classes. *(A dog, a lion, an elephant, a mouse are animals. A cup, a purse, a suitcase, a bowl are containers.)*

3. Rules for some classifications. *(If it can take you places, it's a vehicle. If you put things in it, it's a container.)*

The Information group teaches:

1. Personal and school information. *(The child's first name, whole name; teacher's name; name of school and city.)*
2. The relationship between objects and their parts; the names of parts of objects and their functions.
3. Calendar information. *(Days of the week, months, and seasons of the year.)*
4. Common information about different occupations *(a carpenter, a doctor, a fire fighter, for example)*; common objects and how they are used *(a thermometer, for example, used to measure temperature)*; and natural phenomena *(clouds and the sun are things in the sky, for example)*.
5. Information about different locations *(a farm, a grocery store, a library, for example)* and what is commonly found in each *(cows, sheep, a barn, and a tractor are typically found on a farm.)*

The Applications group expands concepts taught in other groups through:

1. Problem-solving exercises that incorporate previously taught concepts.
2. Exercises that require the child to identify what is absurd about an illustrated situation.

The lessons all require a combination of judgment and then practice in the concept. For example, in the sequence to teach that not-statements are used whenever "no" is said, the children are shown a picture of a boy eating and are asked, "Is the boy combing his hair?" Only the simplest judgment response is required—"No." Then they are asked to make a complete statement, "The boy is not combing his hair."

For some children, these lessons constitute a new language, so the program is arranged to give the child the maximum amount of teacher-monitored practice in each language period. Basic language patterns are used consistently; only when they are mastered are alternatives introduced. The repetition of these patterns has led to the charge that DISTAR is a return to old-style, rote learning. In replying, the authors of DISTAR make a distinction between two types of repetition—rote learning and drill. If practice is required on idiomatic information that has little general utility, it is rote learning and fairly useless. If practice is used to insure student mastery of nonidiomatic, easily generalized patterns, however, then it is drill and this practice is valuable. For example, "not" is an extremely important concept—its utility is not limited to a few peculiar expressions. The amount of practice required by some children to master this concept may seem excessive, but the practice is necessary for some, and it is meaningful—because the content practiced is meaningful.

In Language II (Engelmann and Osborn, 1971) definitions, descriptions, questioning skills, analogies, synonyms, and opposites, and verb tenses are taught. In Language III (Engelmann and Osborn, 1972) children learn to discriminate sentences from nonsentences; to identify subjects, predicates, and verbs; to make subjects and verbs agree; to discriminate among questions, statements, and commands; to punctuate sentences; to use capitals, commas, quotation marks, contractions, and abbreviations; and to identify adjectives and adverbs. The children learn to write first by answering questions about pictures, briefly describing events and objects, and by writing stories. Finally, children are given a problem-solving situation and are asked to identify information provided in a statement as relevant or redundant. They are asked whether deductions based on the information are true, false, or doubtful.

Arithmetic

DISTAR Arithmetic I (Engelmann and Carnine, 1975a) does not start out with memorization of math facts. Rather, the program is set up to teach a way of going about answering such questions as: Seven plus three equals how many? ($7 + 3 = \square$); Six plus how many equals nine? ($6 + \square = 9$). Since all these questions involve quantity—how many— they all can be answered by counting. It is by teaching how counting operations can answer these questions that DISTAR teaches the basis for understanding and remembering arithmetic facts. The following questions and answers are from the DISTAR Arithmetic I Teachers' Guide (Engelmann and Carnine, 1975a, pp. 2–4).

DO THE CHILDREN LEARN TO HANDLE BASIC
OPERATIONS BY ROTE?

No. The children learn a precise strategy for handling basic problems, which will continue to apply later on to problems that are far more complex than those in Arithmetic I.
For example, here is a simple addition problem:

$$5 + 2 = \square$$

The children are taught the following strategy for solving this problem:

1. Find the equal sign, and apply the "equality rule." (You must end up with the same number on this side and on the other side.)
2. Figure out which side to start counting on. The children have learned they can't start counting on the side with a box, because the box doesn't tell how many lines to draw (what number to count to). The side with $5 + 2$ has no box, so counting must start on that side.
3. Ring the side with $5 + 2$ as a reminder to count everything on the *side*.

$$\boxed{5 + 2} = \square$$

4. Determine the operation to be performed. The + tells the children they are "plussing" two, so they draw two lines under 2.

$$\left(\begin{array}{c} 5 + 2 \\ || \end{array}\right) = \square$$

5. Count everything on the side. The numeral 5 in the first group tells the children to count from five. "Fiiivvve . . ." Then they touch each line under 2 and count: ". . . six, seven."
6. Summarize the results. The children ask themselves, "What number did I end up with on the side with five plus two? Seven."
7. Apply the equality rule to balance the equation. According to the rule, you must end up with the same number on both sides. If you end up with seven on the side with five plus two, you must end up with seven on the other side.
8. Write the answer in the box.

$$\left(\begin{array}{c} 5 + 2 \\ || \end{array}\right) = \boxed{7}$$

The children learn similar strategies for analyzing and solving algebra-addition and subtraction problems. All of these strategies are based on understanding the symbols in a given problem: =, $\square$ ("how many"), + or — signs (count forward or backward), and the numerals.

WHAT ARE THE ADVANTAGES OF TEACHING STRATEGIES?

1. A single strategy can be applied to a wide range of problems. For example, once a child has learned the strategy for solving an addition problem such as $5 + 2 = \square$, he can use the same approach to solve other similar problems such as $7 + 5 = \square$, $4 + \square = 7$, etc. He has been taught how to attack the problem. A child who relies on memorizing answers, however, must learn each new fact as a separate entity. The amount of learning involved is enormous and may become overwhelming. (It should be pointed out that *some* children figure out the relationship between addition and counting: Distar Arithmetic teaches *all* children this skill.)
2. If children are taught precise strategies, you will be able to correct their mistakes in a more meaningful way. Consider the situation in which a child arrives at this solution to an algebra-addition problem:

$$3 + \boxed{10} = 7$$

If the child has learned a precise strategy, the teacher can correct the mistake so that he will actually learn something from the correction. The correction would take this form:

Teacher: Erase the numeral in the box. (Wait.)

Teacher: Ring the side you start counting on.
Child: (The child rings 7.)

If there's any confusion at this point, the child can be reminded that he can't start counting on the side with a box because the box doesn't tell him how many lines to draw.

Teacher: What number do you end up with on that side?
Child: Seven.
Teacher: So what number must you end up with on the other side?
Child: Seven.
Teacher: Yes, seven.

If there is any confusion at this point, the child can be referred back to the equality rule.

Teacher: Count everything on the other side.

There are three in the first group, so the child counts from three, drawing lines under the box as he counts to seven.

Child: Thrreee . . . four, five, six, seven.

$$3 + \Box = \enspace \boxed{7}$$
$$| \, | \, | \, |$$

Teacher: What number did you end up with on this side?
Child: Seven.
Teacher: Yes, seven. Look at the problem and tell me what numeral you're going to write in the box.
Child: Four.

If the child responds incorrectly, you can refer him to the rule about the lines under a box:

Teacher: Tell me the rule about the lines under a box.
Child: The lines under a box tell what numeral goes in that box.
Teacher: How many lines are under the box?
Child: Four.
Teacher: So what numeral goes in the box?
Child: Four.
Teacher: Write four in the box. (Wait.)
Teacher: How many do you end up with on the side with three plus four?
Child: Seven.
Teacher: And how many do you plus?
Child: Four.

This correction will facilitate the child's learning and understanding. It will reduce his confusion and clarify the unique characteristics of algebra-addition problems.

3. Teaching precise strategies serves as a logical prerequisite for teaching arithmetic facts.

Consider this situation. A teacher asks a child, "What's seven plus three?" The child answers, "Sixteen." If the child has been taught a strategy, the teacher can say to her, "Figure out the answer." And the child who has mastered the strategy can "figure it out" by starting with a "plus-one" statement she knows and saying a series of addition statements—"7 plus 1 equals 8, 7 plus 2 equals 9, 7 plus 3 equals 10." Being able to say these statements to figure out the answer puts the child in a more comfortable situation. Furthermore, she can "prove" things to herself:

Some children develop strategies intuitively. The DISTAR philosophy holds that children shouldn't be penalized if they lack this intuition. The strategies are, therefore, basic to the program and are presented so that every child can master them.

HOW ARE CHILDREN TAUGHT THE BASIC STRATEGIES?

The elements of each component called for in a strategy are taught separately. An example of a component essential to all of the strategies is the equality rule: You must end up with the same number on this side and on the other side.

The elements that must be taught before the children can apply this rule to simple equations are listed below:

1. Symbol identification (=, □, +, numerals)
2. Meaning of "end up with"
3. Meaning of "this side" and "other side"
4. Meaning of "same number"

Each element is taught separately and mastered. Then the elements are combined slowly, resulting finally in an understanding of the whole component—the equality rule.

The elements listed above are taught as follows:

1. Symbols are introduced slowly in Arithmetic I. For example, by the time the children have reached lesson 45, they have been introduced to only these symbols: 4, =, 2, 6, □, and +.

   The introduction is slow so that every child will master every symbol. The program provides for adequate repetition and drill to ensure that children will probably not confuse the = with the + or the 4 with the 6.

2. "End up with" is taught in a variety of counting tasks before the equality rule is introduced. The children count objects and the teacher asks, "What number did you end up with?" In the rote counting tasks the teacher says, "You're going to count and end up with eight. What number are you going to end up with? . . ."

3. "This side" and "other side" are taught using a simple equation such as ⑦ = □. The teacher points to ⑦ and says, "Read everything on *this side* of the equals." She continues to touch ⑦ . "Now read everything on the *other side* of the equals." The children work many examples like this one. The examples teach the meaning of the words "this side" and "other side."

4. In tasks teaching "same number" the teacher asks, "What's the same number as seven? . . . What's the same number as nine? . . . etc." In another set of exercises the teacher writes 4 on the board. She says, "Tell me if I end up with the same number as four." She draws two lines on the board. "How many lines did I draw? . . . Is that the same number as four?"

A variety of similar exercises are presented to the children. When they have completed the exercises, they understand the meaning of "same number."

After the vocabulary elements have been taught, the children learn how to apply the rule. Here is an example of problems they work on:

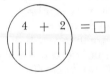

The teacher points to the left side of the equation and presents the rule: "You must end up with the same number on this side and on the other side." Then she touches the lines as the children count. And then she asks, "What number did you end up with on this side? . . . So what number must you end up with on the other side?" The children say, "Six," and the teacher draws six lines under the box and writes the numeral 6 in the box.

After the children master all the components essential to a strategy, they are ready to work problems independently.

The analytical approach that is used to teach the equality rule is used to teach everything the children use in the program—every fact, every bit of information, the meaning of every word, the understanding of every operation.

DISTAR Arithmetic I also teaches a backward counting strategy for solving subtraction problems, simple story problems, more-or-less problems with the < and > signs, 35 addition facts, and ordinal counting. Arithmetic II (Engelmann and Carnine, 1976) covers 60 addition facts, 20 algebra addition facts, and 43 subtraction facts; column addition involving carrying; multiplication with single digit numbers; telling time to the nearest five minutes after the hour; identifying coins and determining the value for different coin groups; making statements of equivalence in metric and standard units; fraction problems—decoding proper and improper fractions, drawing fraction pictures, making more-than and less-than comparisons, and multiplying and reducing fractions; working story problems involving addition and subtraction classification forms, multiplication and algebra multiplication, fractions, coins, and measurement. Arithmetic III (Engelmann and Carnine, 1972) extends the basic operations—adding several multidigit numbers, borrowing, column multiplication, and long division. Story problems are extended to include these operations as well as adding and subtracting fractions with like denominators. Addition and subtraction fact teaching is continued, and multiplication facts are introduced. Formal problem-solving procedures—substitution, terms, analogies, factoring, and algebra—also are introduced.

Reading

DISTAR reading is auditory, phonic, and highly structured. Like other reading programs, its goal is comprehension. And although it includes techniques for teaching comprehension, it does not treat reading initially as a comprehension process. The reason for this ordering of priorities is that a child must be able to *say* the word before the meaning can be considered. A child may comprehend what is meant by the words "house" and "horse"; but if the two words cannot be distinguished in print the ability to comprehend will be poorly utilized. Thus, word identification *must* come before comprehension. DISTAR calls this pre-comprehension skill *code-cracking*. Code-cracking is a collection of sub-skills that together allow a child to decode squiggles-on-pages into words. The following discussion of the code-cracking subskills is taken from the DISTAR Reading I Teachers' Guide (Engelmann and Bruner, 1974, pp. 2–3).

> We can figure out what skills should be taught before children are introduced to word reading by analyzing a simple word such as *mat*. What skills must a child have to "attack" this word and any similar word?
>
> *Symbol Identification.* The children must be able to recognize the letter symbols and produce the sounds they represent.
>
> *Sequencing.* The children need to know the order in which to read the symbols.
>
> *Blending.* The children need to know that a word can be pulled apart by sounding it out and that once a word is sounded out it can be put back together by saying the sounds fast.
>
> *Rhyming.* The children need rhyming skills so that they will be aware of similarities among words.
>
> When the children begin to read words, they use all these prereading skills. They sound out words, blend the sounds together, and then say the sounds fast to come up with the word.

The skills the children need in preparation for reading are taught in the following tracks: Sounds, Symbol Action Game, Say the Sounds, Say It Fast, Sound It Out, and Rhyming.

Sounds. In the Sounds track, the children learn to recognize the symbols and produce the sounds for which they stand. They learn that *a* stands for *aaa* as in *and,* while *ā* stands for the vowel sound in the word *ate.* They do not learn the letter names until they are into the second level of the Reading program. Since the ability to recognize and reproduce sounds is the key element in decoding words—and thus in reading—sounds exercises are taught each day in DISTAR Reading I.

Symbol Action Game. Children learn left-to-right sequence through the Symbol Action Games, which appear in each of the first 24 days of the program. The exercises in this track start by teaching children to sequence two or three actions in time and end by showing them how to follow a sequence of action pictures laid out along an arrow. The skills learned through the Symbol Action Games prepare the children for reading words and sentences from left to right.

Say the Sounds. The children learn how to break a word they hear into its separate sounds through oral exercises called Say the Sounds, a track running from lesson 22 to lesson 45. The teacher gives them a word orally, and they reply by saying the word slowly, one sound at a time. From the first exercise they are taught not to stop between the sounds. After they have said the word slowly, they put it back together again by saying it fast.

Say It Fast. Say It Fast is an oral blending skill that prepares children to put a sounded-out word back together again. In this track the teacher says words at a slow rate, and the children respond by saying the words at a normal rate. If the teacher says, "Listen. Tele—phone. . . What word did I say?" the child should be able to identify the word. He must learn to do this telescoping, or blending, from an oral cue before he can be expected to say words fast after sounding out the symbols that make up a written word. Practice in this type of blending starts on the first day of the program and continues through day 34.

Sound It Out. In the Sound It Out track, beginning at lesson 26, the children do everything needed to read a word except to say it fast. They identify each sound in order and blend the sounds together. The exercises differ from Say the Sounds exercises in two ways:

1. Children are working from written words rather than from words presented orally by the teacher.
2. Children are not asked to "say it fast" after sounding out the written word; later, when they do say the words fast, they will be reading.

Rhyming. Rhyming is introduced at lesson 18, after the children know some sounds and have had some experience with "saying it fast." They read the initial sounds in the rhyming exercises, but the word ending (the rhyming element) is presented orally by the teacher. Rhyming provides children with an additional word attack skill. If a child understands how rhyming works, he can discover the relationship between how words look and how they sound.

After the children learn the prereading skills, they begin reading regular words that begin with continuous sounds. Later they learn to sound out stop-sound-first words and irregular words. Sounding out is used to decode both isolated words and words in stories; later the children identify words without first sounding them out. Simple comprehension questions, written exercises, and spelling assignments also are important components of Reading I. In Reading II (Engelmann and Bruner, 1975) children encounter traditional orthography; learn the letter names; and decode more irregular words, words with common letter combinations, words with common endings, words that end in *e,* and compound words. Comprehension is emphasized more than in Reading I—the children work a variety of following instruction tasks, answer story review questions, and learn to make deductions and apply rules. Reading III (Engelmann and Stearns, 1972) focuses almost entirely on comprehension—teaching the children to read textbooks for new information and to be able to answer concept questions. Although some of the stories are historical or fictional, most involve scientific rules that the children learn to apply. Topics include pressure laws, muscle movement, astronomy, and the atom.

THE CHILD AND DISTAR

The teacher is the only person charged with imparting the academic skills that are essential for a productive life in our highly complex society. Parents, community groups, peers, and counselors all can develop social skills in children and will not be considered remiss if the child is not an academic success. But the teacher who develops only social skills is a failure. There is no other agency but the school that is charged with passing on our academic heritage. For DISTAR's authors, academic achievement is the teacher's primary responsibility, but that achievement does not have to come at the expense of other areas of development. They see no conflict between academic and emotional-social development. In fact, they see them as complementary, rather than conflicting.

The DISTAR programs teach academic skills, but in every learning encounter there are two kinds of learning going on: content-dependent concepts and content-independent concepts. The latter are the concepts the children learn about learning and about themselves such as, "I am a success. I can do it if I try." The DISTAR developers have structured their work so that children learn positive things about themselves and education. In the first place, the content is material children enjoy; the teacher presentations are set up to be fun and fast moving; and the children are warmly praised for the work they do. Because the steps in the program are small enough that children are not faced with a hopeless task, they learn that they *can* do things. They experience success; they come to view themselves as successful people. DISTAR teaching is never punitive; it *is* work, but it is not punitive. If the student isn't "getting it," the teacher leaves it, reworks the presentation, and tries again later. In line with DISTAR's basic premise, the teacher looks at what he or she is doing if a child is not learning. Self-esteem grows from the knowledge that "I can do it." With this program, children have evidence every day that they are competent.

There are some data indicating that child competence leads to a "positive self-image." A recent Abt report (1976) on four-year Follow Through effects found that children in four out of the five DISTAR sites had significantly higher self-esteem measures than did control children. Kim, Berger, and Kratochirl (1972, p. 39) summarized findings from a preschool study using the DISTAR method:

> By using such measures as behavioral observations, teacher ratings, and attendance patterns in the regular program, it was determined that children from the Engelmann prekindergarten program were better adjusted than children from the enrichment preschool or the control group.

All the DISTAR programs have built-in devices to teach children to trust and rely on their own judgment. After a skill is mastered, the teacher plays the "fooler" game in which deliberate mistakes are made that the children have to catch. They learn that it is their judgment of what is going on that is reliable. They trust their judgment, because they *know*, not just because "the teacher says so." Besides experiencing individual accomplishment, they also learn how to work in a group. They experience the satisfaction of group cooperative success—a very important social skill.

There is no DISTAR program to teach children how to play happily together. Nor is there a program to develop creative expression. But if a teacher wished, settings and programs could be developed to accomplish these and other aims, without in any way slighting academic development. These other programs would be a complement rather than a substitute for academic growth. Because of the proven efficiency of the DISTAR programs, the teacher has time for much more than is possible in many traditional classrooms. DISTAR-type programs—and there are other successful programs—have enabled teachers to indulge in a have-your-cake-and-eat-it-too situation unknown before the advent of pleasurable and efficient teaching methods.

REFERENCES

ABT ASSOCIATES, *Education as experimentation: a planned variation model* (Vol. III). Boston: Author, 1976.

BECKER, W. C., and S. E. ENGELMANN, *Technical report 73-2*. Eugene, Oregon: University of Oregon, 1973.

———, *Technical report 1976-1*. Eugene, Oregon: University of Oregon, 1976.

BECKER, W. C., ENGELMANN, S. E., and THOMAS, D. R. *Teaching 1: Classroom Management*. Palo Alto: Science Research Associates, 1975(a).

————, *Teaching 2: Cognitive Learning and Instruction.* Palo Alto: Science Research Associates, 1975(b).

BISHOP, C. H., Transfer effects of word and letter training in reading. *Journal of Verbal Learning and Verbal Behavior,* 1964, *3,* 215–221.

CARNINE, D. W., *Modifying graphemes to increase discriminability.* Unpublished manuscript (mimeo). Eugene, Oregon: University of Oregon, 1973.

————, *Discriminating stimuli that appear between two discriminative stimuli along a numerosity continuum from stimuli that appear beyond a discriminative stimulus.* Unpublished manuscript (mimeo). Eugene, Oregon: University of Oregon, 1974(a).

————, *Effects of teaching rules and component skills on children's acquisition of three fraction operations and in transfer.* Unpublished manuscript (mimeo). Eugene, Oregon: University of Oregon, 1974(b).

————, *Emphasizer effects on children's and adults' acquisition rate and transfer score on simple and complex stimuli.* Unpublished manuscript (mimeo). Eugene, Oregon: University of Oregon, 1974(c).

————, *A comparison of two beginning reading approaches with regard to training time, sounds learned, and transfer scores on regular and irregular words.* Unpublished manuscript (mimeo). Eugene, Oregon: University of Oregon, 1975(a).

————, *Correction effects on academic performance during small group instruction.* Unpublished manuscript (mimeo). Eugene, Oregon: University of Oregon, 1975(b).

————, *Establishing a discriminative stimulus by distributing attributes of compound stimuli between instances and not-instances.* Unpublished manuscript (mimeo). Eugene, Oregon: University of Oregon, 1975(c).

————, Effects of two teacher presentation rates on off-task behavior, answering correctly, and participation, *Journal of Applied Behavioral Analysis,* 1976(a), *9,* in press.

————, *Similar sound separation and cumulative introduction in learning letter-sound correspondences.* Unpublished manuscript (mimeo). Eugene, Oregon: University of Oregon, 1976(b).

CARNINE, D. W., and W. T. FINK, *Increasing rate of presentation and use of signals in direct instruction teacher trainers.* Unpublished manuscript (mimeo). Eugene, Oregon: University of Oregon, 1976.

CHEYNE, W. M., Vanishing cues in paired-associate learning. *British Journal of Psychology,* 1966, *57,* 351–359.

COWART, J., CARNINE, D. W., and W. C. BECKER, *The effects of signals on attending, responding, and following in direct instruction.* Unpublished manuscript (mimeo). Eugene, Oregon: University of Oregon, 1973.

DEY, M. K., Influences of the sequence of similar stimulation of paired-associate learning. *Journal of General Psychology,* 1970, *83,* 255–265.

ENGELMANN, S., *Preventing Failure in the Primary Grades.* Chicago: Science Research Associates, 1969. © 1969, Science Research Associates, Inc. Reprinted by permission.

————, The effectiveness of direct instruction on IQ performance and achievement in reading and arithmetic. In J. Hellmuth (Ed.), *Disadvantaged Children,* Vol. 3, New York: Brunner/Mazel, 1970.

ENGELMANN, S., and E. BRUNER, *Distar ® Reading Level I.* Chicago: Science Research Associates, 1974. © 1974, 1969, Science Research Associates, Inc. Reprinted by permission.

———, *Distar ® Reading Level II.* Chicago: Science Research Associates, 1975.

ENGELMANN, S., and D. CARNINE, *Distar ® Arithmetic Level III.* Chicago: Science Research Associates, 1972.

———, *Distar ® Arithmetic I.* Chicago: Science Research Associates, 1975(a). Copyright © 1975, 1969 by Science Research Associates, Inc. Reprinted by permission.

———, *A structured program's effect on the attitudes and achievement of average and above average second graders.* Unpublished manuscript (mimeo). Eugene, Oregon: University of Oregon, 1975(b).

———, *Distar ® Arithmetic Level II.* Chicago: Science Research Associates, 1976, 1970.

ENGELMANN, S., CARNINE, D. W., and W. C. BECKER, *Continuous Test for Distar Arithmetic I.* Chicago: Science Research Associates, in press.

ENGELMANN, S., and J. OSBORN, *Distar ® Language Level II.* Chicago: Science Research Associates, 1971.

———, *Distar ® Language Level III.* Chicago: Science Research Associates, 1972.

———, *Distar ® Language Level I.* Chicago: Science Research Associates, 1976. © 1976, 1972, 1969 by Science Research Associates, Inc. Reprinted by permission.

ENGLEMAN, S., J. OSBORN, and T. ENGELMAN, *The Teachers' Guide, Distar Language 1: An Introductional System.* Chicago: Science Research Associates, 1969.

ENGELMANN, S., and S. STEARNS, *Distar Reading Level III.* Chicago: Science Research Associates, 1972.

FINK, W. T., *Effects of a pre-correction procedure on the decoding errors of two low-performing first grade girls.* Unpublished manuscript (mimeo). Eugene, Oregon: University of Oregon, 1976.

FINK, W. T., and D. W. CARNINE, Control of arithmetic errors using informational feedback and graphing. *Journal of Applied Behavioral Analysis,* 1975, *8,* 461.

GRANZIN, A. C., and D. W. CARNINE, *Child performance on discrimination tasks: effects of amount of stimulus variation.* Unpublished manuscript (mimeo). Eugene, Oregon: University of Oregon, 1976.

GROBE, R. P., PETTIBONE, T. J., and D. W. MARTIN, Effects of lecturer pace on noise level in a university classroom. *Journal of Educational Research,* 1973, *67,* 73–75.

HYMAN, J., and S. A. COHEN, The effects of verticality as a stimulus property on the letter discrimination of young children. *Journal of Learning Disabilities,* 1975, *8,* 41–49.

JEFFERY, W. E., and S. J. SAMUELS, Effect of method of reading training on initial learning and transfer. *Journal of Verbal Learning and Verbal Behavior,* 1967, *6,* 354–358.

KIM, Y., BERGER, B. J., and D. W. KRATOCHIRL, *Distar Instructional System.* Palo Alto: American Institute for Research, 1972.

KRYZANOWSKI, J. A., *Praise effects on inappropriate behavior during small group instruction.* Unpublished manuscript (mimeo). Eugene, Oregon: University of Oregon, 1976.

McDaniels, G. L., The evaluation of Follow Through. *Educational Researcher,* 1975, *4* (11), 7–11 (a).

————, Follow Through yields new evidence of school effects. *Education Daily,* March 20, 1975, p. 5 (b).

Miles, C. G., Mackintosh, N. J., and R. G. Westbrook, Redistributing control between the elements of a compound stimulus. *Quarterly Journal of Experimental Psychology,* 1970, *22,* 478–483.

Oliver, P. R., May, R. B., and J. Downing, Transfer of grapheme discrimination from cued to traditional orthography. *Journal of Experimental Education,* 1973, *41* (4), 82–87.

O'Malley, J. M., Stimulus dimension pretraining and set size in learning multiple discriminations with letters of the alphabet. *Journal of Educational Research,* 1973, *67,* 41–45.

Prokasy, W. F., and J. F. Hall, Primary stimulus generalization. *Psychological Review,* 1963, *70,* 310–322.

Risley, T. R., and N. J. Reynolds, Emphasis as a prompt for verbal imitation. *Journal of Applied Behavior Analysis,* 1970, *3,* 185–190.

Rosenshine, B., Classroom instruction. In N. L. Gage (Ed.), *Psychology of Teaching: The 77th Yearbook of the National Society for the Study of Education.* Chicago: National Society for the Study of Education, 1976.

Science Research Associates, *Summaries of Case Studies on the Effectiveness of the Distar Instructional System.* Chicago: Author, 1971.

Siegel, M., Teacher behaviors and curriculum packages: Implications for research and teacher education. In L. J. Rubin, ed., *Handbook of curriculum.* Boston: Allyn & Bacon, 1976.

Siegel, M. A., and B. Rosenshine, *Teacher behavior and student achievement in the Bereiter-Engelmann Follow-Through Program.* Paper presented at the annual meeting of the American Educational Research Association, New Orleans, February, 1973. (ERIC Document Reproduction No. ED 076 564.)

Siegler, R. S., and R. M. Liebert, Effects of presenting relevant rules and complete feedback on the conservation of liquid quantity task. *Developmental Psychology,* 1973, *7,* 133–138.

Silberman, H. F., *Exploratory research on a beginning reading program.* Technical Memorandum No. TM-895/100/00. Santa Monica: System Development Corporation, 1964.

Stallings, J. A., and D. H. Kaskowitz, *Follow Through Classroom Observation Evaluation.* Menlo Park, California: Stanford Research Institute, 1974.

Trabasso, T. R., Stimulus emphasis and all-or-none learning in concept identification. *Journal of Experimental Psychology,* 1963, *65,* 398–406.

Twardosz, S., and D. M. Baer, Training two severely retarded adolescents to ask questions. *Journal of Applied Behavior Analysis,* 1973, *6,* 655–661.

Walker, H. M., and N. K. Buckley, *Token reinforcement techniques.* Eugene, Oregon: E-B Press, 1974.

Part III

Systematic
Instructional
Procedures

7

INTRODUCTION

The last three chapters covered information on various techniques and methods for dealing with the problems of the learning disabled child. From perceptual-motor programs to the DISTAR program, many advances have been made in providing educational opportunities and special services to mildly handicapped children. Research to measure the success or failure of these programs often is inconclusive or controversial. Programmatic research with learning disabled children has indicated that no one method or approach works with every child and that every learning problem is unique. The need for individualization of instruction through educational assessment and careful analysis of the resulting data is thus obvious. In special education, children are referred because of a variety of reasons. Often overlooked is one common reason for inadequate performance—an educational program that has not been individualized to suit the needs of individual students. *Learning disabilities often prove to be instructional disabilities.* Overwhelmingly convincing experimental evidence shows that employing almost microscopically precise analysis of individual ability, the systematic arrangement of instruction, and the instructional environment are effective and efficient steps in teaching the learning disabled child. If children with academic and perceptual handicaps are to achieve proficiency in the basic skills, so that advancement in the educational system and then in society is possible, instruction must be designed to the child's specific learning needs.

As the title indicates, we will focus on procedures in this chapter. We will speak about technology. Perhaps this is a good place to insert a cautionary note. It is fair to say that the best technologist in the world may not be a very good teacher if he or she has nothing to teach with the technology, has no particular skills to impart with these procedures. In the early days of applied behavior analysis, when technology was beginning to be applied in practical settings, the major emphasis was on observation of children's responses and on the attempt to strengthen desired responses and extinguish undesirable ones. The emphasis was on the consequences of responses, that is, on reinforcement. But as behaviorists have become more skilled in applying their technology, they also have realized that the whole process could be accelerated by increased attention to antecedent conditions—that is, by building and arranging instructional cues to increase the probability of the correct response occurring. Now, as educators apply behavior principles and use behavioral analysis in classes, they attend to the task of strengthening individualized instructional plans by specifying these cues or antecedent conditions. In other words, the behavior manager needs more than mere technology; he or she also needs subject matter competence so that the content of instruction can be systematically and optimally arranged.

In this chapter we shall present contemporary information on instructional technology, or systematic instructional procedures by which individualization of instruction is possible in nearly every classroom situation. We fully realize that many teachers lack the skills necessary to create individualized programs, but we are attempting to deliver procedures that will facilitate improved instructional capabilities. Educational technology gives today's teachers the opportunity to provide a positive learning experience for nearly every child who enters the classroom and to learn to utilize resource services and personnel to the fullest extent. The system we are presenting is, in one sense, imaginative. Although the Experimental Education Unit of the University of Washington and other such centers throughout the country utilize procedures closely resembling these, the application to public school classrooms and resource rooms is only in its infancy.

Why Systematic Instructional Procedures?

We must differentiate between methods approaches that tend to lock in procedures to conformity and routine, and procedures that, although standardized, provide flexibility in instruction and program design. The successful application of systems and behavioral technology to the classroom gives this flexibility and enhances the flow of information in the teaching-learning process. The systematic procedures of instruction are an attempt to insure naturally reinforcing behavior patterns between teachers and students. Formal and stylized group methods of instruction and classroom management tend to restrict natural, articulate forms of communication. New insights into better ways of intervening with social and academic behavior problems indicate positive trends toward a beneficial means of behavioral change.

Too often the teacher is conceptualized as an actor or actress, or even a salesperson. In reaction to this view of their role, teachers demand to preserve spontaneity in the teaching process without really knowing what is necessary to be a successful teacher. The artistic aspect of teaching is defended by the profession when the discussion of technology and the scientific aspect of teaching begins. But even the artist uses technology in developing a specific craft. Technology is simply the tools and techniques an artist uses in performing his or her specific art. In its original Greek form (technologia), technology referred to the "ordering of an original bit of human artistry in such a way that its makeup might clearly be understood and replicated" (Komoski, 1969). A musician uses a long and rich tradition of ordering sound through scales and notation. Many techniques of practice and drill help the musician master both an instrument and specific musical concepts. A painter uses many tools developed both by artistic masters and by science—color, form, new synthetic materials, new paper and canvas, brushes, and the like. An artist acquires expertise through experience, drill and practice, and experimentation. In all disciplines, all crafts, there exists at least a minimal or baseline set of procedures that everyone can use in transferring skills and expertise to other individuals. Although the technologies of a specific discipline, art, or science are particular to that area, there is a technology, or set of principles and procedures, that is applicable to teaching per se. A technology of teaching is a set of basic organizational principles that are easily mastered and administered to facilitate the teaching-learning process.

Teachers often fail to teach because they have not mastered the tools of observation and organization that point out instructional and curricular failure for individual students. An oft-repeated mistake is teaching to an amorphous group of bodies without considering the individual learning processes that exist within the larger whole. Teaching, in this sense, is impersonal and statistical. The move to individualize instruction in the past decade or so is a move in the direction of humanizing the educational system. However, until fairly recently, although we have had the philosophy, we have not had the technology to apply these ideas. In the area of special education this need has been painfully obvious, and research and development of individual instructional programs have provided not only meaningful data but new technologies that *do* individualize instruction. It is now necessary to bring these advances into the regular public school classroom where the learning disabled child is either overlooked or mismanaged.

The regular classroom teacher must learn the necessary skills to facilitate learning by disabled and mildly handicapped children. Although educators speak about teaching *all* children, the concepts predate the development of workable, effective programs that will bring about changes in the inadequacies of public education. These changes place new responsibilities on both the classroom teacher and the administrator, but this is necessary if we are to solve the problems of specific academic disabilities and perceptual handicaps. And it could be easily contended that if we are not able to solve such basic problems, there is little probability that we can solve problems of greater magnitude.

It is relatively simple to tell others how to behave or what to do in a given situation and construct an artificial reinforcement schedule that will, at most, insure only partial success. It is not so simple, however, to teach others how to observe, gather information, conduct an analysis, make evaluations, and base instructional and programming decisions on the resulting data. Ninety percent of all decision-making in public education takes place in the classroom. Unfortunately, many decisions that affect a child's learning process are made out of expediency or in a random, haphazard manner that does not consider the structure of the situation. Accountability has to take place in the classroom, not as a topic at teachers' meetings. Passing the buck must be replaced by clear, precise, decision-making ability based on empirical data gathered in the classroom. Understandably, if a classroom teacher does not know what to do, and if admitting it somehow casts doubt on his or her ability, easy rationalizations or inattention will occur. One way this happens is that teachers seek diagnostic solace by looking to psychological profiles and assessment of a particular child, becoming convinced that the child is failing because of some medical or psychological dysfunction beyond the expertise of the classroom teacher (Lovitt, 1967).

This type of thinking, and other examples of communication breakdown, reinforce existing patterns of learning problems because no steps are taken to provide special or individualized instruction for the child. The child is forced deeper and deeper into a cycle of failure from which no escape or relief seems possible. The long-lasting effects on the child's behavior patterns, communicative ability, self-concept, and the like should be obvious. This constitutes a special form of what Gregory Bateson (1972) calls a "double-bind" situation. The tacit assumption is that a child is unable to learn, so there is no reason to teach to a particular weakness or to change the nature of the teacher-pupil interaction. The teacher's behavior is biased by this assumption. The child, who does not know directly about the teacher's decision, can receive information only through the teacher's behavior and the communicative signals that take place between them. The child is the victim of circumstance and the structure of the situation, which is beyond his or her power and means to change. Because the child's failure in actuality is being reinforced, rather than systematically modified and changed, the child continually is being punished for a behavioral pattern maintained by the teacher over which the child has no control. The child may be aware of a teacher's biased behavior or of changes in the way the teacher chooses to interact, but there are no available avenues for release from, or modification of, the pattern. The child is required by law, and usually parental demand, to attend school. If the pattern persists, the damage can be nearly permanent.

This is the basic double-bind situation in school classrooms. The double bind may begin to develop in infancy and may be transferred from home to school and public life. Aside from clearly organic dysfunctions, this pattern can be seen as the communicative etiology of learning disabilities. And as such, the mythology concerning the learning disabled child is clarified by analysis of the teaching-learning process and the structure of communicative exchanges between teacher and pupil.

Using Educational Technology

The use of contemporary, advanced technology reveals the inadequacies that often exist in general classroom interaction. Technology applied to the teaching-learning process is a systematic way of designing, organizing, managing, and evaluating human and nonhuman resources in the educational system. Although this may seem a rather all-pervasive definition, it serves the purpose well. A technology of teaching develops the tools and procedures by which teachers and administrators can view the subsystems of the teaching-learning process, including evaluation, measurement, curriculum design, instructional methodology, student needs, levels of experience, and so on. Scientific research has provided data and criteria by which systematic instructional procedures can be developed. The procedures to be discussed have been developed through applying research findings and experimentation in the fields of behavioral science and systems technology. These two fields (as well as related ones) account for a major breakthrough in developing a set of systematic instructional procedures. By no stretch of the imagination is the development complete. This contribution, as well as those of precision teaching, behavior modification, and task analytic research in instructional objectives, are only approximations, only beginnings. In Chapter 3 we discussed briefly the history of the experimental analysis of behavior as applied to education. This is the original experimental work in developing a technology of teaching. This research, coupled with work in other fields, is the basis for a comprehensive educational technology.

If professional educators begin to concentrate on developing sets of procedures that are systematic and universal to the teaching-learning process, the educational system will begin to move toward direct and close approximations of basic procedures that all teachers can use in arranging the instructional situation and making teaching decisions. Administrators, teachers, and parents need meaningful, practical information to plan a child's educational experience. Planning must be flexible enough to provide choice for the child and facilitate change both environmentally and intellectually. Both short-term and long-term goals should be formulated to direct the child's educational experience. And the most efficient way to get where one is going is to have a travel plan.

The Correlation of Behavioral and
Systems Technology

Two separately developed but complementary technologies have contributed to the development of educational technology. The first, behavioral technology, grew out of research in operant psychology in both experimental and applied situations. The second, systems technology, developed from research in areas as diverse as biology and computer science. A synthesis of the two is beginning to provide a comprehensive and integrative system of teaching. We use the concept of the teaching-learning process in bringing together the procedures and ideas of these two technological developments. What we hope for and what we are working toward is a problem-solving technique by which teachers, administrators, and students will be able to discuss learning and the school environment in real terms based on performance data, not hearsay and assumption. Just as administrators have discovered that systems analysis provides the basis for administrative decision-making criteria, so classroom teachers have found that behavioral technologies such as precision teaching provide the basis for instructional decision-making criteria. A synthesis of these technologies into a comprehensive, total program begins to give 100 percent compatibility between the goals of the individual student and teacher, the principal, the district administration, and schools within the district. Using random procedures rather than systematic ones for arranging instructional environments tends to foster waste, and they cost the public precious time and money. Public education is a big business, the biggest business in which the community as a whole is engaged.

America has benefited from systems technology in many areas, such as business, the military, and science. A charge levleed at using technological advances in schools is that it "dehumanizes" the educational process. In fact, systematic organization and administration is a "humanizing process." As we move from the learning environment with the teacher as a manager to the child as a self-manager capable of controlling and making decisions concerning arrangement of the environment, the child's ability to be self-sufficient is enhanced. In education, we need to create a reinforcing system of exchange between individuals that replaces the all-too-often punitive system now in practice. Educational technology offers a problem-solving means to incorporate behavioral management from the classroom level to the administrative level where each level is accountable to the others.

BEHAVIORAL TECHNOLOGY

The Experimental Analysis of Behavior

The experimental analysis of behavior as a scientific discipline has set out to demonstrate the lawfulness of the behavior of organisms as a whole (Skinner, 1953). The function of a scientific analysis of behavior is not to provide another theory *per se,* but to reveal a systematic interpretation of human behavior based on the generalized principles or laws of behavior by which predictions validly can be made. Thus, theory and practice gradually become synonymous. The application of scientific data to a practical situation should prove either the validity or invalidity of the laboratory data obtained to modify or change certain behavior. A synthesis of the laws of behavior based on the independent variables, or the causes of behavior that are external, and the dependent variable, or the effect of predicting and controlling behavior of the individual organism, can be expressed in quantitative terms that yield a comprehensive patterning of the organism as a behaving system.

In an actual classroom situation the process of reinforcement and of controlling the contingencies of reinforcement becomes one of the primary aims of classroom research. Following the basic stimulus-response-reinforcement paradigm, a stimulus is anything in the environment that evokes a response, a specified *observable* behavior. Reinforcement is the presentation of a desirable or rewarding consequence for a response, which increases the probability that the same type of response will be made to the same stimuli in succeeding instances. The reinforcement component of the Skinner paradigm is the key to successful behavior modification. Operant conditioning, or behavior modification, brings behavior under the control of the reinforcer. If a child is reinforced by receiving free time for answering a series of math problems correctly, chances are that he or she will either maintain or improve his or her performance contingent on the free-time reinforcer.

Progressive education has made a humanitarian effort to substitute positive reinforcement for such aversive measures as physical punishment, threats, and the like. Because the control and management of human behavior is at the same time controversial and unpopular, people tend to ignore the fact that we are all engaged in controlling and being controlled each day. By not attending to the controlling elements in our lives, the aversive and indirectly punishing events continue. Punitive contingencies should not be confused with aversive control, through which people are induced to behave in given ways. Punishment is used to induce people *not* to behave in given ways (Skinner, 1971). The double bind in which we often are placed by humanistic philosophy is that while we vigorously defend the basic rights of freedom and dignity, we use punitive contingencies and aversive measures as the major forms of social control. It is somewhat like the parents who grant their child a generous weekly allowance, then keep the money in a jar, saying "That's your money, but don't touch or you'll be spanked." Although many seem to recognize the need for a reinforcing environment, little has been done to provide either methods or technologies that would implement such change. Teachers need to know how and when to use reinforcement, as well as how and when to use punishment. The technology of behavior applied to the classroom begins to supply this information.

Reinforcement Principles

Reinforcement is a procedure through which a given behavior is increased or maintained. There are two distinct forms of reinforcement—positive and negative. Positive reinforcement is the contingent presentation of a stimulus that increases or maintains a behavior. Negative reinforcement is the contingent removal of an aversive stimulus to increase or maintain a behavior. Many of the problems in classroom situations can be handled by using reinforcement procedures to increase the occurrence of already existing behaviors. There are several types of reinforcers as well as several methods of reinforcement that can be delivered systematically.

Positive reinforcement.   When a teacher is interested in increasing low rate behaviors, such as task completion, various academic skills, or group participation, effective positive reinforcers must be found. Basically, presenting a pleasant event after a response increases the probability that the response will recur. The teacher may influence the probability of a child's response to a task; that is, the teacher may affect the accuracy and efficiency of performance by providing rewarding conditions in the classroom.

Positive reinforcement generally can be categorized as primary reinforcement, social reinforcement, token reinforcement, and high strength activities. *Primary reinforcement* means presenting a stimulus that meets a basic life need, such as food, water, and clothing. Many researchers have used primary reinforcement to teach language and physical and social skills to children with severe behavior disorders. Primary reinforcement can be scheduled into the classroom structure in the form of snacks, milk breaks, and lunch on a contingent basis. Small parties can be given to a class based upon the students' attainment of a specific goal. If primary reinforcers are used in the classroom, the teacher must be aware of the critical nature of timing their delivery. If the event is to be reinforcing, it must be a direct consequence of the response. Any type of reinforcement that is too long delayed becomes weak.

Social reinforcement is more effective than primary in achieving behavioral change because of the impracticality of primary reinforcers in the classroom. A traditional form such as grading is an example of social reinforcement. And social reinforcement is a form of conditioned reinforcement; that is, presenting a stimulus, object, or event that through frequent pairing with another stimulus already possessing reinforcing properties has itself acquired reinforcing value. Conditioned reinforcers develop as the individual interacts with the environment Social reinforcement in the form of praise, smiles, or compliments replaces earlier, more primary reinforcers such as feeding and fondling. The frequent pairing of primary reinforcement with praise or attention results in verbal and social events becoming reinforcing by themselves.

With some children, social reinforcers fail to become strong, are not applied to a wide variety of responses, and generalized reinforcers do not develop. When this occurs, the child usually has a variety of behaviors at low levels of development and in various states of deprivation that are resistant to effective reinforcement. Such socially deficient children have extremely limited repertoires of social responses, and the environment exerts very little control over their behavior. Teachers often overlook the fact that some children grow up without experiencing typical combinations of primary and conditioned reinforcers. In such cases, shaping procedures can be implemented. With a child who makes few appropriate reinforceable responses, it is necessary first to evoke behavior that approximates the appropriate behavior and then shape it through a series of approximations until the final appropriate behavior becomes conditioned. Shaping must be planned carefully, beginning with identifying the terminal behavior and specifying the successive approximations to be reinforced.

Often the teacher inadvertently reinforces the very behavior that is undesirable and disruptive in the classroom. This certainly is understandable. The temptation to correct a child who is making loud noises or distracting another child is hard to resist, but attending to the child while he or she is behaving inappropriately certainly does maintain, if not increase, the undesirable behavior. A teacher who responds to Sally's giggling by saying "Stop that giggling and get back to work" will likely use the same response the next time that the situation occurs, if Sally actually stops giggling and goes to work. Actually, the behavior being reinforced and maintained is giggling behavior rather than working behavior, because it is giggling to which the teacher pays attention. Because the giggling behavior is being reinforced by the teacher's attention, Sally will probably emit giggling behavior in the future. To compound the problem, the teacher's conditioned response to Sally's giggling may result in giggling from other children.

A great amount of classroom research demonstrates the use of various social reinforcers in increasing student behavior. The teacher's main objective in using reinforcement is to become established as a positive reinforcer for each child. If positive reinforcement has little effect in maintaining the child's appropriate behavior, environmental conditions must be rearranged so that social behavior becomes a positive reinforcer. If teacher attention, positive or negative, to inappropriate behavior maintains the rate of that behavior, the teacher must withhold or withdraw attention from the behavior and redirect it to other behaviors that need to be strengthened. Far too many children do not respond satisfactorily to "normal" classroom conditions and demands (being able to sit quietly, to attend to work, to complete assignments accurately, to follow directions.) The stimuli fail to reinforce them, and, most unfortunately for the children's learning careers, the teacher never becomes a social reinforcer. These children are not reinforced by coming to school or by responding to academic materials, and if the teacher continues the same patterns for reinforcement, their skill development and academic progress will be slow. To strengthen rates of response to instructional cues, the teacher systematically must identify and apply reinforcing consequences and structure the classroom environment so that each child can plan the natural consequences to maintain appropriate individual academic, social, and verbal behaviors.

One of the most effective procedures in designing a reinforcing classroom environment is the Premack Principle. After extensive laboratory studies, Premack demonstrated that the behaviors one actually engages in may be used to reinforce behavior that occurs less frequently. Applying the principle to the classroom, Lloyd Homme and his associates (1963) showed that using access to high frequency behaviors, such as running and screaming, could be made contingent on performance of low frequency behaviors, such as academic tasks.

There is nothing new about this practice; in fact, Ivar Lovaas (1968) says it is as old as child rearing. When a mother declares "Before you go fishing you must mow the lawn" or a teacher schedules a dance party based on the class meeting a group criterion level, they are employing the Premack Principle. For each child in any classroom, some activities are naturally reinforcing and others are not. One child may find arithmetic, gym, and art reinforcing, but may detest reading and spelling. Another child may be reinforced initially only by sailing plastic boats in the sink and nothing else. Consequently, the classroom must accommodate a wide range of activities and possibilities. Dividing the classroom into high and low strength areas is one method that has been successful (Homme, 1963; Haring and Kunzelmann, 1966). Academic tasks are usually done in the low strength areas where stationary desks or carrels are provided. Desks should be well stocked with whatever materials the child might need as part of learning readiness-for-task procedures. The high strength areas should be arranged for independent, free-time use by the children. Everything should be accessible to them, including equipment and supplies for planned activities and working on projects.

Token reinforcement is another special case of conditioned reinforcement. With token reinforcement, the child is given some small item or marks as a reinforcing consequence for a specific response or pattern of responses. Regardless of what form they take, token reinforcers are exchangeable at a later time for another reinforcing item or activity. Often token systems are used in haphazard ways, such as giving gold stars or tally marks that can be turned in later for a prize. Teachers who use a token system should be aware of its consequences.

Many studies have concerned wide ranges of populations such as psychotic patients (Ayllon and Azrin, 1965); delinquents (Cohen, 1971); behavior problems in public schools (Wolf, Giles, and Hall, 1968; Orme and Purnell, 1968) and in regular classroom settings (Bushell, Wrobel, and Michaelis, 1968). Token reinforcement may be the most flexible reinforcement plan in the classroom. Various kinds of tokens are easily dispensed and easily become conditioned reinforcers. Token systems allow for the individual needs of all the children, and also provide control for satiation and deprivation. A child given only extra gym or art after performing to criterion will be satisfied by these reinforcers, even if those events are reinforcing for a time. Successful token systems provide diverse opportunities that allow the child to choose what to do at the moment, rather than engage in a specific event. Thus, the tokens remain strong reinforcers.

The token system can be incorporated with the use of *high strength activities.* The teacher and the students are thus able to work out extensive lists of activities, events, and conditions having potential as reinforcers in the classroom. The high strength area is gradually developed to provide for all the children's needs and is equipped with games, toys, puzzles, records, and the like. The effectiveness of a token system depends on the backup times and activities available. Delivery of tokens can be combined with individual attention and praise so that social reinforcement is generalized from the token reinforcement schedule.

Scheduling reinforcement. One of the central aims of contemporary educational technology is to carry the principles of behavior to higher levels of generality through cybernetics, development of systematic teaching procedures, and programmed instruction. Any teaching and learning system contains several features. First, it has definite beginning and ending points, definable objectives and a flexible mode of operation that considers the learner's skills or behavioral repertoire. Second, the presentation of materials to be learned (stimuli) is relatively organized, provides for sequential and self-pacing progress by the learner, and leads to some discernible consequence (reinforcement, feedback). Basic to this systematic approach to teaching and learning is, of course, the phenomenon of reinforcement and the delivery of reinforcing consequences.

The careful scheduling of reinforcement and delivery of reinforcing consequences is a crucial phase in implementing a teaching-learning system. An educator can analyze a certain task into sequential steps, design a hypothetically reinforcing environment, and decide on terminal objectives, but if the task is not reinforcing or if reinforcement is not scheduled and delivered in ways that cause behavior to be strengthened and maintained, the system is inadequate. Delivery of reinforcement is systematized in the classroom by use of contingency management. The term "contingency" denotes a relationship that is resultant rather than merely temporal. Nearly all behavior is controlled by contingencies of some nature. Our salaries are contingent on performance. We occupy our homes contingent on mortgage or rent payments as well as taxes. We advance to higher levels of employment contingent on performance, experience, and education. If we observe and analyze our behavior, it is easy to discern the environmental contingencies that control it and make it relatively predictable.

Each of the various types of reinforcement schedules has different properties or effects. For the classroom situation, Skinner's reinforcement paradigm has been modified by Ogden Lindsley (1964), who identified four components of a contingency management system. E^A is the antecedent event, M is the movement cycle or the response to be measured, A is the arrangement of reinforcement or its presentation schedule, and E^S is the subsequent event designated as a consequence (reinforcement) of the response.

$$E^A \quad \rightarrow \quad M \quad \rightarrow \quad A \quad \rightarrow \quad E^S$$

| Antecedent Event | Movement | Arrangement | Subsequent Event |

In analyzing the scheduling and delivery of reinforcement in the teaching-learning system, we are interested in the final two phases of Lindsley's paradigm. Of the many complex schedules of reinforcement that have been discovered, four are basic (Ferster and Skinner, 1957): fixed ratio (FR) and variable ratio (VR), based on number; and fixed interval (FI) and variable interval (VI), based on time.

When reinforcement is contingent upon the emission of a given number of responses before one response is reinforced, the schedule is known as a ratio schedule (Sulzer and Mayer, 1972). On a fixed ratio schedule, reinforcement follows a specific number of responses, and the schedule is identified according to the number of responses required before reinforcement is presented (Haring and Phillips, 1972). A fixed ratio of one to one, or FR-1, is the same as continuous reinforcement (CFR) with reinforcement presented directly after every response. With a schedule of FR-10 (fixed ratio of 10), reinforcement is contingent upon 10 correct responses. The classic example of a fixed ratio schedule is piece-work in industry. When a worker finishes a tenth commodity, he or she is credited with $5. In school, a fixed ratio schedule awards a student points or free time contingent upon completion of a given number of workbook problems.

A more typical reinforcement schedule in many school situations is the variable ratio (VR). The VR schedule programs reinforcement contingent upon a response following a number of responses like a FR schedule; the number of required responses varies over a given range around some average value. Most reinforcement in the classroom, particularly academic work, occurs on a variable ratio schedule. If units in a math workbook vary from four to eight pages with an average of six pages, students would be reinforced toward their final grade upon completion of all the pages of each unit, or by a VR 6 schedule.

Whereas ratio schedules depend on a specific number of responses being emitted, *interval schedules* are dependent upon the passage of a specific period of time. Reinforcement on a fixed interval (FI) schedule follows the first correct response emitted after the specified interval has elapsed. If a teacher decides that a student should spend more time on a reading assignment and less time looking out the window, the student may be reinforced if he or she is reading after five minutes has elapsed.

If the desired behavior, in this case reading, is being emitted after five minutes has elapsed, the student is reinforced. Or the student is reinforced immediately upon the first emission of the behavior after five minutes has elapsed. This is FI-5 or fixed interval, five-minute schedule.

A variable interval (VI) schedule operates in the same way, except that the time requirement is not held constant but is a specified average. Following a variable interval schedule, reinforcement is delivered at irregular intervals. For instance, the teacher may decide to vary the time parameters for modifying reading behavior between 0 and 10 minutes. Research has shown that the rate of responding is more rapid under the variable interval (VI) schedules than the fixed interval. Because the individual is reinforced at random and unpredictable times—sometimes near the beginning of the interval, sometimes toward the end—response patterns are usually emitted at a fairly constant rate and have the general effect of yielding more responses per interval. If the child has no way of telling when he or she will be reinforced for attending to a reading task, it is more likely that the child will keep reading continuously to receive reinforcement whenever it is forthcoming.

The various schedules of reinforcement produce different response patterns. Techniques and research in the experimental analysis of behavior are only beginning to reveal some expected patterns. For practical purposes, a reinforcement schedule specifies conditions under which responses produce a reinforcer. Such conditions are the time that has passed since an antecedent event (dynamic effects), the number of, or temporal patterning of, antecedent events (discriminative effects), or combinations and variations of these conditions (differential effects). The scheduling and delivery determine the way in which the reinforcement contacts the behavior and generates a subsequent performance. Some of the major issues in the analysis of reinforcement scheduling concern the various ways in which dynamic, discriminative, and differentiating processes operate and interact to determine a particular performance (Catania, 1970) and reinforcement history of an individual. The issues are of great importance in the design of teaching–learning systems that systematically reinforce academic and social behaviors. By learning ways to build reinforcement schedules into the teaching–learning system, it is possible to provide reinforcement that is the instructional feature essential to motivating without increasing the tasks of the classroom teacher. Reinforcement schedules are easily designed directly into programmed texts, teaching machines, and even into the available procedures to manage a classroom situation effectively.

A teaching-learning system can reinforce more systematically and can make better use of intermittent schedules than a teacher can (Haring, 1971). But a word of caution—over the years two occurrences in the history of behavioral science have caused some confusion as to the exact nature and utility of reinforcement schedules. The first is the difference in the experimental analysis of behavior, or "free operant research" and behavior therapy. The second is the many varieties, compounds, and permutations of ratio and interval schedules that have been proposed and studied in recent years (Schoenfeld and Farmer, 1970). One area needing work is the synthesis and organization that is more than inventing different labels for schedules or conjuring up new schedules. This problem is amplified by the fact that there seems no limit to the number of schedules that can be devised. Skinner's format for deriving schedules by the criteria of numbers of responses and temporal position (Skinner, 1958) and Schoenfeld and his coworkers' systems in which time was chosen as the structural variable and response number was "treated as dependent datum and not as a criterion for the independent variable of reinforcement" (Schoenfeld and Farmer, 1970) are two attempts at organizing reinforcement schedules. But the science of behavior, if it is to move closer to the goal of revealing a systematic interpretation of human behavior, must work diligently in elucidating the nature of reinforcement schedules and their practical application to social situations such as the classroom.

The developing technology of teaching faces a direct challenge in researching the scheduling and delivery of reinforcing consequences in the classroom situation. For instance, research has shown that ratio schedules generally produce higher rates of responding than interval schedules. The classroom teacher must be aware of what schedules are most effective in modifying behavior. In the next section we will consider the application of various reinforcement schedules in the classroom environment.

FURTHER DEVELOPMENTS

Instructional Programming

Nearly all educators are acquainted with "programmed instruction." Teaching machines, devices that present a series of sequential steps of material, were developed as early as the 1930s by Pressey (1932) and popularized in the 1950s by Skinner (1958) and Holland (1960). In the early 1960s, programmed instruction was hailed by proponents as the answer to individualizing learning so that all children could progress at their own rate, and even slow learning children could achieve high levels of knowledge. As with many other innovations, programmed instruction failed to become an educational panacea. However, it has provided some lasting contributions to systematic instruction.

First, programmed instruction gave the initial impetus toward specifying instructional objectives in terms of overt behavior. Mager (1962) identified the essential ingredients of an instructional objective as being a description of what the learner actually will do to indicate he or she has achieved the desired knowledge; the conditions under which the learner will perform; and the criteria of performance the learner will be required to meet. Such objectives have the advantage of specifying for both the teacher and learner what are to be the final outcomes of instruction. Pragmatically, teachers can use the principles of specifying instructional objectives without using programmed instruction. For example, a first grade teacher may decide that by the end of the year each pupil should be able to write correctly the answers to all 100 of the basic addition facts within three minutes, given a sheet of such facts. Such a statement contains the essential components of an instructional objective and makes the teacher's goal for addition facts explicit.

A second contribution of programmed instruction has been to articulate some practices for developing instructional sequences of materials. Briefly stated, these practices are:

1. Specify the instructional outcome or objective.
2. Provide for overt responding.
3. Analyze the task into small sequential steps (sometimes called task analysis or slicing).
4. Determine the entry behaviors required to initiate the program.
5. Arrange the sequence of instruction to result in a high proportion of correct responses.
6. Provide cues and prompts to teach a concept, withdraw them gradually.
7. Provide for relatively immediate feedback regarding correct and error performance.
8. Establish performance criteria indicative of task mastery.

Evaluation Technology

Another development that contributes to the education of handicapped children is evaluation technology. The reason for evaluation is to facilitate decisions. Educators have been interested in evaluating methods, materials, and practices; group performance; and individual performance. We evaluate educational methods, materials, and practices to determine if they achieve their intended outcome, or if they surpass certain other methods, materials, and practices in effectiveness. We evaluate groups of children to determine if their educational progress is satisfactory according to some criteria. We evaluate individual performance to determine if children are progressing adequately, and even to decide what deficits to remediate. In each instance the implication is that if practices are inferior or if group or individual performance is inadequate, action will be taken to change the practices leading to inferior performance.

If the results of evaluation are to be useful, they must meet certain criteria. First, the goal of evaluation must be specified. For example, one might ask if a certain arithmetic text will, in fact, teach specified arithmetic skills. A test could be constructed to answer that question. One might ask how the pupils in a selected school perform in reading compared to pupils in other schools. Norm-referenced achievement tests sometimes have been used to answer this question. Or one might wish to know if an individual pupil is improving on his or her oral reading performance each day. An appropriate evaluative procedure must be selected or constructed specifically to answer the question.

A second criterion for effective evaluation is a direct measure of the performance required. It would be absurd, for example, to use a reading test to assess math performance. However, many tests used in education have measured skills other than the ones being taught directly. For example, educators have used story problems when they wished to assess computation skills. Only when measures are related directly to the performances to be assessed will the measures provide useful information for decision-making.

A third criterion for evaluative measures is that they be administered soon enough, and frequently enough, so that remedial practices can be implemented. An achievement test given at the end of a school year is not useful for making decisions in time to alter teaching practices for the pupil who took the test during that academic year. To be useful for decision-making, measures should be constructed and administered soon after instruction has occurred, and then repeated frequently.

A fourth criterion is that educational measures sensitively and precisely reflect changes in pupil performance. As an extreme example, a "satisfactory-unsatisfactory" rating of performance is neither sensitive nor precise in reflecting change in pupil progress. Hence, it is not very useful for decision-making.

A fifth criterion for evaluation procedures is their practicality. One of the disadvantages of extensive psychometric evaluations has been their inaccessibility for many pupils. Teachers actually may benefit from information resulting from such evaluations, but if pupils who need the evaluation cannot obtain it, the evaluation is impractical for that teacher and those pupils. Practical measures probably should be available daily in the classroom and should be capable of administration by the teacher or the pupil.

Many of the traditional evaluation measures have been normatively standardized achievement tests, referred to as norm-referenced tests. These measures may be contrasted with criterion-referenced tests. Norm-referenced tests report pupils' performance relative to the average performance of a larger reference group. Such tests do not measure proficiency directly on a given task, but simply describe how a selected group scores on that task and an individual's performance relative to the group. Norm-referenced tests are somewhat inefficient for making decisions about instructional procedures. Criterion-referenced measures, on the other hand, assess pupil performance relative to some standard of performance deemed desirable. When a youngster performs poorly on a criterion-referenced test, information can be drawn directly from the test regarding remedial needs for particular pupils. Criterion-referenced tests are relatively efficient for decision-making.

Evaluators have contrasted formative and summative evaluation. Summative measures simply describe a pupil's or group's performance at the end of some time or project period. Summative data are not useable for decision-making during the time or project period preceding the test. These data may be useful for longer range decision-making. On the other hand, formative measures are used to assess pupil progress periodically throughout a time or project duration. Data are frequently used to assess pupil growth, and alterations are made in the intervention procedures if necessary. Formative data are collected specifically to increase the frequency and the efficacy of educational decision-making.

SYSTEMS TECHNOLOGY

General System Theory

The terms "system" and "systems analysis" have become widely used in fields as varied as medicine, law, education, government, engineering, and architecture. These disciplines commonly have complex problems to be solved and many variables to be coordinated to achieve intended objectives. A system is defined as a complex of interacting elements (von Bertalanffy, 1968). The concept of a system is used to consider two or more activities or elements that can be related functionally to achieve a goal. Systems analysis becomes a process whereby one may analyze an existing system or problem and create a system for solving that problem (synthesis).

The roots of the development of systems theory are complex. From power engineering, such as steam and atomic mechanics, to control engineering, such as missile guidance systems, systems concepts permeate all levels of contemporary society. The basic concepts, however, were developed in biology by Count Ludwig von Bertalanffy. His "general system theory" was advanced before World War I in an attempt to bridge the gap between theory and research practice in biological science. The basis of his theory emphasized that an organism can be considered as a whole or system, and that the main objective of both biological and social sciences is the discovery of the principles of organization at all levels (von Bertalanffy, 1968). The result was the organic model of biology developed by the expansion of conventional physical chemistry, kinetics, and thermodynamics. This synthesis was an initial step in introducing new categories in scientific thought and research that had been neglected in classical science and physics with its strict mechanistic model. Classical science has been interested essentially in two variable problems (cause and effect) and statistical decision-making that framed the problem in terms of alternate and null hypotheses. The classical scientific approach has proved too rigid to deal effectively with multiple–variable problems that occur in everyday life. The controlled laboratory situation is not often available in applied social settings. Systems analysis is the study of process in a systematic manner using specific techniques to identify variables and to measure and analyze the resulting data about the interrelationship of the variables. General system theory holds that any system responsive to its environment evolves a structure unique to its conditions and that structure will resemble its genotypic counterparts only in following similar rules for development (Ammentorp, Daley, and Evans, 1969). No two plants have exactly the same form, but each has similar capabilities, functions, and processes of development; the same is true of human behavioral systems. Organismic processes as a rule are so ordered as to maintain the system (von Bertalanffy, 1968).

The impact of contemporary thought in systems science and cybernetics has resolved a major conflict between behavioral and cognitive psychology. A human being does not so much respond to stimuli as interpret certain states of the environment as posing problems that the individual attempts to solve (Pask, 1969). Certainly, all human systems thus can be considered goal-directed. This consideration is of vital importance to the educator. Children with learning disorders or perceptual or physical handicaps must learn to interpret, intend, and anticipate in relationship to the social and natural environments. The child is not viewed through the blinders of the robot-mechanistic models of classical science, but as an active behavior system in accordance with the organismic-cybernetic models of contemporary science. Every individual has problem-solving potential; education's role is to provide an environment where this can occur naturally and where the learner can take an active part in managing his or her education.

According to the principles of general systems theory and cybernetics, the teaching-learning process is a spiral loop that includes the elements of feedback (learning), feedforward (performance), and reinforcement. The teaching-learning system is characterized by several features—definite beginning and ending points, specific goals and objectives, and flexible modes of operation (systematic instructional procedures) that takes the learner's skills and behavioral repertoire into consideration. The difference between the teaching-learning system and teaching-learning process is that the process is the actual way an individual learns and processes information, and the system is the method or style of instruction. Ideally, there is no difference. However, this is not the case most of the time. The cybernetic and systems approaches state that the behavior of an organism depends on the feedback information available. As we develop more precise instructional procedures we become more adept at reinforcing self-directive behaviors.

The original application of systems technology in education was on the administrative level as a problem-solving strategy. However, developments in cybernetics and task analysis have proved useful in curriculum design, classroom management, and instructional planning. Educational technology approaches human behavior according to the cybernetic model of human development (Haring and Phillips, 1972). The behavior of a system (or organism) depends on feedback information (learning) and the feedforward or information (performance) after the informational input (stimulus) is processed against the existing bias. The Greek root of cybernetics (kyber) refers to a helmsman or steerer, or a controlling agent or element in a system. The minimum elements of a cybernetic system are a "receptor" accepting stimuli or information from the outside as input; from this information a message is led to a "center," which in some way reacts to the message and, as a rule, amplifies the signals received. The center, in turn, transmits the message to an "effector," which eventually responds to the stimulus as output (von Bertalanffy, 1968). The field of cybernetics was pioneered by Norbert Weiner (1950), who generalized the concepts of cybernetics, feedback, and information beyond the limits of technology and applied them to biological and social problems.

The cybernetic nature of the teaching-learning system following Weiner's basic concepts provides an integrative means of viewing the educational system as a whole. It should be stated, however, that cybernetics as the theory of control mechanisms in technology and nature, founded on the concepts of information and feedback, is only part of a general systems theory concerning self-regulating systems. Neither is it true that the cybernetic model utilized as an organizational tool by educational technologists is a complete organismic model. Living systems, human beings included, are open systems, whereas the cybernetic systems and models developed out of Weiner's work are closed. According to von Bertalanffy (1968), the cybernetic model is an advancement of the S-R scheme, with a feedback loop added for self-regulation. Living systems are not mechanistic in that regulative behavior is not determined solely by structural conditions, but also by the interplay and commerce of forces in the environment. Cybernetic systems are "closed" with respect to the exchange of matter with the environment, and open only to information (von Bertalanffy, 1968). This is essential in considering the teaching-learning process, because the cybernetic model does not provide the essential elements of living systems involving growth, development, differentiation, and generalization. Education designed truly to serve human beings and the development of human society is an open, living system maintained by a continuous exchange of components and reordering of structure to facilitate both internal and external change. It is understood that in this open, living system the learner participates in decisions and goal-setting to promote both internal and external change. But the cybernetic model and the process analysis made available through it are key organizing and troubleshooting tools for educators and teachers.

Task analysis. Task analysis and task analytic techniques are not usually considered as developments of general systems thinking and research per se, but the concepts are similar both chronologically and developmentally. Task analysis developed from work on initiating sequential procedures for describing tasks and job criteria. Robert Miller and Jack Foley, working for the U.S. Air Force, began the early work developing task analytic techniques and the first "task taxonomies" (Miller, 1973). As it has developed, task analysis is a detailed description of what a person does or should be doing to perform a task, a job, or to learn a skill successfully. At the same time work on programmed instructional materials was done by behavioral psychologists using principles described by Skinner (1958) in developing teaching machines and systematic arrangement of instructional material. In both the cybernetic and organismic models, behavior is seen as purposive or goal-directed. Education operates on objectives or goals that are often hazy and not well defined. Task and goal analysis provide methods for utilization of resources that produce outcomes defined by goals and educational objectives (Boston, 1972).

Task analysis has four basic steps or components: 1) describing desired outcomes in behavioral terms; 2) naming skills and knowledge involved in the task; 3) naming, classifying, and measuring the functions of each property named in the second step; and 4) development of the course of action. These steps represent one of the best ways of systematizing instruction for the classroom teacher.

Combining cybernetics and task analytic techniques with the principles of behavior makes possible a set of *systematic instructional procedures,* which are further advanced by the synthesis of behavioral and systems technology using the organismic model as an integrative factor. We shall discuss these procedures shortly. For the most part, in education, task analytic techniques have been incorporated into programmed instruction especially in creating linear, self-paced programs. This proved to be too rigid a format that limited complete transmission of information (Miller, 1973). To be effective, a task analysis should consider existing environmental contingencies and the actual performance levels of the individual.

The Process of Analysis

Systems analysis can be used for analysis alone, or to analyze and modify an operation. One goal of analyzing or studying a system might be simply to understand or to satisfy curiosity—as one might study the solar system. A more utilitarian goal is the understanding and evaluation of changes needed to improve a system by manipulating problem elements systematically, rather than in a haphazard, unplanned manner. In both cases systems analysis requires identification of the component parts of an existing system and determination of their relationships or dependencies.

In contrast, when systems analysis is considered as a means of solving a problem, the problem is considered as a whole, then analysis and synthesis take place. In analysis, elements are separated to examine their relationships; in synthesis, elements are combined to create a system. After examining a problem, one may set goals for its solution. For instance, if a student cannot read, a short-range goal is to devise a system for teaching him or her to read. The long-range goal is, of course, that the student will read. After the integration of elements to achieve a goal, the next concern is to determine ways of making that achievement most efficient.

The steps taken in systems analysis include: definition of the problem, collection of information relative to the problem, synthesis of a solution, implementation of the solution, evaluation of the solution, and provision of feedback. Feedback can consist of data that facilitate decisions, or decisions based on the analysis of data.

In many instances the initial definition of the problem is relatively imprecise—for example, Tom cannot read. The second step, collection of information, can be stated in the form of a task analysis—for instance, "What skills essential to reading are missing from Tom's repertoire?" An analysis of his skills may show that he knows the names of most of the letters, but can differentiate the sounds of only some of them. He is capable of making still fewer vowel sounds in response to a visual cue and has only a very small sight vocabulary. After such assessment or diagnosis, one must specify, for each skill or sub skill to be acquired, the behavior to be exhibited, the conditions under which the behavior is to occur, and the criteria for acceptable behavior (Mager, 1962). Additionally, it will be necessary to determine the sequence of skill development through which the pupil will progress.

When the problem has been defined more precisely, one must determine what further information will help the solution. Or once the dependent variable (the skill to be learned) is known, one may ask what independent variables can be used to modify it, and what are the constraints on these variables? Independent variables that influence learning occur in the following categories: the pupil's individuality, the conditions preceding the pupil's performance, the characteristics of the required response, and the conditions following performance. After one considers as many combinations of the above variables as possible to arrive at the best solution, the third step in systems analysis—synthesis of a solution—is approached. Many limits and constraints determining what must and what must not be done will be imposed on the potential solution. One consideration in establishing theoretical options and limits is their impact on organizational and practical issues. For instance, it must be determined whether or not the materials that call for the appropriate response are available and whether the people and cues are the most desirable ones. Is there enough time to provide the appropriate feedback? What reinforcers are available, and what effect will their use have on other children? In many cases the existing constraints will eliminate some possible solutions, perhaps even some of the more desirable alternatives. Regardless, one seeks an alternative that best achieves the solution with attainable or available resources.

When a strategy has been synthesized to meet the problem, the fourth step, implementation, can be initiated. When completed, the strategy and its effects upon the child can be evaluated.

Evaluation, the fifth step, is necessary to know if, or how well, the objective was satisfied. This information is useful in determining alternative action in the event of failure, or in deciding how to approach the next objective. Evaluation also can improve the system. When information on the system's output is returned, it is called feedback. Since the purpose of feedback is to improve the system, it may take place at any time in the system's evolution or between any of its developmental stages.

The quality of the analysis is limited by the amount of data available. For instance, if only posttest scores are available, all that can be determined is how well the objective was met. If an item analysis of the posttest scores is available, it may be possible to see with greater clarity what procedures were not effective. If daily or otherwise frequent data are available, it may be possible to determine why the system was not effective and to make some judgment about its efficiency for the student. When data are accumulated daily, the teacher can watch a student's performance closely and make adjustments sooner.

In attempting to improve the cost effectiveness of a system, any variable in it can be altered. Perhaps the constraints initially set were unnecessarily limiting, or perhaps the objective was not worth its cost. A change could be as simple as telling a child to work faster; it is possible that a change in reinforcers from expendable ones to activities based on the Premack Principle (Premack, 1959) might be a more efficient course of action.

TECHNIQUES FOR EFFECTIVE INSTRUCTION

Because teachers are concerned with changing only a small fraction of the thousands of behaviors in which children engage, they are left with decisions for determining which behaviors to change. Fortunately, society has adopted some general priorities for behavior change. Those areas in which there is broad general agreement include: language and communication skills, preacademic behaviors, academic behaviors, social competencies, physical and mental fitness, and leisure time and recreational activities. Within these general areas, specific behavioral goals can be and have been specified in many school systems throughout the nation.

The more conscientious and precise a teacher is in managing his or her pupils, the greater will be the number of specific child behaviors that can be managed. Even a conscientious teacher is in somewhat of an organizational dilemma for achieving desired change in his or her pupils. The problem is the multiplicity of pupils and the naturally occurring differences among them. Teachers are, on the average, confronted by about 30 children in the classroom. For each youngster, a teacher likely will select several academic areas and social behaviors that need to be modified. This problem is compounded by the fact that children vary, presenting a wide range of differences for teachers to incorporate into planning for behavior change. The available range of educational practices and instructional procedures further complicates things. When the scope of behaviors, pupils, and educational variables that must be dealt with on a daily basis are considered, it is no wonder that teachers often feel frustrated and weary at the end of a day—wondering if any progress has been made with certain children.

For a teacher to achieve a good balance in selecting behavioral goals for individual children and to insure that each child is progressing in those areas of importance for him or her, a teacher must give careful attention to a strategy of instruction and to the classroom and program organization. Let us consider how a teacher can establish a comprehensive assessment-instruction-education plan that combines systems and behavioral technologies.

The teacher's primary goal is to provide conditions that will lead to effective pupil learning. Some of the activities necessary for these conditions are not direct instructional practices. They are considered organizational and administrative. For example, a teacher is responsible for keeping track of attendance, lunch count, attending teachers' meetings, and other routine duties. These activities at times seem trivial to direct instructional practices, but they are essential as part of the organization of the educational system so that direct instruction can occur. A second area in which teachers engage in noninstructional activities is communication with other persons who are important in the child's life. Parents, other teachers, and support personnel all are individuals with whom the teacher must communicate to provide the optimal set of conditions suitable for a child's learning. So that these activities do not consume a disproportionate amount of time in the teaching day, they should be handled in a systematic fashion—therefore, teachers may spend the required time and energy providing specific instruction that children need.

Decision-Making

Much of a teacher's behavior involves decision-making, a selection of alternatives. When a teacher is not aware of this, haphazard and inconsistent decision-making is likely to occur. To teach without a basic strategy as a guide in making decisions is to risk making decisions based on impulse or emotion rather than on a systematic consideration of the consequences involved. Decisions should increase the probability of achieving desired educational objectives. When facing a decision, a teacher needs to consider what will be the likely outcome of available alternatives. If one child continually is talking to another and disrupting a lesson, possible alternatives might be to scold the child, ignore the disruption, or remove the child from the situation. The teacher naturally would like to choose an alternative that would reduce the behavior effectively. Scolding the child could act as positive reinforcement for the talking-out behavior. Patterson and Reid (1970) refer to this as a coercive cycle. The child whose inappropriate talking behavior has been reinforced by teacher attention will emit that same response again (Haring and Phillips, 1972). If the teacher scolds the child once more and this proves ineffective, the disruptive behavior may generalize to other children. A better alternative would be ignoring the talk-outs. If the behavior persists, it may become necessary to remove the child from the situation either by asking him or her to go to another part of the room or to stand in the hall.

The only basis by which the actual consequence of different decisions can be determined is to collect data on how effective certain alternatives were in modifying a specific behavior. To determine empirically whether removing a child from the talk-out situation is more likely to decrease the behavior than scolding, data must be collected on each of the intervention tactics. Once data have been collected across time for particular problems, tactics that have a higher probability of working with children can be identified. However, a teacher should not lean on statistics or habit when working with individual children. The effectiveness of any intervention, whether academic or social, must be verified when applied in a given situation.

The soundness of a decision is determined only by its effect. In the case of reducing a child's talk-outs, the effectiveness of a particular decision is determined by whether or not less disruptive talk-outs occur in the future. If an intervention does not produce the desired change immediately, a teacher should not try another immediately, as an intervention must be adhered to for several occasions to determine its effect. It is best to formulate several alternatives if a child behaves in a given way and to stay with the alternatives consistently to discriminate their effects. If possible, decision points should be anticipated and principles, or rules, established for actual decision-making. Rules generally take the form of "if-then" statements. "If Patty does x, then Y will be done." Doing this, a teacher can anticipate many decisions that will occur during the day. "If Richard disrupts the class, I will do x. If x does not reduce the disruptive behavior, I will do y." If a teacher anticipates a talk-out situation, a simple rule can be formulated. The same procedure applies to academic performance. If a child scores less than 50 percent on a criterion test on math facts, the teacher must select alternative instructional tactics to increase performance. Drill on error problems or additional practice on specific types of problems might be initiated. The general rule could be: if a child achieves less than a specified criterion, learning will continue on current material under varying conditions.

By following a systematic approach to decision-making, a teacher can anticipate many decisions. This should not imply, however, that for every situation there is one proper response. Nor should it be taken to mean that spontaneous behavior in the classroom should be limited or avoided. Considering the number of children and the myriad possibilities of combinations of behavior that children may display, events and situations naturally will occur that have not been anticipated and for which no rule has been devised. In every situation a teacher should consider the effect that his or her behavior will have on the future behavior of the child. Most decision-making involves routine behavior, and the majority of the decisions a teacher must make involves instructional activities. Collecting a daily record of pupil performance provides a good source of information to determine whether specific interventions were effective and whether refinement of a tactic is necessary. Collecting data can serve as a source of positive reinforcement for teachers and also as a means of seeing when change is necessary to increase academic performance or remediate an evolving problem.

Teachers, in many instances, make 90 percent or more of the decisions directly involved with the instructional process. Lovitt (1973) has demonstrated that many behaviors once the exclusive province of teachers, such as selecting, scheduling, presenting, confirming, reinforcing, recording, and evaluating, can be administered by the students themselves. Teachers can specify and plan a decision-making process sufficiently to give some of the responsibility for decision-making and implementation directly to the children. Such self-management aids children in discovering how to organize and manage their own behaviors. There are endless possibilities of how teachers can aid children in learning to make their own decisions. This reduces teacher time for planning and also helps the children to gain a valuable skill—decision-making.

Moreover, if we accept the view that increasing a child's self-managing skills is a legitimate aim of education, then providing as many opportunities as possible for the child to practice these skills is a desirable, not merely expedient, educational activity. A study by Lovitt and Curtiss (1972) indicated that when students select their own contingencies, their academic behavior improves. Lovitt and Curtiss note:

> . . . the person who can control . . . his own behavior may be the person who can assess his own competencies, set his own behavioral objectives, specify a contingency system whereby he might attain these objectives. Translated to school, this might be: one who knew his academic capabilities . . . could arrange . . . steps to achieve a variety of self-imposed objectives, and could grant himself reinforcement on a prearranged schedule to accomplish certain behavior sequences.

A number of investigators have used group contingency systems for promoting self-management; in these studies, a whole group's fate (extension or cancellation of privileges, and so on) depends on the behavior of anyone in the group. In a study by Billingsley and Smelzer (1973), the "behavior game" involved two "teams" within a class having a very high rate of disruptive behavior; the group contingency system worked to reduce these behaviors when the limits of tolerance were clearly specified. Laurence J. Peter (1972) found that the system produced an environment in which students no longer encouraged each other's inappropriate behavior; rather, they encouraged more appropriate behaviors that enabled the class to be fully involved in learning.

Direct evaluation characteristics. It may be useful to discuss some of the most commonly used classroom measures in the light of characteristics that are desirable in direct evaluation procedures for children with academic response deficits. Basically, nine characteristics seem desirable:

1. The behavior being measured should be directly observable. Children's written and verbal responses are the two most common categories of observable academic behavior.

2. The behavioral units should be uniformly and finely defined. For example, "words said" is a reasonably uniform and small unit of behavior with which to measure much oral reading.

3. The behavior being measured should be directly related to the learning objective, and likewise the learning task. This provides direct information on the targeted task.

4. The scale used to represent the performance should have small enough increments so that change can be reflected sensitively. The typical letter grading scale of A, B, C, D, and F has such large increments that much pupil change must occur before it will be reflected in the performance scale.

5. The scale used to represent the performance also should allow measures to vary over a wide range, so that pupil change will not be restricted by a performance ceiling or floor. The performance of a youngster who typically scores 95 to 100 percent correct on weekly quizzes is not free to vary upward to reflect additional improvement. (Contrary to common belief, 100 percent accuracy on a task does not always indicate mastery or proficiency. Consider the child who can complete all of the required addition facts correctly, but who uses fingers or a number line to count out the answers. This child probably would not be considered proficient.)

6. The procedures for collecting the data should be applicable and practical for the classroom. The teacher should be able to administer the procedures as part of the regular instructional routine.

7. The procedures should provide that data be gathered under conditions that are uniform each time measures are obtained. This is necessary so that differences in derived data can be attributed to changes in the learner and not to varying measurement conditions, materials, or time. To insure that measurement conditions are stable, the teacher will want to assure that the content of the measurement tool, the length of time, and the measurement procedures are the same each time performance is measured.

8. The derived data should be reliable. This is largely dependent on whether the observable behavioral unit is clearly defined and data-collection procedures are adequately developed.

9. The derived data should be obtained often enough so that they can be used to show pupil change on a frequent basis and consequently be used to make instructional decisions. Daily performance measures generally meet this criterion best.

Teachers historically have given regular classroom assignments and administered weekly or periodic quizzes. The quizzes often have been considered more valuable than assignments in evaluating whether children actually have acquired the intended information. The raw scores or percentage scores obtained from such quizzes are based on overt pupil performance. The reporting units (that is, percent correct) are based on a uniform scale. Certainly the procedures are practical; teachers have been using them for many years. However, because their content and difficulty levels vary from testing to testing, these measures are not always as indicative of progress as they are of differences in the content and difficulty of the course and tests. Nor are they sensitive to specific learning problems. Such tests often are given infrequently enough so that they are not very useful for altering conditions to improve pupil learning on the included content. Little information is obtained that shows a pattern or trend of failure. Letter grades based on percent scores, and frequently including teacher judgments about effort, are even less useful for making instructional decisions.

Achievement tests, used by many schools to supplement other forms of measurement, are not very helpful in direct instructional decision-making. Usually they are given only annually. They are constructed to sample a very broad amount of information, so they usually do not measure directly the content covered in a course. In fact, professionals become concerned if they feel a teacher has taught to an achievement test. The resulting data also are referenced to normative groups and not to criteria levels of performance. The apparent deficits of achievement tests are due to the fact that they were not designed as a formative tool for the day-to-day instructional decisions with which teachers are faced.

FIVE COMPONENTS OF INSTRUCTION

Educational research is geared to developing a set of precise and systematic instructional procedures. Improvement of traditional instructional techniques occurs through scientifically identifying the major components of instruction and discovering how each operates in establishing an optimum learning environment. Basically, there are five components of instruction: 1) assessment and evaluation, 2) direct and daily measurement, 3) arrangement of instructional cues and curriculum, 4) drill, practice, and application, and 5) reinforcement. In the discussion that follows, these components will be examined at length, with the exception of reinforcement, which has been discussed in detail earlier.

There is no specific order as to which comes first or what sequence is best, but when working with a child who has an academic or social behavior disorder the above sequence seems best. One should not, however, think that reinforcement should come at all phases and that measurement is a continuous function. It is not easy to present these procedures linearly as they are more a helical or cybernetic function than a linear one (Haring and Phillips, 1972). These procedures are quite similar to the applied analysis of behavior, and because they involve direct observation, continuous measurement, and systematic changes in instructional condition, the most functional form of assessment is offered. Assessment and evaluation becomes not merely a task at the beginning of a specific remediation technique, but an integral part of the analysis of direct daily measurement data. Each of the components of instruction work together to bring about change in the targeted behavior of the pupil and reinforce new levels of skill mastery.

The combination of systems and behavioral technologies makes possible the establishment of a comprehensive assessment-instruction-evaluation plan necessary in educating the learning disabled child. The classroom teacher is the target of these procedures, but an understanding of them is helpful to all concerned. Continuous measurement enables the teacher to monitor student performance daily and equips the teacher with hard data on which to defend and explain decisions. This combats a major problem in the classroom teacher's experience—when to make changes and how to justify them.

Assessment and Evaluation

Assessment and evaluation are closely related. Assessment, at least theoretically, determines pupil placement, intervention tactics, and maintenance of performance. It is often assumed that assessment procedures are initiated after a problem has been identified. Then some type of assessment is used that results in an evaluation of a child's performance focusing on specific discovered deficits. One of the goals of developing systematic instructional procedures is the design of an ongoing assessment and evaluation technique that identifies learning problems as they occur. Implicit in such a system is the use of early identification and screening tests. Screening children as soon as they enter the public school system to identify potential learning disabilities as early as possible and to begin the process of individualizing instruction are vital factors in the overall remediation of specific learning disorders. Perhaps the most important information a teacher can have is the current performance level of a child on a specific task. Knowing "where the kid is at," and what he or she is capable of doing, makes programming a much simpler task.

The traditional way of assessing a child has been to administer intelligence, achievement, and personality measures. This usually is done by a psychologist, who makes suggestions about placement based on the test results. A child scoring two standard deviations below the mean on intelligence and achievement tests, and showing no major personality problems, is often placed in a classroom for the moderately or educably retarded. Placement is based on the assumption that such an environment will be more beneficial than putting the child in a classroom not designed for the retarded. Without arguing the validity of such an assumption, it can be seen that making the decision and planning the intervention is not based on educationally relevant data. Intelligence and other related tests often do not identify a child with a specific learning disability. On such tests as the Weschler Intelligence Test for Children (WISC), the only way to pinpoint a problem is by discrepancy among subtest scores, which lead to more testing but not directly to remediation. Methods such as Lovitt's functional analysis procedure (discussed earlier) provide more refined means of assessment that generate educationally relevant data. The intent of this chapter is to offer an instructional system incorporating functional analysis assessment procedures into an ongoing evaluation method that is individualized and sensitive to each child's needs and abilities.

SST-PERFORM PROJECT

The identification of children with specific learning disabilities in the state of Washington began in 1971 with funding from the Child Service Demonstration Program. Although several goals originally were delineated in the project, the greatest contribution is the development of a screening instrument that identifies children operating at one-half or more below the class frequency median in three out of five select movement cycles in kindergarten or four out of seven in grades one through three. These movement cycles include: 1) write x's, 2) mark dots, 3) hear to write number, 4) write number at random, 5) write letters random, 6) draw Harmon circles, and 7) say letters random. Originally, the seven movement cycles (four in the case of kindergartners) were given over a 10-day period. Children performed each movement cycle for one-minute samples. Upon analyzing data from the first two years of operation, project leaders decided to reduce the number of movement cycles to two or three (write numbers random and say words random) to be administered for 10 consecutive days.

The second phase of the project (Precise Educational Remediation for Managers, Perform) has been to design individualized remedial experiences for children identified as performing on basic academic skills at half or less than half the frequency and acceleration of their classmates. In the "acceleration" phase, concern focuses on bringing those children identified as learning disabled in specific areas up to a class performance level. Attempts were made to teach to specific movement cycles using precision teaching methods. Information collected from the screening phase served as baseline data. Direct and daily measurement continued as instruction began.

The most successful contribution of this project is the screening instrument. Children whose performances showed either a consistently low rate or decelerating were identified for further practice on those particular movement cycles. Children who were deficient to the extent that it was likely they would not succeed in the classroom were referred for special assistance. High error rates and low correct rates, of course, indicate a problem. Remedial exercises are then based directly on the child's performance on the screening battery.

Whether or not this type of procedure will be continued is not certain. If the screening instrument can be developed so that it can tentatively identify problems early, further assessment procedures should be developed to identify more precisely specific learning disabilities. The advantage is that these procedures can be used by a trained classroom teacher as a means of ongoing assessment. The movement cycle probe in the SST project is a step toward a comprehensive assessment instrument that is operational and directly applicable to the classroom. The screening instrument is an extension of the probing procedures, which we shall discuss shortly.

GENERAL ASSESSMENT STRATEGIES

Because we are interested in designing individualized instructional programs, those assessment activities relevant to true individualized instruction are discussed here. Assessment directed toward individualized instruction has been the constant theme of the applied analysis of behavior, precision teaching, and other related instructional systems. Also involved in this enterprise is the development of logic or sequence of instruction. Initial assessment and the measurement strategies implicit in the functional analysis of behavior are the keys to this logic. The specific type of assessment strategy suggested here has evolved from Lindsley's Precision Teaching and Lovitt's work in the functional analysis of behavior. A more comprehensive coverage of these considerations can be found in White and Liberty's chapter "Behavioral Assessment and Precise Educational Measurement" (Schiefelbusch and Haring, eds., *Teaching Special Children*, 1976).

Assessment provides data on which to base decisions and make predictions about instruction. Assessment may take three forms: for formulating goals and objectives for instruction, for placement in specific curriculum or instructional sequence, and to determine the "cause" of a particular deficiency. Each type of assessment is needed at different times and under various conditions.

A goal is a general statement about a desired long-term behavioral change. An objective is a much more specific statement derived from the more general goal. An objective should include a statement of pupil response, a description of conditions or the environment in which the response is to occur, and a statement of the criteria for acceptable performance (Mager, 1972). The knowledge of what children are to learn is necessary to arrange the learning environment that will insure progress. Human behavior is goal-directed. Children respond more readily to instruction when they know where they are and where they are going.

Instructional goals for teachers must be complementary to goals selected for children. The general instructional goal can be broken down into several enabling objectives:

1. To assess each child for placement in basic skills.
2. To establish long-range objectives for each child concerning performance at the end of the instructional period.

3. To establish immediate objectives toward the long-range objectives.

4. To write a systematic instructional plan for each child in each subject area covering all conditions (materials, procedures, reinforcement conditions, and evaluation).

5. To obtain performance data on every child at least three times a week.

6. To use performance data to change instruction to facilitate learning either by advancing the child to more difficult material or slicing the material into more easily accessible units of response.

The amount of freedom a teacher will have in implementing these instructional objectives will vary from district to district. Some districts have global goals to be met, but within these broad parameters individual teachers have the freedom to set long- and short-term objectives. When districts do not specifically state criteria for performance, teachers likely will do so in some form or another.

Setting long- and short-range instructional objectives is of great value. If a teacher knows that at the end of a school year a child must be able to read 100 words per minute with 80 percent comprehension in a third grade reader, the scope of instructional activities during the year can be designed to motivate the child toward that goal. The usual procedure for selecting long-range objectives is to define the task on which the child should perform at a given time. Immediate objectives are steps to a larger, long-term objective. Many tasks are sequenced by commercial texts and such texts are acceptable to teachers. They also can break down tasks into sequences that seem natural. Three books of value in learning to sequence instruction are: R. F. Mager's *Goal Analysis* and *Preparing Instructional Objectives;* and R. E. Boston's *How to Write and Use Performance Objectives to Individualize Instruction.*

A diagnostic form of assessment is more useful in setting goals and objectives than a wide-range normative assessment. It is necessary to gain a precise and definitive statement of a child's capabilities and achievement levels. A diagnostic reading test, for example, may show that a child has a sufficient sight vocabulary, but is deficient in phonics skills. Such assessment methods are criterion-referenced, focusing on specific abilities and disabilities and using levels of performance on specific tasks rather than being norm-referenced against a larger statistical reference group. When current performance is stated in relationship to a specified criterion, one knows both what a child can do and how far the child must progress to achieve mastery of the skill.

To place a child in an instructional sequence requires information about the skills and behavior that the child already possesses. Once a specific skill has been sequenced, an assessment of performance on the various levels of the sequence will reveal what the child can and cannot do. To do this, one must determine the "desired critical effect." This means identifying the behavior one desires children to perform and specifying the conditions under which the performance is to occur. A child deficient in naming written numerals can be given a page with numerals written on it randomly. The teacher has decided that proficiency is reading the numerals correctly at the rate of 100 per minute. The critical effect in this case is to read numerals correctly at 100 per minute for one minute. The implications of the concept of desired critical effect are vital to establish ongoing assessment procedures. The time-frame one selects for a particular skill can vary from skill to skill, especially academic and social skills. One-minute to five-minute samples are usually sufficient to assess pupil performance on basic academic tasks. In assessing social behavior such as study actions or attention, a teacher might use longer periods of time. The outcome of the performance a teacher desires to achieve with a child is largely determined by the critical effect that is identified initially.

The forms of assessment used to determine causes for deficient behavior are usually medical or psychological in content. The pursuit of causes, or etiology, has led to a preoccupation with the specific process within an individual, usually neurological in nature, to the exclusion of manipulable or environmental causes. The assignment of causative factors, whether internal or external, is always an inferential process, since it is impossible to replicate organic states or previous learning history. A reading deficit may lead a psychologist to search for intervening neurological or perceptual deficits that cause the reading problem. Although at one level this is truly important, for the classroom teacher such assessment usually fails to provide relevant information.

Probing procedures.   The probing process is the practice of taking a relatively brief sample of a pupil's performance on a standard task under standard conditions. The data from such a probe can be utilized to make decisions about the effectiveness of the instructional procedures used with a pupil. The basic procedure includes the following steps: 1) selection of a sequence of learning tasks against which the pupil will be assessed; 2) selection of specific tasks at different levels of performance, or from different performance areas; and 3) administering brief probes on several consecutive days to determine where in the sequence the pupil will be placed. For example, to determine pupil placement in a reading series, the teacher might take oral reading probes from each of several different levels within the series. Based on the correct and error data obtained on the pupil, and the trend of progress over the first few days, the teacher might select a particular level in which to place the pupil. A similar strategy might be used to decide in which reader series to place the pupil.

Generally, probe materials consist of relatively small, internally consistent units of learning. For example, a probe might consist of all of the basic addition facts, or it might consist only of a selected portion of the addition facts, such as problems with sums of zero to three. Such a probe presents uniform materials for the pupils to respond to. Addition facts, for example, constitute problems of approximately the same length. Probe materials also elicit uniform responses. In other words for each fact to which the pupil must write an answer there is either a one- or two-digit answer. Probing procedures also allow for control of the conditions and the amount of time under which a youngster performs. Probes are generally given in the same manner each day, at the same time of day, and in the same relationship to instruction. In other words, they are always given after, before, or in the middle of the instructional period. They also are generally given for the same amount of time, for example for a one- or two-minute timing. Because both the materials and procedures are uniform from day to day, any changes in performance are expected to reflect changes in a pupil's academic growth. The data can then be used to evaluate pupil progress and the efficacy of whatever instructional procedures are being used.

So that children do not simply memorize the answer or sequence of answers to probe materials, alternate forms are constructed in which the same problems or same class of problems are varied randomly. By following this process, measures can be taken on the same materials, but youngsters cannot simply memorize a sequence of answers. It is also general practice to provide more work than a youngster can perform on a probing task, so that a limiting ceiling will not be set on a pupil's performance. For example, if a one-minute timing is being given on addition facts, the teacher would provide more problems than a youngster could perform in one minute.

The use of probing procedures with direct daily measurement has several advantages over more traditional types of pupil evaluation. First, the teacher is able to construct measurement units or probes that correspond to the actual instructional objectives used in the classroom. Second, probes provide uniform measurement for individual pupils within each learning step. Third, a display of data taken from probes enables a pupil to see daily progress, rather than simply work through materials. Fourth, controlled probes enable a classroom teacher to collect reference data in regard to typical child performance on specified learning tasks.

In math, one could use a similar strategy. Arithmetic might be sequenced into rote counting, counting objects, addition, subtraction, multiplication, and division processes. Each of these general tasks would be refined further into its component parts. Addition processes, for example, might be subdivided into basic facts, two-column problems without carrying, and so on. This repeated division of tasks into smaller and more homogeneous subtasks can be carried as far as necessary for effective assessment.

It would be extremely cumbersome to ask a pupil to perform all math tasks to determine his entry point in an instructional sequence. Therefore, a few probe sheets from a wide variety of tasks can be selected, and performance data on these tasks can be obtained. On these selected sheets the data usually will sort into three groups: those tasks on which the child readily meets proficiency criteria; those tasks on which errors are made on most items; and those tasks on which the child passes some items and makes errors on some others. The teacher can then select additional probe sheets for tasks near the child's point of transition from

Write Numbers, Random

INTAKE ☐ RETURN ☐ FOLLOW-UP ☐   Date_____ Correct_____ Error_____

3	8	9	5	7	2	4	3	0	1
—	—	—	—	—	—	—	—	—	—
7	5	4	9	3	2	0	1	3	2
—	—	—	—	—	—	—	—	—	—
8	3	5	1	6	0	2	6	7	3
—	—	—	—	—	—	—	—	—	—
4	9	8	5	6	0	2	1	3	7
—	—	—	—	—	—	—	—	—	—
9	4	5	2	0	1	4	5	3	8
—	—	—	—	—	—	—	—	—	—

Figure 7.1a. *Academic Probe.*

Developed by Experimental Education Unit, College of Education and Child Development
& Mental Retardation Center, University of Washington, Seattle, Washington.

Addition, Facts

INTAKE ☐ RETURN ☐ FOLLOW-UP ☐   Date _____ Correct ____ Error ____

2 +3	1 +9	2 +2	1 +1	6 +1	2 +9	7 +1	3 +9	1 +5	2 +6
1 +2	1 +3	2 +5	1 +0	1 +4	8 +2	7 +2	8 +1	2 +0	4 +2
3 +4	8 +3	5 +3	3 +0	7 +5	4 +4	7 +3	5 +0	4 +5	4 +7
3 +6	5 +6	4 +8	5 +8	4 +3	5 +5	4 +0	3 +3	9 +4	6 +4
9 +6	9 +3	9 +7	7 +7	9 +0	8 +8	8 +5	9 +9	6 +6	6 +9
8 +9	7 +0	9 +5	8 +6	0 +8	6 +7	6 +0	7 +8	7 +4	5 +7

Figure 7.1b. *Academic Probe.*

Developed by Experimental Education Unit, College of Education and Child Development
& Mental Retardation Center, University of Washington, Seattle, Washington.

competency to failure. Of course, if the teacher already is familiar with the range of tasks the child has performed, that information can be used to guide his or her initial selection of probe sheets.

Suppose we wished to assess a pupil's entry point in the math sequence previously described. For initial data we might select the following probe sheets:

1. Write numerals.
2. Count objects (dots).
3. Addition facts.
4. Subtraction facts.
5. Multiplication facts.
6. Division facts.

If a pupil met proficiency criteria on the first three tasks, erred on all items of the last three tasks, and completed only a few items correctly on the subtraction task, we probably should select additional probe sheets from the more complex addition tasks. By using such a funneling process, we are able to focus on a pupil's precise entry point for the arithmetic program.

Direct and Daily Measurement

Earlier, we discussed the assessment procedures involved in a functional analysis of behavior. Taking baseline data as to the performance level of a child on a given academic behavior is the initial step in setting up an effective measurement system. Probing procedures also provide baseline data to inform the teacher of the level on which a child is capable of performing. The functional analysis of behavior technique is used often in clinical schools or experimental situations with children referred from public schools for academic or social learning disabilities. The following procedures are nearly the same, but are applicable to public school settings. Once a learning disability exists, it is an educational management problem, and the child is best served if remediation can be a direct part of the public school experience. This is best for the child in terms of reinforcement potential and for the community in terms of cost. It is more expensive to operate sophisticated referral centers than to develop and implement procedures to educate the child with a learning disability in the regular classroom.

Before discussing the tools for taking continuous data, we need to consider several concepts.

Movement cycles. The behavior to be changed must be precisely identified and defined before beginning instruction or remedial intervention. The term usually used for such a precise educational target is a "movement cycle," which is a statement of observable behavior that contains movement, is controlled by the child, is countable, and is repeatable. In the case of academic movement cycles, teachers can pinpoint such behaviors as "saying letters," "writing numerals," or "listing names of capitals." With social movement cycles, behavior such as "hitting a peer," "getting out of seat," or "talking out" can be pinpointed. "Movement cycles" is the initial phase of establishing behavioral objectives. Once a target behavior or movement cycle is defined, modification procedures can be used either to accelerate or strengthen the behavior, or decelerate or weaken it.

Pinpointing movement cycles in the classroom is essential for the investigation of a standardized system of classroom measurement. When a movement cycle is defined, one knows what exactly to count and measure. It is important that the behavior being targeted involve "doing" or movement. It is also important for the teacher to try to pinpoint what the child should be doing rather than what is not being done. An academic behavior can be seen in terms of acceleration and deceleration. If a child is deficient in oral reading, a pinpointed behavior could be "reads words orally correctly." This is an acceleration of behavior. The deceleration target would be "reads words orally incorrectly." If a child reads one sentence from a reader correctly as defined in the movement cycle, this action constitutes the completion of one movement cycle. If the sentence is read incorrectly, the emission of the behavior is zero.

Rate or frequency data. The basic datum used in systems that are extensions of the experimental and applied analysis of behavior is the rate, or frequency, at which a behavior occurs. Determining the rate of performance requires taking the total of movement cycles that have occurred and dividing by the total time.

Rate is one of our most important measures, as this statement reveals:

> The rate at which events occur is an extremely important consideration in human affairs. In health, we are concerned about blood pressure or rate of abnormal cell growth. Financially, we watch with concern the rate at which we earn money, spend money, and pay interest; economists carefully study the rate at which our economy expands. The rate of occurrence of disasters such as automobile accidents, fires, and floods is of great concern to those affected (Cohen, Gentry, Hulten, and Martin, 1972).

It is a child's rate of response on given academic tasks that determines the conditions the teacher will set up to change the behavior. Traditional measures of academic success such as percentage scores do not reveal as much about change over time as do rate data. Percentage data permit us to compare situations in which there have been differing numbers of *opportunities* to respond; whereas rate data include the *time* allowed or taken in actual responding. Instead of dividing the actual number of events (or movement cycles) by the time taken, percentage data are obtained by dividing the actual behaviors by the number of possible behaviors, for example, the number of answers by the items on the test.

It is possible also to obtain percentage scores when taking rate data, but not vice versa. Focusing on obtaining rate data, the teacher will attempt to measure performance daily. This replaces the traditional pretest, posttest technique, where a test is administered before instruction and after instruction, and inferences are drawn from comparisons of the two scores. If a child fails to learn or is confused during instruction but does not ask for help, the teacher may overlook the problem. By taking daily samples of performance, the teacher is able to see if change is occurring and to make adjustments in curriculum, instructional procedures, or reinforcement if necessary.

Desired rate. Educators have in recent years advocated a mastery learning approach to instruction. Mastery or proficiency criterion is usually expressed in percentage terms, for example, "The pupil will write 98 percent of the add facts correctly." Desired rate is one way to define the goals toward which a pupil is to work. Desired rate is basically the number of movement cycles per minute that a teacher wants a child to attain. Several methods can be used for determining desired rate. A teacher can set a rate arbitrarily based on what is thought to be reasonable. This is not advisable except to begin developing approximations toward more appropriate desired rates. Previous performance on similar movement cycles or material can be used as the pupil moves on to a more difficult level. Another method is to use peer performance as a criterion level for setting an instructional objective for a child. By using probes and establishing baseline performance level on a given task, the teacher can determine a reasonable criterion for the child to work toward by gauging the trend and rate of performance. We shall discuss the establishment of desired rate more fully when trend analysis is discussed. For the present, it should be understood that in setting instructional objectives the teacher should use actual performance data.

Accuracy. Not only must a teacher have a means of accelerating the rate of a child's performance, but procedures also must be available to improve the quality of academic work. A comprehensive measurement system must reveal both rate and accuracy scores. Accuracy generally is expressed in terms of percent correct. In a direct daily measurement system, both aspects of rate and accuracy (quantity and quality) are retained. By comparing the rate of correct responses and the rate of errors, one can obtain a relationship that reveals accuracy. We shall discuss this in greater detail shortly.

Endurance and generalization. It is important to know the rate and accuracy of a child's academic performance, and it is essential to know if an individual can maintain performance over time and can generalize one skill to another context. Learning a skill in one context is probably of little use unless that skill can be generalized to other areas. A child's ability to generalize probably is dependent on the strength of the cues and the association the child has with the cues, as well as on the child's endurance. A teacher must consider carefully the length of time a child is asked to perform on certain tasks, the way in which the learning task is structured, and the length of time the teacher observes the child's performance. Endurance can be aided by altering a pupil's performance level, altering the consequences of performance, or by lengthening performance time. Once a learned skill exemplifies endurance, generalization to other contexts should be attempted. This is done by altering the curriculum or the context in which the specific skill is performed and measuring the pupil's success or failure.

Collecting data.   Probes and initial assessment procedures give the teacher baseline data by which specific movement cycles can be pinpointed for change and terminal goals set for instruction. Classroom research in various systems of data collection has produced a set of procedures used in experimental schools at the universities of Washington, Oregon, and Kansas, as well as in public schools working with them. The procedures offer practical, precise assistance to teachers in the process of individualizing instruction. For the teacher confronted with one or more learning disabled children in the classroom, these procedures are vital in guarding against both learning failure and instructional failure. It also has been found that students easily can learn to collect and chart their own data, thus allowing the teacher time to give attention to curriculum and individual instruction. Daily charting tells the students and the teacher exactly what is happening in various areas of academic behavior. Self-charting enables students to become more self-sufficient and to learn to monitor and control their behaviors in a wide variety of situations.

The three tools a teacher must use for taking continuous data in the classroom are the plan sheet, the event sheet, and the six-cycle, semilog graph paper.

Plan sheet.   The plan sheet is the basic tool for developing an overall teaching strategy. It has five basic components: 1) the program, 2) the programmed event, 3) movement cycle, 4) arrangement, and 5) arranged event. Figure 7.2 is a composite of several plan sheets currently in use. Basically, the plan sheet describes the conditions and procedures to be used with a pupil in the above five areas. All elements of the instructional process likely to affect pupil performance should be included in the plan sheet.

Systematic planning of pupil programs probably implies actually writing down a teaching plan, considering all of the environmental elements that a teacher feels are relevant to initiating learning. Systematic planning has several advantages over cursory or unsystematic planning, even though the initial cost in teacher time may be greater. The advantages include the following: 1) a well-specified planning format can insure a systematic and orderly consideration of elements of instructional importance and can reduce the probability of overlooking some important component; 2) by establishing a systematic plan and adhering to it, the teacher is better equipped to evaluate the influence of specific instruc-

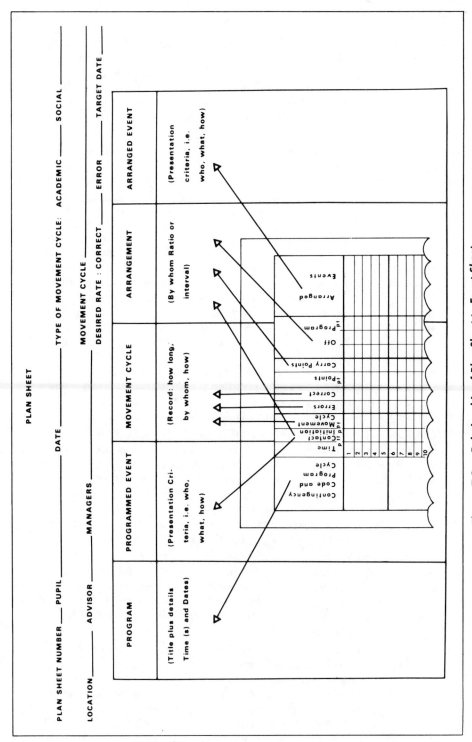

Figure 7.2. *Relationship of Plan Sheet to Event Sheet.*

CDMRC Media Services.

tional components and the efficacy of the total plan with children; 3) a written plan can constitute a permanent record of the conditions under which a child or children performed; and 4) such a plan allows other educators to implement the same instructional plan with the child, or more broadly to replicate the plan with the same or other children.

A systematic plan should allow at least for the consideration of the following elements.

1. *Program.* The program is the overall instructional setting. Three key components of the program are instructional objectives, setting, and curriculum. Immediate *instructional objectives* should be stated in such a way that the teacher can assess whether or not the pupil is progressing toward the objective. Generally, an objective should include all three of Mager's criteria—a statement of the observable behavior to be performed, the conditions under which the child must perform, and the criteria for success. Some of the elements of the setting may affect pupil performance. Examples are: the number of other children present during instruction, a child's location and position in the classroom, the time of day that a program is presented, and the general noise level of the classroom. Of course, other possibilities might be considered. Some of the more obvious aspects of curriculum that might be recorded include: the type of material (programmed or conventional), the content of the program, the format of the display, the type of display, whether the program is commercial or teacher-made, the title of the materials, the author, the publisher, the book or material number, and the grade or difficulty level of the material.

2. *Programmed event.* Procedural considerations include those aspects of instruction that relate to presentation or to the teaching methods used with pupils. They include such elements as who or what will present the material, how it will be presented, how many examples will be presented, what type of special teaching tactics might be used (such as manipulating cuisinaire rods), how many practice problems a pupil will perform, what instructions are given, what material the pupil is told to work, and how long a pupil is told to perform.

3. *Movement cycle.* The observable behavior of the pupil to show that the material actually is being learned ordinarily should be specified. Usually the behavior will be the same as that specified in the learning objective. The units of behavior to be counted should be indicated. For example, on math problems, will each digit be counted or only each complete answer?

4. *Evaluation.* Ongoing evaluation should be a part of the total teaching plan. It has been the authors' experience that unless evaluation issues are planned along with the instructional process procedures, evaluation is not always performed systematically. The following questions might be considered for formative evaluation procedures: What type of data will be collected? What behavior will be monitored? Who will count and time performances? What data-collection tools and proce-

dures will be used? How will data be displayed and used? Who will be responsible for displaying and utilizing data? What decisions are to be made from the data? What are the decision-making rules to be employed? Who will be responsible for insuring that data are used for decision-making?

5. *Arrangement.* Behavior consequents should be planned as systematically as instructional procedures. There are several distinct classes of consequents: correction of work performed, social approval (such as teacher praise), point or token reinforcement followed by backup reinforcers, primary reinforcers such as food, contingency contracts, and the opportunity to advance to new learning tasks.

In writing an arrangement description, it is important to specify the relationship of the consequents to the pupil performance. For example, if a pupil is on a point system to earn free time, it is important to state the number or rate of responses that earn points. Usually such relationships are stated as the ratio of responses to points, for example, 50:1. Sometimes, however, rate contingencies are specified, such as 50 words per minute correct earn 5 points.

6. *Arranged event.* It is important to specify the reinforcing event upon which pupil performance is contingent. For example, if a student is to receive 10 minutes free time for completing 20 correct math problems, this should be clearly stated. This event is dependent upon the student's completing the movement cycle specified in the numerical relationship of the arrangement.

Originally the plan sheet was developed by Ogden Lindsley (1969) and further refined by Eric Haughton (1969) and by several people at the Experimental Education Unit at the University of Washington (Kunzelmann, Cohen, Hulten, Martin, and Mingo, 1970). Lindsley's original formulation (containing five of the above elements of writing a systematic plan) was called the *IS-DOES* formula—the IS refers to planning and describing environmental events that might have an effect upon behavior; DOES is identical in structure except that it is composed of those events identified as having an effect upon the pinpointed behavior. In other words, the IS part of the formula simply refers to what is going on. Altering any part of the IS equation will produce a change in the movement cycle being measured. The change is recorded in the DOES equation, that is, the part of the plan that appears to change behavior. When writing a plan, one is preparing the IS phase of the formula; when the child attempts to perform the task, the DOES part occurs. In this way a teacher easily can separate what is assumed from that for which specific evidence exists. The DOES part becomes active only after collecting and analyzing data. Then evidence of the effect of the IS equation either is verified or disproved by the DOES, or what actually happened.

Event sheet. The event sheet is used for actual recording of performance in the classroom. An event sheet packet containing name, date, and curricular programming is placed on a pupil's desk before each instructional day. The event sheet represents some aspects of the child's behavior over a period of time. Figure 7.2 shows how the five columns of the event sheet relate to the plan sheet. The event sheet represents the relationship between some aspect of the child's behavior and the arranged event (Mingo, 1970).

Either the teacher or the pupil can record each bit of data. On the far left of the event sheet is a column to record the Contingency Code and the Program Cycle. The Contingency Code basically refers to the programmed and arranged events. The Program Cycle is a programmed event occurring in some temporal order. (Examples of program cycles are Sullivan Math, Lippincott's Basic Reading, and Physical Education.) Next is the time column. One column represents one hour, or 60 minutes. For every minute of the day there is a space to record the events that take place in the child's environment, which are described on the plan sheet.

The Contact Initiation column is for recording the type of contact between the pupil and teacher, as well as the time such contact occurred. Four kinds of contact are possible—P, T, PT, TP. Code letter P represents a situation in which the child initiates contact with the teacher. If the child raises a hand or asks for assistance, this is considered child-initiated contact. If the teacher contacts the child without being asked, this is teacher-initiated contact. The code for this is the letter T. Contacts can be arranged in advance. A teacher can tell the child to raise his or her hand after completing a certain amount of work or when an impasse is reached. This is a teacher-arranged contact and is represented by PT. An example would be to say, "Complete this list of add facts and then raise your hand." Students can arrange contacts in advance also. A child can tell the teacher, "Come back when I finish this page," or "Check my work at ten after." This contact is coded TP.

One of these types of contacts should be specified on the plan sheet in the programmed event. This is circled on the event sheet when the lesson begins. The teacher has only to make a slash in the approximate time space whenever contact is initiated. The contact initiation is related directly to the plan sheet to either the programmed or the arranged event. The contact either comes before the movement cycle or before an arrangement based on the movement cycle. If the plan were for the pupil to raise a hand after completing 10 problems, the TP code would be circled. If a contact is made that is not in the plan, the type of contact is written in the time space instead of a slash mark.

In the Movement Cycle column, the exact movement cycle should be recorded. If the program cycle is Sullivan reading, the movement cycle to be counted could be "say words," "say sounds," "say the names of letters," "draw lines," and so on. Teachers are encouraged to develop codes for recording movement cycles that are helpful and tailored to their own needs. These suggested codes are by no means the only possible ones.

When the teacher corrects a pupil's work, correct and error data are recorded in the columns provided. (The column next to correct and error allows space for points correct according to the arrangement.) The first column explains who made the arrangement—pupil or teacher. If the teacher is to describe the amount of points awarded, T is circled. If the pupil is to decide, P is circled. Points are awarded on either ratio or interval schedules. Assume that a teacher arranged with a pupil that points for correct spelling would be earned on a three-to-one ratio. For every three correctly spelled words, the child would receive one point. When correcting work, the teacher or student makes a slash in the points column according to the arrangement, then marks the amount of points in the next column.

The Off Program column designates whether or not the child chooses to utilize points earned under the arrangement plan. The middle number of the contingency code indicates the arrangement. For example, the contingency code is 514. The first digit (5) indicates the kind of contact that occurred. The second digit, or 1, shows that the teacher arranged to give the student points on a predetermined schedule. The last number (4) represents the Off Program column. The 4 indicates that the pupil can specify cash-in of earned points based on a number of accumulated points. This means that the pupil is able to specify when to go "off program" and spend the points earned.

The final column, Arranged Events, indicates for what the pupil chooses to use the points. This gives the teacher space to record the actual subsequent event. The student can use points for free time, trinkets, gym, or can accumulate points continuing to another program. Teachers can develop many types of choices for cash-in of points that allow the children to select reinforcing events.

Charting—six-cycle, semilog graph paper. The final phase of direct daily measurement is the presentation of data through charting. The charting system to be discussed provides a continuing, easily accessible record of changes in behavior as they occur. The basic tools for charting are six-cycle, semilogarithmic chart paper, a rate plotter, and a trend line acceleration finder. Six-cycle log paper was developed by Dr. Ogden R. Lindsley and his associates for use in classroom situations. The vertical axis of this type of chart features six exponential increments ranging from 0–1,000 movements per minute broken down into six cycles—.001–.01, .01–.10, .10–1.0, 1.0–10, 10–100, 100–1,000. The horizontal axis represents 140 days, or 20 weeks, of graphing. The basic difference between six-cycle and arithmetic papers is that semilog paper shows the rate or percent of change. As stated previously, rate is the basic measure of performance in developing systematic instructional procedures. The six-cycle, semilog charting method graphically illustrates change as it occurs and offers a sound data base for making educational decisions.

Nearly all learning disabled children are deficient in basic perceptual or academic skills. In providing a learning experience that attempts to remediate these deficiencies, it is not difficult to program instruction so that resulting daily data are in terms of correct and error over time. This is done by precisely defining movement cycles and counting the occurrence over a set period. However, collecting a ream of data is useless without a method of analyzing them. This method of charting and analysis is an attempt to provide a set of standardized procedures for recording educational data. It is no mere conjecture, as the method is employed extensively across the country. Once a person gets accustomed to using six-cycle charting, it becomes quick and easy. Even children can use it.

The vertical lines on semilog chart paper are day lines. The dark vertical lines are Sunday lines; the lighter ones are the other days of the week. Data can be graphed either by beginning the chart at the first Sunday of the month or by beginning with the first Sunday of the week in which the data was collected. The date of the initial Sunday is written at the top of the chart. Successive calendar days can be counted and marked in units of 10 by using the scale at the top of the paper corresponding to the day lines.

The horizontal lines of the chart are the *rate* or *frequency lines*. They are divided into cycles. The vertical sequence of numbers to the left of the lines represents the number of movement cycles per minute. The cycles are in a "multiply" arrangement, from 1 to 1,000 and in "divided" arrangement from 1 down to the bottom. The three "multiply" cycles are 1–10, 10–100, 100–1,000 movement cycles per minute. Since six-cycle chart paper shows proportional amounts of change in the first multiply cycle, each rate line shows an increase of one movement cycle per minute over the next. From 10–100 each rate line shows an increase in 10 movement cycles per minute; from 100–1,000 shows increases of 100.

Going down the chart from 1, each cycle represents division. From 1 to 0.1 movement cycles per minute is a divide by 10, with each rate line decreasing one-tenth. The next "divide" cycle is divide by 100, with each rate line decreasing by one-hundredth. The final full cycle is a divide by 1,000, from .01 to .001, with each line decreasing by one-thousandth. It is important to remember that this chart shows *frequency* data, because it is, in reality, impossible to count or observe behaviors fractionally. The divide cycles mean that a behavior occurs at a rate of .05, or .3, or .007. At a rate of .01 movement cycle per minute, one behavior happens once every 10 minutes; at 0.5 movement cycles per minute, one behavior occurs every 2 minutes.

The six complete cycles plus one fractionary cycle complete the chart. The final cycle represents one movement every 24 hours, or 1,440 minutes, and allows charting of movement cycles that occur only once a day.

All pertinent administrative information is recorded in appropriate spaces along the bottom of the chart. The Behavior box identifies who is performing the movement cycle, and Age and Label give additional information about the behavior. The Movement Cycle space identifies the specific behavior being recorded and when it is to be recorded. The Charter refers to the person who charts the movement cycles; the Manager is the person responsible for changing the behavior, usually the teacher; the Advisor is the person assisting the manager, a resource teacher or

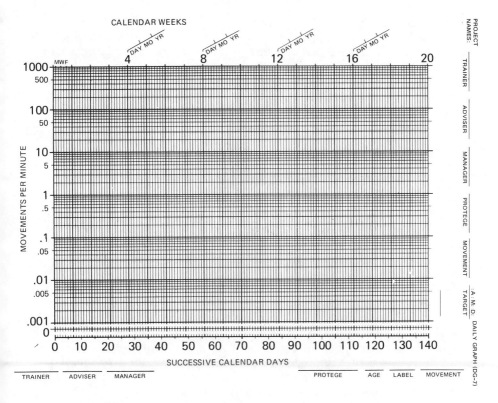

Figure 7.3.

Reprinted by permission of Behavior Research Co., Box 3351, Kansas City, Kansas 66103.

consultant; and the Supervisor is the person of administrative responsibility such as the principal. The Agency box is for recording the school or clinical unit where the instruction or remediation takes place. The blank for Depositor refers to the person responsible for submitting the information to the Behavior Research Company Behavior Bank in Kansas City, Kansas, if such deposits are being made.

On a logarithmic scale there is never an absolute zero point, so that the location of any given data point indicative of movement cycles per minute will vary as the amount of time varies. To note the time as a constant, the *record floor* must be computed. The record floor shows the time a movement cycle lasted. It is placed at the lowest possible performance rate that can occur over a specific length of time. The lowest rate other than zero is always one movement cycle for the time observed. For example, if a child's oral reading rate is timed for 2 minutes, the lowest possible frequency is 1 word per 2 minutes, or ½ word per minute, or .5 words per minute. Having computed this, the record floor is recorded on the chart by drawing a line from the Monday line to the Friday line of the week being charted. If there is a change in the amount of time a given task is observed, a change in the record floor also is necessary.

An easy, quick method of finding the record floor is by using a *rate plotter.* The scale on the clear plastic rate plotter is logarithmic like the chart paper. On the rate plotter, number of minutes are written beside horizontal lines. To find the record floor, the time value on the plotter is placed next to the one rate line of the chart and the record floor is read at the arrow on the rate plotter (see Figure 7.4).

Once the record floor has been located, the *frequency data* can be charted. Frequency data are of two kinds, correct (acceleration) or error (deceleration). Using the rate plotter and plotting from the record floor, recording the data is an easy process. Placing the *plot here* arrow next to the record floor, the numerical value of the counted responses is located on the rate finder and plotted on the graph directly to the left of the plotter. Correct rates are recorded with a dot or small filled-in circle; error rate is recorded with a small triangle or an X.

Days on which data are collected are referred to as *rated days.* Days on which movement cycles may have occurred but were not counted are *ignore* or *no-count* days. It is usual to connect data points from day to day. Correct data points are connected from the center of the circle, and error data points are connected from either the apex of the triangle or the cross point of the X. If a no-count day occurs between two rated days, the two data points are connected by a line. However, if no data can be collected due to absence, program change, or the like, the data points are *not* connected by a line. This is referred to as a *no-change* day and indicates that the movement cycle did not happen.

The *phase change lines* (see Figure 7.5) are the symbols for illustrating a change in the program condition under which the movement cycle is performed. When environmental contingencies are changed, the phase change symbol is used and a short descriptive phrase is inserted under the "roof" of the line. The line is drawn one-half day before the first rated day on which data will be collected under the new program conditions.

Two additional charting conventions are frequently used—*record ceiling* and *desired rate symbols.* The record ceiling indicates the rate limit. The symbol for record ceiling, a heavy horizontal line from Friday to Monday at the determined maximum rate, is used any time that some condition sets an upper limit on performance. For instance, if a movement cycle is being recorded every five seconds and each time it is observed it is occurring, the maximum count that could be obtained in a 60-second period would be 12. The record ceiling would be 12 per minute, that is, 60 seconds/5 observations = 12 observations per minute. Desired rate is a symbol for aims of instruction. This is indicated by placing the X on the rate and date that has been set as the aim.

It may seem that these procedures are difficult and time-consuming for the teacher, but, in fact, they are simple enough for kindergarten and first grade children to chart their own data (Bates and Bates, 1971). A positive benefit of pupil *self-charting* is that the very process of becoming

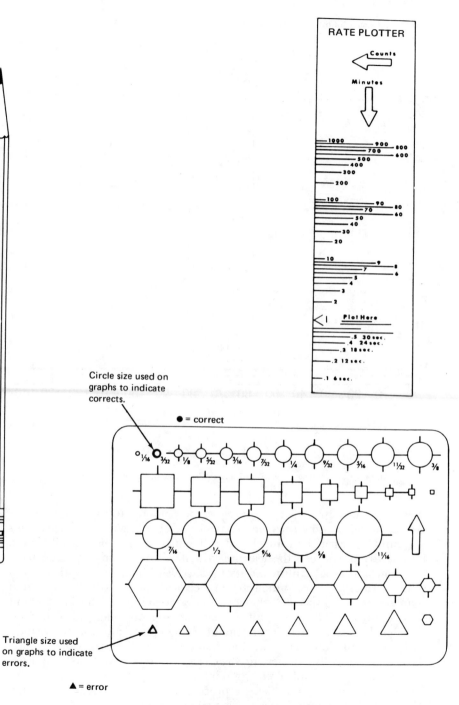

Figure 7.4. Tools for Plotting.

CDMRC Media Services.

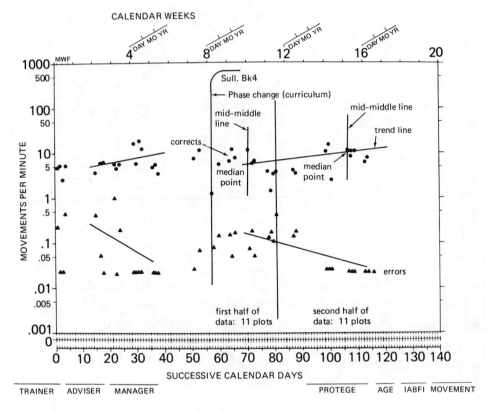

Figure 7.5.

Reprinted by permission of Behavior Research Co., Box 3351, Kansas City, Kansas 66103.

involved in measuring personal progress becomes rewarding and leads to a greater understanding between behavior and its consequences. This helps the child to learn self-control and self-management. Distractibility and impulsivity often keep the learning disabled child from acquiring basic academic and social skills necessary for successful interaction with self and others. Projects that help the learning disabled child to develop attention span and focus on specific behavioral and academic problems bring about change quickly. Ultimately, all teachers agree about one goal of instruction—make the child independent of the teacher and able to perform without instructional cues or aids. Using systematic instructional procedures and gradually transferring the chart tasks to the students are powerful remedial tools and a potent reinforcement measure. However, this book and the description of these procedures are by no means good substitutes for in-service training and actual experience working with persons acquainted with the procedures. Therefore, no information as to how to instruct students in self-charting will be included. Teacher preparation programs in regular and special education are in many cases moving to introduce courses in applied behavior analysis, including procedures mentioned in this chapter. Other programs are introducing the principles of behavior into already existing courses. As well as teaching these topics and providing students with opportunities to apply the principles in N of 1 (single-subject) studies, training centers are increasingly emphasizing systematic application of instructional technology (including systematic teaching, task analysis, and other structured ways of arranging instructional cues). We would like to suggest these volumes for readers who are not receiving formal instruction in applied behavior analysis: *Changing Children's Behavior* (Krumboltz and Krumboltz, 1972); *Parents Are Teachers* (Becker, 1971); and *Behavior of Exceptional Children* (Haring, 1974); and *Exceptional Teaching* (White and Haring, 1976).

Once data have been graphed, the pupil's performance must be interpreted to determine the amount of progress. *Data-analysis* procedures are designed to allow the teacher a dynamic picture of current pupil performance on target behaviors and to predict future performance based on these data. No extensive knowledge of statistics is necessary to analyze data charted on six-cycle paper. Because of the structure of the paper and the methods of data collection, merely looking at the chart can indicate improved performance. But "eye-balling" data is not sufficient. Analysis of a trend line is necessary to achieve a more precise evaluation.

The procedure for *trend analysis,* or establishing trend lines, is simple. For any given group of data, the data must be divided into two equal parts, and the median and midmiddle points of each half established. The median is found by counting from the top or bottom to the center horizontal position of the data. A straight horizontal line is drawn separating the two halves of the data. If an unequal number of data plots occurs, a vertical line is drawn through the median plot. The midmiddle line is located by finding the median plot on either side of the center vertical line. The trend line is drawn by connecting the two midmiddle points (see Figure 7.5). The data yielded by a trend line is, for the most part, descriptive information that shows whether pupil performance is decreasing, increasing, or holding constant.

The central reason for implementing a direct daily measurement system is to improve the quality of educational decision-making. Once data on a child's performance are obtained, the teacher must be able to evaluate the data to make further plans, to adjust instructional techniques, and to exchange ineffective curriculum. To see improvement, the teacher must determine trends along two dimensions of performance, namely the rate and accuracy, and the comparison of change in performance over time. Improvement is occurring when the data reveal that the level of the child's performance is accelerating. The trend of performance refers to the line of progress as seen when data are charted and displayed. A trend has three possible directions. First, a target movement cycle can remain the same. Second, it can be decreasing or decelerating. Third, the trend can show acceleration or increase in the movement cycle.

Trend analysis gives the teacher a sensitive indicator of a pupil's past and present performance rates, which are a sound basis on which to make decisions on curriculum material or reinforcement changes in the pupil's program. One tool that can be used to determine trend direction and power is the *Acceleration Finder,* a clear plastic strip produced by Behavior Research Company (see Figure 7.6). Positive acceleration is determined by placing the Acceleration Finder on the graph so that its X1 point covers the median midpoint of one side of the data. To determine decelerating slopes of a decrease in frequency, the Finder is inverted so that X^{10} part of the right-hand scale is on the bottom.

After the Acceleration Finder is placed correctly on the data, it is

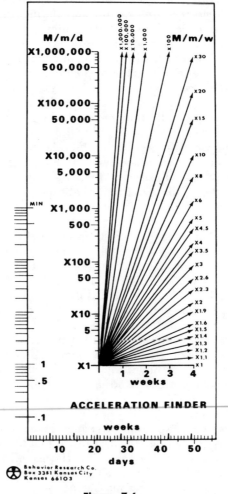

Figure 7.6.

Reprinted by permission of Behavior Research Co., Box 3351, Kansas City, Kansas 66103.

read by following the line that covers the trend line to the arrowhead. Increase is indicated with a X before the number, and decrease is shown with a ÷. At least five data plots should be shown to make such an analysis and are usually the basis for making a phase change. However, an analysis of the effects of phase changes calls for a comparison of prephase change trends with postphase change trends. Such comparison tells the teacher how much effect an instructional or curricular change has had on a pupil's performance over time. It is possible to make projections from accumulated data before actually implementing an instructional change. This is done by extending the acceleration line beyond the data until it reaches the desired rate or frequency established for that academic task. This method determines when a criterion will be met according to the acceleration or acquisition rate. Next, the teacher must determine whether or not this is reasonable. Will it take too long? Should the pupil's performance be accelerated? Should the program remain unchanged?

The decision to continue the program does not automatically mean that all will run smoothly. Often the first few days of instruction produce a rate of increase above average. The first projection, therefore, will probably be inaccurate, and adjustments must be made. This is to be expected. If the trend slope appears to be changing away from the projection, the process of projection should be adjusted to the new data. Rate tends to become stable or flatten out as instruction continues. If the trend plateaus below desired rate, either instructional change is indicated or the aim is set too high.

Summary.   One of the most difficult problems a teacher using systematic instructional procedures faces is determining desired rates and aims. Perhaps only experience with these procedures produces a teacher whose instruction is precise and efficient and who can use such procedures naturally and routinely. Changes in programming and instruction are almost limitless. The boundaries of innovation to aid a child's learning process is set only by the limits of the teacher's imagination and decision-making capabilities. Taking continuous data and recording them each day provide the teacher with direct information as to how a pupil is performing, so guesswork and haphazard planning are at least somewhat reduced.

These procedures are not perfected completely, but advances continue. Only practice makes perfect. Teachers who work to correct instructional disabilities become precision teachers. Although several specific pieces of 'hardware' involved in the technology of teaching have been suggested, the emphasis is on application of instructional procedures. Let us now discuss some actual instructional techniques.

Arrangement of Instructional Cues and Curriculum

MOTIVATING PERFORMANCE

One of the more important tasks for a teacher is to "motivate" pupil performance. Traditionally in education, motivation is conceptualized as an "inner state," which refers to a generalized state of being for a given child. Hence, a child has high or low motivation depending upon the ability to internalize. The ideal state of being motivated is where the child is eager to perform whether or not praise or material reward is given. The idea of extrinsic reinforcement is seen as too manipulative. In any event, considering motivation as a generalized, internal condition, one child is seen as motivated and another as unmotivated, depending on the teacher's interpretation of each child's attitude toward an assignment. Often we have tried to "enliven" instruction to arouse student interest and to sustain motivation. To do this, teachers have resorted to animated lectures, the use of audio-visual materials, novel presentations, classroom discussions, and a wide variety of other instructional tactics.

Perhaps it would be useful to clarify what educators commonly have meant by motivation. A child is often thought to be motivated if a task is begun promptly after an instruction is given, if the task is worked on consistently, if minimal teacher supervision is sought and given, and if a reasonably high amount of production on the task is achieved. An additional dimension usually considered is the quality of work. In other words, pupils who are well motivated are frequently thought of as producing "good quality work." Other peripheral components of motivation commonly are considered, such as appearing very interested in the assigned activity. A student who asks many questions, who approaches the teacher to ask for advice on an assignment, and who is good-natured about his or her school tasks frequently is considered more motivated than a student who appears totally uninterested.

Despite the fact that educators generally have thought of motivation largely as a function of the interest a teacher is able to generate in curriculum, research based on performance data indicates that very nearly the opposite is true (Ferriter, Buckholdt, Hamblin, and Smith, 1972). That is, motivation is reasonably specific to a given task and it is largely dependent upon the consequents following an individual's performance. It is reasonable to assume that an individual who works consistently at a task, who responds at a reasonably high rate, and who ends up with a large amount of work accomplished is motivated to perform that task. Quite extensive research indicates that "motivated" performance can be generated and maintained on most tasks simply by providing for appropriate reinforcement to occur contingent upon the desired behavior.

From the original research of Ferster and Skinner (1957) discussed earlier, four principles specifying the arrangement of consequences in relation to pupil behavior have been identified. The first principle is positive reinforcement, which occurs when a desired event is presented to an individual contingent on a behavior, and the behavior increases in frequency. We can say that candy positively reinforced asking "May I have a piece of candy," if the behavior increased when we presented candy to an individual. Negative reinforcement, the second principle, occurs when the termination or withdrawal of some event increases the frequency of a behavior. For example, if a classroom of youngsters became very quiet immediately after a teacher said "Please be quiet," and the frequency of the teacher's statement increased, we would say that negative reinforcement of the teacher's behavior had occurred. Third, positive punishment is applying an aversive event to decrease the frequency of a behavior. The practice of slapping a small child's hand when a hot object is reached for might decrease the frequency with which the child reaches for hot objects. This would be called positive punishment. Fourth, negative punishment is the practice of withdrawing a desired event to decrease the frequency of a behavior. For example, if every time a teen-ager drives over the speed limit, his or her parents take away car privileges for several days, this is an example of negative punishment. These constitute the four basic ways in which subsequent events can increase or decrease the frequency of a behavior, and they are closely tied with the motivation of pupil performance in a classroom.

There is a fifth way to decrease performance or to decrease pupil motivation—withdraw any positive reinforcement that might have occurred contingent on the behavior. Very frequently, when positive reinforcement is withdrawn, behavior gradually will diminish. This process is called extinction.

Another aspect of consequent events or reinforcement that should be considered by the classroom teacher are contingencies of reinforcement or schedules of reinforcement. As discussed earlier, this refers to the relationship between a behavior and the reinforcers or consequents that follow behavior. As mentioned earlier, five schedules are commonly used: 1) a one-to-one or fixed ratio schedule; 2) a variable ratio schedule; 3) a fixed interval schedule; 4) a variable interval schedule; and 5) a differential reinforcement schedule.

Practically speaking, teachers have several areas they can use to reinforce behavior and increase response output. To review: the first is primary reinforcement; second is token reinforcement; third, social reinforcement; fourth, contingency contracting; fifth, performance feedback.

Some of the reinforcement approaches suggested are unnatural because they do not occur spontaneously in children's customary day-to-day living. Others are quite natural in the sense that smiling, giving social approval, and performance feedback are events that commonly do occur in children's lives. It is sometimes necessary to use artificial or constructed reinforcement to initiate high rates of pupil behavior, but these gradually can be exchanged for more natural reinforcement approaches without resulting in a decrease in pupil performance. It is desirable to use natural reinforcement whenever possible and/or to build in artificial means of reinforcement that will have to be withdrawn subsequently. When artificial or synthetic means of reinforcement are necessary, it is best to move to natural reinforcement contingencies as quickly as possible.

FORMULATING AND IMPLEMENTING PROCEDURES
FOR INSTRUCTIONAL MANAGEMENT

Instructional management is defined as the comprehensive process of systematically arranging components of the educational environment so that children will learn effectively. Two critical components of instructional management are arrangement of instructional cues and environment and a variety of teaching procedures.

When arranging instructional cues and curriculum, it is necessary to consider goals, objectives, and curriculum selection. Arranging the actual physical environment will be considered in the next chapter. The final component of instruction is the actual hardcore instructional techniques—drill, practice, and application, and their effect on the child's performance.

Establishing instructional objectives.   We have emphasized that education and society have defined broad educational goals. As we said, a goal is a statement of long-range directions and aims, usually in general terms. An aim is a much more specific statement. It may be derived from a general goal, and it includes three essential characteristics: a statement of a pupil response (movement cycle), a description of the conditions under which the response is to occur, and a statement of the criteria for acceptable performance. It is essential to develop precise instructional objectives for both the learner and the curriculum used for instruction. Only if teachers know precisely what children are to be learning will the learning environment be arranged so that pupils will progress efficiently. Teachers easily can determine when children have achieved desired instructional outcomes if these outcomes are stated clearly and precisely. Curricular materials usually are selected to teach children the information or skill chosen as part of their learning objectives. It is reasonable to expect that the objectives the material is intended to teach will coincide with the learner objectives that a teacher has for a pupil.

Within the established goals, teachers have freedom in specifying instructional objectives. However, society and education have established broad parameters that are narrowed by school district philosophy and policy. The specific freedom a teacher has to establish objectives will come from several sources. First, there may be areas of concern in which districts have not formulated general or specific policies. In general, teachers will have freedom to formulate general and specific objectives in these areas. Second, districts will have identified general goals and specific objectives, but may have specified their details inadequately. For example, if a district has indicated that physical fitness is a goal, but has not defined behaviors indicative of physical fitness, a physical education teacher may have the freedom to specify such behaviors. Or if oral reading is a behavior specified as important by a district, but the criteria for performance are not stated, a teacher likely will have the freedom to do so. Finally, as noted earlier, where individual pupil differences exist that do not fall within district guidelines, teachers usually are expected to deal with those differences. In actual practice, teachers have considerable freedom to specify and formulate objectives.

It is useful for teachers to specify both long-range and immediate instructional objectives. Longer range objectives help teachers to arrive at a determination of the important directions for individual children. For example, if a teacher knows that a child must be able to read 100 words per minute at 98 percent accuracy in a fourth grade reader within one year, that knowledge will guide the teacher in selecting the scope of instructional activities during the year. Or if a teacher knows that a handicapped teen-ager will be working in an environment where a variety of safety signs will have to be known, the teacher can arrange for those signs to be learned instead of other reading materials that may be less useful to the student.

Longer range objectives can assist teachers in formulating immediate objectives. If a child who must read at fourth grade level within a year is deficient in second and third grade sight vocabulary, or basic phonic skills, the teacher may set immediate instructional objectives that lead to the longer range objective. An immediate objective or aim, for example, could be to learn a selected list of sight words at 100 percent accuracy within a specified time.

Establishing the conditions under which performance will occur and the criteria for acceptable performance are tasks that should be taken seriously. For example, it may be important to specify the number of new items to be included in a specific learning objective, since this may have considerable influence on how a child performs on the task or how rapidly new knowledge is acquired. Similarly, the criteria for acceptable performance can be very significant. For a child to learn math facts to 100 percent accuracy may seem desirable, but the youngster may not retain that knowledge unless the facts are learned both to 100 percent accuracy and to a correct performance rate of at least 30 facts per minute. Criteria levels for proficiency performance have not been established authoritatively to date, but evidence indicates that speed and accuracy are influential in children's retention and ability to use knowledge in alternate situations (Haring, 1971).

Selecting curriculum for instruction. Ideally, instructional materials should possess a number of characteristics. Let us consider the basic ones. Perhaps most important is whether or not the materials include the same content as the learning objectives selected for the child. In practice, this has been difficult to achieve for several reasons. Education has not given teachers precise and comprehensive information regarding learning objectives in different subject matter areas. Teachers have been left to select or devise their own objectives—a task of such large proportions that they rarely have either the time or expertise to complete it. Also, most textbooks to date have been ambiguous regarding the objectives to which the book teaches. Therefore, it has been difficult to relate textual materials to the objectives a teacher has selected. Finally, in those cases where objectives have been well specified (such as in programmed learning materials), they have not always coincided with teacher-selected objectives. In most cases, teacher and textbook objectives differ to a greater or lesser extent.

A second desirable characteristic of instructional materials is that they break a learning task into small, sequential steps appropriate to the learner. Traditional textbooks frequently have provided a potpourri of steps and sequences that can be achieved satisfactorily by only a small majority of pupils. Programmed textbooks have provided a much clearer delineation of tasks and their sequences. However, most programmed texts have been linear; that is, they provide the same sequence of tasks for each person and do not allow for rapidly learning pupils to bypass unnecessary frames, or do not require slowly learning pupils to repeat frames. Rarely have curricular materials broken learning tasks into small sequential steps that allow the learner to advance through the tasks according to individual pupil mastery of each step.

Third, instructional materials should provide for overt or active response on the part of the pupil. Research has not been decisive in favor of overt responding, but there are a number of reasons for requiring it. It is only through overt performance that the teacher actually can observe that pupils have reached their learning objectives. When pupils perform overtly, it is possible to complete an analysis of errors, which can lead to their remediation. It is possible to reinforce overt responses, thus assuring that a pupil is actually working on desired learning tasks. It is virtually impossible to be sure that a pupil actually is studying prescribed material if the pupil is simply staring at a book.

Fourth, pupils should not be "locked into" certain overt responses. In other words, the curriculum or machines or teachers should not control the presentation of material so that the child's response rates are restricted. In basic academic skills, proficiency seems partially related to speed or fluency, which implies a free response rate. On more complex curricular tasks, it is a waste of time for the child to wait for the next instructional item. Subjectively, it probably is frustrating to many learning disabled children to have to wait for instruction.

A fifth characteristic of curricular materials is that they allow for relatively easy, immediate correction and feedback to the pupil. One of the strongest arguments in favor of programmed materials has been the ease of obtaining immediate correction and feedback. With many other materials, however, it also is possible to procure or construct answer keys that pupils can use to correct their own performances. Besides enhancing pupil learning, pupil correction procedures relieve teachers of potentially time-consuming tasks and allow them additional time to manage the various aspects of the learning environment.

A sixth characteristic is that materials must allow individualization of performance. This means that each child is allowed to respond individually, is placed in materials at his or her own level, and is allowed to advance to subsequent task levels when proficiency on the current task is demonstrated. The typical use of traditional or programmed textbooks has not provided true individualization.

Seventh, instructional materials should specify the prerequisite knowledge required to enter the program. On some tasks of a hierarchical nature the prerequisite skills are readily apparent. For example, it is clear that complex addition tasks require knowledge of basic facts, number recognition, and such. However, it is not always evident which reading level is required for completion of a social studies assignment.

Eighth, the format for instructional materials should be clear and presented consistently. In terms of pupil performance, the format should not lead to errors that are extraneous to the desired learning task.

There are probably a variety of other features that characterize good instructional materials. Ultimately, of course, the important criterion is whether or not the materials allow specified learning objectives to be achieved. Until further research verifies the exact characteristics of "good" instructional materials, we must rely on those characteristics that have a partially empirical and logical base.

In practice, the actual selection of instructional objectives and relating the objectives to instructional materials is less precise than the previous discussion indicates. Teachers who select their own objectives have two alternatives: they can construct their own teaching materials, commonly seen with instruction in basic skills, where teachers have made their own work sheets based on a sequence of objectives most suitable to their own needs; and teachers can select pages or segments of materials from published texts, duplicating books, and other sources following their own instructional objectives sequence. Using this approach, teachers frequently build files of materials to match their instructional sequences.

On the other hand, teachers may follow the sequences selected by the author of an instructional program. In that case, it is important to inspect the program and insure that the sequence of objectives the publisher lists actually coincides with the sequence the material covers. In evaluating pupil performance with commercially produced texts, the teacher is well advised to construct small tests, or probes, that cover the content of the objectives included in the text. These tests can be used to measure performance on a daily basis directly on the material covered in the text. If the material on the probe is mastered, the teacher knows that the child is ready to advance to the next instructional objective. If the child fails to achieve criterion performance on the probe, even after completing the textual material, the teacher knows that additional instruction is necessary.

Drill, Practice, and Application—Hardcore Instruction

Teachers have rarely had systematic guidelines for the selection of instructional procedures. On the one hand, the selection of procedures has been unsystematic and random, so that their efficacy with individual pupils has been difficult to assess. On the other hand, procedures sometimes have been so rigidly prescribed, such as with espoused teaching methods, that teacher flexibility in altering instructional procedures for individual differences in pupil performance has been restricted severely. An adequate conceptualization of the types of teaching procedures available should provide guidance for systematizing the selection of procedures, and increase the repertory of alternatives that a teacher has for specific instructional tactics.

For our purposes, we have divided the instructional act into five phases (which we refer to as "hardcore" instruction). These are: (1) modeling, (2) demonstration, (3) drill, (4) practice, and (5) application. The actual phases of the instructional act in the basic literature on teaching are rarely described or defined clearly.

Initial contact between student and teacher in the case of remediation of a specific academic deficit is accomplished most successfully through a model. With *modeling techniques,* the teacher can set up a response using some type of media or three-dimensional model that is easily perceived by the student. The greater the difficulty a child has in sensory reception, the more concrete the model should be. The actual model can range from a visual display to a visual-auditory display to a tactical model. Examples of models are flash cards for word or number drills, color sheets for color discrimination, three-dimensional tactile-kinesthetic letters and numbers, and a tape recording to vowel sounds. The possibilities are limited only by the teacher's imagination and ingenuity.

Two kinds of modeling should be differentiated. The type just described is *perceptual modeling* and involves an actual display of the desired performance, live or mediated (McDonald, 1972). There are also *symbolic models,* in which an expected response or task is described in words. When working with children with academic deficits or perceptual handicaps, a stimulus model should engage the child's perceptual apparatus directly. In this way the child receives as much direct information as possible about the task without having to interpret either an oral or written description of what is expected. The next step is *demonstration,* showing the required response using the model. Providing a child with the exact response allows him or her to imitate the task and begin the process of close approximation that makes up the drill phase. An example would be simply presenting a child a flash card with the letter A printed on it and the teacher saying the sound of the word. These two initial phases of hardcore instruction give the child clear and simple directions and cues as to the exact nature of the learning task. Often it is wise to explain to the child briefly what is going to happen even before presenting the model and demonstrating it. The exact nature of the model and the task should be included on the plan sheet; if it becomes necessary to check back to see how the process of remediation took place, an exact record exists.

Drill exercises give the child an opportunity to approximate the model by repetition. Such repeated responses provide for closer and closer approximations to criterion performance and for immediate teacher reinforcement of correct responses. Drill exercises long have been acknowledged as important for learning basic academic skills, developing short- and long-term retention, and later generalizing learning skills to other contexts. Systematic drill provides for more rapid acquisition toward proficiency on basic academic skills. Since acquisition of performance proficiency or criteria is the central focus in working with learning disabled children, slicing the response requirements into readily accessible sequences and providing systematic drill exercises is essential. Drill usually is provided until mastery at a 100 percent correct response rate is achieved.

Skills gained through drills can be transferred into more complex situations calling for *practice*. It is important to note that drill of a skill on one hand might constitute practice on a simpler or subordinate skill. The conceptualization of whether an instructional activity constitutes drill, practice, or application depends on the particular instructional unit under consideration. For example, drill on a series of c-v-c phonetically regular words might constitute practice for specific vowel sounds.

Practice is, therefore, a more complex instructional phase than drill, requiring the child to use skills gained in other drills in combination. For example, drills on short vowel sounds until reaching criterion level is a prerequisite for practice of words incorporating the vowel sounds. Continued practice provides maintenance of the learned response or skill. Children tend to learn more easily when practice develops systematically out of contact with concrete models and experiences.

Practice on academic or perceptual skills leads to generalization. Learning is not a process limited to making responses that have been conditioned under a certain set of circumstances. Academic and social behavior generalizes from a specific conditioned stimulus to a similar stimulus. To illustrate, consider the teacher attempting to teach the concept of "redness." The teacher holds up red and green circles and asks the child to point out the red one. When the child has given the correct response, he or she is ready to generalize the concept of redness to other objects.

A large part of instruction is devoted to developing generalizations. Application provides a context in which the child can make generalizations, having mastered a specific skill through drill and practice. For instance, once a child has mastered vowel and consonant sounds and has achieved a criterion performance rate as a basal reader, a situation should be provided where the child can read for pleasure or learn to read outside a structured instructional situation.

The use of drill, practice, and application usually can follow in that order. In other words, drill will usually precede practice on a specified task. When mastery has been obtained on drill, the pupil is ready to practice the skill in more complex material. When proficiency has been achieved at the practice level, the pupil is ready to apply the newly learned skill in a novel context in more advanced material. The use of instructional procedures out of such a sequence can lead to the pupil's failure to make adequate progress on many learning tasks.

Actually, instructional texts constitute a teaching procedure. However, the mere use of texts, without considering additional instructional procedures, has at least two major dangers. First, textbooks rarely provide the exact amount of drill, practice, and application appropriate for each individual. Although some pupils will receive approximately the amount of instruction they need, others will receive too much or too little. Second, textbooks frequently move children too rapidly to the application components of instruction, without adequate preparation at the drill and practice levels.

The systematic use of instructional procedures ordinarily will lead a teacher to provide initial drill on an activity. Such drill need not be unimaginatively conceived and applied. Specific drill procedures might range from repeated performances on a work sheet, the use of flash cards, presentation of material on the language master, manipulation of beads or rods, and the selection of multiple choice answers. It is important to establish criterion levels of performance, so that the teacher and learner have an idea of when a youngster is ready to move from drill to practice exercises. The exercises may use the same or similar procedures as drill, or they may incorporate more complex tasks where the skill being performed may be used with less redundance. Finally, the application of the skill in new learning is important. For example, the use of newly acquired reading skills to enjoy a story or to acquire new information is a crucial step in natural positive reinforcement for engaging in preliminary drill and practice exercises. The teacher should be careful to arrange sequences of drill, practice, and application in small units, so the learner will move through the complete cycle to the frequent application of newly learned skills. This procedure will reduce much of the need for extrinsic reinforcement.

EVALUATING THE INSTRUCTIONAL PLAN
IMPLEMENTED WITH A PUPIL

One of a teacher's most important tasks is the evaluation of pupil performance on the total teaching plan implemented with the pupil. Evaluation consists of determining whether pupils are adequately progressing toward their objectives and when they have reached them. The entire evaluative process depends on knowing precisely what the aims are for a pupil and the rate of progress that the pupil is expected to maintain enroute to the objective.

On basic skills, such as learning basic math processes, phonics skills, sight vocabulary, and given reading materials to proficiency, there are four ways to determine criterion rates or aims (and each has advantages and disadvantages):

1. Experts often have recommended criterion performance levels on basic skills for both fluency and accuracy. For example, many informal reading inventories list the number of words per minute that children should be able to read at different grade levels, as well as the percent of correct performance. For those who prefer, aims can be stated simply as the number of required correct and error answers per minute.

2. Performance of competent peers—for example, if the best readers in a second grade class read at 80 correct words, with about 2 errors, per minute, perhaps a teacher would select aims comparable for less proficient peers. One should be cautious in using such an approach, since typical performance may not be necessarily proficient performance.

3. Assess the effect of different performance rates on subsequent learning tasks. Suppose a child learned add facts to three at 20 correct answers per minute, and on his or her add facts to four, five, and so on, it took progressively longer to achieve the same rate of performance. The teacher would have some evidence that the low rate of performance on the simpler tasks impeded acquisition of a more complex performance. The teacher might wish to establish higher performance levels and see if the youngster's rate of progress improved. In actuality, this type of design to determine proficiency rates is complex and requires repeated measurement with many pupils over a period of time. Eventually, it may be one of the more fruitful ways to study proficiency performance.

4. Ratio analysis. Suppose an adult can write numerals at 120 digits per minute and can perform addition problems at 60 digits per minute. A teacher might decide that a youngster who can write 80 digits per minute should be able to write answers to the same math problems at 40 digits per minute. The formula for such ratio analysis is:

$$\frac{\text{Adult write number}}{\text{Adult computation rate}} : \frac{\text{Child write number}}{\text{Child computation rate}}$$

Given any three of the four bits of information, the teacher can determine the fourth bit.

Once performance aims have been established, teachers have relatively straightforward criteria for advancing a child to subsequent tasks. The teacher simply decides in how many days the pupil must achieve the proficiency criteria, then implements the decision.

Even after determining criteria for advancing to new tasks, teachers are still faced with decisions about adequacy of progress toward the specified performance criteria. Essentially, determining adequacy of progress enroute to objectives consists of deciding the minimum amount of progress acceptable each day. The teacher must allow for some variability in pupil performance, so that one day's low performance, for example, is not a cause to make major revisions in the child's instructional program. The minimum celeration procedure described by White and Liberty (1976) is one way to assist in making decisions enroute to objectives.

When pupils fail to progress adequately toward their objectives, teachers are faced with decisions about instructional plans. As a general rule, only one change should be implemented at a time. Unless the plan is grossly inadequate, relatively small and simple changes in it might account for significant changes in pupil performance. With one pupil, for example, the teacher simply switched from marking errors to circling correct answers, and the pupil's performance began to improve dramatically. By making only one change at a time, a teacher will be able to assess the effect of specific instructional and management tactics on an individual youngster's learning rate.

SUMMARY

Arranging environment and instructional conditions so that learning disabled and mildly handicapped children can be educated in regular classrooms is an educational problem for classroom teachers and for administrators. The need for individual programs for these children is obvious when initial assessment reveals that actual performance is significantly below that of the other children. While writers of education texts have been talking about individual instruction, the actual logic of management and the instructional procedures and materials that this requires have not been discussed thoroughly or implemented in the schools. The procedures developed in the application of behavioral and educational technologies have provided some guidelines to achieve individualization. Almost all of what are considered direct instructional programs utilize components of instruction necessary for teaching children individually. Direct instruction encompasses the philosophy of teaching as well as an instructional strategy that involves:

1. Providing specific attention to each child in the classroom.
2. Measuring initial performance directly.
3. Specifying instructional aims individually.
4. Arranging a specific program of instruction.
5. Measuring the child's performance directly and daily.
6. Making decisions on the basis of the child's performance.
7. At the end of specified periods of time, evaluating the child's performance on the basis of stated criteria.

It has been shown that the procedures discussed in this chapter can be applied in regular and special classrooms and that they contribute dramatically toward providing teachers with basic guidelines for tailoring instructional programs for their children (Haring, 1969; 1971).

By the very nature of their profession, teachers are interventionists. They are charged with changing children's behavior toward increasing skills and social effectiveness. The more proficient the teacher becomes in arranging the many crucial instructional events, the more effective the process of education. Planning and organization are the very bases for systematic instruction.

Teachers have used lesson plans for many years, but these plans frequently become less and less specific as the school year passes. Yet the basic plan of instruction, as well as the organization by which instruction proceeds, provides the course and the structure for implementing change when necessary.

Probably among the most important behavioral acts that the teacher displays in the classroom is that of making decisions. The more consistent the teacher is with respect to decision-making, the more predictable the decisions will be. Ninety percent of the instructional decisions that affect the child in the classroom are made by the teacher. It is essential, therefore, that these many daily decisions are correct ones. Although a few errors naturally will be made, a strategy to increase the accuracy of decisions is very important. Basic guidelines must be utilized in decision-making. For example, one decision that affects instructional programs and procedures should be made on the basis of individual direct measures of a child's performance. Here, using performance data as the basis for instructional decisions significantly reduces the error and advances the instructional program toward better and better approximations. It also is essential that the classroom situations requiring decision-making be anticipated and general rules be established to guide the decisions. Of course, emergencies do occur that are difficult to anticipate, but guidelines should be followed that lead to increasing the accuracy and appropriateness of a decision.

The total process of decision-making, implementation, and management can be assisted greatly if the teacher will specify this process clearly enough to give some of its responsibility to the children. Even where children make their own decisions, there are certain important guidelines to follow:

1. Do not offer a youngster a choice that does not exist.
2. Do not suggest a consequence that cannot be imposed.
3. Avoid narrow alternatives to only aversive choices.
4. When possible, offer a choice of two or more viable alternatives.

The information gathered by teachers on pupil performance is and always must be the basis for instructional procedures. Evaluating the effectiveness of drill, determining the application of drill to practice, maintaining continuous records of a child's performance throughout learning are the bases for instruction. Direct, daily measurement of academic responses recorded and displayed individually by charts has been the single most important development in individualizing the instructional process. This formative evaluation procedure has given the teacher information that leads to more precise prescriptions for use in selecting instructional materials, drill and practice procedures, and reinforcement contingencies. These direct, repeated measures of child performance on instructional activities provide daily performance records, which have significantly increased instructional precision and have resulted in surprising effectiveness in increasing children's response rates, leading to more proficiency in learning academic skills.

Another very important development to come out of direct measurement of responses is probing. Probing procedures are a way for teachers to determine at any time the most appropriate placement of the child on instructional materials, the need for additional drill, and many other instructional decisions. Probes, for example, might consist of all the basic add facts or only a selected portion of them. Probes can control the uniformity of materials as well as the uniformity of responses. When probes are used for determining child progress, the teacher may take a one- or two-minute sample of performance on a particular subject each day at the same time of day in the same relationship to instruction. These probes can be used effectively to sample performance once learning has taken place. Probes are an efficient way of getting information about how well previously learned tasks are being maintained. The use of probing procedures on a daily basis has several advantages over more traditional types of pupil evaluation:

1. Teachers are able to construct probes that correspond to objectives.
2. Probes provide a uniform measurement.
3. Probes taken daily enable a pupil to see daily progress.
4. Controlling probes enables a classroom teacher to collect data on specified learning tasks.

Systematic planning for instruction is a vital process in any form of instruction. Planning allows the teacher to implement the same instructional program with the child, to replicate this program with other children, and to maintain a constant set of conditions on which the instructional program is based. A systematic plan should include the following:

1. The setting in which the plan is implemented should be described specifically and should include the number of children, child location, time of day the program is presented, general noise level of the class, and all other conditions describing the setting.
2. The curriculum, type of materials, content of the program, format of the display, and type of display must be included in the plan.
3. Procedural considerations include those aspects that guide the teacher as well as instruct the child.

4. The observable behavior (movement cycle) that the child will perform is specified.
5. Ongoing evaluation should be a part of the total teaching plan.

Motivation or reinforcement remains a basic component in effective instruction; however, motivation as a concept has been a source of great confusion. Many teachers believe that children should be motivated intrinsically, but how to achieve this ideal state is not clearly understood. Motivation is a lay term used to describe the eagerness, or lack of, with which a child pursues tasks. Actually, children's performances can be related directly to the consequences of their performances. It has been well established that a high rate of performance by children can be acquired and maintained on almost all tasks by arranging appropriate contingencies of reinforcement. Arranging reinforcement for children is as much an individualized process as is the instructional program and procedures to be used. In this summary, we would like to reiterate the kinds of reinforcement discussed earlier:

1. Positive reinforcement—occurs when a desired event is prescribed to an individual contingent on a behavior, and the behavior increases in frequency.
2. Negative reinforcement—occurs when terminating or withdrawing some event increases the frequency of a behavior.
3. Positive punishment—occurs when applying an aversive event decreases the frequency of a behavior.
4. Negative punishment—occurs when withdrawing a desired event decreases the frequency of a behavior.
5. Extinction—occurs when positive reinforcement is withdrawn, and the behavior gradually diminishes.

The most basic reinforcement schedules successfully used in classrooms are:

1. *Fixed ratio*—a child is reinforced for a fixed number of correct responses.
2. *Variable ratio*—a child is reinforced for a varying number of responses.
3. *Fixed interval*—a child is reinforced on the basis of a time interval.
4. *Variable interval*—a child is reinforced on the basis of an interval of time that varies.
5. *Differential*—a child is reinforced differentially depending on whether or not he or she meets a specified criterion.

Applying reinforcement principles on a very systematic basis usually will produce changes in behavior toward the desired rate. Children who exhibit a low rate of performance on individually and appropriately arranged instructional tasks may require specifically constructed conditions for reinforcement. However, after the child's response rate accelerates and remains high, more natural reinforcing events can be explored. It is desirable to use natural reinforcement whenever possible, because the natural environment—for which the child is being prepared—is where he or she must behave appropriately.

Instructional management is the comprehensive and systematic process of arranging components of the educational environment to increase the proficiency of children's learning.

Besides reinforcement, four basic instructional components have been formulated to implement effective instruction. They are:

1. Assessment of pupil performance. All assessment is performed to make determinations about pupil placement, intervention, and maintenance of performance. Assessment takes at least three different forms—to help formulate goals and objectives for a pupil; for placement in specific curricular or instructional sequences; and for determining the causes of deficient performance.

2. Direct and daily measurement. Evaluation consists of determining whether pupils are progressing adequately toward their objectives. The process depends on having precise information about behavioral aims that the pupil must reach and the rate of progress toward the objective on a daily basis.

3. Arranging instructional cues and curriculum. An instructional objective is a specific statement including three essential characteristics—a statement of a pupil response; a description of the conditions under which the response is to occur; and a statement of the criteria for acceptable performance. Selecting curriculum for instruction requires very careful consideration. Instructional materials must meet eight conditions, qualities, or characteristics. They must:
   a. include the same content included in the learning objectives specified by the teacher;
   b. slice the task into small, sequential, equal slices appropriate to the learner;
   c. provide for overt responding from the child;
   d. not control the rate of the child's responding;
   e. allow for relatively easy and immediate correction and feedback to the pupil;
   f. allow for the individualization of pupil performance;
   g. specify the prerequisite knowledge required to enter the program; and
   h. be clear and consistently presented. The format should not contribute to errors irrelevant to the desired learning task.

4. Selection of instructional procedures. The wise selection of instructional procedures really should increase the teacher's flexibility rather than reduce it. A full knowledge of the many types and arrangements

of available teaching procedures gives any teacher a wide selection of appropriate tactics. The three main types of instructional procedures are drill, practice, and general application of information and skill. Drill procedures might range from repeated performance on a work sheet, the use of flash cards, presentation of material on the language master, and/or the selection of multiple choice answers. Practice exercises may utilize the same or similar procedures as drill or they may incorporate more complex tasks, which use the skill acquired through the drill activities. Application is the use of the skills acquired through drill and practice in performing complex tasks.

It should be kept in mind that the five components of systematic instruction are not a linear function, but rather are a helical, cybernetic process. The way in which one sees this process potentially affects the implementation and use of these procedures. All the components work together to form a constantly changing and evolving process. For learning disabled and mildly handicapped children, systematic instructional procedures offer individualized instruction based on the principle of positive reinforcement. School failure caused by rigidity in programming and instructional methodology can be alleviated by using the suggested procedures to meet the growing challenges of society. Schools must become truly accountable for providing experiences directly relevant to the basic democratic ideals of our society. Progress has been made in teaching the learning disabled child in special education and experimental classrooms. Now, the task is to bring these advances into the reality of public education.

REFERENCES

AMMENTORP, W., M. F. DALEY, and D. N. EVANS, Prerequisites for systems analysis —analytic and management demands for a new approach to educational administration. *Educational Technology,* 1969, *IX,* no. 8.

AYLLON, T., and N. H. AZRIN, The measurement and reinforcement of behavior of psychotics. *Journal of the Experimental Analysis of Behavior,* 1965, *8,* 357–383.

BATES, S., and D. F. BATES, ". . . and a child shall teach them," Stephanie's chart story. *Teaching Exceptional Children,* Spring 1971, *3,* 111–113.

BATESON, G., *Steps to an Ecology of Mind.* New York: Ballantine Books, 1972.

BECKER, W. C., *Parents Are Teachers.* Champaign, Ill.: Research Press, 1971.

BILLINGSLEY, F. F., and S. SMELZER, *A Group Contingency System: An Analysis of Component Effects.* Working Paper No. 3. Seattle: Experimental Education Unit, College of Education and Child Development and Mental Retardation Center, University of Washington, 1973.

BOSTON, R. E., How to write and use performance objectives to individualize instruction, Volume I: *How to Analyze Performance Outcomes.* Englewood Cliffs, N. J.: Educational Technology Publication, 1972.

BUSHELL, D., P. WROBEL, and M. MICHAELIS, Applying "group" contingencies to the classroom study behavior of preschool children. *Journal of Applied Behavior Analysis,* 1968, *1,* 55–61.

CATANIA, A. C., Reinforcement schedules and psychological judgments: a study of some temporal properties of behavior. In Dr. W. N. Schoenfeld, ed., *The Theory of Reinforcement Schedules.* New York: Appleton-Century-Crofts, 1970.

COHEN, H. L., *Motivationally Oriented Designs for an Ecology of Learning.* Paper presented at the American Educational Research Association Meeting, New York, February 1971.

COHEN, M. A., N. D. GENTRY, W. J. HULTEN, and G. L. MARTIN, Measurement of classroom performance. In N. G. Haring and A. H. Hayden, eds., *Improvement of Instruction.* Seattle: Special Child Publications, December 1972.

FERRITER, D. E., D. BUCKHOLDT, R. L. HAMBLIN, and L. SMITH, The noneffects of contingent reinforcement for attending behavior on work accomplished. *Journal of Applied Behavior Analysis,* 1972, *5,* 7–17.

FERSTER, C. B., and B. F. SKINNER, *Schedules of Reinforcement.* Englewood Cliffs, N. J.: Prentice-Hall, Inc., 1957.

HARING, N. G., *The Application of Functional Analysis of Behavior in a Natural School Setting.* Final Report Grant No. OEG-0-8-070376-1857(032). Washington, D.C.: U.S. Department of Health, Education, and Welfare, Office of Education, 1969.

———, A project to provide additional education for experienced teachers to improve learning conditions for handicapped children in regular classrooms. Final Report, Project No. 577001, 1969–71. Experimental Education Unit, College of Education and Child Development and Mental Retardation Center, University of Washington, Seattle, Washington, 1971.

———, ed., *Behavior of Exceptional Children: An Introduction to Special Education.* Columbus, Ohio: Charles E. Merrill, 1974.

———, *Investigation of Systematic Instructional Procedures to Facilitate Academic Achievement in Mentally Retarded Disadvantaged Children.* Final Report Grant No. OEG-0-9-572167-4270(030). Washington, D.C.: U.S. Department of Health, Education, and Welfare, Office of Education, 1971.

HARING, N. G., and H. KUNZELMANN, The finer focus of therapeutic behavioral management. In J. Hellmuth, ed., *Educational Therapy,* Vol. I. Seattle: Special Child Publications, 1966.

HARING, N. G., and E. L. PHILLIPS, *Analysis and Modification of Classroom Behavior.* Englewood Cliffs, N. J.: Prentice-Hall, Inc., 1972.

HARING, N. G., and R. L. SCHIEFELBUSCH, eds., *Teaching Special Children.* New York: McGraw-Hill, 1976.

HAUGHTON, E., *Counting Together: Precision Teaching Rationale.* Eugene: Department of Special Education, University of Oregon, 1969.

HOLLAND, J. G., Teaching machines: an application of principles from the laboratory. *Journal of the Experimental Analysis of Behavior, 3,* 1960, 275–287.

HOMME, L. E., P. C. DI BACA, J. V. DEVINE, R. STEINHORST, and E. J. RICHERT, Use of the Premack principle in controlling the behavior of nursery school children. *Journal of the Experimental Analysis of Behavior,* 1963, *6,* 544.

KOMOSKI, P. K., The continuing confusion about technology and education or the mything-link in educational technology. *Educational Technology,* 1969, *IX,* 70–74.

KRUMBOLTZ, J. D., and H. B. KRUMBOLTZ, *Changing Children's Behavior.* Englewood Cliffs, N.J.: Prentice-Hall, Inc., 1972.

KUNZELMANN, H. P., M. A. COHEN, W. J. HULTEN, G. L. MARTIN, and A. R. MINGO, *Precision Teaching—An Initial Training Sequence.* Seattle: Special Child Publications, 1970.

LINDSLEY, O. R. Direct measurement and prosthesis of retarded behavior. *Journal of Education,* 1964, *147,* 62–81.

LOVAAS, O. I., Some studies on the treatment of childhood schizophrenia. In J. M. Shlien, ed., *Conference on Research in Psychotherapy,* Vol. 1. Washington, D. C.: American Psychological Association, 1968.

LOVITT, T. C., Assessment of children with learning disabilities. *Exceptional Children,* 1967, *34,* 233–242.

————, Self-management projects with children with behavioral disabilities. *Journal of Learning Disabilities,* 1973, *6,* 135–150.

LOVITT, T. C., and K. CURTISS, A contingency management classroom: basis for systematic replication (four studies). In N. G. Haring and A. H. Hayden, eds., *The Improvement of Instruction.* Seattle: Special Child Publications, 1972.

MCDONALD, F. J., Behavior modification in teacher education. In C. E. Thoresen, ed., *Behavior Modification in Education: The Seventy-Second Yearbook of the National Society for the Study of Education.* Chicago: The University of Chicago Press, 1972.

MAGER, R. F., *Goal Analysis.* Belmont, Calif.: Fearon Publishers, 1972.

————, *Preparing Instructional Objectives.* Belmont, Calif.: Fearon Publishers, 1962.

MILLER, R. B., Task analysis: sources and futures. *Improving Human Performance,* 1973, *2,* 5–27.

MINGO, A. R., A program for teaching data collecting on the event sheet developed at the Experimental Education Unit. In H. Kunzelmann, and others, *Precision Teaching—An Initial Training Sequence.* Seattle: Special Child Publications, 1970.

ORME, M. E. J., and R. F. PURNELL, *Behavior Modification and Transfer in an Out-Of-Control Classroom.* Paper presented at the American Educational Research Association meeting, Chicago, February 1968.

PASK, G., Cybernetic in the behavioral science of the cybernetics of behavior and cognition; extending the meaning of "goal." In J. Rose, ed., *Progress in Cybernetics.* London: Gordon and Breach Social Pub., 1969.

PATTERSON, G. R., and J. B. REID, Reciprocity and coercion: two facets of social systems. In C. Neuringer and J. L. Michael, eds., *Behavior Modification in Clinical Psychology.* Englewood Cliffs, N.J.: Prentice-Hall, Inc., 1970.

PETER, L. J., Developing cooperative social behavior. In N. G. Haring, and A. H. Hayden, eds., *The Improvement of Instruction.* Seattle: Special Child Publications, 1972.

PREMACK, D., Toward empirical behavior laws: 1. positive reinforcement. *Psychological Review, GG,* 1959, 219–233.

PRESSEY, S. L., A third and fourth contribution toward the coming "industrial revolution" in education. *School and Society,* 1932, *36,* 668–672.

SCHOENFELD, W. N., and J. FARMER, Reinforcement schedules and the "behavior stream." In W. N. Schoenfeld, ed., *The Theory of Reinforcement Schedules.* Englewood Cliffs, N.J.: Prentice-Hall, Inc., 1970.

SKINNER, B. F., Teaching Machines. *Science,* 1958, *128,* 969–977.

————, *Beyond Freedom and Dignity.* NewYork: Alfred A. Knopf, 1971.

SULZER, B., and G. R. MAYER, *Behavior Modification Procedures for School Personnel.* Hinsdale, Ill.: The Dryden Press, Inc., 1972.

VON BERTALANFFY, L., *General Systems Theory.* New York: Braziller, 1968.

WHITE, O., and K. LIBERTY, Behavioral assessment and precise educational management. In N. G. Haring, and R. L. Schiefelbusch, eds., *Teaching Special Children.* New York: McGraw-Hill, 1976.

WIENER, N., *The Human Use of Human Beings; Cybernetics and Society.* Boston: Houghton and Mifflin, 1950.

WOLF, M. M., D. K. GILES, and V. R. HALL, Experiments with token reinforcement in a remedial classroom. *Behaviour Research and Therapy,* 1968, *6,* 305–312.

Classroom
Administrative
Organization
8

In developing a comprehensive and interlocking school system program that works both to prevent and to remediate learning disabilities, there must be a flow of information on and to all levels of the system. The growing technology of teaching draws from research findings in operant psychology, systems analysis, and cybernetic and information theory. It attempts to synthesize the goals of individualized instruction and development of precise, instructional, and evaluation techniques, requiring expansion of administrative decision-making strategies, into an integrative model whereby a total system analysis is possible on all levels— the individual student and teacher, the classroom, the school, the district, the state. Emphasis on efficient and direct administrative decision-making, and attention to planning, design, and accountability for administrators in general, have emerged from questions originally raised in relation to providing educational opportunities for exceptional children and equal opportunities legislation. It is in the hazy, uncertain area of learning disabilities where the once nearly separate entities of special and general education meet, either to collide in discord or to synthesize into a workable and synergistic system capable of handling the problems of the learning disabled child.

Some readers may wonder why this much space is devoted to a discussion of administrative organization in a text whose audience is largely teachers or teacher trainees. In the first place, we expect that many of the teacher trainees who read this volume eventually will become administrators, or at least have administrative responsibilities. But we also expect, and certainly hope, that administrators will want to read the volume. However, our main purpose in including this discussion derives from our belief in an open system of communication: we think that although administrators are generally expected to understand teachers' activities and problems, the understanding should go both ways. We are not describing an impossibly "ideal" world of education; rather, we believe that our suggestions are workable and that, to a very large degree, they can work through open exchanges of ideas and information. We would like to suggest to the teachers in our audience that if what they read in this chapter seems logical, and if they support our suggestions, they should share the text with the administrators with whom they work.

As stated before, a case easily can be made for viewing any specific learning disability as a programming inequity on some level of the teaching-learning system. A system (a term that has become a most fashionable catchword of the technological era) can be defined as a "complex of interacting elements" (von Bertalanffy, 1968). According to von Bertalanffy, this means that the behavior of any individual part of a system being studied is unique to that particular system. It is important that one think in terms of relationships within a system to discover the unique operating properties of each part or element in it. Various mathematical equations can define a system applicable to many areas of information flow from general principles of kinetics to demographic problems. From this more formal definition of a system, the isomorphic and synergistic nature of the "laws" governing the behavior of systems in general become organizing principles both for understanding existing systems and for the design of new systems. Systems that have evolved for social purposes and that do not obey the generalized principles of system behavior and cybernetics are pathological, and an analysis of the various levels of the system, the interrelationships and information exchange within a system, may reveal the nature of the pathology. As a society grows and evolves, many of the forms of social control and information exchange prove ineffective. As the relationship of the social environment we create and the natural environment that supports it becomes more obvious, the pathological features of human implemented systems and the means of correcting them become more accessible. From new information about the functioning of a system and its subsystem, maps of improved information flow can be developed. The subject matter of cybernetic exploration and systems analysis is not events or objects, but the information "carried" by events and objects (Bateson, 1972). An integrative operational model and its supporting technology applied to educational systems must consider the hierarchical nature and informational flow necessary for applying the model in school settings.

The administrator is, in a very real sense, an information flow evaluator, a troubleshooter involved in the management of change. The administrative role is that of evaluating specific areas of the whole system, from both statistical and behavioral analysis, and making decisions on change based on the data. Systems analysis techniques, knowledge of human information processings potentials, computer technology, and the use of systematic daily data collection are attempts to reduce uncertainty in the decision-making process for educational administrators. Too often when someone in a hierarchy acts on either insufficient evidence or contradictory information, double-bind situations are created in which further action elsewhere in the hierarchy is reduced in clarifying the decision or attempting efficient action, or action is inhibited by the contradictory or illogical nature of the decision. Such knots (Laing, 1970) or double binds (Bateson, 1969) block information flow in the teaching-learning system; only through data provided by an efficient evaluative process can decisions be made to facilitate change.

The evaluation process provides information relating to the internal functioning of a system through feedback, or environmental information that affects control of that system. The process is applicable to all levels of a given system. We have discussed techniques of evaluating individual student performance and designing individual programs that facilitate learning at the child's own rate and performance level. The administrator must be responsible for a much broader, macroscopic view of the educational hierarchy. Not only must the administrator be aware of educational and emotional needs of individual students and teachers, but he or she also must be aware of physical, financial, curriculum, and programming needs; facilitation of information flow; and decision-making within the concerned school or district.

Dr. Laurence Peter caused a minor uproar in 1969 with his Peter Principle; his theory of incompetence at given levels of a hierarchy, as reasons for mismanagement, is applicable in terms of decision-making in public school systems. Dr. Peter's principle, in fact, was developed as a result of work in a public school system. It simply states: In a hierarchy, each employee tends to rise to his or her level of incompetence; every post tends to be occupied by an employee not sufficiently competent to execute its duties (Peter, 1969). Although we may deny that we have "peaked out" in our present jobs or have plateaued at our level of incompetence, at least a partial truth is contained in the Peter Principle. That is, many people in a given hierarchy such as public education have not been trained to make decisions quickly and efficiently. Making decisions does not always require reflexing to a set pattern or routine. In fact, a person who makes decisions easily has the flexibility and training that makes him or her responsible to the needs and desires of the hierarchy in which he or she serves. Mismanagement and incompetence are corrected as information flows freely through a system and is made available when decisions must be made.

The learning disabled child well may be the victim of incompetence and mismanagement in the public education system. Dr. Steven Forness (1972) advanced the idea that many mildly retarded children were "casualties of the present educational system." Five factors were held responsible for misplacing children in special education classes:

1. Ignorance of motivational and situational aspects of mental retardation.
2. Lack of systematic early identification.
3. Misapplication of elemental social reinforcement techniques.
4. Lack of administrative support.
5. Organizational structure of special education.

The first three factors have been discussed in earlier chapters, but the last two are important in considering the role of administration in organizing classroom environments as a part of the entire educational system. In analyzing the operation of a system and attempting to cite weaknesses, it is best to point out obvious constraints that exist. Forness (1972) indicates what may be one of the most damaging constraints in the educational system:

> One such constraint is the consultative-evaluative bind posed by the role of the school principal. Aside from the occasional visit from a supervisor of curriculum, the beginning teacher must look largely to the principal for day-to-day consultation regarding problems which arise in the classroom; yet it is the principal who also has responsibility for evaluating teacher progress toward tenure. A teacher who feels less than competent in dealing with a problem child in her [or his] classroom has generally three alternatives: ignoring the problem, talking it over with a colleague, or taking it up with the principal . . . to take the problem to the principal, however, is to admit one's incompetence to the very person from whom teachers spend a great deal of effort trying to hide their incompetence. Asking for help is viewed as an admission that one lacks the competence necessary to manage one's own classroom.

This conspiracy of silence often is furthered by the principal's fear that referrals for psychological testing and consultations may be interpreted as administrative incompetence and inability to manage the educational problems in the school. The child is clearly the victim. By the time the problem is severe enough to warrant consulting the school psychologist, the only alternative is special class placement. This usually is done for one of two reasons. First, the traditional training of a school psychologist does not emphasize curriculum and classroom management, and the child's diagnosis is not always educationally relevant (Lovitt, 1967). Second, the school psychologist too often tests a child specifically to determine whether special class placement is warranted or not. If it is, according to the standards of testing used, the child is placed in a special class where the necessary remedial instruction may or may not be received. If the child is referred to the regular classroom, the teacher usually is not given any helpful information with which to design remedial programs.

These constraints have become directly relevant in the light of several court decisions regarding special education placement and labeling, psychodiagnosis, and parent involvement in the educational process

(Cruickshank, 1972). In the case of *Hobson* v. *Hanson,* Judge Skelly Wright (269F. Supp. 401, 1967) ruled that the method of testing used in Washington, D. C., public schools was a violation of the due process clause of the Fourteenth Amendment to the Constitution. Other court cases have appealed methods of labeling and tracking used to place children. Many times school districts choose to settle out of court. The constraints pointed out by Forness are echoed by Cruickshank (1972):

> Suffice to say that poorly prepared teachers are a primary reason for this situation. . . An uninformed public school educational leadership regarding this complex issue is another reason for program failures. Unsophisticated school psychologists, still married to a mental age and an intelligence quotient, instead of the qualitative diagnosis blueprints of child capacities, produce sterile information which assists no one, teacher or child or parent.

To add to this dilemma, many states have passed education-for-all legislation, which guarantees all children, regardless of race, creed, or handicapping condition, an education in the public school system. To make this a reality for children who traditionally have been placed in institutions or denied access to public education, the borderline cases—the learning disabled and the mildly handicapped—must be handled in regular classrooms to free the special education services for the severely physically handicapped and mentally retarded.

Special education's role has been one of "fix and return," or as Evelyn Deno (1970) states, special education operates under the "statue of liberty" philosophy. "Give me your defective, defeated, and unwanted and I will love and shelter them." This approach has proved futile (Simches, 1970; Lilly, 1970). Special education services have given regular education a scapegoat with which to hide its failure to provide the quality individualized instruction that is necessary to remediate even minor academic behavior deficits and perceptual handicaps. Doing so, special education has reinforced the status quo of a system that should be challenged to change. Of course, not all special educators have been ignoring the problems and inequities. Change is taking place, but institutional change is a slow process.

By utilizing developments in behavioral and systems technology, many of the defects and constraints in the present educational system can be corrected. We have presented information about systematic instructional procedures that produce data directly related to making educational decisions.

ROLE OF THE PRINCIPAL

Principals are responsible for the success or failure of a general school program. The principal, however, does not stand alone in the school as the one who makes decisions and sets policy. The entire staff, classroom teachers and supportive services, must provide the principal with information and specification of problems. As the failure to identify what to teach basically stems from failure to identify the responses that a skillful teacher makes to facilitate learning, failure in administrative decision-making and classroom organization stems from not precisely identifying the events that facilitate successful administration of programs and collection of data. Evaluation of the success or failure of a general program or a specific child's performance must be made on environmental data about what is occurring, not on assumptions or expectations about what should be occurring.

Within the field of special education, a movement has begun to integrate exceptional children into the regular school programs. The problem of learning disabilities points out the need to reevaluate general educational programs, because it is estimated that 20 percent of the children now in public schools have been affected by some specific perceptual, motor, cognitive, or behavioral deficit that restricts learning. In 1969 parent groups, congressional legislative committees, and professional educators in special education pointed out that 40 percent of the children considered handicapped do not receive service from state and local education agencies. Administrative understanding of learning disability problems and serving learning disabled children within the regular school classroom are necessary to develop integrative programs and curriculum design that have the capability to prevent and to remediate specific learning problems.

If a technology of teaching and a science of education are to be effective, certain concepts must be replaced and transformed in the light of scientific advancements. The concept of the principal as headmaster does not create a free flow of information in a teaching-learning system, and does not provide a means of change through feedback of data from the classroom teacher to the principal for evaluation. The central administrative function of the principal has been one of discipline rather than of managing change. Rigidity within an information system reinforces miscommunication between various levels. To facilitate the flexibility for information flow that enhances the differences within a system and allows for organization and growth, it is necessary that communication networks be open and self-corrective.

If information is stopped or parcelled out in contradictory ways, the feedback mechanisms by which the system self-corrects are reduced. The principal or administrator must insure flexibility within the school system. This is done by considering the ecology or balance of the system in terms of the growth potential and tolerance to change within it. Gregory Bateson (1972) notes that flexibility is to specialization as entropy is to negentropy (information). Flexibility is defined as uncommitted potentiality for change. As entropy is a measure of disorganization, flexibility is necessary to balance the process of specialization, which tends to solidify or make a system rigid. Flexibility insures information flow throughout the system.

The integration of special children into the regular classroom through individualized instruction, continuous measurement, and contingency management were discussed in the previous chapter. The principal, often with the aid of data evaluators and computers, must be able to make decisions concerning placement, redesign of specific programs, curriculum effectiveness, and teacher behavior from the data generated in the classroom by individual pupil and teacher performances. The administrator is responsible for creating and maintaining an interrelated data base for decision-making that is tailored to the particular situation, needs, and environmental factors of the school and district.

The headmaster concept of administrative function can and does limit the feedback potential of a hierarchical teaching-learning system as existing in public education. In a hierarchical situation, such as the public schools, the lower levels of the decision-making process offer feedback data to higher levels, so that information is flowing between all levels of the system to enhance change and adaptation to novel situations. Several models have been offered that illustrate workable schemes considering these points.

A PROPOSED MODEL SCHOOL DISTRICT

We now present an integrative model based on the central processing paradigm and cybernetics, using criteria from models developed by Foley (1970) and Vallet (1969). A change of focus is needed in establishing the behavioral criterion for this mode. First, in beginning to see the educational system as an organismic or as a biological rather than a machine model, we postulate a life-death cycle. Otherwise, an educational system is cyclic and operates in complete cycles with clear-cut beginning and ending points. Therefore, the system can be analyzed. Second, the central processing model postulates that change is a constant function. An educational system changes and adapts by assimilation (making internal changes by encoding environmental events) and accommodation (making external change by adjusting to the prevailing environment). These processes by which a system adapts to the environment strengthen the organizational potential and increase the ability for regulation and control within the structure. The third criterion is feedback, which provides an evaluative process by which information is cycled and recycled into the system to facilitate adaptation. The survival of a given system is contingent upon its ability to change under various environmental conditions, and to process the environmental information necessary to make internal adjustments within the system. These internal adjustments generally occur through feedback information that controls and monitors the amount and kind of environmental data the system receives. The final criterion, closely related to feedback, is that of reinforcement. The process of reinforcement is basic to all social systems. Feedback is information provided concerning performance, whereas reinforcement is a result or reward that increases the probability of a specific response reoccurring. Behavior and performance is increased or maintained by reinforcement procedures and schedules. The administrative role in reinforcement is sometimes difficult to define or elucidate. But as the classroom teacher offers reinforcement to the individual student for performance on academic and social tasks, so must the principal and administrators reinforce the teachers for successful performance as the community reinforces the system by continued support. In an educational system that utilizes advanced technologies, this central processing of environmental data that directly affects the system's survival potential comes from individual decision-making capacity and the use of computers to correlate and synthesize information from the various levels of system hierarchy.

Rather than developing a macroscopic abstract model of a general educational system, a model for a single school with relations to district and state levels is more accessible. In the central processing model of perception, our anchor level is the individual neuron; in this adaptation of the model our anchor level is the individual child. In this way the central processing model of perception and the active behavior system concept interlock providing a solid base from which to work. The central processing paradigm places the main focus on the individual student and the student's educational and social needs. We have already discussed the individualization of instruction that can be used by the regular classroom teacher to prevent and remediate learning disabilities. When these techniques are implemented in a school, the principal has clear, concise data about student performance on individual and group levels. Data from the classrooms concerning individual performance on a daily basis make decision-making and control of change procedures much easier and efficient for those in administrative positions. The classroom teacher, who makes decisions on many matters by evaluation, relieves the administrator to perform other activities and to administer on a more personal level to teachers and students. For the learning disabled child, this means the possibility of more adult attention and direct tutorial help.

An integrated model of administrative and classroom organization. This model, in actuality, is a metaprogram, or a program about programming an educational experience. A metaprogram allows better observation of the behavior of the whole system and increases the predictability of events within the system. We consider three specific levels of the teaching-learning system. The first is the school and the communication network involved in the school subsystem. The second is the district, or local administrative level. The third is a composite of state and national functions, including the public, the government, and the professional categories. The interaction or communication between these subsystems and within subsystems is organized by principles of order and structure, which are fundamental to communication and information theory. The main purpose of this model is to provide a context for understanding the hierarchical arrangement of the teaching-learning system as it generally exists in our society today. A secondary purpose is to elucidate the communication networks by which information is transmitted, and, where possible, to elucidate contradictions or biases that limit sets of alternatives from which choices are made and individual differences are facilitated. This model provides for feedback loops necessary for the system to adapt to environmental stresses from the natural and social environments. In this way uncertainty in decision-making and about responsibility for a particular decision is reduced. A note of warning is necessary, however. The world of action, experience, organization, and learning cannot be mapped completely onto a model that excludes propositions about the relation between classes of different logical types (Bateson, 1972). That is to say—this model in no way is comprehensive or all-embracing, and it does not include all possible levels of interaction. For instance, it should not be assumed that "higher" levels of a hierarchy have direct control over the behavior of "lower" levels; they have only a higher or more comprehensive information processing capability. A system such as we are considering is in a constant state of growth and development, and it uses information to help the lower levels—the children—to become more efficient data processors and to gain information that aids in controlling their behavior.

The key to this organismic model is the process of evaluation by which information is provided to decision-makers. Everyone in the teaching-learning system must make decisions on various levels. Administrators, both on the school and district levels, must make the majority of decisions pertaining to total programming and financial outlays. The evaluation system in the model is designed as a total program evaluation process, making recommendations and responding to problems anywhere in the system. Such a specific evaluative process would correlate data and give information to appropriate levels for implementation. This creates a relatively new task—program evaluation. Such personnel would provide information directly to administrators about general program effectiveness, need for specific changes in programming, and to correlate data from various levels.

Evaluation takes place on all levels of the system, functioning much in the same way as discussed in the previous chapter. The process and evaluation systems shown in the model are administrative means of collecting data on the operation of the entire district. It is important that these functions be implemented, and the most effective means is computerization. The central output data of the school system are changes in individual student behavior. This information can be centrally processed and evaluated, and overall changes in district policy and programming can be made from this data base. The administrative data base for both principals and higher level administrators is individual child behavior and performance. Using systems analysis techniques and theory, program failure and waste are reduced through more efficient and effective control of actual operations. It also is likely that new design for programs and curriculum change to attain desired goals will be achieved with less expenditure of human and financial resources. The basic reason for the ability to perform these managerial miracles is the reduction in uncertainty concerning consequences of individual action in decision-making.

The two-dimensional diagram (Figure 8.1) is actually a poor model of the functioning of such a system. One must imagine a four-dimensional model in which all possible channels of communication are represented. For instance, the diagram shows only two channels of information flow from the school to the district. In fact, many could and do exist. It is likely that resources and supportive staff have open channels to the evaluation and process of the district. The principal certainly functions as a member of the district administration. Most districts are controlled further by the policies set by the board of education or the school board, who are elected officials. If hierarchical, bureaucratic systems are to function for the stated goal of educating each child, the specialization of talent and effort that is demanded must be supplemented with an open access to information on which decisions can be made without threat of reprisal and with sufficient data.

The immediate benefit of implementing this model is the creation of links between levels or categories that are dynamic rather than static. Input into such a system consists of more than pupils. Community input,

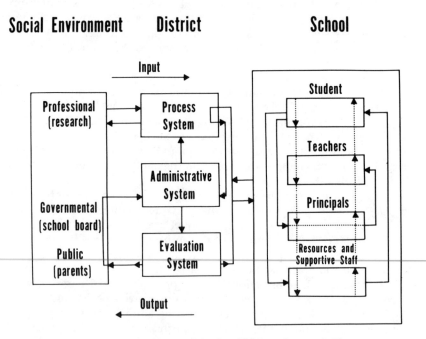

Figure 8.1. *An Integrated Model of Administrative and Classroom Organization.*

CDMRC Media Services.

professional input, environment constraints, and other variables are aspects of input. Community input is vital to total programming. The educational needs of the community are better met when input information from the community is made available. This model provides open channels for expression of needs by the community—parents, professionals, business people, and government. Curriculum design that meets community educational needs must receive input from outside the educational system. In this model, process is the structured differentiation of function organized to produce change in input variables (Foley, 1970). Administrators at different levels serving different structures naturally have different needs. To meet these needs, evaluation must produce information related to the function of particular decision-makers. Output information provides data about changes occurring at various levels, whether pupils, curriculum, finance, or facility. Output information is vital to the administrator in setting and analyzing system goals.

It is beyond the scope of this volume to judge whether or not the present administrative structures and organizational plans function to facilitate quality education. If one accepts even a few of the research report assertions, such as those in the Coleman Report (1966) and others, it is obvious that change is necessary. The concern here is improving the delivery of services to the learning disabled and mildly retarded, within the context of the public education system. As we have said, public education in contemporary urban society is big business, perhaps the biggest, most important business in which the community as a whole is engaged. By utilizing financial planning, materials acquisition and distribution, and personnel administration developed in industry, and by allocation of responsibility to decision-making levels where the decisions take place, administrators on the district level can remain close to the actual task of instruction.

Perhaps the most profitable change can occur in our concepts of how an educational system functions. The cybernetic-organismic model is an important improvement conceptually, for it provides a degree of flexibility not always present.

CLASSROOM ORGANIZATION

It would be naive to assume that teachers have not had their own systems of organization in the past. Teachers and educational systems have promoted certain types of classroom organization, planning, and management based on a number of considerations. One major factor in educational and classroom organization is administrative effectiveness; in other words, classrooms have been organized to facilitate the effective administration of instruction and management of resources. For example, a traditional type of administration is for a superintendent to supervise principals, who in turn supervise a number of teachers in their buildings, who in turn may each teach 25 to 30 children. Also, administrative organization often has dictated that certain schedules of teaching be followed. For example, certain academic subjects must be followed by recess, physical education, music, lunch hour, and so on.

A second major factor influencing teacher classroom organization is the traditions established by education in general or by a school or school system in particular. Only the unusual teacher implements an organization and management system that deviates from the one traditionally used in his or her school or district.

A third factor frequently affecting teacher organization for planning is the problem of managing the social behavior in the classroom. In other words, teachers have organized space and scheduling of activities through the day to result in effective behavior control of the pupils. In many instances, the criteria for organization have been strongly influenced by behavioral management and perhaps less by the desired instructional outcomes.

A fourth factor, which has had considerable influence in recent years for classroom organization and management, is the notion of innovation. One emphasis in American education for many years has been to implement "innovative" practices. Innovation frequently originates from a philosophy or from a social or educational critic with the hope of improving the educational environment. Some innovations have been worthwhile and others have not.

A fifth, and frequently overlooked, factor affecting teacher organization, planning, and management is the effective attainment of learning objectives important to the individual pupils. In other words, children attend school to learn to perform better in academic and vocational tasks, and to communicate with others more effectively. It would seem reasonable, therefore, that effective learning for each pupil be a major consideration in teacher decisions about classroom organization, management, and planning.

There are several ways in which classrooms traditionally have been organized. One kind of organization, not used as frequently as it once was, is teaching the same material at the same time to the entire classroom. In this situation, teachers may lecture on the material to be covered, then assign from a test a common task to the entire class. Pupils complete the task and turn in their papers; the teacher grades the papers and returns them the following day, with grades ranging from zero to 100 percent.

A second kind of classroom organization is "grouping." Teachers divide classes into two or more groups of children, working at different placements within a curricular series. For example, a fast reading group might be in a higher level reader, and the middle and slower groups would be placed in lower level readers. In all fairness to this practice, the groups are usually designated by labels such as bluebirds, blue jays, and blackbirds rather than high, middle, or low. Grouping is an effort to place children more nearly according to performance level, and thereby provide instruction more suited to individual needs. With this process the group generally advances through the assigned curriculum together.

A third kind of organization, an attempt to achieve even more individualized instruction, is the arrangement of learning stations where children can go to perform selected tasks individually and at their own pace.

A fourth type of classroom organization and management is "team teaching." One rationale behind this approach is that teachers can assume teaching responsibility in those areas in which they are most competent and, by thorough preparation and organization, can present a better instructional program than in situations where they try to teach many topics, perhaps less well. Generally, the emphasis in team teaching has been on improving the effectiveness and efficiency of the presentation, and not necessarily on better evaluation of pupil performance.

The apparent motive in these organizational arrangements has been to increase the effectiveness of instruction for individual children. Two of the components involved in these efforts are to increase the effectiveness of delivering instructions to children and to tailor instruction individually to children's needs. However, few teachers have individualized instruction effectively for each child in all of the vital academic areas.

Educators have not discussed the implications of implementing truly individualized instruction. If a teacher actually individualized planning for each pupil in 6 different areas of performance, and that teacher had 30 pupils in the classroom, he or she would have nearly 200 individual plans and programs. To implement such a large number of individual programs successfully appears to be an overwhelming task, one which partially explains the failure of education to implement individualized instruction effectively. However, with effective management, individually tailored programs are feasible and practical, and they have been implemented successfully in an increasing number of regular and special classroom settings throughout the country.

In the administration of instruction, a distinction should be made between management and operation. Operation is defined as achieving an objective through one's own efforts; management is defined as achieving an objective through the use of resources and the efforts of others. Through operation one directly engages in tasks designed to achieve an objective. The practical way an individual can increase performance is by expending more time and enegry practicing the tasks involved. This naturally limits improvement through operation. However, in management one can achieve many more and greater objectives by increasing the amount of time, effort, and resources applied to a problem through coordinating the efforts of other individuals. It has been useful to apply the principle of management, as opposed to operation, to the instructional process. As long as teachers use operations, they will be frustrated because of the finite amount of time they can spend on an almost infinite amount of work to be achieved with so many pupils. By using a management approach, however, teachers will be able to multiply the results of their own behavioral expenditures many times over.

Basically, a management approach involves:

1. Identifying the general goals one wishes to achieve.
2. Specifying the goals in terms of objectives that will lead to achievement.
3. Identifying the activities and necessary resources to achieve the specified objectives.
4. Delegating responsibility for engaging in those activities to reach the objectives.
5. Systematic analysis of progress toward objectives.

In a management system, the person responsible for the management obviously must have individuals to whom responsibility can be delegated. In many classrooms, the only individuals a teacher has are the children being taught. The children themselves, in such a case, have a role in the management of their own learning to achieve educational objectives. This has the obvious advantage of also teaching children to be agents in managing their own education. In other cases, teachers have additional individuals who can assist in management, such as teacher aides, secretaries, and volunteers.

Classroom ecology.   The ecology of the classroom comprises two general levels important in considering systematic programming. The first level is the physical environment—the shape and size of the room, arrangement and placement of desks and chairs, supplies, recordkeeping equipment, display media, and the location of work and activity areas. Structuring the physical environment is necessary for certain learning disabled children who are hyperactive or lack the attention skills necessary for learning basic academic tasks (Haring and Phillips, 1962; Hewett, 1964; Haring and Phillips, 1972). The use of carrels, for instance, often is necessary to keep external distractions to a minimum.

An effective and reinforcing technique often employed for learning disabled children is dividing the room into high and low strength activity areas (Homme, and others, 1963; Haring and Kunzelmann, 1966). This application of the Premack Principle provides a specific area for academic tasks, which are usually low strength behaviors, and other areas for high strength behaviors, which usually involve open play, individual or group projects, and spaces for science and arts and crafts.

Arranging the classroom into high and low strength areas results in a natural structure in which effective contingency management can be implemented. The physical environment in a real sense contains the contingency system that is managed through systematic instructional procedures. A teacher familiar and at ease with such an environment can deliver instructional cues in such a way that each student receives the necessary amount of attention for individual progress. Team teaching, classroom aides such as parents or volunteer college students, or even peer tutors, are of further benefit, as are electronic display media in language and communication centers, and television or other media. The high strength activities are then used to reinforce the low strength ones. When a student successfully completes a daily math assignment, for example, access is granted to a high strength activity, usually chosen by the child.

The influence of the physical environment in learning and gaining communication skills cannot be overestimated. Flexibility is the key to successful environmental planning. The administrator, too often worried about damage to school property or maintaining order in the classroom, often does not provide adequate reinforcement to a teacher who has made the environment more flexible, thus facilitating behavior change in more children. We do not know how many learning disabilities actually can be blamed on instructional or administrative failure. We do know that applying systems technology in organizing better educational opportunity means specification of objectives not only for the student, but for the teacher, the principal, the administration, and the overall school program. Goal-directed learning necessitates goal-directed administration. Precise programming means precise teaching.

The second basic level of classroom ecology is the instructional environment, which we discussed earlier. The teacher and administrator should make the reinforcing nature of the physical and instructional environment work together. The curriculum, the instructional methodology, the physical features of the classroom, plus the children and teachers, are an integrated whole that is the learning environment. We can differentiate any given environment into many separate categories, but unless the categories are recognized as subsystems in a greater whole system, programming and management errors can be made easily and unconsciously. One of the greatest problems facing the total programming needs of the educational system is the tendency of those advocating technological innovation to divide the environment into specific functions, but not to provide for information flow between the subsystems.

One way to design an environment that is a cohesive, functioning whole is by using free time as a reinforcer through the Premack Principle. Some research projects (Lovitt, Guppy, and Blattner, 1969; Hopkins, Schutte, and Garton, 1971) have demonstrated clearly that free time is an effective means of increasing academic performance. Systematic and structured academic instruction seem to work best when performance is contingent on student selection of free-time activity. Thus, balance is achieved between activities that necessarily are highly structured, such as specific remedial exercises, and flexible, free-time activities. The relationship of the instructional environment to the physical environment has not been researched fully as yet. However, as behavioral research in natural school settings evolves, these relationships become clearer and more accessible for use in designing better, more positively reinforcing school environments.

The educational system and the classroom make up one of the major environments in which a child's behavior is shaped. To grow and evolve with the needs of contemporary society, the educational system must implement changes that enhance the cybernetic nature of that system. In recent years the applied analysis of behavior has provided empirical, systematic, and generalizable techniques for describing and controlling behavior-environment relationships in education (Zifferblatt, 1972). Using and emphasizing the procedural and methodological similarities between systems and behavioral technology on an administrative level in the design of curriculum, information flow, and environment can be one of the greatest preventives to learning and instructional disabilities to date.

Learning Resource Centers

Beginning with Strauss and Lehtinen (1947) and Cruickshank and his associates (1961), the concept of structure has been used to provide educational experiences for a wide range of behavioral and academic deficits. Research with "engineered classrooms" (Hewett, 1968; Haring and Lovitt, 1967) resulted in a strong basis for an ecological approach to classroom organization. The concept of the resource room was developed to provide a specialized instructional center for direct remediation of behavioral and academic deficits (Connor and Muldoon, 1967; Vallet, 1970; Reger and Koppman, 1971). The resource room, if it is to be effective, should be an educational laboratory where precise assessment and presentation, and immediate feedback, can be delivered. Much criticism has been leveled at special education services that remove children from the regular classroom and place them in special self-contained classes for the entire school day. The resource room offers an alternative to removing children with learning problems from the classroom and placing them in an environment that may do little to remediate the problems.

A learning resource center is staffed by a resource teacher or educational technologist, who is trained in working with children with specific academic deficits and/or behavior problems. Such an educational specialist can function in a number of ways within the school district program. First, such personnel would be responsible for managing the learning resource centers in one or more school facilities, working with students whose special needs could not be met in the regular classroom. Second, such personnel would help teachers in the regular classroom, providing information on methods and procedures for remedial help and classroom management. In this role, the resource teacher is an itinerant special assistant to teachers to aid in designing individualized programs for children whom the regular teacher feels need help. This role also provides in-service training for regular classroom teachers through the resource teacher's expertise in applying advanced educational technology. Such teacher consultant services bring new and sharper skills to the teacher and also bridge the gap between the traditional psychological services offered by school districts.

In a research project conducted in the Clover Park School District, Tacoma, Washington (Haring, 1971), five self-contained special education classes were closed after an intensive training sequence for resource teachers using systematic instructional procedures. As a result of the service by the first generation of resource teachers trained, the project continued, resulting in 926 academic and social interventions, 561 students returned to regular classrooms, and the discovery that many students referred to special classes needed no intervention at all, only systematic behavioral management and individualized instruction.

The resource room-resource teacher model is neither a panacea nor a replacement for special self-contained classrooms. A resource room program is an excellent opportunity to offer direct services to children and teachers, and to effect changes in the educational programs through other teaching and local administrators (Reger, 1972). For the child with a learning disability, whether a perceptual, academic, or behavioral deficit, resource teachers and special remedial techniques offer improved opportunities for educational and vocational advancement.

Early Childhood Assessment—A Preventive Strategy

Although each learning disability is a unique phenomenon, it is important that educators, administrators, and teachers design public school programs that are flexible enough to meet the needs of children with a broad scope of potential learning problems. Total school programming is necessary on a district and statewide basis. The focus of designing an integrative, multidisciplinary program always should be on the child and the interactions that occur between children and between children and staff. Schools exist to educate children, but a look at many organizational flow charts indicates that the most overlooked component is often the child. Problem-solving strategies will be more successful the closer they are applied to the problem. Classroom problems are best solved in the classroom. Direct intervention and remediation work better than administering many and diverse psychological and perceptual tests. Administrators should be aware of as many options as possible and become familiar with advanced remedial strategies and educational technology.

As stated before, there are probably as many categories of learning disabilities as there are conditions that create them. One administrative strategy that is both preventive and remedial is early childhood assessment. Most children enter public education at the kindergarten level, so it is well to provide services that can uncover potential problems. In the Model Preschool Center at the Experimental Education Unit of the University of Washington, a technique is proving useful in identifying potential handicapping situations. In preschool, the children are routinely presented with preacademic skills training and social and communication opportunities that allow the teacher to monitor their development—a task that is not as difficult as it may seem to a teacher who has never done it consciously (Hayden, Haring, Allen, Rieke, and Dmitriev, 1972). Keeping simple behavioral data on a child's interaction can provide useful diagnostic information that leads to identifying potential learning problems.

Early remedial help can prevent the problem from becoming worse and can aid in the child's growth. Early childhood education also gives children enriched perceptual and communication skills training that perhaps may not be experienced in other environments. Although not much information exists to validate this assertion, it is certainly plausible that many learning disabilities develop from environmental conditions, such as reinforcement history, lack of perceptual opportunity, or poor instruction. As soon as a child enters public education, the system can and should begin to make every possible effort to provide him or her with an enriching environment and opportunity to learn.

One problem must be pointed out. As we have noted many times before, definitions of learning disabilities tend to vary from state to state. Under federal legislation, a specific learning disability is defined as "a disorder in one or more of the processes involved in understanding or using language, spoken or written." Included in this category are the traditional labels of developmental aphasia, dyslexia, minimal cerebral dysfunction, and auditory and visual handicaps. These problems are starting to be seen as discrepancies between apparent potential and performance. Early childhood education begins the process of providing experiences and skills that aid development and prevent such problems. However, only by using direct, daily measurement and probing procedures can a teacher quickly discover when problems occur. So many causes and interrelated conditions can be responsible for a learning problem that the best method of dealing with it is to detect it as soon as it shows up in the child's performance.

Good teaching is the best preventive measure. Using systematic instructional procedures prevents children from being reinforced for inadequate or poor performance, and reduces the probability of the teacher's overlooking an academic deficit.

Systems Approach to Management as Applied to Administration

The procedures that an administrator uses in applying the systems approach to problem-solving is similar to the way any other person would apply the concept. The application of systems technology to administration differs basically in respect to the details and content of materials with which the administrator deals. The administrator must orchestrate material, financial, and human resources to achieve the finest education possible for the children under his or her responsibility. This means that the community and the school personnel must agree on the objectives the children are to reach. Once this has been done, a needs assessment can be initiated. This is not an easy task, since there are a wide variety of social, academic, and vocational goals to be met. One approach is to assign to the staff the task that would first use techniques to cover a wide range of abilities. Once areas of deficits have been identified, more intensive informal assessment could be initiated to pinpoint precise needs.

Knowing the needs and resources, the administrator and the staff plan their allocation. This may mean that special curriculum and materials must be generated. If this is the case, Program Evaluation and Review (PERT) techniques are helpful. In using PERT procedures, the enabling objectives or steps enroute to finishing the project are defined. Then their relationships are established, which ones are dependent and which ones are not dependent on others. They are then arranged in a temporal flow pattern with due dates set up at each step. With the task sequencing established, personnel allocations can be made. It may be discovered that one person is a key to several tasks. This probably will necessitate that the initial time estimate be adjusted.

Allocation and implementation activities must be monitored to see what changes should be made as conditions change. Monitoring can be done informally at some levels or at meetings at other levels; however, where there is a large volume of data, such as pupil status and progress, formal reports should be made. Unfortunately, pupil performance long has been expressed normatively. Now, with the emphasis on behavioral objectives and direct daily measurement, it is possible to monitor pupil progress by accomplishment of distinct tasks or goals. With this kind of information, projections can be made about pupils' progress and what their needs will be. As a result the administrator may wish to reassign pupils or establish resource rooms to provide special assistance to those in need before they drop very far behind. Behavioral objectives and direct daily measurement allow reports to be functional for decision-making rather than just descriptive nonfunctional public relations statistics.

An educational system is designed to help students acquire certain behaviors. When direct and daily measurement is implemented in the classroom as a means of performance measurement, it can be reported to administrators as a basis for problem-solving and decision-making. If daily pupil performance data are used to make administrative decisions, some general requirements should be met. First, the collection of such data should result in little increase in demands upon teacher time and energy. Second, the data should provide information specifically related to decision-making and should provide feedback about the results of decisions. Third, since different types of decisions necessitate different types of data, data summary and reporting systems must be flexible (Zelman, 1972).

Systems approach to managing education.   The general steps that a research coordinator goes through in using the systems approach to manage research are similar to the steps anyone else would go through—setting goals, objectives, and such. The task of applying the systems approach in education differs in the details that must be considered in setting the goals and organizing for their achievement. Considering educational activities as a system becomes more imperative as the complexity of the problem and the size of the staff increase. This is particularly true with programmatic research projects, which provide for several research activities focusing on one common problem where a number of projects are conducted concurrently. An essential characteristic of programmatic research is the organizational approach that is used. If education is to use the scientific method to build a basic body of knowledge about the teaching-learning process, ideally it should become research oriented. Although this does not always appeal to educators, the fact is that it is perhaps the only proven method of problem-solving currently available. An educational system that is research oriented and data based attempts not only to educate the children it serves, but also to constantly generate information that allows it to evolve and grow, overcoming defects and meeting new problems. Systematic instructional procedures are the result of careful and systematic investigation of classroom variables using the techniques of applied behavioral analysis.

The first step in developing a research project is to establish the goal. Likewise in educational planning, all relevant goals must be carefully defined. The goal may be selected on the basis of what is determined to be important, or it may be what some funding agency deems desirable, or both. The next step would be to review the literature. Now the objectives can be defined and design considered. When developing designs, the constraints of the resources have to be considered—population availability, personnel, space, and so on. Once the design has been established, the steps of implementation can be delineated, responsibilities assigned, and a PERT chart developed. Examples of some possible steps are getting clearance to use subjects, acquiring or developing materials to be used, selection of measurement instrument, informing computer programmer of needs, and training of research assistants. As the program progresses, unanticipated factors will develop, requiring changes in some of the previously planned activities.

Information on the unanticipated factors may come from within or outside the system. An example of an influencing factor outside of the research project is the funding agency requesting additional information. Surprises within the organization may be that one team is taking longer than expected to achieve a critical objective necessary for the progress of the other teams, or the findings of one team may influence the work planned for another.

In a public school system, the implementation of systematic instructional procedures and data-based decision-making is analogous to setting up a research program. This is no easy matter and is not accomplished overnight. But it is a direct way to discover defects in the operation of the school system, and the information generated will hopefully be of assistance in finding ways to make necessary changes.

The system must be able to adapt dynamically to these changes. To do so, it must be informed. The cybernetics of internal feedback may be accomplished by periodic meetings and reports. Often appropriately designed forms will reduce the burden of the reports. Care should be taken to avoid having to meet or report so often that there is no time to do any work. When the feedback rate is too high, another potential danger is encountered. This danger is that the system will become too sensitive and change directions too fast. In technical terms this is called "porpoising," because of the bouncing nature of the interaction. This is analogous to driving a sports car after driving an old truck—there is a lot of wasted, dangerous, inefficient motion. Therefore, a compromise must be reached between too sensitive a system and one that is too sluggish, both of which have similar dangers. One caution to be taken in setting up the PERT chart is not to overlook the final reporting considerations, leave enough time, do as much as possible without waiting for the final data, and prepare for enough secretarial support. This period is the most critical in terms of time and is often overlooked, leading to a terminal rush and an inferior product in spite of all the quality that may have preceded it.

THE USES OF COMPUTERS IN EDUCATION

One common characteristic of systems in education, be they administrative, instructional, or research, is the flow of information. It often comes into a central location in a raw, unprocessed form from a variety of sources. To draw any conclusions or make any data-based decisions, the data must be analyzed or reduced, and a report of that processing must be made available. Computer systems increasingly have been pressed into service to assist in handling the increasing volumes of data.

When computer systems are integrated into the overall information system, attention should be given to certain considerations. Electronic Data Processing (EDP) can be considered a subsystem of the overall information system. As a result, its development follows the systems approach. Hence the first consideration is, what is it to do or what are the characteristics of the reports to be generated, how often are they to be generated, what initiates their generations—a fixed passage of time, an exception condition, or a call from a user? Are the format and content constant, or will it be desirable for the user to specify content? Is the format to be restricted to $8\frac{1}{2}''$ x $11''$ dimensions for direct copying and dissemination, or can the entire width of the computer printer be used? The point to be made is that detailed consideration of the output will guide the selection of what information is to be collected and how it is to be processed. The more attention given to output in the beginning, the faster the project will be operational, and the better the morale of those working on the project.

Knowing what data have to be collected to produce the desired output, attention can be addressed to how and when they will be collected. The data-processing industry has developed, and is continuing to develop, techniques to facilitate data collection. In general these techniques range from real-time interaction through on-time data collection, and remote to local input, storage, and retrieval. Each approach has its advantages and disadvantages, and the selection depends on the requirements and economics of the overall system. For example, if fast turnaround time is needed for relatively small amounts of data, and the funds are available to support it, a remote terminal such as a teletype may be used with the computer in a real-time interactive mode. At the other end of the spectrum, when data can be collected over a long time prior to being processed, and a response time of hours or days is acceptable, a local input, processing, and output mode may be used.

Regardless of the input-output technology, forms often insure the correct sequence and complete collection of the necessary data. The form design should be done in conjunction with the computer programmer to determine the sequence of questions, type of response, and amount of data to be allowed. The first draft of the form should be tried out on the population who will be filling it out. After a few (perhaps 10) people have filled it out, the errors and omissions should be studied to determine how the form can be revised to reduce or avoid these mistakes. White space, boxes around sections, proximity of related items, and the wording of instructions are items to consider changing.

Computers have been applied in education to assist learning, administration, and research. Classically, their use in research and administration has been as a number manipulator to solve statistical inventory or accounting problems. Their application to instruction has included direct instruction of pupils via computer-aided instruction (CAI), computer-managed instruction (CMI), and computer-generated tests. In computer-aided instruction, the computer asks the pupil a question and waits for a response. After the response is given (generally typed), the computer evaluates it and presents the next question based on the accuracy of the previous response. CAI, although effective, has proven too costly for most schools to use. CMI employs the computer in a less sophisticated but more functional way to meet such requirements of individualized instruction as selection of materials and activities, pupil evaluation, and pupil record-keeping.

A system under development at the Experimental Education Unit (EEU) is designed to have the characteristics of a CMI system (Haring, 1973). It also is designed to assist administrators and researchers, as well as the teachers and children. In principle, it will accept daily data from the classroom on dependent variables along with less frequent data on the constant conditions and changes in the independent variables. The system will then make reports to teachers and administrators on pupil progress. The program is capable of accepting criteria that will cause an exception report (alarm) if the child is not progressing adequately. In time, after enough histories have been collected, it is hoped that prescriptions for a new child to the school can be made by matching individual characteristics to those of other youngsters in the history file, and then picking the program combinations that worked best for individuals with similar problems.

CONCLUSION

We cannot view the educational system as separate from either the social system or the natural environment. Changes are necessary in our thinking and perception of the relationship of human beings to the environment. As Gregory Bateson (1972) points out, "The creature that wins *against* its environment destroys itself." Understanding that the goal of *ecologically harmonious behavior*—that is, establishing behavior patterns where balance between natural and social environments insures growth and differentiation—should be the goal of each individual and the systems with which we apply technological advances to help solve our problems. The learning disabled child is a casualty of the present education system. We force children into failure patterns and cycles that demean the individual's ability to develop in an integrated manner. And we do it daily. This occurs not because of malicious or unhumanistic intent, but because the ways in which we teach children are in need of change.

One great advancement in public education to date has been the application of the systems approach of problem-solving in administration and research. A complementary and more and more compatible set of procedures is being developed by research in behavioral technology. It is well possible that a synthesis of these two technologies may take place in the field of education. New administrative strategies designed to improve and redesign the educational system to the advantage of the individual student naturally will use both behavioral and systems technologies. Already in use in education are information management and control systems originally developed by application of cybernetic and general systems concepts to business and industry. Another field showing parallel development is in psychological theory in the development of the notion that the human being is an adaptive organism in a continually evolving environment and psychology is the study of possible relationships and interrelationships of human society and the environment (von Bertalanffy, 1969; Bateson, 1972).

In discussing both systematic instructional procedures and classroom administrative strategies, the impact of behavioral and systems technologies in the development of educational technology is beginning to show. Focusing on the notion that a disability lies within the environmental events that a child experiences rather than the neurological and biochemical structure of the child, educators may begin to design and produce educational systems that prevent and remediate academic learning disabilities, perceptual handicaps, and various developmental disabilities. Eileen Allen (1967) points out that the effectiveness of systematically using social reinforcement that exists naturally in the environment is a powerful means of modifying academic learning problems. Using both systems and behavioral technologies in designing and redesigning the ecology of the learning environment is one proven way to carry effective planning to higher and higher levels of generalization. With these advanced technologies, a school district, the administrators and teachers, the supportive staff, the parents, and the children can work together to avoid the programming inequities and instructional disabilities that produce and maintain many learning problems.

REFERENCES

ALLEN, K. E., The strengthening of adjustive behaviors through systematic application of reinforcement procedures. In *International Convocation on Children and Young Adults with Learning Disabilities Proceedings.* Pittsburgh: Home for Crippled Children, 1967.

BATESON, G., *Double Bind,* 1969. Paper presented at a symposium on the Double Bind, sponsored by the American Psychological Association, August 1969.

————, *Steps to an Ecology of Mind.* New York: Ballantine Books, 1972.

COLEMAN, J. S., E. Q. CAMPBELL, G. J. HOBSON, J. McPARTLAND, A. M. MOOD, F. J. WEISFELD, and R. L. YORK, *Equality of Educational Opportunity.* Washington, D. C.: USGPO, 1966.

CONNOR, E. M., and J. F. MULDOON, Resource program for emotionally disturbed teenagers. *Exceptional Children,* 1967, *34,* 261–265.

CRUICKSHANK, W. M., Some issues facing the field of learning disability. *Journal of Learning Disabilities,* 1972, *5,* 380–388.

CRUICKSHANK, W. M., F. A. BENTZEN, F. H. RATZEBURG, and M. T. TANNHAUSSER, *A Teaching Method for Brain-injured and Hyperactive Children.* Syracuse, N. Y.: Syracuse University Press, 1961.

DENO, E., Special education as development capital. *Exceptional children,* 1970, *37,* 229–237.

FOLEY, W. J., The future of administration and educational evaluation. *Educational Technology,* 1970, *10,* 20–25.

FORNESS, S., The mildly retarded as casualties of the educational system. *Journal of School Psychology,* June, 1972, *10,* Pt. 2, 117–126.

HARING, N. G., *The Application of Functional Analysis of Behavior by Teachers in a Natural School Setting.* Final report of Grant No. OEG-0-8-07-0376-1857 (032). Washington, D. C.: U. S. Department of Health, Education, and Welfare, Office of Education, 1969.

————, *A Program Project for the Investigation and Application of Procedures of Analysis and Modification of Behavior of Handicapped Children.* Annual report for Grant No. OEG-0-70-3916 (607). Seattle: Experimental Education Unit, University of Washington, and Washington, D. C.: Department of Health, Education, and Welfare, 1973.

HARING, N. G., and H. KUNZELMANN, The fine-focus of therapeutic behavioral management. In J. Hellmuth (Ed.), *Educational Therapy,* Vol. 1. Seattle: Special Child Publications, 1966.

HARING, N. G., and T. C. LOVITT, Operant methodology and education technology in special education. In N. G. Haring and R. L. Schiefelbusch (Eds.), *Methods in Special Education.* New York: McGraw-Hill, 1967.

HARING, N. G., and E. L. PHILLIPS, *Analysis and Modification of Classroom Behavior*. Englewood Cliffs, N. J.: Prentice-Hall, Inc., 1972.

——, *Educating Emotionally Disturbed Children*. New York: McGraw-Hill Book Company, Inc., 1962.

HAYDEN, A. H., N. G. HARING, K. E. ALLEN, J. RIEKE, and V. DMITRIEV, Systematic observation: a valuable tool in recognizing potentially handicapping conditions in young children. *Newsletter*, University of Washington, College of Education, Seattle, Spring 1972.

HEWETT, F. M., A hierarchy of educational tasks for children with learning disorders. *Exceptional Children*, 1964, *31*, 207–214.

——, *The Emotionally Disturbed Child in the Classroom: A Developmental Strategy for Educating Children with Maladaptive Behavior*. Boston: Allyn and Bacon, 1968.

Hobson vs Hanson, 269 F Supp. 401 (D.C.D.C.), 1967.

HOMME, L. E., P. C. DE BACA, J. V. DEVINE, R. STEINHORST, and E. J. RICKERT, Use of the Premack Principle in controlling the behavior of nursery school children. *Journal of the Experimental Analysis of Behavior*, 1963, *6*, 544.

HOPKINS, B. L., R. C. SCHUTTE, and K. L. GARTON, The effects of access to a playroom on the rate and quality of printing and writing of first- and second-grade students. *Journal of Applied Behavior Analysis*, 1971, 4, 2.

LAING, R. D., *Knots*. New York: Pantheon Books, 1970.

LILLY, M. S., Special education: A teapot in a tempest. *Exceptional Children*, 1970, *37*, 43–49.

LOVITT, T. C., Assessment of children with learning disabilities. *Exceptional children*, 1967, *34*, 233.

LOVITT, T. C., T. E. GUPPY, and J. E. BLATTNER, The use of free time contingency with fourth graders to increase spelling accuracy. *Behaviour Research and Therapy*, 1969, *1*, 155–156.

PETER, L. J., and R. HULL, *The Peter Principle: Why Things Always Go Wrong*. New York: Morrow, 1969.

REGER, R., Resource rooms: change agents or guardians of the status quo? *Journal of Special Education*, 1972, *6*, 355–359.

REGER, R., and M. KOPPMANN, The child oriented resource room. *Exceptional Child*, 1971, *37*, 460–462.

SIMCHES, R. F., The inside outsider. *Exceptional Children*, 1970, *37*, 5–15.

STRAUSS, A. A., and L. E. LEHTINEN, *Psychopathology and Education of the Brain-injured Child*. New York: Grune and Stratton, 1947.

VALLET, R. E., The learning resource center for exceptional children. *Exceptional Children*, 1970, *36*, 527–530.

——, *Programming Learning Disabilities*. Palo Alto, Calif.: Fearon Publishers, 1969.

VON BERTALANFFY, L., *General Systems Theory*. New York: Braziller, 1968.

ZELMAN W. N., Increasing the availability of pupil performance information for administrative decisions. In N. G. Haring and A. H. Hayden (Eds.), *The Improvement of Instruction*. Seattle: Special Child Publications, 1972.

ZIFFERBLATT, S. M., Behavior systems. In C. E. Thoresen, ed., *Behavior Modification in Education*. Chicago: The University of Chicago Press, 1972.

Afterword

A Parent's Thoughts for Parents and Teachers

DOREEN KRONICK, M.A.

TO THE PROFESSIONAL

There always will be parents of exceptional children who are unprepared to face their child's limitations. They displace their disappointment in their child onto the educational system and blame slow development on current class placement. On the other hand, thousands of parents harbor justifiable concerns around their child's placement and the quality of help that is offered. It is too easy an escape for educators to attribute all parental concern to lack of acceptance of their child's limitations. It is simpler to state that parents are unrealistic than it is to take a long, hard look at the ways in which the educational process meets or fails to meet a child's needs. Today's educational rhetoric professes individualization, but practices it to a lesser extent.

What, then, does this mean? Professionals view the inception of services within the boundaries of community resources, funds, availability of professional staff, training facilities, and similar considerations. They tend to view services in their own frame of reference, which sufficed until recent years and was not providing services to the learning disabled. Parents see only their child's needs. They are apprehensive that their child's life will be a nightmare of profound frustration, emotional disturbance, and very limited opportunity. Traditionally, our communities offer too few educational facilities for the handicapped, although the moral obligation to provide opportunity for all children to maximize their abilities, regardless of the limitation to their potential, often has been verbalized. We say one thing, do another, and the children fall in the middle. How can we deny to intelligent youngsters with good prognosis the opportunities within regular and special education to become more functional persons?

During the years in which parents seek ways to solve the acute problems of their learning disabled child, they rarely know to whom to turn. In their search for help they tend to receive a series of diagnoses, which are disposed to reflect the diagnostician's bias as much as the child's actual symptoms. It is not uncommon to have the same child diagnosed as autistic, aphasic, cerebral palsied, retarded, and "the only thing the matter with that child is the mother." The terms "brain damage" and "brain injury" frequently are used as descriptive labels for a set of behaviors, with little proof that the behaviors are caused by actual damage. Dyslexia, in its original context, referred to congenital "word blindness." Now it is the label loosely attached to any child who has difficulty reading or spelling and who comes in contact with professionals and schools who are partial to that term.

Prognosis tends to be equally inconsistent. Predictions for the same child can vary from "institutionalization" to "the child will grow out of it." The irony of these predictions is that learning disabled children can learn a great deal, yet often do not outgrow their disabilities completely.

Long after parents have ceased shopping, professionals ply them with mixed messages. They are burdened by the diagnoses and prognoses of educators, vocational guidance personnel, school psychologists, and family physicians. They are faced with the serious dilemma of not knowing which message to believe or which advice to follow. If parents follow advice suggesting that the disability no longer exists, and thus urge their child into areas in which coping is difficult, incalculable harm can follow. Conversely, if a no-longer existent disability is perpetuated, the parents indulge in unhealthy behavior and the child is done a grave injustice. If a child is given a diagnosis that differs from the one expressed and practiced by the parents, the parent-child relationship can be seriously undermined. Failure to follow the advice of school psychologists or guidance counselors places parents and child in a difficult situation, yet following advice that does not seem in the child's best interests is not defensible either. Seeking a professional opinion outside the school system may not be the answer, since some school boards will consider only the diagnoses of their own staff members.

As frustrating as parents' attempts have been to obtain meaningful diagnoses, it nonetheless remains easier to secure a diagnosis than ongoing, comprehensive treatment. Certainly, a proliferation of treatment programs has sprouted up around the country. Some of these programs offer treatment that tends to be costly, time consuming, and frequently thinly related to the child's disability. Furthermore, such treatment too often neglects the total child—dealing solely with articulation, eye-movement, coordination, and so on. However, diagnosis persists as the favorite professional activity. One winter, each professional who addressed our local parents' association was given the topic "home management." One professional, a pediatrician, actually lectured on "home management," whereas the others talked about how they diagnose children. The inter-agency study on the needs of Canadian children with emotional and learning disorders states:

> Our field visits revealed a much greater availability of assessment or diagnosis than treatment. There is no doubt that it is easier to diagnose than to treat emotionally disturbed children, but there may also be a tendency on the part of clinicians to be satisfied with the intellectual excitement of grasping the dynamics of the case and to avoid the exacting task of becoming involved in a therapeutic process which may be long and arduous.

> This shortage of treatment and the isolation, selectivity, and scarcity of children with emotional and learning disorders, means that a heavy burden rests on the families and school personnel who are responsible for the day-to-day care of these children. This has led to some particular problems between community health services and schools which have further frag-mented the delivery of care and hindered the development of comprehen-sive services for children.

Communities and professionals frequently are aware that present models of service and professional practice fail to meet the ongoing needs of the few children served and altogether neglect the needs of most persons in the community requiring such services. Some parents, respond-ing to the failure of authorities to provide consistent support and direction, have assumed a pseudoprofessional role. They acquire impres-sive bodies of knowledge to steer their child intelligently through the maze of mixed diagnoses and copious treatment possibilities. Nonetheless, this pseudoprofessional role is greatly resented by many professionals.

Both professionals and parents seem to lack the creativity to assess and mobilize such human resources as housewives, retired teachers, secondary and college students, and persons in related and helping pro-fessions, who could assist the learning disabled throughout their lives. Thus we expect that a diagnosis, or a year in a special class, will be the total solution for an acute problem. This simplistic attitude shelters us from the necessity of becoming involved with the more careful planning requisite for long-term care.

One obvious example where parents have used pressure to further questionable services has been in the push for segregated classes. Most parents realize that a very small segment of the learning disabled popula-tion requires special class placement. We parents also recognize that the majority of the learning disabled would have their needs met more adequately within the typical classroom with the backup support of consultant, itinerant, resource, and crisis personnel. The provision of service within such a model would maintain our children in their neighborhood schools and provide help within an expanded framework of normalcy. In other words, "this is a normal child who learns dif-ferently," or "this is a normal child who requires more assistance." Most of us are aware that the provision of services within the regular classroom is the only way we can hope to offer help to all the learning disabled children requiring it.

Nonetheless we continue to pressure for special classes because they are more tangible and easier to obtain. To serve the child within the standard classroom, we need to reexamine teacher training, pupil-teacher ratio, and consider developing more backup personnel. Because it is so much easier and faster to convince school boards to initiate one or two additional segregated classes, we cling to that outmoded model. Hence we perpetuate the visible symbol of the success of our efforts, rather than work to obtain the slower but sounder route.

Educators and parents do not always agree on the concept of adequate special education services. A child may be given two remedial reading periods weekly, which the parents, in their desire for speedy results, see as inadequate (which they may or may not be). A learning disabled child with normal intelligence who is experiencing difficulty academically may be placed in an auxiliary class where teaching occurs at a slower pace to accommodate children with various types of handicaps. The educators feel that the pressure has been removed from the learning disabled child and that an expensive and valuable service is being offered. The parents feel that the child will receive little specific remediation in such a setting and that insufficient learning will take place. They fear that the child is being forced into a limited stream and that future vocational opportunity and life style will be curtailed by such a placement. Learning disabled youth of secondary school age may be limited in the ways they express themselves and may be competent in a restricted number of areas. Because their abilities are not generalized, it is the common practice in North America for educators to place such youth in nonacademic or semiacademic streams.

The Subtle Forces At Work

Parents have focused their frustration and anger on the obvious issues, such as inadequacy of services, because they do not always consciously perceive, properly assess, or delineate the subtle and negative aspects of the social environment. Nonetheless, and possibly because of the elusiveness of these experiences, the environmental forces are equally debilitating. Many professionals and others tend to deny these aspects of our experience. It is important that they begin to recognize them as a significant force in the adjustment of child and family.

Typically, the learning disabled infant and preschool child seems to progress largely within the continuum of normal development. Family and community have normal expectations for the child, and the child assumes that he or she will be able to realize those expectations. Simultaneously, the child internalizes the fact that our society places less value on the less functional individual. Even if the family discovers in preschool years that the child is disabled, they frequently suppress their fears, furthering the myth and expectation of normalcy. However, the realization that the child is different emerges in the early school years. How, then, is adjustment to the conflicting identities possible? There is the ideal self, developed in the family and internalized by the child, of being like everyone else, and the new self, furnished by educators and peers, of being a less able person. The likelihood of making an early and realistic adjustment is slim. Generally, parents discover the existence of this handicap at the same time that the child becomes aware of having difficulties. Parents are so self-concerned at that time with their own need to come to terms with the loss of expectations that they tend not to recognize the child's behavior as an expression of internalized fears, confusion, and questions about these newly discovered inadequacies. The parents even may resent and punish the child's behavior.

Educators, peers, relatives, family friends, neighbors, and acquaintances fail the child in providing consistent, reliable feedback. Since we shape the concept of ourselves from the feedback of human interaction, we truly handicap such a child by feeding such mixed messages that it is impossible for a realistic self-concept to emerge. At times the child is praised for achievements which do not merit praise and at times penalized for levels of achievement when the best effort possible has been given.

Peers are quick to label the child "spas," "retard," and "mental." Educators resist the existence of a learning disability and are likely to view the child as spoiled, lazy, underachieving, or bad. Relatives and family friends tend to reject the idea of a disability, stating that the child obviously is intelligent and therefore can't be disabled. Parents also take a varying period of time to accept realistic limitations concerning their child's future. Their adjustment is hampered greatly by their confusion, created by the inclusion of a variety of disabilities within the category "learning disabilities." Consequently, prognosis varies so markedly that some learning disabled eventually obtain Ph.Ds and others progress minimally. The literature describing achievement frequently omits the type of disability involved. In any event, the matching of disability to prognosis for the learning disabled remains a crude art. Some fathers and mothers view the same child differently—one parent sees the child as handicapped and the other perceives only normalcy. Each parent may feed the child very different messages at different times, because the parent's acceptance is tempered by dreams of normal achievement. Thus, the father insisting that his son is a "normal, all-round boy" may readily fault the child for lack of coordination and achievement. The mother, appearing to make a good adjustment to the handicap, may spend years telling the child that he is not university material, yet inform him of all the college courses in which he could enroll. This polarization of the parents' image of their child creates tremendous confusion in terms of individual development of expectations and self-concept.

Our culture guards well the secret that all parents harbor mixed feelings about their children. We foster the myth that all our feelings about our offspring are positive ones. This allows us no accepted, or guilt-free, outlet for our disappointments or occasional rejections. Our ambivalence may start at birth when we are disappointed that the baby has Uncle Charlie's nose and mother-in-law's forehead. Later we may be disappointed if our daughter is loud and bossy, when we prefer polite, ladylike little girls. Our baby fails us if he or she does not walk or talk as quickly as other babies, is not well behaved in front of people or in public, or shatters the stereotype by behaving in any way different from our expectation of the ideal child. For example, if a small boy climbs a tree and gets dirty in the process, that may be very acceptable to some of us because little boys in our society long have been expected to be "all boy." Similarly, a family that is proud to have an "all boy" son is bound to be disappointed and feel rejection toward a son who is fearful and fastidious. To complicate this picture further, we expect our children at an early age to learn that one behavior pleases us in one situation, and the opposite behavior is expected in another milieu. Summarily, then, we perpetuate a fairy tale, that by producing a child, parents automatically are pleased with every facet of personality and appearance. In reality, however, parents tend to accept and reject a variety of attributes based upon their past experiences. Because we feel that it is wrong to have an aversion to any facet of our children, we tend to produce compensatory behavior. For instance, if we don't like one of our children's looks or some aspect of behavior, we compensate by spoiling the child.

In a similar vein, we feel that intensely hostile feelings toward our children are shameful, even if those feelings are triggered only by specific occurrences. I was amazed when a friend of mine commented, "Sometimes I could kill my kid." What a relief it was to learn that other mothers feel murderous impulses on occasion!

These ambivalent feelings that we harbor toward our children assume an added degree of significance with a learning disabled child. We still are disappointed that Aunt Sally's stubbornness, Uncle John's overbite, and our spouse's stubby fingers were inherited. But added to these are the gamut of feelings engendered by producing a less able child, running from our reactions to any maladaptive behavior to our feelings about society's reaction to our child and us.

Learning disabled children generally are not as efficient as other children in perceiving situations in which they find themselves. They have difficulty comparing the current situation to past experiences and storing it for comparison with future events. Similarly, they find it difficult to match and store responses so that they can recall a favorable response to one situation for use in a similar situation, or to be certain to avoid reusing undesirable behavior. Just as they tend to have difficulty matching auditory and visual configurations, they have a hard time matching experience with experience, response with response, and experience to response. If the adult reaction to a situation does not follow the behavior immediately, some learning disabled children will not associate the response to the behavior. Some children are so deficient in their ability to make certain kinds of associations that they even are unable to relate immediate adult response to their behavior. Furthermore, impulsivity, anxiety, and hyperactivity are such powerful urges that they prevent some children from producing appropriate behavior, even when the children are aware of the behavioral expectations. Therefore, they will continue to behave inappropriately some of the time. This tends to be extremely embarrassing to even the most enlightened and objective parents. Consider the mother's feelings when her child pulls the groceries off the supermarket shelf and responds to her efforts at suppression by throwing a tantrum in the middle of the aisle. She suspects that everyone who happens on the scene thinks that she has raised an ill-mannered child. In her embarrassment she may resort to anything to end the tantrum, from physical violence to bribery. Later she feels guilty that she reacted impulsively, with no appreciation of her child's needs. Then she is angry at her child for being different, for placing her in an uncomfortable, face-forfeiting situation and impelling her to react immaturely. Hostility and rejection, being unacceptable emotions, necessitate replacement, so the parent substitutes with overprotection, extra mothering, overindulgence, or inconsistent handling.

Learning disabled children generally do not show the lack of affection, communication, or affect associated with exceptionalities such as autism. Typically, they exert tremendous effort to relate and communicate. However, processing difficulties and hyperactivity may distort interaction, result in inappropriate affect, and reduce the incidence of giving or receiving affection. I recall a little boy who was so hyperactive that he never stopped moving to hug and kiss his parents, or allow them to cuddle him. Another lad was so confused by body gestures that he flinched whenever anyone attempted to put an arm around him, mistaking the affectionate gesture for a blow. Language processing problems can interfere with understanding or expressing verbal affection. Thus, with some of these children, the ability to receive or give affection may be reduced, and, in time, parents may respond by offering less affection. Some of these children are egocentric and fail to see situations as they relate to others. Thus, they fail to praise or express interest in others' interests. Their language tends to be boring and repetitive. Consequently, they are unrewarding family members and friends and are not sought out in that context.

There is a constancy to our days and years. They are variations on the theme in which our child's disability produces a succession of confrontations with our culture, which exacts prescribed behavior and production on demand. Each confrontation reverberates to the parents and each produces hostility and impotence. What *can* one do about a child who says the wrong things at the wrong time to the wrong people? Or the child who doesn't conform to the lock-step demands of the school? Or the child who disrupts family outings? Pretty explanations about learning disabilities are not sufficient to reverse the outsider's expectations and reactions. Our children spend their childhood and adolescence unwittingly alienating themselves from peers, educators, friends, and neighbors. The parent who can handle such alienation without negative feelings toward the child is unique indeed! So we are angry at the youngsters and compensate by being oversolicitous. Meanwhile the child doesn't know where he or she stands.

Let us progress to our child's hostility. No child or adult can fail to be frustrated and angry at a world that rejects people and is oblivious to individual needs. Yet parents continue to perpetuate the myth that life for children in North America, and especially the United States, is honey and roses. Any attempt on the child's part to shatter this dream is countered by our anxiety and denial. Many of us will admit that our own childhoods were far from utopian, yet we refuse to believe or share our children's concerns about theirs.

"The other kids don't like me," he states.

"Sure they do," you retort, instantly terminating the discussion.

"The teacher picks on me," he complains.

"All teachers treat all children the same way," we answer.

The child gets a painful sore. We wash and bandage it and state, "There, it feels better now." How can the child reconcile a parent's statement with reality, which is that the sore still hurts?

There are two facets to this. The first is our naive belief in the inherent justice of an unjust world, and our simplistic image of a child's world in which all adults and children are kind, loving, and friendly. The second is that by our denial of what our child perceives as reality, we protect ourselves from having to face the unpleasantness that the child experiences in life.

Thus we play a game entitled, "As long as we never mention our child's disability, we can pretend it isn't there." The rigid rules of silence demanded by this game are adhered to readily by outsiders, who are more comfortable pretending that the disability is nonexistent than facing its actuality. When parents are confronted directly with this noncommunication, their excuses typically are: "I don't know what to tell him," or "She knows that she's different; I don't have to tell her," or "He has never asked us what's wrong with him." The person who can't escape the disability is the child. He or she faces ineptitude at every turn, yet we don't clarify it. Thus anxieties and shameful feelings build up. Eight-year-old Jennifer told me that children who don't read then never learn to read. Ten-year-old Clifford said that people who don't read are "mental."

We drag our children to test after test. They have wires attached to their heads and numerous other unexplained and frightening procedures foisted on them. Some communities still resort to hospital admission for a period of observation and diagnosis. Then we begin our round of treatment centers. The child is subjected to a new assortment of boring and often demeaning techniques. Once again, no explanation is offered. What does the child assume as this process goes on—that the deficit must be severe to warrant such a large degree of silent anxiety and time and effort?

Parental pressure on the child to conform is linked to the denial process. Our culture has minimal tolerance for the person who acts differently or learns differently or more slowly. Parents are desperately anxious to achieve conformity before severe societal restrictions are imposed. This creates unusual pressure upon their children to be other than what they are. "Behave before the neighbors demand that we move." "Pass your year in school so you won't be put in the dummy class." "Be a good boy in school so they won't expel you." "Treat the teacher and principal with respect." "Don't break the law or you'll be jailed." Conform, conform, conform. Don't be you, be a stereotype.

Inability to meet educational demands in the narrow confines within which the demands are made and within the allotted time is to invite penalty. Since the learning disability often prevents compliance, the child is penalized. Hence the manifestations of the disability are punishable, and since the disability is the child, the child's reality is being denied. In their eagerness to have their child meet standardized academic expectations, parents too frequently allow injustice to continue without intervention, rationalizing that the school knows best. Even the most knowledgeable parents tend to support the school system. We are aware that our child must fit into existing molds, since, indeed, there are few educational alternatives.

All our remediation focuses on making the learning disabled child the same as everyone else, and parents embrace this worthwhile goal with zeal. "If you spend one more hour a day crawling, eye tracking, memorizing words, fitting puzzles, or matching objects, you, too, can achieve the ultimate goal of being like everyone else." It is a graphic illustration of our readiness to revert to primitive behavior wherein a few rituals performed daily are believed to achieve magic results. The tragedy of this approach is that this goal rarely is achieved. We work to develop a skill in a child only to discover the need for that skill has been replaced by the need for another. We remediate an area of deficit with ferocity, only to discover that the ability has not been generalized sufficiently to enable the child to handle more complex learning in that deficit area. Thus the child with poor ability to organize visually and spatially may become a whiz at assembling puzzles and matching shapes, yet flounders when confronted with geometry. The child who has trouble remembering how to spell words may become a passable speller of English, yet be unable to spell words in a foreign language.

I would hope that we could continue to furnish our children with the basic skills required to cope in our society. However, I wish that we could free ourselves of the illusion that we must fashion them in the mold of "the North American child of the year." Our efforts might be spent more productively attempting to educate our schools and communities to respect, provide for, and maximize the contribution of the child who is different.

Adults and children are uncomfortable with the person who is even minimally different in conduct from society's norm. It is fascinating to watch a group of children meet a learning disabled youngster. The learning disabled child emanates only the subtlest message of being different, yet is excluded by the others. The child, sensing the rejection of a peer or adult, suspects that something is grossly different and less acceptable about him- or herself as a person. The response to this rejection is to try so hard to act "normally" that resulting anxiety tends to create even more abnormal behavior, and it additionally reduces the ability to process the experience and respond appropriately. On the other hand, the child may internalize the message about being different and act the part of clown, fool, or disruptive youngster. In the latter instance, the popular myth that a disabled person must appear obviously impaired, and cannot essentially be intelligent and functional, is actualized. By reducing opportunities whereby the learning disabled can be themselves, eventually it is not too difficult for them or others to lose contact with the "real child." The youngster is placed further off-balance by patterns of abilities and disabilities. One parent aptly described the dichotomy when he commented that "Mark never knows where he fits into the scheme of things."

In this manner we play our games of professional-parent polarization, denial, ambivalence, compensation, and stereotyping. The joker in the pack is the child, who finds it impossible to extract a constant, honest, and discernible self-image. I suspect that these communication factors play a more important role in the creation of the distorted self-image of the learning disabled than the cause-effect relationship of poor body image to poor self-concept.

Parents too often have been recipients of varying diagnoses with no meaningful direction or ongoing support. They have had to cope with professional hostility, rejection, withholding of information, withholding of services, red tape, and hardening of categories and services that professionals perceive as ideal, but prove less than workable. Added to this are community denial, rejection, and withholding of outlets for parents' feelings. Yet no child or parent can show his or her accumulation of feelings resulting from years of such experiences without being labeled neurotic, and, in the parent's case, the cause of his or her child's disability.

Ten Suggestions to Professionals

Professionals can begin to reduce parental alienation by considering some of the following:

1. Refer the child to a diagnostician whose orientation is relating diagnosis to living, rather than being involved in exotica such as localizing brain lesions or finding finger agnosia.
2. Treat the parents as intelligent, and their observations and child-rearing practices as worthy of consideration. Rather than assume that their anxious behavior is neurotic, assume that in most cases it is an

unneurotic reaction to their cumulative past experiences (only a few of which have been mentioned in this chapter).

3. Teach parents how to relate treatment to disability and assist them in their initial efforts to obtain treatment. If treatment is unavailable, teach the parents how to obtain additional facilities in their community.

4. Be accessible to the parents on an ongoing basis to be consulted as problems arise, or refer them to a professional who will undertake this role.

5. Recognize that a diagnosis performed in a relatively short period of time may not be accurate. Be open to change your opinion.

6. Since diagnoses are fluid and some learning disabled children make amazing gains in I.Q. levels and in academic ability, do not close out a child's opportunities.

7. If you describe behavior rather than label, there will be less likelihood that a label will follow the child. Make your descriptions understandable to lay people. If your description has not been simple enough for the parents to understand and, in turn, to explain to their child, it has been too complex. Be certain that the parents understand the disability. It may need to be explained several times.

8. Reassess confidentiality. Does it serve primarily the needs of child and parents or is it designed to enhance professional aloofness and mystery? Does confidentiality equip the parents with enough information to seek appropriate, ongoing services for their children? Does it allow for information-sharing with persons who are prepared to help the child? Finally, does a parent have a basic right to know what is the matter with his or her child?

9. Familiarize yourself with services in your community. When you refer a child to the fanciest status quo service, you may not be referring the best service.

10. If you have any commitment to the validity of services for the learning disabled, roll up your sleeves and fight for them. At times the fight will follow acceptable channels and at times it might take another form. However, that is the way that change comes about in our society. Professionals must stop feeling that they are above struggling for improved services.

TO THE TEACHER

Teachers tread a fine line between their desire not to worry parents about minor concerns and the necessity of determining the point at which a concern becomes sufficiently significant to share with parents. Therefore, teachers may not request a conference as promptly as some parents feel they should. Conversely, they may bring problems to the parents' attention that parents feel incapable of solving. The teacher anticipates the forthcoming parents' conference with a tinge of apprehension, wondering what the parents of the learning disabled student will be like and how they will react to a resumé of their child's difficulties.

Parents who have been exposed to several parent-teacher conferences liberally laced with their child's nonconformity, develop a generalized dread of all such conferences whether or not the dread currently is justified. One mother, upon learning that she was pregnant after her other children were grown, complained that she was prepared to handle being awakened at night and washing diapers, but simply could not face 13 more years of parent-teacher conferences. Learning disabilities are such subtle deviations that parents of the preschool learning disabled child may have nursed hidden fears that their child was atypical, while clinging to the hope that the child would meet the challenge of the school experience and emerge as normal, if not superior. The request to attend a parent-teacher conference threatens to shatter that last hope. Thus the parent arrives at the classroom tense and defensive.

One of the typical parental reactions to a description of the child's maladaptive behavior is impotence. Parents rarely know what can be done to change Johnny from a boy who runs around the classroom and calls out answers to a well-behaved child. How, too, can parents alter conditions such as "Tom writes sloppily; he won't stay between the lines," or "Sue could do better," or "Mary is an underachiever," or "Bob forgets instructions." In frustration, parents are likely to return home and lecture or punish the child. This, of course, is unlikely to alter the child's modus operandi, particularly if the deviant behavior is attributable to an intrinsic disability or lack of individualized programming.

A few minutes spent at the beginning of the conference in pleasant interaction may help to reduce parental anxiety. It helps, too, to begin the conference talking about the child's positive attributes and reassuring the parents that no current plans to have the child repeat the grade or be transferred to the slow learners' class are being made. Since the child's behavior may not be a reflection of the manner in which the parents raised the child, it is important that the teacher avoid describing it in that context. Some parents feel that some teachers have difficulty communicating. If the parents sense that efforts emanate from a genuine desire to help (not suppress or exclude) children, the majority of parents will be only too grateful to cooperate.

Some parents may project their child's failures onto supposed inadequacies of the teacher, school system, number of children in the classroom, and similar considerations. Although in some instances this is obvious rationalization, it frequently contains more than a grain of truth. A teacher working within the typical pupil-teacher ratio of our classrooms may be unable to meet a child's special learning needs. Furthermore, the teacher may not have the background to assess individual learning styles and teach to them. In those instances, parental concerns are not a reflection of the teacher's adequacy. Rather, they may be a realistic assessment of gaps in teacher training, sufficiency of consultative services, and pupil-teacher ratio. Therefore, the teacher should resist viewing the parent's protests as an attack on teaching ability, and instead see them as an expression of a realistic need for backup assistance for both the teacher and student. Then the first step has been taken toward the procurement of assistance.

Similarly, some teachers hesitate to refer a child for help, because they feel that they have failed when they are unable to help the child themselves. Some principals also display a reluctance to use ancillary services. Educators commonly seek outside assistance only when the problem is acute, at which point the child may be so defeated that removal from the normal classroom is necessary. This is unfortunate because early referral not only increases the likelihood that remedial help can begin within the standard classroom, it means as well that the child is more likely to respond readily to remediation. Learning disabled students who receive remedial help early in their school careers are less likely to have severe secondary emotional problems.

The learning disabled child is not retarded but rather possesses normal intellectual ability in many functional aspects. The basic problem is a deficient ability to organize—and hence remember—one or more facets of the sensory or temporal-spatial world. The majority of learning disabled children can spend their school years in standard school streams if they receive remedial help before they become overwhelmed. Many will always need individual help. Such approaches will differ from child to child, and most children do not need unreasonable effort on the teacher's part. In fact, they are likely to require less effort than might be involved in providing individualized instruction in the classroom for a child with another type of handicap. Yet because many teachers do not believe that learning disabilities are a genuine handicap, they deny the child any consideration. "I can't let Jane take more time to write her assignments; that would be favoritism." One teacher used to give Norman about 90 percent on every test, then subtract 25 marks for spelling—Norman's ability to remember visual sequences was so poor that he was unable to spell. Another teacher forced her student to hold his sloppy assignments in front of the class so that his classmates could laugh at his lack of neatness.

Both teacher and student can enjoy a comfortable school year if a special education consultant will familiarize him- or herself with the student and design an approach that takes into account the student's abilities and disabilities, as well as the teacher's resources. Outside assistants, such as older students, volunteers, or parents, can shoulder some time-consuming chores, such as reading assignments to the child or taping lessons. Supervised volunteers have been used effectively in many communities to provide individualized remediation. The nurse's office, school library, and teachers' lounge can be retreats for the learning disabled child when stress begins to accumulate.

Some educators are fearful of spending too much time with the learning disabled child. They have commented that, in such a situation, the child will know that he or she is different—of course, the child already knows that. However, relief will be immense if the child is given demands that can be met, rather than having to face the daily terror of unachievable demands. Teachers are often concerned that the other pupils will want similar privileges, but most pupils tend to accept an explanation of the extra time with a child with different needs. If consideration is shown to individual differences among students, they will not resent efforts to meet another student's needs.

Adults view rewards in terms of absolutes. We never comment to the grimy child, "Isn't that great! You're twice as clean as you were yesterday," or remark, on seeing a sloppy assignment, "That's good; it's much neater than your last paper," or congratulate the child who has succeeded in reducing ear-piercing shouts to a low scream. Either the child is clean, writes neatly, talks softly, or he or she continues to be penalized. It may have taken great effort for the child to produce an assignment less sloppy than the previous one. It may not compare in neatness to other children's work, but then one child's coordination may not be comparable to the other's.

A learning disabled child reaches school age with the cumulative experience of six years of not being able to meet expectations. Many attempts have merited disapproval. In school this pattern is perpetuated or even accelerated. Achievement is considered in terms of set goals. It is more difficult to think, "He (she) is reading a little better," than "He (she) is not progressing as well as the third reading group." Learning disabled children have managed not to succeed in so many ways that it doesn't seem worth their efforts to try, since they are slapped down for most attempts. Therefore, if we want them to retain motivation, we must be prepared to acknowledge partial success. The partial success of the learning disabled may represent far more effort than the polished success of other children.

Many learning disabled children have great difficulty manipulating spoken or written language. Language usage may be garbled and agrammatical, disorganized, and misspelled. The primary consideration of the teacher should be whether the child knows the academic material, regardless of how it looks. If the child demonstrates knowledge of the material, credit is due. If the teacher is able to help the child structure verbal responses, they may become more discernible. Similarly, the child might profit greatly from help in organizing notes to provide anchors and guidelines around which to build academic material.

Begin work at the child's level. Frequently, learning disabled children fail to acquire a sound grounding in a subject, so that successive teachers fruitlessly attempt to impart sophisticated concepts on a faulty base. A child's age or grade placement is not necessarily indicative that basic early learning has been integrated. Some learning disabled children require extensive multisensory experiences, augmented by spelling rules, before they master rudimentary spelling. Others require long periods of work with concrete materials before arithmetic can be mastered.

Goal-setting motivates the learning disabled child to initiate and control individual academic progress and assists him or her in developing a realistic concept of what he or she can and cannot do. It allows the student to express and work for goals that are individually important and to assess individual levels of progress. This changes education from an unpleasant and often unrealistic extrinsic demand, to be resisted because its meaning and level have little relationship to the child, to rewarding individual effort. It commits the child to a specific academic program and alters the typical approaches to the learning disabled, which impose controls from without, and makes the child responsible for controlling his or her own behavior and progress.

Learning disabled children are so used to a life of punishment that they have little hope and sometimes much resistance. They tend to see punishment as something that they deserve because they are disabled. The child is unlikely to want to invest energy in a program that promises more defeat and pain. Before punishing a learning disabled child, it is vital to determine whether his behavior is a result of unrealistic demands. For example, if the child has a three-minute attention span and is expected to sit still and complete a half-hour assignment, restless or hyperactive behavior will signify the inability to meet the demand. The child who feels progress is being made in a program is more likely to be committed to that program than to one that consistently penalizes him or her for not meeting demands.

If a child is experiencing academic difficulties, it is important to first rule out problems of eyesight, hearing, nutrition, allergy, and general health. Even if the child has a known learning disability, physical problems can compound the difficulty. If the teacher is scheduling a hearing test, the test should be arranged so that the ability to hear running speech is determined, not just a pure tone test.

Many learning disabled children tend to be literal and concrete. When the teacher tells the class that a mathematics problem will not be explained again, a nonhandicapped student usually can appeal by stating something like, "Miss Jones, I know that you said you wouldn't explain this again, but I was absent yesterday. Could you give me a little help?" However, the learning disabled child does not have the subtlety to evolve such an approach, and is left agonizing in confusion and the certainty that it won't be reexplained. Thus, current confusion is added to past confusions, with the cumulative result that the child feels overwhelmed. Do you remember days in secondary school when you were burdened with about eight hours of homework? You would figure out which teachers were likely to check the homework the following day, complete their assignments, and defer the others. The learning disabled child, on the other hand, returns home distraught by the prospect of eight hours of homework, literally feeling compelled to do it all. We more or less breezed through school by perceiving and playing the angles. I learned that one geography teacher divulged the content of all his exams in his preexam review periods. Subsequently, I studied only the material that was covered in those periods. The grade eleven English teacher enjoyed effusive essays, and I plied her with as much schmaltz as she enjoyed. It took only one disastrous experience to learn that the grade twelve teacher preferred straightforward material. The learning disabled are not as skilled in ferreting out the subtleties and nuances of each situation, nor can they make changes with ease. Therefore you, the teacher, should clarify for them what you really mean and what you really want. Check with them frequently as to whether they have understood a lesson, and don't let them lag in understanding assignments. When they become depressed and discouraged, they become anxious and confused; thus, the discouragement is compounded.

Many learning disabled children tend to be so disorganized that they do a poor job of planning their homework. They may return home from school intending to complete their assignments, then suddenly realize that bedtime has arrived and the assignments have not been started. Encourage the child to set aside a specific time each afternoon for homework. You may have to review the things done between school's end and bedtime, and draw a schedule for each activity. The learning disabled child needs help to plan guidelines for assignments and determining the length of time each assignment should take.

Dr. Alice Thompson, Department of Special Education, Southern Illinois University, commented in a letter to me: "An urgent matter is the current tendency to consider brighter children more valuable or worthy than duller ones. Most teachers are infected with the notion that it is more important to develop the best in bright children than the best in duller ones. Since learning disabled children are often mistaken for dull, they are often discounted, too. It is no part of democratic principle to assume that bright people are 'better' than duller ones, or worth more, or more important. But it is obvious that many teachers do not think it worth their while to elicit the best of which the duller are capable. They tend to disregard, if not actually to show contempt for, those who do not learn quickly. Since life is surely valued for its feeling components, its satisfaction and happiness, we cannot suppose that the subjective experience of the less capable is of less importance than that of others. And there is no evidence to suggest that the plodders and the uneven learners make little contribution to the society. It is a vicious and insidious situation."

TO THE PARENT

Much parental frustration can be reduced by "learning the angles." It will take many years of effort before we are able to effect global changes in professional attitude and services. In the interim, we have to live with imperfection. Therefore, our only way to cope is to develop techniques that will maximize our use of current resources.

Diagnosis

Our first step, of course, is to secure a meaningful diagnosis, consisting of an easily understood description of the child's areas of strength and deficit and the ways to adapt to these difficulties. A diagnosis is not complete unless the parents are told of its implications for school programming and placement and home management. Parents should be directed as well to community resources, such as speech therapy, physiotherapy, and recreation programs that would be beneficial to their child. There should be direct contact between the diagnostician and the child's school, so that the diagnostician can interpret findings in relationship to the academic program. It seems to be necessary to have our children "labeled" to enroll them in our category-bound services. However, a diagnosis that consists of a label alone, and omits a description of behavior and management, tells nothing. After all, what does learning disabled, brain injured, slow learner, emotionally disturbed, and such really say? We receive such a label and return home, supposedly enlightened, only to realize that the youngster still is hyperactive, nonverbal, or can't read—and we still don't know what to do.

A good diagnostician is a professional who will respect the parents' need and ability to help their child, and is prepared to meet with the family periodically or refer them to a person who can assume that role. The diagnostician will assist in coordinating the child's habilitation program, particularly if it involves the use of several community resources. Typically, the psychological assessment, which forms the core of the diagnosis, is done by an educational psychologist. He or she may carry out the above mentioned role, or may do so in conjunction with other professionals.

A neurologist, psychiatrist, pediatrician, or general practitioner might use an educational psychologist for the basic assessment, and handle the interpretation to the family, direction for home and school management, and other considerations as delineated above. Therefore, it is not the professional specialty that will enable us to find a helpful diagnostician, but the orientation of the particular individual.

Too often in the past parents have encouraged unhelpful diagnosticians to continue their practice of noncommunication and nondirection by flocking to them for diagnoses and reimbursing them for not sharing their findings. We should consider seriously not rewarding this kind of behavior if we wish it to change.

How, then, are we to find a diagnostician who will meet even a few of the criteria I have mentioned? One fruitful source of referral might be your local parents' association. They generally are aware of the elements of a meaningful diagnosis and can direct families to appropriate professionals. Failing that, parents are justified in asking a professional what is involved in a diagnosis. We can ask whether findings are shared with parents and direction offered in planning a school program. Such questions may arouse the ire of some professionals, which would be a good indication of their feelings toward parents. Regardless, it is better to be the recipient of their anger than to expose parents and child to another upsetting and useless experience.

Various professional roles. A neurologist primarily is oriented to clarifying the absence or presence of neurological damage or disease. It would seem to be particularly important to seek a neurological examination if any of the following possibilities are under consideration:

1. The onset of the disability is sudden in a child whose developmental pattern has met normal milestones to date.
2. There is a sudden severe change in the child's behavior.
3. The child complains of headaches or has seizures or convulsions, or subclinical seizures are suspected.
4. The physician wants to investigate the possibility of a medical condition such as hyper- or hypoglycemia.
5. The physician feels that the child might benefit from drug therapy.

However, too frequently the child's physician or the parents seek a neurological examination expecting that it will be an assessment. Typically, the sum total of the examination is a statement of whether or not the child is brain damaged. Many neurologists do not seem heavily oriented toward treatment, so that the diagnosis often contains little or no direction, and the parents are disappointed. The basic confusion emanates from the referring physician's interest in, and parental curiosity about, the etiology (cause) of the problem. Some physicians don't seem to realize that their curiosity is academic, since we are unable to treat cause, be it brain damage, genetic, or deprivation. Treatment is confined to symptoms, and we do not treat symptoms differently when the cause is different. Further, satisfying curiosity and securing a diagnosis of brain damage can result in extensive parental guilt, focused on their supposed role in causing the damage. The energy expended on this guilt could be channeled more productively.

It is important, at this juncture, to clarify some issues about brain damage. Neurologists readily state that their tools are crude. There are people who show no signs of dysfunction, yet have abnormal EEGs; on the other hand, some people who are strongly suspected of being brain damaged pass a neurological examination with flying colors. Autopsies have revealed surprises, in that functional people at times have brain damage and brain damaged persons occasionally have lesions in far different locations of the brain than would be suspected by their symptomatology. A few diagnosticians use the label "brain damage" or "brain injury" as a descriptive term to apply to any child who shows the behaviors associated with learning disabilities. If the same child were seen by another diagnostician, it is likely another label would have been used. Parents who belong to associations for brain injured children do not necessarily have brain injured children, any more or less than do members of associations for children with learning disabilities. Prognosis is not related necessarily to the stated presence or absence of brain damage. It is associated more readily with such issues as the severity and location of the dysfunction, intelligence, emotional intactness, motivation, and opportunity.

In summary, then, neurologists play an important role in ruling out progressive diseases and treating some chronic disorders. In general, they should not be sought to provide a definitive assessment and follow-through. Exceptions may be neurologists employed by school systems and those who have developed a special interest in learning disabilities.

Some child psychiatrists have particular interest in and knowledge of learning disabilities. Many of these professionals admirably provide diagnosis, support, and direction for families in conjunction with an educational or clinical psychologist. The majority of psychiatrists, however, do not have special orientation to learning disabilities. Some still feel that all behavior is learned behavior, meaning that it is a result of the environment. Psychiatrists with this orientation have given years of psychotherapy to some learning disabled children and their families, working with their feelings and interactions, without changing the basic disability. It commonly is said that they make their patients into well-adjusted failures. Furthermore, they may engender unnecessary parental guilt. It is true that many families develop neurotic patterns of coping with the stresses of the disability, but they should not be blamed for creating it. It probably is accurate to state that the majority of families of the learning disabled, as well as the learning disabled child him- or herself, could profit from some psychotherapy. When a psychiatrist is sought for counseling, spare yourself aggravation and frustration by consulting one who will concede that some learning disabilities have an organic base.

In this section I have suggested briefly the orientation of psychologists, neurologists, and psychiatrists. If you match what you are seeking with the professional area of expertise, you more likely will be pleased with the end result. It is only when we continue to harass the neurologist for habilitation, or the psychiatrist or pediatrician for remediation, that we may be programming for failure.

Parents have as much obligation as professionals to handle themselves appropriately in parent-professional interaction. A few parents can antagonize a professional, who then may be "turned off" on parents, to all our detriment. The parent may have been the recipient of much professional misdirection and little help. However, past experiences were not brought about by the current professional whose services are being sought. Neither is the professional responsible for all the misdemeanors of fellow professionals. Therefore, if your approach is angry and accusing, the professional is likely to react negatively to you, and consequently will be of little help. The hostile, attacking parent stomps from professional to professional loudly protesting that no one is interested in his or her child. The professionals feel that there seems to be little purpose in trying to help such a neurotic, rigid parent or to help a child whose home life is so unhealthy.

Treatment

Parents tend to find themselves in even more difficulty in the treatment maze than in diagnosis. At some point we are furnished with a diagnosis that sounds like our child, and our search ends. However, we are bombarded endlessly by treatment possibilities, each one sounding more promising than the one before. It takes superhuman effort to resist such programs, because we tend to feel that each new treatment entity may hold the clue for our child's cure. And so most of us try too many approaches. We drag our child from place to place and invest much time and money, only to find in the end that little meaningful change has resulted. What criteria can parents use to guide them through this web of confusion? Learning disabilities are not one handicap but a cluster of handicaps housed under one roof. The common denominators are gross, at best, being presumed brain dysfunction, some aspects of normal intelligence, and difficulty in organizing some facet of one's sensory or spatial-temporal world. A treatment program that benefits a language handicapped child may be of no use to the poorly coordinated, highly verbal youngster, and vice versa. Just as epilepsy, cerebral palsy, mental retardation, and learning disabilities may be caused by brain damage, the areas of the brain that are damaged are not necessarily the same, nor are the symptoms. Thus we have no reason to assume that the same treatment will benefit them all. However, some treatment models are given to children of every exceptionality whose family decides to embrace that treament modality. The results are many disappointed families.

It is known that our abilities to process our visual, spatial, and temporal world are interrelated. The accuracy with which one has sorted out the body's size and shape and related it to the size and shape of things in the environment is connected with the general ability to perceive and organize one's self in the environment. However, we frequently are unsuccessful in effecting a transfer from motor learning to generalized learning through formal remediation. Hence, if a child has difficulty perceiving auditory material, there may be a theoretical rationale behind giving motor therapy. In reality, unless the child is uncoordinated, in which case a motor program would seem indicated, the child's time may be better spent receiving remediation in auditory perception.

Remediation should relate to real life. If the child has problems perceiving sounds, practice in perceiving language and environmental sounds should be given. If trouble perceiving the size and shape of the body is discovered, the most meaningful puzzle will not be a wooden one of various shapes and sizes, but the body itself.

How much remediation and from whom? Some parents are so desperate to "cure" their child quickly that they suffocate the youngster with a killing remedial program. Social learning, fun, and the skill of learning how to use one's free time are sacrificed to the "good of remediation." I know one very uncoordinated little boy who didn't talk until age five. He still has considerable difficulty comprehending spoken and written language. His parents have convinced themselves that all he has is a five-year maturation lag. They state that he is going to be a professor, and to that end they awaken him at six a.m. daily to begin his grueling remedial program. His parents have embraced every therapy that has crossed their path, and they augment their son's remediation with music lessons, French and Hebrew lessons, and Sunday school. I predict eventual disaster. This little boy now is having severe tantrums as a reaction to the pressure. He may erupt in a massive explosion or his parents may fall apart when their son does not become a professor.

If your child currently is in a learning disability class, consult the teacher about additional remediation. The teacher may feel that the student receives sufficient remediation and pressure in the classroom, in which case, *respect* the teacher's judgment and take a vacation from remediation. If the child has been in a learning disability class in the past or received itinerant remedial help, once again the teacher is a good source of direction and should be able to guide you concerning how much remediation should be undertaken, what kind, and even possibly direct you to a tutor or treatment personnel. If your child has not received any special help from the school system, the special education consultant may be able to direct you to sources of aid. In the absence of a consultant, you might seek the advice of the school psychologist. Your local parents' association should be in a position to direct you to effective treatment programs. Naturally, if you have been sufficiently fortunate to find a professional who will provide ongoing help, certainly involve him or her in the planning role. If you find yourself dragging your child to a succession of treatments that seem to be of little benefit, and can find no one to direct you, acquire the knowledge yourself. Familiarize yourself with the particulars of your child's disabilities and find treatment directly related to those deficits.

The end goal of remediation should not be elimination of the deficits, since that seems unrealistic. A more accessible goal is to bring the child to the point where sufficient skills are gained to cope with modified school demands. An equally unrealistic goal of remediation is to hope to bring youngsters to the point that they fit into the lock-step demands of our education system without any difficulty. Consequently, part of parents' energies should be redirected toward educating the educators. Hopefully, this would enable our children to progress in their strong areas without being held back by their deficits. They would be allowed to demonstrate their knowledge by whatever means they are able. They would not be penalized for their disabilities in expression, be they in organization, language usage, spelling, or penmanship. Hence, we establish realistic remedial goals and should include the child in goal-setting and planning modes of remediation.

How much time for remediation and for how long?   The amount of time that should be devoted to remediation revolves around a multiplicity of factors and will vary from family to family. The overall consideration should be: how much time and money can be diverted to remediation without depriving either parent or any of the children, including the handicapped member, of resources that should be directed toward maintaining a well-balanced life? If some remediation must be forfeited and if your child goes through life a little more handicapped because of it, it still may be more than outweighed by the advantages of leading a well-rounded childhood and learning respect for people's global needs, including the other children, yourselves, and the child's. You can deny some of your own' or your family's needs for a period of time without obvious consequences. However, if you function in such a lop-sided manner for an extended period, something will be lost or reaction will occur. Your temporal needs, and those of your family, are sufficient time for rest and nourishment, time to spend with each other one at a time and together, time spent with contemporaries, and time alone, relaxing and pursuing one's interests. Once you have met everyone's temporal needs, you freely can devote leftover time to remediation.

The amount of time you spend at home in formal remediation, and indeed whether you should do anything, should depend upon how well you and your child can handle formal work together at that stage. I have found that I could work well with my children at certain points and that trying to work formally with them at other times bordered on disaster. My efforts invariably failed if I tried to sandwich some remediation into a busy day. I invariably would react impatiently to my son's apparent slowness or ineptitude. It was far better to live with my guilt over omitting that day's remediation than to create a situation of mutual frustration and disappointment. I found, too, that my children were well motivated toward sustained effort at some junctures of their childhood, whereas at other times they became frustrated one or two minutes after we started to work. At those times remediation was far more effective if handled by an outsider.

Many parents don't work well with their own children because they become disappointed and impatient with their efforts. If you are one of those parents, don't feel that you are failing or that you have to work with your child because all the parents you meet at the gross motor program say that *they* work with their offspring two hours daily. Relax, most of them probably are exaggerating. Furthermore, many probably work poorly with their children, doing them a great disservice. If you don't work well with your child, *don't*. Either hire someone to do it or forget it. It is important that you spend time with your child that is mutually enjoyable. Don't jeopardize that by conveying messages that he or she is stupid and clumsy.

When planning your child's total remedial program, take into accout how much can be handled emotionally. If one of you is high-strung, pressure-sensitive, or easily upset, the remedial demands should take that into account. Dispensers of treatment techniques rarely do consider such factors, so you, the parent, must.

Many learning disabled children do not acquire social skills unless they receive coaching throughout the sequence of social development. Therefore, some parental time should be devoted to this. In the final analysis, this will be a more important skill for adult adjustment than academic learning. The child should have ample opportunity to develop global interests and aptitudes, to substitute for a deficient ability to obtain information from reading and experience. Parental time devoted solely to remediation neglects these vital aspects of a child's development.

Remediation should not be prolonged indefinitely. Certainly our children will continue to progress with sustained remediation, but at what price? If a child has received remediation for several years, the choice should be given whether it should be continued in adolescence. If the learning disability is discovered in adolescence, the child likely may elect to receive essential help. If not, externally imposed help will be of minimal value. On the other hand, if hundreds of hours have already been devoted to special assistance, the child may choose to channel all energies toward coping with the stresses of adolescence. The parents must respect such a decision and its implications. Thus, if the child is a poor speller at age 15 and discards remediation, the parents must accept the likelihood that he or she will be a poor speller at 40. Even were remediation continued, the child likely will continue to be a poor speller, so one has to weigh maximum effort against minimal gains. Additional criteria should be, is the child's spelling understandable, and if not have other acceptable modes of communication been developed? In a similar vein, if one or both of the parents have devoted several hours weekly for an extended time to remediation, and is weary, he or she, too, has a right to close the book and live easily with that decision.

I made the decision when my son was age 13 that he and I had sacrificed enough of our lives to remediation. Once we had reached that choice, my relief was immense! No more running, seeking, pushing, prodding—life was lovely! It wasn't an easy decision to uphold against the school psychologist who decided that my son, at age 18, needed help with reading comprehension (he didn't), and others who were ready to suggest what he needed, rather than consider what had gone into him to bring him to that point. He attended a residential school for the learning disabled for the latter half of his grade twelve year. They sidestepped our decision about remediation and gave him individual help with visual memory and spatial organization. Within the warm, accepting school atmosphere, in which he felt comfortable with the curriculum and demands, he responded well. I noticed several positive changes. Nonetheless, in our community he had been faced with considerable academic and social stress, so that to continue remediation would have been unfair.

Now that my experience of raising young learning disabled children is behind me, I can confess to many things. One of my easiest confessions is of the crushing boredom generated by many of the remedial techniques. If I was bored, my children with their short interest spans must have been frantic! Finally, out of sheer need for variety, I discarded all formal remediation, except some academic work, and replaced it by integrating the same concepts into everyday life. I doubt that anyone could state that my children benefited less by walking across fallen logs, on stepping-stones, or along raised curbs than they did by walking along a walking board. Nor can one dispute that they gained as much by a game of "I baked a cake and in it I put". . . than they would by textbook auditory sequential exercises. Certainly I discarded the discipline of performing each task for 15 minutes daily. Who is to say, however, whether a child benefits more by performing a structured, meaningless task for a specified period of time, or by practicing what is needed to learn, in a less regular fashion, in the context of real living? There is no magic formula to guarantee that if you perform such and such a remedial exercise for x period of time daily, a specified result will accrue. Consequently, I contend that formal remediation is a good beginning but poor nourishment for an extended period. The secret behind the success of informal remediation is to become intimately familiar with your child's deficits and use ingenuity to incorporate remedial concepts into the chores and games of living.

One general goal for most families might be to excite your children around the versatility of our language. Learning disabled children may use large words, yet may not be aware of the adaptability of language and how it can serve us. This was graphically displayed to me by my group of very verbal learning disabled campers who were making catalogues. I encouraged them to describe the articles for sale so enticingly that people could not resist buying them. Regardless of my encouragement, their descriptive vocabulary seemed limited to "nice" and "beautiful." When children forget the names of things (nouns and pronouns), substitutes are not easily found. Consequently, we can readily spot the deficit and label it "anomia," "auditory retrieval problem," or Dr. Bateman's apt tags of "sticky bucket" or "leaky bucket." However, children can disguise a serious lack of verbs, adverbs, and adjectives without its being obvious. Have you ever tallied the number of times your children substitute "get" for a more appropriate verb?

Play word games. There are good formal ones such as "Scrabble" and "Anagrams," and hundreds of informal ones that you can "cook up" from the environment. Our family plays games involving rhyming, punning, synonyms, antonyms, idioms, categories, descriptive words, and such. Often in the course of a game we will talk about the origin of the word, or the origin of the animal, custom, piece of furniture, or whatever we are discussing. To corroborate what we are saying, we look the words up in a dictionary or encyclopedia. My two language handicapped children write poetry and our dysphasic son is an incredibly skilled punster. Our family custom is *never* to purchase an invitation, birthday, or anniversary card, but always to design and write our own. These games never are a chore because we play them for fun. This means that if we don't feel like playing, we don't. We encourage our children to talk with us. We plan events and later enjoy reminiscing about them. You can incorporate number and spatial concepts equally well into everyday activities. Long after formal remediation has stopped, these games can continue.

The home, a sanctuary. Animals face a world of survival of the fittest, returning home to lick their wounds. People hurt our feelings, the boss has been unjustly angry at us, our mother-in-law has been too critical, we had an argument with the store clerk, so we return home for solace. Everyone needs a harbor with its promise of warmth, acceptance, and understanding. The learning disabled person's need is even more profound. They will be misunderstood even more than others, and injustice awaits them at school and on the street. Their catalogue of daily hurts even are augmented by strangers, who are ready to chastise with "why don't you watch what you're doing?" to impatience with jerky speech or a groping for words. The child who retreats from a punitive world has no sanctuary in a home where parents are demanding, pressuring for performance, attempting various remediations, and burdening him or her with the conflicts of parental overinvolvement, underinvolvement, recriminations, anxiety, and other not uncommon reactions. Regardless, the child is aware that there is no escape. No child is equipped or allowed to be self-sufficient in our society. The learning disabled youngster is aware of his or her additional vulnerability, and clings to the port where storms rage unabated. This is, of course, untenable for anyone. Hence, our most primary goal must be to insure that the home is a relaxed and pleasant place, a source of strength to the child. It should not shield the child from the world but give the courage to cope with it. This means that the child must feel like an accepted, valued member of the family, sharing plans, decisions, special occasions, and concerns. I strongly feel that the home must be the child's anchor and that other considerations are secondary. Therefore, if you have to discard home remediation to create this kind of atmosphere, then discard it.

In our culture, we tend to respect the important people more than the unimportant, those with titles or money more than the have-nots, bosses more than servants, adults more than children, with children in the immediate family being at the end of the continuum. What funny customs they are indeed, and certain to be a source of amusement for sociologists of the future. The next time your child drops something, spills something, forgets to bring the right texts home for homework, consider your verbal reaction. Not only would you not say those things to the president of the United States or to your minister if he came to dinner, you would not react that way to a nonstatus adult visitor. We treat our children disrespectfully, discrediting everyone's right to spill, break, or forget something on occasion. We tend not to respect their observations and often their feelings. Ironically, we expect them to respect us and all other adults. If you want your child to feel like a person of worth, show it. If you want your child to acquire intrinsic respect for others, it must be learned at home. To say one thing and act another makes little sense for all children and no sense to the literal learning disabled child.

SOME GENERAL RULES OF THUMB

If the child is so retarded academically that by adolescence even simple spelling or computation is a chore, and there is no intensive remedial course available, perhaps an occupational course is the best solution.

If, on the other hand, the child can handle several aspects of a secondary academic program, that opportunity should be kept open. Keep as many doors open for as long as the child is able to cope. This rule applies to learning disabled children of all ages. (Our school system had no learning disability classes, but I refused to permit the board to place my intelligent son in a slow learner class. In our community, placement in such a class leads to secondary occupational courses, and I would not allow that kind of terminal decision to be made for an eight-year-old.) If the child is unable to cope, determine whether it is the total curriculum or whether the child feels defeated because difficulty is experienced in one or two subjects. Are the problems a result of difficulty in comprehension and memory or the way in which the subject is taught and the teacher's demands? Norman was a good biology student until grade twelve, at which time he became balky and discouraged. Investigation uncovered the fact that his biology teacher depended heavily on graphs, which collided with Norman's deficits in spatial organization. Fifty percent of the biology classes were laboratories, in which the students were expected to work in pairs. No student ever chose Norman as a partner, and the teacher said that he was uncooperative because he would not work with anyone.

To sort out which aspects of the "not coping" are related to the child's deficit, which would respond to altered demands or interpretation, as contrasted with problems related to teaching methods and orientation, the parents may need the help of the guidance counselor, school psychologist, or special education consultant. The consultant customarily is not used in this context on a secondary level, and you will create a new and valuable precedent.

If you learn that the child truly cannot handle the subject, do not demand continuance, even if it is required for college entrance. However, if it can be handled with more structuring, understanding, or modified input or output, the above mentioned ancillary personnel can be pressed to work with the teacher to design a more manageable approach.

At the beginning of a school year, teachers often are not apprised of the student's special needs. This frequently is true in elementary school, and invariably true on a secondary level. The information may be in the child's file, but not everyone reads that. Hence, if you want to insure that your child will receive the necessary understanding, meet with teachers at the beginning of each school year, all of them together if possible, separately if not. Explain briefly and simply, without emotion, your child's strengths and deficits. Determine as best you can the demands of each subject, and explain to the teacher involved your perception of your child's ability to meet those demands. Perhaps you and the teacher can evolve a few simple methods by which small modifications or extra structure will enable success. Alternatively, perhaps the special education consultant can take on that role. Make the demands on the teacher realistic and easy to execute. Most elementary and secondary school classrooms have a large complement of students, so to expect time-consuming individualization is unrealistic.

Use ingenuity to arrange the extra crutches the child requires. Perhaps they might be a parent or older student reading assignments nightly, or having you tape the lesson, which the child listens to with earphones in school the next day. Try to have someone other than the teacher shoulder time-consuming extras.

Explain the disability to the teacher in terms that can be accepted. If the concept of a problem in terms of auditory discrimination cannot be accepted, tell the teacher your child is hard of hearing. If a 'gross or fine motor problem' cannot be accepted, explain that the youngster has minimal cerebral palsy. We parents of the learning disabled tend to cringe at the labels attached to what we perceive are lower status disabilities. Nevertheless, if a more familiar label will elicit understanding, use it.

Teachers, like other professionals, become turned off by the anxious, pressuring, and hostile parent. Don't tell a teacher how to teach. Present a picture of your child's disabilities and suggest that together you possibly might develop methods to help the child. You have a right to expect the teacher to accept the existence of your child's disability, and you have a right to expect that respect will be shown to all of your children, with ridicule being something not to be tolerated. Your child has a right to be protected from demands that cannot be met, yet be expected to work fully to meet realistic demands. It is not uncommon for parents to allow children to be exposed to demands that they cannot handle, at the same time requesting exemption from tasks that are within their capabilities. You do not have a right to expect teachers to devote appreciable periods of time to your child alone, nor do you have a right to expect a teacher to institute an extensive remedial program if no support, back up assistance, or direction is received from the school system.

Parents often ask my advice about the advisability of allowing their child to be placed in a learning disability class. They are concerned about the social isolation from neighborhood children that is created when a child is bused to an out-of-district school. They are afraid that their youngster will be picked on by peers and stereotyped as "the kid in the dummy class." These concerns are valid, but they must be weighed against the remedial opportunities of a learning disability class and removal from a classroom situation that may have become totally overwhelming and discouraging. Hopefully, the special class placement is considered transitional. Thus, the parents can exert extra effort to involve their youngster in neighborhood social activities, so that contact with former and future schoolmates is maintained.

To parent a learning disabled child is to shoulder an added burden of hurt, disappointment, and frustration. It demands of a parent maturity, involvement, and fortitude. Our reactions are intensified; each slight toward our offspring cuts us deeply; each kind gesture evokes lifelong appreciation. We encounter some thoughtless people but also a few wonderful ones, who put forth the extra effort to be helpful. Best of all, we have the opportunity to share the unfolding development of a child progressing from uneven functioning to confident coping. The challenge is ours, and so are the rewards.

Index

Abel, D., 139
Abeson, A., 15
Ability and process training, 130
  criticism of, 138
Abt Associates, 138, 139, 169, 171, 199
Academic achievement, measurements of, 99, 100
Academic achievement tests, 119–20
Academic disorders, 39
Academic learning theory (*See* Learning Theories)
Academic probe, 238 (*fig.*)
Acceleration Finder, use in trend analysis, 254–55
Acceleration phase, SST-Perform project, 234
Accuracy, as direct measurement, 241
Achievement level, in developmental strategy, 49
Achievement tests, 100
  use in direct instructional decision-making, 231
Achieving Perceptual Motor Efficiency, 29
Actions, skills taught in DISTAR, 189
Administration:
  classroom organization, 285–90
  general considerations, 276–77
  Peter Principle, 277
  proposed model school district, 281–85
  role of principal, 279–81
  systems approach to management, 292–95
Administrator, as information flow evaluator, 276–77
Agnosia, 39
AKT multisensory approach, 136
Allen, Eileen, 297
Allen, James, 125
Allen, K. E., 291
Allocation activities, in administration, 293
"All-or-none" theory of learning, 68, 69
Allport, G. W., 62
American Institute for Research, 169
Ammentorp, W., 222
Anderson, W. F., 130, 131
Animal Intelligence, 70
Animal psychology, Thorndike's work, 70–71
Anna State Hospital, 75

"Annoyer" connection, 71
Antecedent conditions, strengthening of, 206
Antecedent events, analysis of, 107–8
Anticipation method, Ebbinghaus, 80
Antigravity process, 29
Anton Brenner Gestalt Test of School Readiness, The, 121
Aphasia, 41
  Wepman's research on, 39
Application, as instructional phase, 263, 264
Applications group, skills taught in DISTAR, 190
Applied research, compared to basic research, 83
Apraxia, 39
Aptitude-Treatment Interaction (ATI), 102, 144–47
  and learning disabled children, 149–50
Aristotle, 61, 62
Arithmetic skills, remedial suggestions, 152, 156
Arithmetic teaching program, DISTAR, 187, 191–96
Arnold, C. R., 66
Arranged Event:
  as component of plan sheet, 242, 245
  as event sheet component, 247
Arrangement, as component of plan sheet, 242, 245
Arter, J. A., 145
Arthur, B., 129
Arthur Point Scale of Performance Tests, 118
Artley, A. S., 125
Assessment:
  in early childhood as preventive strategy, 291–92
  forms of, 234
Assessment and evaluation, 270
  general assessment strategies, 234–36
  general and traditional considerations, 232–33
  as instructional component, 231
  probing procedures, 236–39
  SST-Perform project, 233–34
Assessment-instruction-education plan:
  development of, 227
  establishment of, 232

331

Association for Children with Learning Disabilities (ACLD), 11
Associationism, 77
  development of tradition, 61–63
Associative mastery, repetition as factor in, 151
Attention level, in developmental strategy, 49
Attributes, proliferation of in child, 35
Auckerman, R. C., 142
Auditory perceptual training and reading remediation, 132–35
Auditory perceptions, slow development of, 3
Auditory-visual integration, and reading disabilities, 135–37
Auditory-vocal functioning tests, 101
Awareness, as skill, 132
Ayllon, Teodoro, 7, 75, 214
Ayres Space Test, 119
Azrin, Nathan, 75, 83, 214

"Backward learning curves," 78
Baer, Donald M., 79, 83, 84, 177
Baker, R. D., 143
Balow, B., 131
Bank Street College, New York City, 169
Bank Street College of Education, E-B D.I (Univ. of Oregon), 172fn
Bannatyne, A., 129, 138
Barrett, L. S., 104fn
Barsch, Raymond H., 8, 23, 33
  approach to learning process and perceptual-motor activity, 27–29
Baseline, establishment of for behaviors, 106–7
Baseline assessment, 86
Basic arithmetic operations, as taught in DISTAR, 191–92, 194–95
Basic cognitive structures (See Intelligence)
Basic Concept Inventory, 97, 99, 101, 120
Basic research, compared to applied research, 83
Bastain, H. C., 37
Bateman, B. D., 8, 9, 10, 39, 58, 95fn, 123, 123fn, 126, 129, 130, 137, 139, 145, 326
Bates D. F., 250
Bates, S., 250
Bateson, Gregory, 208, 276, 277, 280, 283, 297
Beck, G. R., 7
Becker, Wesley C., 17, 47, 66, 85, 128, 169, 170, 171, 172, 173, 174, 176, 178, 179, 186, 187, 253
Beery, K. E., 96
Beery-Buktenica Test of Visual-Motor Integration, 97, 99, 118
Beginning reading:
  analysis of, 140–41
  processes, 148–49
Behavior:
  analysis of components, 107–8
  applied analysis of, 83–86
  Cratty's integration and differentiation model, 34–36
  experimental analysis of, 81–83
  functional analysis of, 106–109
  Skinner's study of consequences of, 74–75
  Skinner's view of, 73
Behavior analysis, as research design, 78–79
Behavior Analysis Approach (Univ. of Kansas), 172fn
"Behavior game," 229
Behavior modification, 209
  development of techniques, 75
  strategy, 48–50
Behavior of Exceptional Children, 253
Behavior Research Company, 252, 254
  Behavior Bank, 249
Behavior-to-be-learned, survey instruments, 105–106
Behavioral abilities, effects of brain lesions on, 44–46
Behavioral components assessment, 86–87
Behavioral intervention, charting as aid in effectiveness of, 51
Behavioral learning theory, definition, 61
Behavioral objectives, movement cycles, 239–40
Behavioral technology:
  correlation with systems technology, 210
  experimental analysis of behavior, 210–11
  reinforcement principles, 212–18
Behavioral theory approaches, 21

Behavioral theory approaches (*cont.*)
  Forness, 50–52
  Hewett, 47–50
Behaviorism:
  early research: Watson and Guthrie, 67–70
  emphasis of research, 66–67
  experimental analysis: Thorndike and Skinner, 70–76
  Hullian theory—behavior therapy, 76–78
Behaviorist tradition, development of, 62–63
Bellevue-Wechsler intelligence test, 42
Belmont, L., 135
Bender, Lauretta, 42
Bender Visuo-Motor Gestalt Test for Children, 98, 103, 118, 131
Benton, Arthur, 43, 118
Benton Revised Visual Retention Test, 118
Bentzen, F. A., 26
Bereiter, Carl, 128, 166
Berger, B. J., 169, 199
Berliner, D. C., 145, 150
Betts, M. L. B., 81
Bijou, Sidney W., 83, 84, 138
Billingsley, F. F., 229
Binet, 44
Biology, and general system theory, 221–22
Birch, H. G., 9, 22, 40, 135
Birnbrauer, J. J., 84
Bishop, C. H., 186
Blake, Kathryn A., 80
Blank, M., 135
Blattner, J. E., 289
Blau, H., 136
Bleismer, E. P., 144
Blending:
  definition, 4
  as skill, 196
Blom, G. E., 129
Blumenfeld, S. L., 148
Bock, R. D., 38
Body image, concept of, 42
Boll, T. J., 45
Bond, G. L., 139, 148
"Bond-protecting reinforcement," Guthrie's term, 69
Boring, Edwin C., 61, 64, 67, 69
Boshes, 40
Boston, R. E., 224, 235
Botel Reading Inventory, 119
Bower, E. M., 47
Bowers, Judy, 4, 5
Bracht, G. H., 145
Broca, 44
Bruner, E., 177, 196, 198
Bruner, Jerome S., 64, 64fn
Bruninks, R. H., 145
Buckholdt, D., 256
Buckley, N. K., 178
Bureau of Education for the Handicapped, 13
Bursuk, L. A., 145
Burton, E., 142
Bushell, D., 214
Buswell-John Diagnostic Test for Fundamental Processes in Arithmetic, 120

C-A-C probes, 5
Cahen, L. S., 145, 150
Cain-Levine Social Competency Scale, 105, 122
Calfee, R., 131
California Achievement Test, 100
California Association for Neurologically Handicapped Children, 11
California Process Model (California State Department of Education), 172fn
Carnine, Douglas W., 165, 165fn, 175, 177, 178, 179, 180, 181, 184, 185, 186, 187, 191, 195, 196
Carr, 65
Carrels, use of, 288

Carroll, J. B., 137
Carson, G., 135
Catania, A. C., 217
Categories test, 98
Cats, experiments with, 71
Cave Schools, 23
C-C-V-C probes, 5
"Center," in cybernetic system, 223
Centering Process, 29
"Central language imbalance," Weiss' term, 41
Central processing model, of diagnosis, 102
Cerebral palsied children, studies on, 25, 26
Chalfant, J. C., 12
Chall, J., 139, 144
Change, in processing model, 281
Changing Children's Behavior, 253
Chapman, R., 131
Characteristics, in concept analysis, 183–84
Charting:
    basic tools, 247
    as direct daily measurement, 247
    use of in shaping classroom environment, 51
    use of six-cycle semilog graph paper, 247–53
Cheyne, W. M., 186
Child, as anchor level in educational system model, 282
Child Service Demonstration Grants, 14–15
Child Service Demonstration Program, 233
Children with Learning Diabilities Act (1969), 13–14
C-I-C probes, 5
Clark, A. D., 10
Clark, C. R., 149
Classification, skills taught in DISTAR, 189–90
Classification of Exceptional Children Project, 8
Classroom, remediation within, 154–55
Classroom environment:
    Montgomery County study, 26
    shaping of, 23
Classroom management, charting behavior, 50–52
Classroom organization:
    administrative effectiveness, 285–86
    attaining learning objectives, 286
    classroom ecology, 288–90
    early childhood assessment as preventive strategy, 291–92
    influence of traditions, 286
    innovation, 286
    integrated model, 282–85
    learning resource centers, 290–91
    management approach, 287–88
    social behavior, 286
    systems approach to management, 292–95
    types of, 286–87
    use of computers in education, 295–96
Classroom settings, use of applied analysis of behavior in, 84–85
Clements, Samuel D., 8, 11
Clover Park School District, Tacoma, Washington, 290
Clustering, in perceptual conditioning, 142, 143
Code-cracking, as pre-comprehension skill, 196
Cognition, Getman's definition, 32–33
Cognition sequence, Barsch's theory, 28
Cognitive-perceptual functioning model, 102
Cognitive theory, definition, 61
Cognitively Oriented Curriculum (High/Scope), 172*fn*
Cognitivists, 63–66
    concept of gestalten, 63–64
Cohen, M. A., 229, 240, 245
Cohen, S. A., 126, 129, 138, 151, 185
Cohn, R., 105
Coleman Report, 285
Columbia Mental Maturity Scale, 117
Common task teaching, as classroom organization, 286
Communication:
    Barsch's term, 28
    visualizations as, 29–30
Communication skills, remedial suggestions, 157
Compensatory model, for prediction of ATIs, 146
Comprehensive treatment, difficulty of securing, 304–5
Computer-aided instruction (CAI), 296
Computer-generated tests, 296

Computer-managed instruction (CMI) system, 296
Computers, use of in education, 295–96
Concept analysis:
    DISTAR, 181–84
    programming techniques, 184–87
Conditioned reinforcers, 212, 213, 214
Conditioning, 77
Conformity, and learning disabled child, 311–12
Connectionist theory (See Associationism; Behaviorism)
Connor, E. M., 290
Consequent events, analysis of, 108
Contact Initiation, as event sheet component, 246
Content-dependent concepts, in learning encounter, 198
Content-independent concepts, in learning encounter, 198
Context clues, in reading programs, 149
Contiguity, definition, 68
Contiguity theory of learning, Guthrie's formulation, 68–70
Contingencies of reinforcement, 82
    in Skinner's model, 74–75
Contingency Code, as event sheet component, 246
Contingency contracting, 257
Contingency management system:
    Lindsley's, 82–83
    and reinforcement schedules, 215–16
    analysis of, 108
Continuous reinforcement (CFR), 216
Corrections, as DISTAR technique, 176–78
Correlation, as type of research, 78
Council for Exceptional Children (CEC), Division for Children with Learning Disabilities, 8, 11
Covarrubius v. San Diego Unified School District, 15
Cowart, J., 179
Cratty, Bryant, theories and concepts of, 34–36
Criterion rates, ways to determine, 265
Criterion-referenced assessment, 235
Criterion-referenced tests, 100–101, 220
    DISTAR, 187
Cronbach, L. J., 150
Cross-modal transfer problems, 135
Cruickshank, William M., 9, 16, 21, 23, 279, 290
    research and theories, 25–26
Cues and curriculum arrangement, 270
    establishing instructional objectives, 258–59
    as instructional component, 231
    motivating performance, 255–57
    selecting curriculum for instruction, 259–61
Curriculum (See also Teaching methods)
    selection characteristics, 259–61
Curriculum innovation, movement toward, 72
Curtiss, K., 229
C-V-C probes, 5
Cybernetic-organismic model, of educational system, 282–85
Cybernetic systems, minimum elements, 222–23

Daley, M. F., 222
Data-analysis procedures, general considerations, 253
Data collection:
    charting—six-cycle, semilog graph paper, 247–53
    event sheet, 245–47
    plan sheet, 242–45
Decision-making:
    as basic teacher behavior, 227–29
    process summarized, 267
Decoding:
    task analysis of, 148–49
    taught by DISTAR, 186
Deductive behavior theory, 76–78
Definition:
    and identification techniques, 97
    value of, for teachers, 6
De Hirsch, Katrina, 98, 99, 121, 144
    work on language disorders, 41–43
Delacato, C. H., 129, 131
Demonstration, as phase of instructional act, 262
Deno, Evelyn, 279
Derby, Janet, 123*fn*

Description of Objects, skills taught in DISTAR, 189
"Desired critical effect," in skill sequencing, 235–36
Desired rate, as way to define goals, 241
Desired rate symbols, in charting, 250
Detroit Tests of Learning Aptitude, 99, 121
Deutsch, Cynthia, 9
"Developmental lag," Frostig's term, 33
Developmental Psychology Laboratory, Univ. of Washington, 84
Developmental strategy, Hewett's model, 47–50
Developmental teaching, compared to remediation, 126–27
Dey, M. K., 186
Diagnosis:
  illustrative example, 103–4
  inconsistencies of, 304
  preschool, 96–99
  psychoeducational models, 102–4
  school-age children, 99–101
  securing meaningful, 319–20
Diagnostic and Remedial Spelling Manual, 120
Diagnostic generalization, as assessment procedure, 87
Diagnostic language tests, 120–21
Diagnostic-remedial approach:
  to learning problems, 102–4
  to reading, 130–38
Diagnostic research, 59
Diagnostic Test to be Administered by Teachers to Discover Potential Learning Difficulties of Children, 122
Diagnostic tests, 119–20
Diehl, K., 139
Differential reinforcement schedule, 257, 269
Digital conception, of learning, 68
Dillard, H., 122
Direct and daily measurement, 267–68, 270
  accuracy, 241
  data collection:
    charting—six-cycle semilog graph paper, 247–53
    event sheet, 245–47
    plan sheet, 242–45
  desired rate, 241
  endurance and generalization, 241–42
  as instructional component, 231
  movement cycles, 239–40
  rate or frequency data, 240–41
  trend analysis, 253–55
Direct evaluation procedures, characteristics, 229–31
Direct instruction (*See also* Direct Instructional System for Teaching Arithmetic and Reading—DISTAR)
  elements, 266
  program, 128
Direct Instruction Follow Through Program, 165*fn*
Direct Instructional System for Teaching Arithmetic and Reading (DISTAR), 139, 142, 143, 149, 151, 156, 165, 165*fn*, 166–99
  as alternative and preventive to conventional remediation, 165–66
  arithmetic teaching program, 187, 191–96
  the child and, 198–99
  concept analysis, 181–84
  conceptualization of, 168–69
  effectiveness data, 169–76
  Follow Through Groups' data, 171–76
  language teaching programs, 187, 188–91
  and learning disabilities, 166–69
  programming techniques, 184–87
  reading teaching program, 196–98
  teacher training, 180–81
  teaching techniques, 176–80
  typical classroom situation, 168
Directionality, development of, 24–25
Disadvantaged children, use of DISTAR with, 168–69
Discrimination, as skill, 133
Discrimination analysis, as core of DISTAR programming, 182–83
Discrimination process, assumptions based on, 77
Discriminations, and DISTAR programming, 184–87

DISTAR Arithmetic I Teachers' Guide, questions and answers from, 191–95
Division of Innovation and Development of the Bureau of Education for the Handicapped, 81
Dmitriev, V., 291
Dolch Basic Sight Vocabulary Test, 120
Doll, E. A., 48, 122
Dollard, J., 81
Dolphin, Jane, 25, 26
Doren, M., 120
Doren Diagnostic Reading Test, 120
Dorfman, N., 145
"Double-bind" situation:
  as block to information flow, 277
  and failure cycle, 208–9
Downing, J., 185
Drader, D. L., 135
Draw-a-Man test, 97, 117
Drill exercises, as phase of instructional act, 263, 264
Drill, practice and application, as instructional component, 231
Drugs, and behavior control, 6–7
Druliner, Patricia, 165
Dunn, L. M., 6, 104*fn*
Durkin, D., 120
Durrell Analysis of Reading Difficulty, 119
Durrell-Sullivan Reading Capacity and Achievement Tests, 120
Dyadic unit, analysis of, 108–9
Dykstra, R., 139, 148
Dyslalia, 41, 42
Dyslexia, 37, 41, 42, 43
Dyslexia Schedule, 99, 122
Dyspraxis, 42

Early childhood assessment, as preventive strategy, 291–92
Easter Seal Research Foundation, 11
Ebbinghaus, Herman, 80
EDC Open Education Model, Interdependent Learning Model (NYU), 172*fn*
"Educable retarded," as label, 15
Education-for-all legislation, 279
Education system, damaging constraints, 277–79
Educational tasks, Hewett's hierarchy of, 47
Educational techniques and programs, planning procedures, 101–106
Educational technology, use of, 209
Educator, view of child's problem, 9
Effect, law of, 71
"Effector," in cybernetics system, 223
Ego orientation, 42
"Égrule" approaches, to remediation, 150
Eimas, P. D., 132
Eisenson, J., 121
Electronic Data Processing (EDP), as part of overall information system, 295
Elementary and Secondary Education Act (ESEA), 13–14
Ellis, H., 79
Emotional disturbances, development of educational strategies for, 47–50
Empiricism, 61
Endogenous retardation, 8
  definition, 22
Endurance, as assessment tool, 241–42
"Energy surround," Barsch's term, 27–28
"Engineered classrooms," 290
  first uses of, 23, 25
Englemann, Siegfried E., 17, 85, 99, 105, 120, 126, 128, 129, 139, 166, 167, 169, 170, 171, 172, 173, 174, 175, 176, 177, 178, 179, 186, 187, 188, 191, 195, 196, 198
Englemann-Becker Corporation, 165*fn*
Englemann-Becker Direct Instruction Model, 169, 170, 171, 172, 172*fn*
Enriching Perception and Cognition, 29
Entropy, as measure of disorganization, 280
Environment:
  effects of free operant behavior, 75
  emphasis upon, 63
Environmental planning, in classroom, 288–90
Erickson, Eric, 48
Errors, teachers' response to in DISTAR, 177–78

Estes, William K., 62, 65, 70, 77, 78
Etiological approach, to reading remediation, 128–30
Etiology, definition, 7
Evaluation:
  as component of systematic plan, 244
  in educational system model, 283–84
  of instructional plan, 264–66
  in system analysis, 225–26
Evaluation procedures (*See also* Diagnosis; Tests)
  direct, 229–31
  functional analysis, 106–9
Evaluation technology criteria, 219–21
Evans, D. N., 222
Evanston Early Identification Scale, 122
Event sheet, components and use of, 245–47
Examining for Aphasia, 121
Exceptional children, integration into regular programs, 280–81
Exceptional Teaching, 253
Exercise, Thorndike's law of, 71
Exogenous retardation, definition, 8, 22
Experimental Education Unit of the Child Development and Mental Retardation Center, 84, 85, 85*fn*, 86
Experimental Education Unit (EEU), University of Washington, 4, 206, 238, 245
  Model Preschool Center, 291, 296
Experimental psychology (*See also* Psychology)
  history and influence on educational practices, 59
Experimental psychology design of research, 78
Exploration level, in developmental strategy, 79
Extinction, 257, 269
Extrinsic motivation, 52

Factor analysis, and Cratty's model, 34–35
Fading procedure, in DISTAR techniques, 185
Failure, as factor contributing to learning disabilities, 3
Family problems, use of operant techniques in, 85
Farmer, J., 218
Feedback:
  allowing for in curricular materials, 260
  as DISTAR technique, 176–77
  in educational system, 281–82
  in systems analysis, 225, 226
  in systems theory, 222
Feedback mechanisms, Kephart's concept and remedial programs, 25
"Feedback perturbation," learning disabilities as, 28
Feedback system, Barsch's theory, 28
Feedforward, in systems theory, 222
Fernald, G., 127, 135
Ferriter, D. E., 256
Ferster, C. B., 216, 256
Fertman, Joan C., 116
Field theory (*See also* Cognitive theory)
  compared to learning theory, 65
Figure-ground, as skill, 133
Fink, W. T., 178, 180
First Grade Screening Test, 122
Fischer, R. A., 79
FIX connection, in S-R, 80–81
Fixations, 32
Fixed interval, 269
Fixed interval (FI) schedule of reinforcement, 216–17, 257
Fixed ratio (FR) schedule of reinforcement, 216, 257
Fixed ration, 269
Flesch, R., 139
Flexibility, definition, 280
Florida Parent Education Model (Univ. of Florida), 172*fn*
Focus, as skill, 132
Foley, Jack, 223
Foley, W. J., 281, 285
Follow Through, 169, 170, 171, 172, 173, 174, 176, 199
"Fooler" game, 180, 199
Formal classroom management, as restrictive, 206–7
Formative evaluation, 220–21

Formula Phonics, reading program, 143
Forness, Steven, 277, 278, 279
  views on classroom management, 50–52
Foundation of Educational Therapy for Children, 33
Fractions, taught by DISTAR, 186
Franklin-Pierce School District, Tacoma, Washington, 153
"Free operant research," and behavior therapy, 217–18
Free time, as reinforcer, 289
Freer, F., 145
Frequency:
  definition, 67
  law of, 71
Frequency data:
  as assessment tool, 240–41
  in charting, 248, 250
Freud, Anna, 48
Freud, Sigmund, 48
Frostig, Marianne, 9, 102
  visual perceptual theories, 33–34
Frostig Developmental Tests of Visual Perception, 97, 99, 103, 118, 130, 131
  areas measured by, 33–34
Frostig remedial program, 104
Full Range Picture Vocabulary Test, 117
Fuller, R. Buckminster, 17
"Fun" teachers, as DISTAR concept, 180
Functional analysis:
  assessing behavioral components, 107–8
  as basis for prescriptive educational methods, 23
  dyadic unit, 108–9
  as evaluation method, 106
  generalization of evaluation, 109
  obtaining baseline data, 106–7
  procedure, 233
  steps in, 106
Functionalist-behaviorist tradition, in America, 65

Gagne, R. M., 62, 74, 80, 81
Gallagher, J. J., 102
Garry, R., 61, 66, 76
Garton, K. L., 289
Gates test series, 100, 119
Gates Word-Matching Test, 98
General Motor System, in Getman's model, 32
Generalization:
  as assessment tool, 241–42
  development, 263
  as step in processing information, 87
Genetic fallacy, 69
Gentry, N. D., 240
Gestalt psychology, 22, 23
  as basis for de Hirsch's work, 41–43
  compared to behaviorist research, 66–67
  development of in America, 63–64
Getman, G. N., visuomotor training program, 29–33
Getman remedial program, 104
Gibson, E. J., 149
Giles, D. K., 214
Gillingham, A., 135
Gilmore Oral Reading Test, 119
Glass, G. G., 142, 143
Glass's perceptual conditioning approach to reading, 142–43
Gleitman, L., 132, 137, 141, 142, 143, 149
Goal, definition, 234
Goal Analysis and Preparing Instructional Objectives, 235
Gobar, A., 64, 69
Goldstein, K., 44
Goldstein, Kurt, 21, 22
Goodman, L., 131, 145
Gordon, Ira, 169
Gorton, A., 135
Government agencies, interest in children with learning disabilities, 11–12
Graham, F. K., 118
Grasp reflex, 30–31
Gray, B. B., 143
Gray Oral Reading Test, 100, 119
Greenfield, P. M., 64*fn*
Grobe, R. P., 177

Group contingency systems, for self-management, 229
Group-control group research design, 79
Group responses, in DISTAR, 179
Group tests, 99
Grouping, as classroom organization, 286–87
Guilford, 44
Gunzburg, H. C., 122
Guppy, T. E., 289
Gurren, L., 144
Guthrie, Edwin, 62, 63, 65, 68, 69, 70, 71, 74, 76, 77
Guttman, N., 81

Hagin, R. A., 132, 144
Halgren, M. R., 33
Hall, J. F., 185
Hall, R. E., 15
Hall, Vance, 84
Hall, V. R., 214
Hallahan, D. P., 21, 23, 25
Halstead, 44
Halstead-Wepman Aphasia Screening Test, 121
Hamblin, R. L., 256
Hammill, D. D., 104fn, 130, 131, 132, 137
Handwriting skills, remedial suggestions, 152, 156–157
Hardcore instruction, 261–66
Harding, C. J., 145
Hare, B., 137
Haring, Norris G., 10, 12, 13, 66, 84, 85, 95fn, 97, 143, 214, 216, 217, 222, 227, 232, 234, 253, 259, 266, 288, 290, 291, 296
Harlow, H. F., 81
Harper & Row basal level readers, 5
Harrigan, J. E., 131
Harris, A. J., 137, 138, 145
Harris, Florence, 83, 84
Harris Tests of Lateral Dominance, 118
Harvard University, 75, 84
Hauck, M. A., 84, 143
Haughton, Eric, 245
Havighurst, 48
Hayden, A. H., 84, 291
Headmaster concept, of administrative function, 280, 281
Hedrick, D., 121
Hegge, T., 136, 143
Heilmuth, Jerome, 30, 31
Heineman, C., 45
Hellmuth, J., 122
Hewett, Frank M., 288, 290
    work with emotionally disturbed children, 47–50
"High frequency behaviors," awareness of, 51–52
High strength activities, and token reinforcement, 215
Hill, W. H., 61, 64, 67, 69
Hobbes, Thomas, 61
Hobbs, Nicholas, 8
Hobson v. Hansen, 15, 279
Holland, J. G., 218
Home, as sanctuary, 327–28
"Home management," 304–5
Home School Partnership (Southern University and A&M College), 172fn
Homme, Lloyd E., 214, 288
Hopkins, B. L., 289
Horne, D., 33
Horst Reversals Test, 98
Hostility, in child, 310
House, Betty, 77, 78
How to Write and Use Performance Objectives to Individualize Instruction, 235
Hughes, A., 144
Hull, Clark L., 62, 65, 76, 77, 78, 81
Hullian theory, 76–78
Hull-Spence theory, applications of, 77–78
Hulten, W. J., 240, 245
Hume, David, 61
Hurlburt, M., 143
Hyman, J., 151, 185
"Hyperactive" children, 6
    control by medication, 7
Hyperkinesis, 41
Hypothetico-deductive system, as research method, 79

Identification, versus remedial reading, 125–26
Identification Process, 29
Identification techniques, related to definition, 97
"If-then" statements, and rules, 228
Ignore days, in charting, 250
Illinois Test of Psycholinguistic Abilities (ITPA), 33, 38, 38fn, 39, 97, 99, 101, 103, 104fn, 105, 121, 129, 137, 138
Immediate objectives, formulation of, 259
Implementation, in systems analysis, 225
Implementation activities, in administration, 293
Individual responses, in DISTAR, 179
Individual tests, 99
Individualization, curricular materials allowing for, 260–61
Individualized instruction:
    attempts at, 3–4
    as classroom organization, 287
    general considerations, 206
    recent move to, 207
Informal remediation, 326–27
Information collection, in systems analysis, 225
Information flow:
    importance of in classroom ecology, 289, 290
    in school model, 284
Information group, skills taught in DISTAR, 190
Inhelder, B., 64fn
Innate Response System, in Getman's model, 30–32
Innovation, influence on classroom organization, 286
In-program tests, DISTAR, 187
Input modalities, disorders of, 39
Input-output technology, of computers, 295–96
Instructional act, five phases of, 262
Instructional approach, to research, 59
Instructional components, summarized, 270–71
"Instructional disability," and teaching obligation, 7
Instructional environment, as classroom ecology level, 289
Instructional materials, characteristics of, 259–61
Instructional objectives:
    definition, 218–19
    establishment of, 258–59
    setting long- and short-range, 234–35
Instructional procedures (*See also* Systematic instructional procedures) selection, 270–71
Instructional Words, skills taught in DISTAR, 189
"Instructionally disabled" children, 4
    compared to "learning disabled" child, 4–6
Intellectual potential, measuring discrepancy between academic achievement and, 99, 100
Intelligence, as innate, 58
Intelligence tests, 99, 116–18
"Interest maintainers," pictures as, 149
Interference, in learning association, 80
Interval schedules, of reinforcement, 216–17
Intrinsic motivation, 52
Introversion-extroversion traits, studies of, 145
IQ, study of changes, 22
IS-DOES formula, 245

Jacobs, J. N., 130
James, William, 70, 79
Jansky, J. J., 98, 121, 144
Janssen, D., 145
Jeffery, W. E., 186
Jenkins, J. R., 145
Jennings, 65
Jipson, J. A., 145
Johnson, D., 130, 148
Johnson, D. J., 132, 144
Johnson, O., 40, 41
Johnson, Steven M., 85
Jones, A. W., 129
Jones, Lyle V., 38, 39
Journal of Applied Behavior Analysis, The (JABA), 83
Journal of the Experimental Analysis of Behavior, The (JEAB), 83
Jusczyk, P., 132

Kaluger, G., 104fn
Kandel, G., 135

Kandel, H., 7
Kane, E. R., 33
Kansas School of Education, 84
Kant, Immanuel, 63
Kaskowitz, D. H., 169
Kass, C. E., 15, 39, 137
Keepes, B. D., 145
Kendall, B. S., 118
Kent Series of Emergency Scales, 117
Keogh, B. K., 131
Kephart, Newell C., 9, 22, 23, 27, 32, 33, 48, 118, 131
  concepts and research of, 24–25
Kephart's motor-perceptual remediation, 109, 131
Kidder, J. D., 84
Kim, Y., 169, 199
Kindergarten Evaluation of Learning Potential (KELP), 122
Kinesthetic teaching methods, 26
Kinesthetic tracing technique, 127
Kingsley, H. L., 61, 66, 76
Kirk, Samuel A., 8, 9, 23, 33, 99, 105, 121, 130, 136, 143, 144
  theories and concepts of, 37–39
Kirk, W. D., 33, 136, 143
Klesius, S. E., 131
Koffka, Kurt, 63
Kohler, Wolfgang, 41, 63
Kolson, C. J., 104*fn*
Komoski, P. K., 207
Koppitz, E. M., 131
Koppman, M., 290
Kottmeyer, W., 126
Krager, J., 7
Kratochirl, D. W., 169, 199
Krippner, S., 131
Kromick, Doreen, 303
Krumboltz, H. B., 253
Krumboltz, J. D., 253
Kryzanowski, J. A., 178
Kunzelmann, H. P., 214, 245, 288

Labeling:
  by peers, 307
  consequences of, 6–7
Labeling litigation, 15–16
LaBerge, D., 149
Laing, R. D., 278
Lamb, G. S., 148
Landsman, M., 122
Langford, W. S., 98, 121, 144
Language, Barsch's view of, 28
Language and Thought of the Child, 64*fn*
Language Development-Bilingual-Education (South West Laboratory), 172*fn*
Language Development of the Preschool Child, The, 98
Language disabilities, remediation of, 37
Language disability theories (*See* Psycholinguistic approaches)
Language Modalities Test for Aphasia, 39
Language skills, remedial suggestions, 152, 157
Language teaching programs, DISTAR, 187, 188–91
Language versatility, as remediation, 326
Larsen, S. C., 104*fn*, 130, 131, 132, 137
Laterality, development of, 24
Latin, as formal learning discipline, 72
Law of effect, as primary law of learning, 62
Law of effect theory, 71, 73, 77
Layman, D., 7
Learning:
  definition of gestalt tradition, 63
  digital conception of, 68
  as problem-solving behavior, 74
  research in, 59
  transfer of, 79
Learning behavior:
  classroom teacher's awareness of, 60
  levels of, 60
  study of, 59
Learning curves, 73–74
Learning-deficiency premise, 127
Learning disabilities:
  appearance of term, 20
  as category, 22
  confusion surrounding, 9–10

Learning disabilities (*cont.*)
  definition, 14
  definition disagreement, 124
  determining, in school-age children, 99–101
  DISTAR approach, 166–69
  early labels, 6
  educational appraisal of, 95–110
  educational definition, 8
  factors in choice of procedures, 95
  factors responsible for misplacing children, 277–78
  as "feedback perturbation," 28
  general rules: thoughts from a parent, 328–30
  how and what to teach child, 105–6
  identifying potential in preschool years, 96–99
  as instructional disabilities, 205–6
  Kirk's stand on, 38–39
  Lovitt's diagnostic and assessment procedures, 86–88
  major trends, 21
  rejection of labels, 307–8
  parental pressure to conform, 311–12
  parent-teacher relationships, 313–18
  as phenomena, 3
  rejection of labels, 307–8
  team approach to, 29
  varieties and types, 10
Learning Disabilities: Educational Principles and Practices, 41
"Learning disabled," as label, 15
Learning disabled child:
  ambivalent feelings toward, 308–9
  as challenge to learning principles, 58
  compared to "instructionally disabled" child, 4–6
  within continuum of normal development, 306–7
  differences in reading abilities, 149–52
  home as sanctuary, 327–28
Learning Disorders, 30, 31
Learning Methods Test, 101, 120
Learning objectives, as classroom organization factor, 286
Learning Quotient, Myklebust's measure, 40–41
Learning resource centers, 290–91
Learning set, 81
Learning theories:
  associationism, 61–63
  cognitivists, 63–66
  compared to field theory, 65
  definition, 61
  history of, 60, 61, 66–78
  Hullian—behavior therapy, 76–78
  research designs, 78–88
Learning Theory and Mental Development, 78
Learning to Read: The Great Debate, 139
"Learning triangle," Hewett's term, 50
Lefever, D. W., 9, 33
Lefford, A., 40
Leford, H. G., 9
Left-Right Discrimination and Finger Localization Test, 118
Legislation:
  Child Service Demonstration Program Grants, 14–15
  Children with Learning Disabilities Act (1969) and Title VI, 13–14
  labelling and tracking litigation, 15–16
  and public education, 12
  special education laws, 13
Lehtinen, L. E., 290
Lehtinen-Rogan, Laura, 8, 22, 23, 24, 25
Leibniz, Gottfried Wilhem von, 63
Leiter International Performance Scale, 118
Lerner, J. W., 125, 139, 144
Letter discrimination, teaching of, 129–30
Letter naming, as skill absent from decoding analysis, 148
Level of reading readiness traits, studies of, 145
Liberty, Kathleen, 4, 6, 234, 266
Liebert, R. M., 177
Life-death cycle, of educational system, 281
Light reflex, 30
Lilly, M. S., 279
Lincoln-Oseretsky Motor Development Scale, 118
Lincoln Primary Spelling Test, 120

Lindsley, Ogden R., 75, 82, 83, 84, 107, 216, 234, 245, 247
Lippincott phono-linguistic program, 139
Locke, John, 61, 62, 63
Loeb, 65
Long-range instructional objectives, setting of, 234–35, 259
Lorge-Thorndike Intelligence Test, 117
Lovaas, Ivor, 214
Lovell, K., 135
Lovitt, Thomas C., 7, 84, 86, 87, 88, 107, 108, 109, 143, 208, 229, 233, 234, 278, 289, 290
Low frequency behaviors, 52
Low-income Follow Through students, data on, 171–76
Low performing children, and signal effects, 179

Mackintosh, N. J., 185
"Madison Avenue" approach, to remedial programs, 10
Madsden, C. H., 66
Mager, R. F., 218, 225, 234, 235
Management, systems approach to, 292–95
Management approach, to classroom organization, 287–88
Mankinen, M., 145
Mann, L., 130, 132
Marianne Frostig Center for Educational Therapy, 33
Martin, D. W., 177
Martin, G. L., 240, 245
Maslow, A., 48
Maslow, P., 33, 34
Mastery level, in developmental strategy, 49
Matthews, M., 139
May, R. B., 185
Mayer, G. R., 216
McCarthy, Dorothea, 98
McCarthy, James J., 11, 14, 20, 23, 33, 38, 66, 99, 121
McCarthy, Joan F., 11, 14, 23, 30, 39, 66
McDaniels, Garry, 169
McDonald, F. J., 262
McGettigan, J., 137
McGrady, H. H., 135
McIntosh, D., 6
McIntosh, D. K., 104fn
McKee, G. W., 33
McKee Inventory of Phonetic Skill, 119
McLeod, J., 39, 99, 122
McMenemy, R., 126
Meaning-emphasis approach, to reading, 148
Mecham, M. J., 121
Mecham Verbal Language Development Scale, 101, 121
Medication (See Drugs)
Memory:
  studies of, 80
  underlying SOS program, 133
Memory-for-Designs Test, 118
Merrill-Palmer Scale of Mental Tests, 116
Meshoulam, U., 135
Meshover, L., 120
Metaprogram, for teaching-learning system, 282–85
Metropolitan Achievement subtests (MAT), 170, 171, 172, 174, 175
Metropolitan Achievement Test (MAT), 100
Miami Linguistic Readers, 5
Michaelis, M., 214
Miles, C. G., 185
Mill, James, 61
Mill, John Stuart, 61
Miller, C. Arden, 12
Miller, Neal, 77
Miller, N. E., 81
Miller, Robert B., 223, 224
Mingo, A. R., 245, 246
Minimal brain damage, 22
  use of concept, 45
Minimal brain dysfunction (See also Brain injured child), 51
  acceptance of term, 11
  first recognition of, 37
  task forces to study, 11–12

Minimal Brain Dysfunction: National Project on Learning Disabilities in Children, 95fn
"Minimal cerebral dysfunction," as term, 8
Minnesota Percepto-Diagnostic Test, 118
Minnesota Preschool Scale, 117
Miron, M. S., 38
Misiak, Henry, 61, 63
Modality instruction, and reading, 144–45
Modeling techniques, 262
Money, J., 119
Monitoring, in management system, 293
Monroe Diagnostic Reading Tests and Supplementary Tests, 119
Monterey Reading Program, 143
Morency, Anne, 9
Morse-Carey amendment, 14
Motivation, 269
  definition, 256
  and reinforcement schedules, 257
  techniques, 255–57
"Motive satisfiers," 62
Motor activity, utilization of, 23
Motor Activity and the Education of Retardates, 36
Motor control, Kephart's theories, 24–25
Motor education, Cratty's stance, 34–36
Movement behaviors, analysis of, 108
Movement cycles:
  as component of plan sheet, 242, 244
  definition and pinpointing, 239–40
  as event sheet component, 246–47
  in SST-Perform project, 233
Movement Efficiency (See Movigenic theory)
Movigenics, 27
Movigenic theory, 28, 29
  basic constructs, 27
Mowrer, O. H., 77
Moyer, S. C., 145
Mueller, Max W., 79, 81
Muldoon, J. F., 290
Multisensory approaches, to remedial reading, 135–37
Multiword responses, and DISTAR techniques, 177
Myklebust, Helmer R., 102, 132, 144
  psychoneurological model of learning, 39–41
Myotatic reflex, 31

National Advisory Committee on Dyslexia and Related Disorders, 124
National Follow Through Evaluation, 170, 171, 172, 173, 174
National Institute of Neurological Diseases and Blindness, 11
National Society of Crippled Children and Adults, 11
Negative punishment, 257, 269
Negative reinforcement, 256–57, 269
Negative transfer, 79
Negentropy, 280
Neurological and Sensory Disease Control Program Division of Chronic Diseases, U.S. Public Health Service, 11
Neurological test results, interpretation and understanding of necessary, 44–46
Neurologist, role of, 320–21
Neuropsychiatric Institute School, Center for Health Sciences of U.C.L.A., 48, 50
Neuropsychological approaches, 21
  general considerations, 43
  Reitan, 44–46
Neuropsychology Laboratory, Child Development and Mental Retardation Center at the Univ. of Washington, 44
Neurotic learning inhibition, 51
Neville, D. D., 145
Newcomer, P. L., 104fn, 137, 145
Newland, T. W., 103
Niles, J. A., 145
Nixon, Richard, 13
No-count days, in charting, 250
Nonsymbolic disorders, 39
Norm-referenced testing instruments, 100–101, 220
Number of Words test, 98

Ocular Motor System, in Getman's model, 32

O'Donnell, P. A., 131
Off Program column, as event sheet component, 247
O'Keefe, R. A., 142
Oliver, P. R., 185
Oliver, R. R., 64*fn*
Olson, D. A., 135
O'Malley, J. M., 186
Operant behavior, compared to respondent behavior, 74
Operant conditioning, 211
  Skinner's laws of, 73–75
Operant conditioning techniques, 62
  development of, 75
  to modify behavior problems, 84–85
Operants, definition, 74
Operation approach, to classroom organization, 287
Order activities, in SOS program, 134
Order level, in developmental strategy, 49
Organic brain damage, 22
Organismic-cybernetic models, of contemporary science, 222–23
"Organizing the stimuli," stage in SOS program, 133
Orme, M. E. J., 214
Orton, Samuel, 43
  remediation programs of, 37
Orzeck Aphasia Evaluation, 121
Osborn, J., 188, 191
Osgood, C. E., 38, 39
Otto, W., 126, 129
Output modalities, disorders of, 39

Pacing, as DISTAR technique, 176–77
Paired-associate learning research, 80–81
"Pals," in formula phonics, 143
Parent and professional groups, 12–16
Parent groups, growth of interest and pressure, 10–12
Parents:
  advice to, 318–28
  and diagnoses and prognoses, 304–305
  view of educational services, 303–304
  views toward teachers, 313–18
Parents and Teachers, 85
Parents Are Teachers, 253
Parsons Language Sample, 101, 120
Pask, G., 222
Pate, J. E., 122
Patterson, Gerald R., 85, 227
Paul, J. L., 26
Pavlov, Ivan, 62, 65, 67, 69
Peabody Picture Vocabulary Test, 117
Pediatric Language Disorder Clinic, Columbia Presbyterian Medical Clinic, 41
Peer performance:
  as criterion level, 241
  as rate determiner, 265
Pelt, D. V., 38
Pencil Mastery test, 98
Percepto-cognitive system, Barsch's theory, 28
Perceptual, definition, 9
Perceptual and Motor Development in Infants and Children, 36
Perceptual event, definition, 32
Perceptual models, 262
Perceptual-motor and visual theorists (*See* Psychoeducational approaches)
Perceptual-motor awareness, Kephart's theories, 24–25
Perceptual process, Cratty's theories, 34–36
Perceptual tests, 118–19
Perceptual visual training, and reading remediation, 130–31
Perceptually handicapped, definition, 9
Performance, motivation of, 255–57
Performance feedback, 257
Performance rates, as criterion, 265
Personalogical variables, 146–47
Peter, Laurence J., 130, 229, 277
Peter Principle, 277
Peterson, W., 122
Pettibone, T. J., 177
Phase change lines, in charting, 250
Phillips, E. L., 66, 216, 222, 227, 232, 288
Phoneme features, attendance to relevant, 150–51

Phoneme-grapheme correspondences:
  multisensory approaches to, 135–37
  teaching of, 129–30
Phonics approach:
  to reading, 139
  to remedial reading, 136–37
Phonics Knowledge Survey, 120
Phonics program, 37
Physical environment, as classroom ecology level, 288–89
Physician, view of child's problem, 9
Piaget, Jean, 33, 48, 64, 64*fn*
Picture and/or "context" reading, as skill absent from decoding analysis, 149
Plan sheet:
  advantages, 243–44
  components, 242
  elements to be considered, 244–45
  IS-DOES formula, 245
Plasticity, concept of, 42
"Pointly Rule," 150
Poritsky, S., 131
"Porpoising," of educational system, 295
Positive punishment, 257, 269
Positive reinforcement, 212, 256–57, 269
"Positive self-image," child competence and, 199
Positive transfer, 79
Practice, as instructional phase, 263, 264
Prather, E., 121
Preacademic responses, and pressure on child, 4
Precise Educational Remediation for Managers, Perform:
  acceleration phase, 233
Precision teaching, 84, 209
  assessment strategy, 234
Predictive Index, The, 98, 99, 121
Preferential model, for predicting ATIs, 146–47
Pre-first grade programs, remedial, 155
Premack, D., 214, 226
Premack Principle, 52, 214, 226, 288, 289
Prereading skills, defined, 140
Prerequisite skills, specified in curricular materials, 261
Preschool Attainment Record, 122
Preschool years, identifying potential learning disabilities in, 96–99
Prescriptive teaching, 130
Pressey, S. L., 218
Pretest-posttest research design, 79
Primary reinforcement, 212, 257
Principal, role of, 279–81
Principles of Psychology, 79
Probing procedures, 268
  sheets, 238 (*fig.*), 239
  steps, 236
  use with direct daily measurement, 237
Problem definition, in systems analysis, 225
Process of Education, The, 64*fn*
Professionals:
  suggestions for from parents, 312–13
  view of educational services, 303–304
Prognoses, inconsistencies of, 304
Program, as component of plan sheet, 242, 244
Program Cycle, as event sheet component, 246
Program Evaluation and Review (PERT) techniques, use in management, 293, 294, 295
Programmed event, as component of plan sheet, 242, 244
Programmed instruction, 75, 81, 218–19
Programmed textbooks, advantages, 260
Programming techniques, DISTAR, 184–87
Progress Assessment Chart, 105, 122
Progressive education, and positive reinforcement, 211
Project Follow-Through, 139
Project 100,000, 125
Prokasy, W. F., 185
Psychiatrists, role of, 321
Psychodynamic-interpersonal strategy, 48
Psychoeducational approaches, 21–36
  Barsch, 27–29
  Cratty, 34–36
  Cruickshank, 25–26
  Frostig, 33–34
  Getman, 29–33
  Kephart, 24–25
  Werner and Strauss, 21–24

Psychoeducational diagnostic models, 102–104
Psycholinguistic approaches, 21
  de Hirsch, 41–43
  Kirk, 37–39
  Myklebust, 39–41
  Orton, 37
  Wepman, 39
Psycholinguistic process, Kirk's model of, 37–39
Psycholinguistic training, and reading remediation, 137–38
Psychological test results, interpreting and understanding of necessary, 44–46
Psychologists, role of, 321
Psychology, associative and cognitive traditions in, 60–66
Psychology of the Child, The, 64*fn*
Psychometric phrenology, 130
"Psychoneurological learning disability," Myklebust's use of term, 40
Psychopathology and Education of the Brain-Injured Child, 22
Punishment, view of, 211
Purdue Perceptual-Motor Survey, 118
Purnell, R. F., 214
Pursuits, 32

Quick Phonics Readiness Check for Retarded Readers, 120
Quick Screening Scale of Mental Development, A, 116
Quizzes, use in evaluation, 231

Rabe, E. F., 145
Radler, D. H., 24
Ragland, G. G., 39
Rate data:
  as assessment tool, 240–41
  in charting, 248
Rate plotter, use of in charting, 250
Rated days, in charting, 250
Ratio analysis, as determination, 265
Ratio schedules of reinforcement, 216–17
Ratzeburg, F. H., 26
Raven Progressive Matrices, 117
Readiness tests, 121–22
Reading:
  analyses of beginning, 140–41
  need for remedial programs, 124–25
Reading abilities, remediation of, 123–24
Reading achievement traits, studies of, 145
Reading Disorders in the United States, 124, 125
Reading drills, 136–37
Reading process, de Hirsch's analysis of, 42–43
Reading programs, task-analytically derived, 141–43
Reading remediation:
  approaches:
    auditory-visual integration, 135–37
    diagnostic-remedial, 130–35, 138
    etiological, 128–30
    psycholinguistic training, 137–38
    task-analytic, 138–44
  aptitude-treatment interaction, 144–47
  compared to developmental teaching, 126–27
  fourth approach, 147–52
  needs, 124–26
  philosophy of, 127–28
Reading task, analysis of, 139
Reading teaching program, DISTAR, 196–98
Reading, Writing, and Speech Problems in Children, 37
Rebus writing, 149
Recency, definition, 67
"Receptor," in cybernetic system, 222–23
Reciprocal reflex, 31
Record ceiling, in charting, 250
Record floor, in charting, 249–50
Reed, Homer, Jr., 44, 46
Reed, J. C., 145
Referent groups, role of in detecting learning disabilities, 101
Referral assessment, 87
Reflexology, Watson's study of, 67
Reger, R., 290, 291
Regional Resource Center for Handicapped Children (Eugene, Ore.), 4
Reichstein, J., 102

Reid, J. B., 85, 227
Reinforcement:
  contingencies of, 74–75
  definition, 212
  as DISTAR technique, 176, 178
  Guthrie's rejection of, 69
  as instructional component, 231
  need for in reading remediation, 151
  as primary aim of classroom research, 211
  in systems theory, 222
"Reinforcement overkill," 52
Reinforcement principles, 212–18
Reinforcement schedules, 75, 215–18, 269–70
  and motivation, 257
Reinforcement system, analysis of, 108
Reinforcement theory, 62
Reitan, Ralph, 43
Relevance-to-teaching position, on etiology, 129–30
Remedial model, for ATI prediction, 146
Remedial reading, vs. learning disabilities, 125–26
Remedial Reading Drills, 136, 143
Remediation (*See also* DISTAR; Reading remediation), 123–56
  delivery of services, 153–55
  focus on conformity, 311–12
  how much and from whom, 322–23
  how much time and for how long, 324–27
  of skills other than reading, 152–53
Remediation techniques, Kirk's, 38–39
Repetitions, need for greater in order to achieve mastery, 151
Research designs:
  applied analysis of behavior, 83–86
  assessment of children with learning disabilities, 86–88
  experimental analysis of behavior, 81–83
  paired-associate research, 80–81
  transfer of training, 79–80
Resnick, L., 123*fn*
Resource room concept, 153–54
  use of program, 290–91
Respondent behavior, compared to operant behavior, 74
"Responding to stimuli," stage in SOS program, 132–33
Response, selecting materials which provide for, 260
Response behaviors, analysis of, 108
Response level, in developmental strategy, 49
Responsive Environment Model (Far West Laboratory), 172*fn*
Reward, Hewett's definition of, 50
Reynolds, N. J., 177
Rhyming:
  DISTAR track, 197
  as skill, 196
Richards, L. S., 10
Richardson, Elliot, 8
Ridgway, R. W., 97
Rieke, J., 291
Right-to-Read program, 139
"Right-to-Read" speech, 125
Ringler, L. H., 145
Risley, Todd R., 79, 83, 84, 177
Roach, E. G., 118
Road Map Test of Direction Sense, 119
Robbins, M., 131
Robeck, M. C., 122
Robinson, H. M., 130, 145
Rogers, D., 131
Rosenshine, B., 178, 179
Rosenstein, J., 102
Ross, A. O., 140, 147, 149
Roswell-Chall Auditory Blending Test, 101, 119
Roswell-Chall Diagnostic Reading Test of Word Analysis Skills, 119
Rotations, 32
Rote learning, compared to DISTAR, 190
Rozin, P., 131, 132, 141, 142, 143, 149
"Ruleg" approaches, to remediation, 150
Rupert, H., 144
Ryckman, D. B., 104*fn*

Sabaroff, R., 145
Sabatino, D. A., 132, 145
Saccadics, 32

Safer, D., 7
Salomon, G., 146, 147, 150
Salvia, J., 130, 137, 138
Samuels, S. J., 126, 148, 149, 186
Sarason, S. R., 22
Saretsky, G., 139
"Satisfier" connection, 71
Say It Fast, DISTAR track, 197
Scanning, as skill, 133
Schech, V. G., 120
Scheffelin, M. A., 12
Scheidler, E. P., 129
Schiefelbusch, Richard L., 47, 84, 95*fn*, 234
Schoenfeld, W. N., 218
School-age children, determining learning disabilities in, 99–101
School district, proposed model, 281–85
Schutte, R. C., 289
Science Research Associates, 165*fn*, 169
Scientific method, use of, 58, 59
Screening, 232
Screening instrument, SST-Perform project, 233–34
Screening program, preschool, 96–97
Screening tests, 121–22
Screening Tests for Identifying Children with Specific Language Disability, 99, 121
Sealey, Leonard, 169
Sears, R. R., 48, 77
Selective attention deficits, 147
Self-charting, benefits, 250, 252
Self-concept, difficulties of developing, 307
Self-management skills, and decision-making, 229
Semel, Elinor, 127, 132, 133
Semmel, M. I., 104*fn*
Sense activities, in SOS program, 134
Sensory-neurological strategy, 48
Sequenced Inventory of Communication Development, The (SICD), 121
Sequencing, as skill, 133, 196
Services, inadequacy of, 304–306
Shafto, F., 7
Short-range instructional objectives, setting of, 234–35
Siegel, M. A., 177, 178, 179, 181
Siegler, R. S., 177
Sievers, Dorothy, 38
Sight-word recognition skills, 140
Signals, as DISTAR technique, 176, 178–79
Silberman, C., 10
Silberman, H. F., 186
Silver, A. A., 132, 144
Simches, R. F., 15, 279
Siqueland, E. R., 132
Six-cycle, semilog graph paper, use of in charting, 247–53
Skeffington, A. M., 29, 30
Skill acquisition, Watson's treatment of, 67
Skinner, B. F., 17, 62, 63, 65, 70, 73, 74, 75, 76, 78, 81, 82, 83, 84, 88, 211, 215, 216, 218, 224, 256
Slingerland, B. H., 99, 121
"Slow learner," 6
 as label, 15
Slow Learner in the Classroom, The, 24
Smelzer, S., 229
Smith, C. M., 145
Smith, I. L., 145
Smith, L., 256
Smith, P. A., 103
Snow, R. E., 122
Social behavior, as factor in classroom management, 286
Social competence tests, 122
Social level, in developmental strategy, 49
Social reinforcement, 212–14, 257
Sound It Out, DISTAR track, 197
Sound-Order-Sense (SOS) Auditory Perception Program, The, 127
 features, 133–35
 stages, 132–33
Sounds, DISTAR track, 198
Sound tasks, in SOS program, 134
Southern Illinois University, 318
Sowell, V., 131
"Space world," Barsch's term, 28
Spache Diagnostic Reading Scales, 119

Special Child in Century 21, 122
Special education:
 beginnings of field, 9
 continuing pressure for classes, 305–306
 factors responsible for misplacing of children in classes, 277–78
 integrating exceptional children, 280–81
 problems with laws and definitions, 13–15
 resources in, 59
 role of, 279
Special Motor System, in Getman's model, 32
Specific learning disability (SLD), 6
 definition, 9
"Specific reading disability," Orton's term, 37
Speech-Auditory Process, 29
Speech delay, 41, 42
Speech Motor System, in Getman's model, 32
Speer, O. B., 148
Spelling skills, remedial suggestions, 152–53, 156–57
Spence, Kenneth W., 77
"Splinter skills," 32
 Kephart's theories, 25
Spradlin, J. E., 120
Sroufe, L., 6, 7
SST-Perform project, 233–34
Stallings, J. A., 145, 169
"Stamping-in":
 Skinner's study of, 74
 of S-R connection, 71
Stanford Achievement Test, 100, 175
Stanford-Binet Intelligence Scale, 97, 99, 116
Stanford Research Institute, 169
Starlin, C., 148
Starter/101 reading program, 142
Startle reflex, 30
Stato-kinetic reflex, 31
"Statue of liberty" philosophy, of special education, 279
Stearns, S., 198
Steger, B. M., 135, 145
Stewart, D., 139
Stewart, M., 6, 7
Stillman, B., 135
Stimulus events, analysis of, 107–108
Stimulus generalization, 81
Stimulus predifferentiation, 81
Stimulus-response, and theory of contiguity, 68–70
Stimulus-response (S-R) connections, "stamping-in" of, 71
Stimulus-response events, precise analysis of emphasized, 70
Stimulus-response models:
 basis of, 61–62
 further work, 62–63
Stimulus-response reinforcement paradigm, 76
Stimulus-response (S-R) research:
 paradigm, 65
 Pavlov, 67
 Watson, 67
Stimulus-response scheme, cybernetics as advancement of, 223
Stimulus-response unit, in Hullian theory, 76, 77
Stotsky, R., 131
Strauss, Alfred A., 8, 21, 24, 25, 290
 research and concepts of, 21–24
Strength areas, division of classroom into high- and low-, 288–89
"Strephosymbolia," 37
Strother, Charles R., 9, 102
Structure, of educational situation, 50
Studies in Cognitive Growth, 64*fn*
Stylized group instruction, as restrictive, 206–207
Subsequent events, analysis of, 108
Substitution, principle of, 68
Success, and DISTAR program, 198–99
Sulzbacher, S., 7
Sulzer, B., 216
Summative evaluation, 220–21
Symbol action game, DISTAR track, 197
Symbol identification, as skill, 261
Symbolic disorders, 39
Symbolic models, 262
Synthesis, in systems analysis, 225
Synthesizing, as skill, 133
System, definition, 221, 276

Systematic instructional procedures:
assessment and evaluation, 232–39
behavioral technology, 210–18
cues and curriculum arrangement, 255–61
direct and daily measurement, 239–55
drill, practice, and application, 261–66
evaluation, 264–66
evaluation technology, 219–21
five components, 231–32
programmed instruction, 218–19
rationale for, 206–209
systems technology, 221–26
techniques for effective instruction, 226–31
Systematic plan, components, 268–69
Systematic planning (*See* Plan sheet)
System theory, 221–24
development of, 221–22
general approach, 222–23
Systems analysis, process of, 224–26
Systems approach, to management, 292–95
Systems technology:
correlation with behavioral technology, 210
task analysis, 223–24

Taguc, C. E., 84
Tannhauser, M. T., 26
Tarnapol, L., 37
Task, Hewett's term, 50
Task analysis, 130, 209
beginnings of, 72
development and steps, 223–24
and reading remediation, 138–44
Task Force I, 11
Task Force II report, 10, 12
Task Force III, 12
"Task taxonomies," 223
"Teach to strength," 105
"Teach to weakness and improve it," 105
Teacher training, DISTAR, 180–81
Teachers, parents' views toward, 313–18
Teaching:
decision-making as basic behavior, 227–29
technology of, 207–209
understanding administration, 275–76
using educational technology, 209
Teaching-deficiency premise, 127–28
"Teaching disabilities," 147
Teaching-learning process, according to general
systems theory, 222–23
Teaching-learning system:
levels in model, 282–83
reinforcement scheduling in design, 217–18
*Teaching Method for Brain-Injured and Hyper-
active Children, A*, 26
Teaching methods:
Barsch's space-movement orientation, 28–29
Cruickshank's evaluation of, 26
Teaching Special Children, 234
Teaching strategies, advantages of DISTAR
arithmetic, 192–94
Teaching techniques, DISTAR, 176–80
Teaching the Retarded, 80
Teaching universe, considerations determining,
183
Team teaching, as classroom organization, 287
Templin-Dailey Screening and Diagnostic Tests
of Articulation, 121
Tests:
academic achievement and diagnostic, 119–20
criterion-referenced, 220
diagnostic language, 120–21
DISTAR, 186–87
in DISTAR concept analysis programming,
186–87
intelligence, 116–18
norm-referenced, 220
perceptual-visual-motor, 118–19
Predictive Index: identification of learning
disabilities, 98
problems with interrelating findings, 104
readiness and screening, 121–22
related to auditory-vocal functioning, 101
social competence, 122
used in assessing academic achievement, 100
use of in developing remedial programs, 33–34
used in kindergarten, 99

Tests (*cont.*)
used in psychological assessment of suspected
learning disabilities, 97
Textbook objectives, critique of, 259–60
Theory, definition, 61
Theory and Practice of Early Reading, 123*fn*
Thomas, B. A., 66
Thomas, D. R., 85, 186
Thompson, Alice, 318
Thorndike, Edward L., 62, 63, 65, 70, 71, 73, 74,
77, 79
Thurstone, 44
Time Appreciation Test, 117
Title VI (SECEA), 13–14
Tobias, S., 144, 150
Tobin, A., 121
Token economy systems, of reinforcement, 75
Token reinforcement, 214–15, 257
Tolman, Edward, 64, 81
Tonic neck reflex, 30
Topography, of relevant behaviors, 107
Toward a Theory of Instruction, 64*fn*
Trabasso, T. R., 185
Tracking litigation, 15–16
Traditions, as influence on classroom organiza-
tion, 286
Transduction process, Barsch's theory, 28
Transfer of training research, 79–80
"Traumatic dements," characteristics of, 21
Treatment, parents' problems with, 322–28
Trend analysis, procedures, 253–55
Trial-and-error learning, 62
Tufts-New England Medical Center, 44
Tucson Early Education Model (Univ. of
Arizona), 172*fn*
Twardosz, S., 177
Tyler, J. L., 145

Understanding the meaning, stage in SOS pro-
gram, 133
U.S. Air Force, 223
U.S. Armed Forces, 125
U.S. Constitution, 15
Fourteenth Amendment, 279
U.S. Department of Health, Education, and Wel-
fare, 8, 11, 124, 125
Office of Education, 11
U.S. Office of Education Primary Reading
Studies, 139
University of Kansas, 84
University of Oregon, 85, 165*fn*
Direct Instruction Model (*See* Engleman-
Becker Model)
University of Washington, 7, 83, 84

Vail, E., 143
V-A-K (Visual, Auditory, Kinesthetic) approach,
135
V-A-K-T (Visual, Auditory, Kinesthetic, Tactile)
approach, 135
Valett, R. E., 106, 281, 290
Vallett Developmental Survey of Basic Learning
Abilities, The, 105, 122
Vandever, T. R., 145
Variable interval, 269
Variable interval (VI) schedule, of reinforcement,
217, 257
Variable ratio, 269
Variable ratio (VR) schedule of reinforcement,
216, 257
Variables:
dependent and independent, study of, 59–60
discovery of as task of experimental behavior
analysis, 82
and teachers, 166–68
Vellutino, F. R., 135, 138, 145
Venezky, R. L., 131, 140, 141
Verbal association studies, 80–81
Verbal labeling problems, 135
Vigorito, J., 132
Vineland Social Maturity Scale, 105, 122
Visual-motor perceptual training, and reading
remediation, 130–31
Visual perception:
areas measured in Frostig test, 33–34
slow development of, 3

Visual processes, model, 29, 30 (*fig.*)
Visual training, and reading remediation, 130–31
Visualization, Getman's definition, 29–30
Visualization Systems, in Getman's model, 32–33
Visuomotor complex, model of, 30–33
Visuo-motor tests, 118–19
Visuomotor training program, Getman's theories, 29–33
Vocal encoding subtest, 101
Von Bertalanffy, Count Ludwig, 17, 221, 222, 223, 276, 297

Walker, H. M., 178
Watson, James B., 62, 63, 65, 67, 68, 69, 70, 71, 74
Waugh, R. P., 145
Wayne County Training School, 21, 23, 24
Webb, W. W., 122
Wechsler, D., 33, 44
Wechsler Intelligence Scale for Children (WISC), 33, 97, 99, 103, 116, 233
Wechsler Preschool and Primary Scale of Intelligence (WPPSI), 97, 117
Weener, P., 104*fn*
Weider, S., 135
Weikart, David, 169
Weiner, Norbert, 223
Weiss, 41
Wepman, Joseph M., 9, 33, 38, 121, 144
  speech disorders model, 39
Wepman Auditory Discrimination Test, 33, 98, 121
Werner, Heinz, research and concepts of, 21–24

Wertheimer, Max, 41, 63, 64
Westbrook, R. G., 185
Westman, J. C., 129
White, Owen, 85, 85*fn*, 234, 253, 266
Whitehill, R. P., 145
Whittlesey, J. R. B., 33
Whittlesey, R. B., 9
Whole-word approach, to reading, 139, 148
Why Johnny Can't Read, 139
Wide Range Achievement Test (WRAT), 100, 120, 170, 171, 172, 173, 174, 175
Wiederholt, J. L., 130, 131
Wiegerink, R., 104*fn*
Wilson, J. A. R., 122
Wolf, Montrose M., 79, 83, 84, 214
Woodcock, R. W., 149
Woolston, J., 145
Word games, as informal remediation, 326–27
Word Recognition Tests (I & II), 98
Word Reproduction test, 98
World War I, 21, 221
Wright, Skelley, 15, 279
Wrobel, P., 214

Yarborough, B. H., 144
Yesseldyke, J. E., 130, 137, 138, 145

Zeaman, David, 77, 78
Zeaman-House theory, of discrimination, 77–78
Zelman, W. N., 293
Zero transfer, 79
Zifferblatt, S. M., 290
Zurif, E. B., 135